WITHDRAWN

Crosscurrents / MODERN CRITIQUES

Harry T. Moore, *General Editor*

GRAHAM GREENE
the Entertainer

Peter Wolfe

WITH A PREFACE BY

Harry T. Moore

SOUTHERN ILLINOIS UNIVERSITY PRESS
Carbondale and Edwardsville

FEFFER & SIMONS, INC.
London and Amsterdam

To my sons
Philip Graham Wolfe
and
John Bennett Wolfe
(too much, a bit)

823.91
Gr

L. 4.77

154595

Contents

Preface

The status of Graham Greene among modern novelists is a matter of continuing disputation. A few years ago, in London, a friend of Greene's assured me that Greene is a far better writer than Conrad.

Over the years, most of us have accepted Greene's division of his work into novels, short stories, essays, travel books, and plays, along with what he called entertainments. At least that's the way his writing was denominated at the front of his books, evidently Greene's own classification. But a surprise came with the publication, in 1969, of his novel Travels with My Aunt: here the entertainments were assembled in the category headed "novels."

Professor Wolfe (of the University of Missouri at St. Louis) deals specifically with the books Greene used to call entertainments; before this, they haven't received the emphasis of a separate study. This study begins with some comments about that disputed status of Greene, noting that "only a solid, far-ranging artistry could admit so many critical approaches; only a warm human touch, coupled with a keen understanding of modern life, could win such a wide popularity." And it quotes Greene as saying, in 1961, that the entertainments were a relief from the prolonged tension brought on by the writing of novels.

Many of us who have read Greene with enthusiasm

over the years have seen some of the excellent films made from his novels, such as Our Man in Havana, featuring Alec Guiness. And we will welcome a study such as the present one, particularly when we will find it sharply written, with useful critical designations. Professor Wolfe proposes that Greene is in the front rank of writers in English of our time. He has made out a good case for Greene before presenting this conclusion, having taken us through the Greene world of sinister intrigues, masquerading agents, and complicated psychological events. After going through Peter Wolfe's book, most of us who know Greene will see him in a newer perspective, heightened by Dr. Wolfe's valuable analyses.

HARRY T. MOORE

Southern Illinois University
March, 21, 1972

Acknowledgments

The author and publisher join in expressing their thanks for permission to quote copyrighted passages from Graham Greene's work to the following: Mr. Graham Greene, Laurence Pollinger Ltd., William Heinemann Ltd., The Bodley Head Ltd., Miss Monica McCall of International Famous Agency, and The Viking Press. We must also thank Mr. Stephen Goode for allowing us to reprint the first chapter, "The Entertainer's Art," which appeared in slightly altered form in *Studies in the Twentieth Century* under the title, "Graham Greene and the Art of Entertainment."

Special thanks are owing to Don Crinklaw and James Tierney for their kind help with organization and style; to Audria Shumard for typing the manuscript; to Norma Stine for supplying both background data and critical insight; and to the University of Missouri–St. Louis for grants to cover expenses connected with the manuscript's preparation.

The combined help of the following people amounts to a major contribution: Geraldine Adams, Jack T. Carmody, John Hudson, Josephine Reid, Jo Ann Leichliter, Claudia Marchese, Elizabeth Gaston, Joyce Katz, Clyde D. Whelan, and Theol Midd.

1

The Entertainer's Art

Graham Greene is too controversial to be called a classic. Critics have not only disputed the artistic merit of his work; they have also quarreled about the nature of his leading subjects and themes. David Pryce-Jones starts his 1963 book on Greene by acknowledging the puzzling character of Greeneland–that grim territory staked out and mined by Greene over a career that spans thirty books and forty-odd years: "Few writers have provoked such contradictory assessments during their life times as Graham Greene." [1] William Birmingham, in his 1952 bibliography of Greene, refers more expansively to his ability to bewitch the critical mind: "Critical estimates of Greene have run the gamut. We hear him called an artist and a hack, a penetrating Catholic and an unconscious Sartrean, in fact almost any pair of irreconcilables that can be named." [2] Nor does his personal life help us label him a burnt-out Catholic, a Manichean, or an artist-craftsman in the Jamesian tradition. John Atkins, his most subjective critic, finds ambivalence in all Greene does, and Philip Stratford finds that his practice of fusing his private life with his art fits no critical system. [3]

Fortunately, Greene's critics have not tried to cut him to a pattern. Nor have their readings of Greene been dull, forced, or superficial. Allott and Farris's *The Art of*

Graham Greene (1951), the first and maybe still the best book on Greene, charts the growth of his leading themes. Atkins's psychodynamic *Graham Greene* (1957, revised edition, 1966), if erratic, is both revealing and exciting. Later studies of outstanding merit include A. A. De Vitis's *Graham Greene* (1964), a balanced, lucid survey of Greene's books, and Philip Stratford's *Faith and Fiction: Creative Process in Mauriac and Greene* (1964), which makes fine theoretical use out of Greene's literary and film reviews. Greene has also been discussed with real distinction in articles. In different ways, Zabel and O'Faolain make excellent observations about his ability to combine spirit and documentary matter. Elizabeth Sewell, working on a smaller scale, channels his preoccupation with waste and decay into an encompassing metaphysic; Ian Gregor, in a biographical essay, anchors his leading ideas in a symbol from his childhood—the green baize door that divided the noisy students' quarters at Berkhampstead School from the serene living arrangements of the school's headmaster, Greene's father.[4]

How has Greene managed to provoke such high-quality criticism? And what of the criticism's conflicting nature? That these questions arise affirms his standing as a major writer. Graham Greene has written more good books than any other living English novelist; he has spoken wisely in many different voices on a wide variety of subjects; called England's most popular literary export to America, he has a wide and faithful readership. There is something for everybody in Greene; if not God's plenty, his world has many colorful sides. Referring to "his insistent carnality" and "the intensified drive of Greene's sexual urge," Atkins makes sex the driving force in Greene; De Vitis claims his chief subject is God; reversing this view, Greene asks to be read as a political writer.[5] Only a solid, far-ranging artistry could admit so many critical approaches; only a warm human touch, coupled with a keen understanding of modern life, could win such a wide popularity. Greene not only perceives his data freshly and sharply; he also shapes them artistically to the services of prose narrative. That nonacademics read him with both profit and pleasure speaks for his ability to grip the reader; that he has provoked wide critical attention reflects his ability to sustain this grip.

Greene's success can be explained in part by his possessing a mind big and generous enough to include opposites. Let us look at some of these opposing forces: David Lodge has spoken of the way Greene "shapes a vividly particularized narrative around a thematic abstraction," and Herbert Haber has mentioned the bedrock of primitivism that underlies his sophisticated technique.[6] Other tensions include a grim overview that accommodates bright spots of comedy and an ability to do metaphysics in a journalistic idiom. Besides being one of today's most somber writers, Greene is also one of the funniest. A relentless tracer of natural effects to their supernatural causes, he makes for quick, lively reading. Then there are the displaced, self-divided characters who cry out in vain for their struggles to end. Reality decrees that they keep struggling; life contains no clear victories or defeats, as man is fighting a war that will never stop. Curiously, the upshot of all this wreckage is a powerful unity. Even though it can look like punishment, God's mercy is infinite. Greene's seedy, guilt-clawed world moves toward spiritual solidity. Martyrs die for noble causes; it takes God to die for the run-down and corrupt. If the halfhearted clay peopling Greene's fiction is redeemable, then nothing is wasted and nobody is overlooked.

Controlling and resolving this dance of dualisms is a novelistic instinct, that genius for storytelling that has kept narrative art alive since Homer. Nobody knows better than Greene that the artist's first job is to show life, not to expound an idea. In a 1939 film review, he spoke of the importance of revealing, rather than reporting, a situation: "Argument is valueless in fiction unless it is dramatic and individualized." [7] By catching ideas on the wing, Greene resists substituting concept for character. Appropriately, both Christianity and art stress the primacy of the individual over the group. Just as God, according to St. Augustine, loves each of us as an only child, so must the artist root himself in human individuality. It is not surprising that the moral issues rising from *The Third Man* and *Our Man in Havana* make sense both theologically and aesthetically. Greene makes his literary labors a function of prayer by executing his themes as human dramas.

Nowhere in Greene's work do human energies pulse more vividly than in his entertainments, or lighter fiction. The entertainments have given pleasure to many readers over the years. Harvey Curtis Webster's dismissal of them as escape fictions which violate probability and trade on sensationalism stands in the critical minority. Richard Boston and Wilfrid Sheed both prefer entertainments like *The Ministry of Fear* and *Our Man in Havana* to novels like *Brighton Rock, The Heart of the Matter,* and *The End of the Affair.* Anthony Burgess— who, like Greene, often uses melodrama as a vehicle for metaphysics—praises the technique of the entertainments: "they are superbly written and their engineering is masterly." Albert J. Guerard, writing on Conrad, defines the entertainment form as a high-level thriller for thoughtful readers.[8]

Greene's novels and entertainments are generically alike, as outcroppings of the same mind. But criticism must sometimes work from the genus through the species to study variants of the species. This sort of attention has not been given the entertainments. Even when critics discuss them, they do so perfunctorily, preferring to dwell on the novels. The remarks they do make are marred by the same faults they attribute to the entertainments when comparing them to the novels —loose interior logic, surface dash, scamped construction, and a giving in to topicality. Important questions about the entertainments have gone unanswered in the wake of this casualness. Is the chief difference between the novels and the entertainments philosophical or technical? Does the novel-entertainment division devised by Greene smack of lecturing the reader, as Atkins believes? [9]

These questions are hard. Greene's original twofold grouping, first of all, has not kept pace with his artistic growth. Secondly, his own statements about the grouping reveal very little. In a 1955 radio interview, he told Walter Allen what we already knew—that the entertainments stressed physical action rather than psychic inwardness:

> In one's entertainments one is primarily interested in having an exciting story as in a physical action, with just enough character to give interest to the action, because you can't be interested in the action of a mere dummy. In the novels I hope one is primarily interested in the character and the action takes a minor part. [10]

His 1961 statement on the subject of his two fictional categories has a different emphasis. His entertainments, Greene says, both whet his appetite for raw sensation and offset the psychological stress he works under while writing his novels:

> The strain of writing a novel, which keeps the author confined for a period of years with his depressive self, is extreme and I have always sought relief in "enter-

tainments"—for melodrama as much as farce is an expression of a manic mood.[11]

The passage says something important about the way Greene works. His novels do demand more from him than the entertainments: while *The Quiet American*, a short novel, took three years to write, *Orient Express*, which extends to about the same length, took only nine months. But beyond providing this glimpse into the writer's workshop, the passage has little value. It does not, for instance, distinguish between genesis and execution in the entertainments; certainly, Greene's craving for physical activity does not externalize itself in slipshod rhetoric and plot construction. And it overlooks the further distinction between artistic integrity and commercialism. The neat formality of Greene's manic-depressive dualism goes against the truth that art stems from an urge to express self, while entertainment expresses a desire to amuse others.

It is time to look at Greene's categories historically. In *Journey without Maps*, a diary of his 1935 safari through Africa, Greene says he wrote *Orient Express* (1932) because he needed money. His calling his fourth full-length fiction an entertainment grates, as if Greene the artist were condemning the commercial work of Greene the writer-merchant. By 1938 a major change in attitude occurs. In *Brighton Rock*, he found that he had carried the materials of his popular fiction—the murder, the police chase, the cinematic rendering of the contemporary landscape—beyond the purview of the ordinary thriller. The book, called by Kunkel "a supernatural 'cops and robbers' story," [12] first came out in the United States as an entertainment; later, when it became popular, Greene decided to call it a novel. The change has proved wise. *Brighton Rock* matches its unified setting to a severe, vertical execution of plot—Pinkie Brown's practice, after Macbeth, of committing successive crimes to cover up previous ones. The demonic hero, the twin theme of salvation and damnation, and the probing treatment of Nelson Place, the Catholic slum in Brighton where Pinkie and his bride grew up, give Greene's longest book an urgency absent in *Orient Express* and *This Gun for Hire*, the two earlier entertainments.

Greene's next change in attitude toward his two fictional categories occurs in 1970 with the publication of *Travels with My Aunt*. Through 1969 and the *Collected Essays*, the card page of all Greene's books since 1932 had divided Greene's book-length fiction into novels and entertainments. *Travels with My Aunt* dissolves the division, listing all the longer fictions chronologically as novels. The first hint of this dissolution comes, perhaps, in this passage from *The End of the Affair* (1951): "We are not hurt only by tragedy; the grotesque too carries weapons, undignified, ridiculous weapons." The strange 1964 play, *Carving a Statue*, which treats a farcical sculptor who comes to tragic grief, continues to redefine comedy and tragedy along modern lines. Greene says in his preface, "I have always believed that farce and tragedy are far more closely allied than comedy and tragedy." *The Comedians* (1966) expresses this belief novelistically. Its interplay of burlesque, slapstick, and terror brings it closer to the entertainment form than any other Greene novel. Gainsaying comparisons, the work refuses to distinguish morally between different kinds of human endeavor. With *Travels with My Aunt*, the term *entertainment* disappears. The book's light, playful tone generates neither terror nor tension. Relying upon its loose picaresque frame and upon Greene's winking partnership with the reader, this charming suspense comedy sets no exciting artistic challenges. Greene's billing it as a novel sidesteps the questions of narrative craft and thematic bite.

But what of these questions? The best way into the

entertainments is through the entertainer. Writing on Evelyn Waugh, Steven Marcus defines the entertainer as a raconteur rather than a fabulist. Instead of probing either a private or collective unconscious, the entertainer stays near the surface of life. Instead of analyzing experience, he describes it in a lively, colorful way.[13] A performer, then, he is also a showman whose brief turn constitutes a sketch rather than a demonstration. Now, entertaining an audience takes as much dramatic skill as either reforming one or making one think. The entertainer has to gain both the confidence and good will of a mixed group. Billy Rice, the music-hall veteran in John Osborne's *The Entertainer*, says rightly that an entertainer needs personality, insight, and character; he must have these assets in order to get the audience on his side: "A real pro is a real man. . . . He's like the general run of people, only he's a lot more like them than they are themselves." [14] Like Billy Rice's music-hall routines, Greene's entertainments are short, usually under two hundred pages. To score early with an audience and to follow up his early advantage, the entertainer needs a thorough working knowledge of his craft. Greene's entertainments reach a wide audience without sinking to the level of pulp fiction; they are surface narratives whose irony and sharpness of detail saves them from superficiality.

Greene knows that controlling the reader's responses depends upon the ability to control one's materials. His praise of Ford Madox Ford's craftsmanship applies as much to himself as to Ford: "He [Ford] was not only a designer; he was a carpenter: you feel in his work the love of the tools and the love of the material." [15] The tight economy of design and the clean narrative follow-through of the entertainments certify Greene a master craftsman, too. A seasoned professional, he roughs out a narrative curve and then fits his data into their proper place within the curve or sequence. He gives his minor characters personalities; he touches in local color vividly; he alternates pleasingly between dialogue and description; danger stabs out of his most commonplace situations. Everything contains the seeds of terror; everything is subject to sudden change. A character can unknowingly spark a series of events that reshapes other lives, the supreme example being the exertions of James Raven, the demonic harelip killer in *This Gun for Hire*, which prevent a European war. To blame Greene for mounting this kind of excitement is to blame him for not boring the reader.

A child pushed from a top-floor window, a man literally frightened to death, an amnesia victim driven to madness by his keepers at a mental hospital, "the smashed dreary city of Vienna" during the four-power occupation—these are some of the data making up Greene's entertainments. Although they fit no rigid pattern, the entertainments usually revolve around a male character with the chance to save. But the potential savior is not only a man with a mission; he is also a man on the run. The urgency of his situation—that of working alone with his life on the line—evokes the reader's sympathy. In *The Confidential Agent, The Ministry of Fear, The Third Man*, and *Our Man in Havana*, the hero's exertions carry the added reward of winning the girl. Yet this last-chapter concession to a happy ending is usually blunted. Here is Kunkel on the subject of Greene's bittersweet finales: "Even when lovers are brought together in the final chapter . . . their happiness is shadowed, and they are not allowed to expect much from life." [16] The hero's exertions produce even less. At the most, they amount to holding actions or stalemates; the evil that spurs the hero to act remains basically untouched by his efforts. The attempts of the title character in *The Confidential Agent* to buy British coal may have lengthened his country's civil war; Rollo Martins enters *The Third Man* too late to prevent the deaths caused by Harry Lime's penicillin racket; Jim Wormold's lucrative go-around with spying brings about the death of one good friend and several strangers in *Our Man in Havana*.

When asked in 1956 about his use of the adventure-story format, Greene said that the thriller reflects life today:

> I couldn't help smiling to think of the many readers who have asked me why I sometimes write thrillers, as though a writer chooses his subject instead of the subject choosing him. It sometimes seems as though our whole planet had swung into the fog belt of melodrama.[17]

Auden, whose ability to put the death's-head rattle into the light lyric resembles Greene's blends of journalism and eschatology, said in his *New Year Letter* that life today is like a police melodrama: "The situation of our time/Surrounds us like a baffling crime." The use of trained technicians as spies, the mounting tension generated by the specter of war, and the liberties government security agencies take with private citizens express both the pervasiveness and the contagion of violence. The Nazis and the Communists made everything possible in the 1930s, the setting for Greene's first four entertainments. Even in England, life resembled a thriller: spies, murder, and hair-breadth escapes became facts of daily life. Thus Greene's entertainments reflect contemporary history better than his novels. Taking place in a climate of war, they drip disaster. If a war is not already going on, one is either about to ignite or has just ended. Nobody is safe. The war mood infects peaceful men (D. in *The Confidential Agent*, Arthur Rowe in *The Ministry of Fear*, Jim Wormold) like a disease.

Modern man's bent for violence reflects a larger, more terrifying truth—the nearly boundless potential for evil in human nature. The dark shadows cast by Greene's fiction spread to both the political and the supernatural spheres. The battlefield metaphor undergirding Greene's 1934 novel *It's a Battlefield* applies universally. Here is Greene commenting in *Another Mexico* (1939) on the inescapability of pain and strife:

> The world is of a piece, of course; it is engaged every-where in the same subterranean struggle, lying like a tiny neutral state, with whom no one ever observes his treaties, between the two eternities of pain and—God knows the opposite of pain, not we. . . . There is no peace anywhere where there is human life.

Man creates this endless struggle. If Greene is a political writer, his subject is God's politics. Man's social arrangements express only a minor aspect of the struggle. Although there is no neat separation, Greene has always stressed what man is rather than what man does. A great deal has been said about his description of Henry James as a writer obsessed with a Judas complex. Yet treachery runs high in *his* work, too. His first novel, *The Man Within* (1929), has for its protagonist a man who has betrayed his mentor and fellow smuggler; "The Basement Room" (1935) centers on a young boy who betrays his best friend; Conrad Drover betrays his brother in *It's a Battlefield* (1934) by sleeping with his wife. And as late as 1968 Greene said of Kim Philby, the Soviet intelligence officer who served as British security chief, "He betrayed his country—yes, perhaps he did, but who among us has not committed treason to something or someone more important than a country?" Life is a web of treason. People cannot act without betraying or being betrayed.

Greene's boyhood reading of Marjorie Bowen's *The*

Viper of Milan convinced him that ours was a fallen world. By a fallen world, he literally means a world smirched by original sin. Again, quotations from different stages of Greene's career express his belief in man's inborn depravity. *The Confidential Agent* (1939) refers to "the guilt which clings to us all without our knowing it," and *Loser Takes All* says, "No machine is perfect; in every join, rivet, screw lies original sin." The 1959 drama, *The Complaisant Lover* also joins sex to sinfulness with the wordplay, "the root of all evil," made on the name Clive Root—Root being both the title character and, as an adulterer and bookstore owner, a dispenser of knowledge. In a 1936 film critique, Greene complained: "The kindly, optimistic Liberal temperament does not recognize the Fall of Man." A 1938 book review carries the point further: "The creative act seems to remain a function of the religious mind. Maugham the agnostic is forced to minimize." [18] Human acts only take on importance when they refer to God—that is, to a God who punishes and rewards. Greene's 1945 essay on François Mauriac complains that recent British fiction has neglected man's tie with God. Novelists nowadays substitute psychology and technical adroitness for supernatural values. The substitution both dwarfs their characters and takes away their individuality:

> With the death of James the religious sense was lost to the English novel, and with the religious sense went the sense of the importance of the human act. It was as if the world of fiction had lost a dimension: the characters of such distinguished writers as Mrs. Virginia Woolf and Mr. E. M. Forster wandered like cardboard symbols through a world that was paper thin. . . . [Trollope's] ungainly clergyman . . . exists in a way that Mrs. Woolf's Mr. Ramsay never does, because we are aware that he exists . . . in a God's eye.

The famous essay, "The Young Dickens" (1950), in which Greene accuses the author of *Oliver Twist* of Manicheism, sharpens the religious focus. Dickens saw supernatural good warring with supernatural evil for the possesion of man. Whereas the evil characters in *Oliver Twist* grip us, the good ones are dim and sugary. The happy ending convinces nobody: evil and nightmare form the narrative core of *Oliver Twist,* and the novel's value lies in the tension generated between what happens (the triumph of goodness) and what we believe (the supremacy of evil). Greene's diabolism goes beyond that of Dickens. Oliver turns up in Fagin's den, and Pip finds his great expectations soiled by crime. But these underworld ties are both passive and involuntary. Greene's heroes sin actively. What is more, they are usually quiet, peaceful men. D., Arthur Rowe, and Henry Scobie of *The Heart of the Matter* are all good men who perform evil deeds. Humanity is so corrupt that its noblest undertakings end in filth and pain: "Courage smashes a cathedral, endurance lets a city starve, pity kills." D., Rowe, and Scobie feel corrupt, as if they are carrying something lethal from which they must protect others. Like Wormold in *Our Man in Havana,* they cannot move without causing pain. But the pain is not gratuitous. "With suffering," says Dr. Colin in *A Burnt-Out Case,* "we become part of the Christian myth." Greene uses suffering to bring the human and the divine together. Just as the crucifixion is the central nerve of Christianity, so does suffering bring us near Christ in His passion. Although rooted in everyday life, Greene's characters move on a large, terrifying canvas. Because their acts matter to God, their conduct can decide their eternal lot, and suffering can be their privilege as well as their punishment.

The supernatural reverberations of human conduct generate enormous suspense. Technically, this suspense is hard to manage, a fact that divides the entertainments, with thier fast-moving melodramatic plots, artistically from the novels. In place of in-depth character portraits, Greene must hammer narrative intensity out of journalistic materials. He usually focuses upon an immediate public danger—the armaments buildup in *This Gun for Hire*, Fifth Column activities during the London blitz in *The Ministry of Fear*, and the black-market traffic after the 1939–45 War in *The Third Man*. Keeping his eye on his audience like any other good entertainer, he interweaves his journalistic materials with a love story. Whatever subtlety or profundity gets into the entertainments he smuggles in. Narrative tempo demands that his characters reveal themselves quickly and definitively. Once they indulge in long self-inventories, they both undermine pace and blur the journalistic focus.

Now a detective novel is not the same as a thriller, or "blood," even though both forms fit into the category of crime fiction. The detective novel is an intellectual puzzle; it belongs in the camp of riddles and has, in its purest form, a rigid design. The first chapter states a problem in the form of an unsolved murder; the middle chapters, a tracery of clues, motives, and alibis, close in on the problem. The solution comes in the last chapter, which also includes a demonstration of the collected evidence and the apprehension of the criminal. The detective is a logician or reasoning machine who stands outside the plot.

Greene's belief in original sin carries the entertainments beyond the crime-puzzle formula. Man has offended God, and no difference can obtain between detective and criminal in a world of offenders. The hunted man and the avenger of society are one: Raven kills for money; D. works for an insurrectionist army; Rowe is a mercy-killer; Wormold undermines government security. By rejecting the analytical thrust of detective fiction,

Greene makes evil a force beyond the reaches of analysis. Evil cannot be driven out by reason; it must be fought with both mind and body. Nervous energy and physical stamina count as much as intelligence in the righting of a wrong. They also involve the reader more. As has been suggested, Greene respects his readers and takes special pains to gain their imaginative participation. His handling of documentary data represents a side of this attentiveness. There are few technical details in Greene to slow down dramatic movement. Although most of *Orient Express* takes place on a train, the book says little about railroad management. Nor does the plot depend on a close knowledge of railway transportation, in contrast to the crime fiction of Freeman Wills Crofts. No hawk-faced sleuths bent over microscopes people the entertainments, either. Greene's rejection of artists or mechanical virtuosos as protagonists, then, knits philosophy with technique.

A major benefit gained by avoiding technicians and technical expertise is narrative drive. The heroes of the entertainments are amateurs, not professionals. Ignorant of official procedures, they freely bypass red tape and chains of command. The rift between their private motives and an orderly professional method (the police usually take part in the action) creates opportunities for irony. *This Gun for Hire* and *Brighton Rock* both ask the Hegelian questions: Does the outlaw preserve the law by breaking it? Can he hasten needed social reform? Do his efforts make him a metaphysical necessity? Besides extending the frontier of the thriller, Greene's heroes, by fighting evil privately rather than collectively, create a climate where anything can happen. Not only do they cause us to wonder what metaphysical sense their crimes make; their rashness also puts them in constant physical danger.

Speaking of Greene's outlaws, G. S. Fraser calls the

entertainments "straight thrillers" and puts them in the tradition of John Buchan's *The Thirty-Nine Steps* (1915). The line of influence stretching from Buchan to Greene, although overlooked by most, is important. In a 1940 review, Greene praised Buchan's originality in stitching character and incident to plot: "John Buchan was the first to realize the enormous dramatic value of adventure in familiar surroundings happening to un-adventurous men." The assessment is correct. In *The Three Hostages* (1924), Buchan's hero, Richard Hannay, speaks of "the intractable bedrock of commonplaceness in me," and he describes himself thus in *The Thirty-Nine Steps*, a book whose commonplace settings include street parades, public meetings, and music halls: "Here was I a very ordinary fellow, with no particular brains, and yet I was convinced that somehow I was needed to help this business through—that without me it would all go to blazes." [19]

Although, as a religious writer, he plays the thriller game for higher stakes, Greene follows Buchan in conferring importance upon ordinary people. What survives in the entertainments is the everyday. It is more solid than the exceptional; it lasts longer; there is more of it. Quin Savory, "The Cockney Genius" of *Orient Express*, whose books sell in the hundred thousands, is "extraordinarily commonplace in appearance." In the film, the porter says of the third man who was with Harry Lime when Harry supposedly died, "He was just—ordinary." The secret message in Hitchcock's *The Lady Vanishes* (1938), for which several characters risk their lives, turns out to be a scrap of a popular song. Accordingly, the political maneuvering and violence of *The Ministry of Fear* begin in a misunderstanding about an ordinary cake.

When violence lashes out of the ordinary, it is all the more sinister for having commonplace origins.

Mabel Warren, the tenacious newspaperwoman in search of good copy, closes in on her quarry in *Orient Express* as "danger in the form of an English spinster a little drunk with gin." On his way to kill a man, Raven "looked like any other youngish man going home after his work. . . . He moved steadily up the street like hundreds of his kind." William Carter, the man sent to Havana by "the other side" to murder Wormold, seems as ordinary as his name. His "common-or-garden Nottwich face" sends the mind to "the English midlands, English snobbery, English vulgarity, all the sense of kinship and security the word English implied." Carter causes several deaths, and he has the doggedness to shoot Wormold after his plot to poison him fails. Even though Carter's bullet misfires, Greene's argument hits home: when terror erupts from common clay like William Carter, we are immobilized. To be attacked by Carter is like being attacked by reality. We can never feel safe again, and we lose faith in the arrangements of civilization to protect us. Nothing is safe with Carter prowling around. Carter murders our trust in everything and everybody.*

In "The Lost Childhood" (1947), Greene says that Visconti, the villain of *The Viper of Milan*, taught him that evil exists objectively in the world. He gives his phrasing of the revelation an odd concluding twist: "As for Visconti, with his beauty, his patience, and his genius for evil, I had watched him pass by many a time in his black Sunday suit smelling of mothballs. His name was Carter." Atkins says that Carter was a schoolmate, now dead, who bullied Greene.[20] Although not used this way consistently, Carter symbolizes for Greene tough, intractable reality. He gets into the children's story, *The Little Steamroller*; into short fiction, like "The Blue

---

* See Graham Greene, *A Sort of Life* (New York, 1971), p. 82.

Film," "Mortmain," and the privately published *The Bear Fell Free*, where he has sex with the wife of a dead friend; and into the books, *This Gun for Hire*, *Brighton Rock*, *The Heart of the Matter*, and *The Third Man*.

There is more to reality, though, than Carter. The power of ordinary life to burst forth sometimes works for joy and hope. "The Devil—and God too—had always used comic people, futile people, little suburban natures and the maimed and warped to serve His purposes," writes Greene in *The Confidential Agent*. The divine makes no exclusions: either all of life falls under God's (or the Devil's) rule, or none of it does. If everything is grist to the divine mills, then the supernatural may bite into the natural order at any time and change it completely. Greene's faith in the interpenetrability of the natural and the supernatural comes through most clearly in the short story, "The Hint of an Explanation" (1948). The story centers on the doctrine of transubstantiation—God coming to life in the commonness of baker's dough. A freethinking baker named Blacker asks a Catholic boy to get him a wafer given at holy communion. A man who works all the time with unsanctified dough, Blacker becomes obsessed with the holy wafer and first cajoles, then threatens the boy to give it to him. Blacker's urgings drive home the truth that the commonplace acquires monumental importance when touched by God. Out of them comes the boy's decision to become a priest.

The priest's memory of the sticky wad of dough he refused his persecutor has a barbed ambiguity typical of Greene: "I knew that this . . . was something of infinite value—something a man would pay for with his whole peace of mind, something that was so hated one could love it as one loves an outcast or a bullied child." Specific religious materials (the sacramental wine in

The Power and the Glory, the Host in *The Heart of the Matter,* baptism in *The End of the Affair*) belong more to the novels than to the entertainments. This comparison holds good elsewhere. While the novels deal seriously with spiritual problems, the entertainments have a secular slant. But since God is the focus of all Greene's work, they too touch upon religion. There is no neat split between the subject matter of the novels and that of the entertainments. The difference in attitude toward subject matter is also one of degree rather than of kind. The entertainments break from the novels only from the standpoint of angle and emphasis; the two modes use the same forms and materials, but slant them differently. De Vitis gives the spectrum its correct shading: "What in the entertainments is a religious sense becomes in the novels a religious theme." [21]

John Buchan is not the only writer of popular adventures who influenced Greene's thriller-entertainments. There is also Edgar Wallace. To appreciate the force of this influence, let us put it within the larger picture of Greene's literary sensibility. In short, what serious writer, we wonder, would fall under the influence of a hack like Wallace to begin with? To ask this question is to forget that the thriller or adventure tale is a respected literary form in England; that Greene honestly believes Rider Haggard, Anthony Hope, and Buchan to be great writers; and that he can both attack Hitchcock and use many of the devices and conventions found in Hitchcock's films.

Greene's literary opinions are found mostly in reviews. Much more idiosyncratic than academic, they reflect an instinctive response. Instead of setting up critical touchstones, Greene often digresses from the work he is reviewing to give his own ideas about the writer or the writer's subject, and these digressions contain his most exciting observations. A literary artist, he brings an insight to his reading beyond the powers of the ordinary reviewer. Many of his judgments, which sounded reckless when he made them, have stood up with time. For instance, he said of Henry James in 1936, when James was unpopular, "He is as solitary in the history of the novel as Shakespeare in the history of poetry." And it was not as easy in 1939 as it is today, first, to single out *The Good Soldier* and *Parade's End* as Ford Madox Ford's best work and, next, to call them "novels which stand as high as any fiction written since the death of James." Some of these judgments encroach upon prophecy, like his saying of Elizabeth Bowen's technique in 1935—that is, before the publication of either *The House in Paris* (1936) or *The Death of the Heart* (1939)—that "no writer since James has proved capable of a more cunning evasion." Some of his judgments are silly, like his calling Virginia Woolf's picture of Regent Street in *Mrs. Dalloway* "a charming whimsical rather sentimental prose poem" (1945); some of them still sound electric, like his terming Conrad Aiken in 1935 "perhaps the most exciting, the most finally satisfying of all living novelists."

What is remarkable about these judgments is the flexibility and openness of mind underlying them. This same freshness informs Greene's literary borrowings. T. S. Eliot's influence in Greene's *The Potting Shed* or J. B. Priestley's in *The Complaisant Lover* is not surprising: Eliot and Priestley have been forces in the British theater since the 1930s. But that Greene should borrow from the absurdists and the drama of noncommunication in *Carving a Statue* causes real wonder. Only an extraordinary freshness and freedom of spirit would permit an established artist to learn from colleagues thirty years younger.

Thus Greene knows better than to sneer at popular commercial fiction: as his plays show, no artist can miss a chance either to deepen his vision or to refine his technique. Few writers in our century have earned more money writing fiction than Edgar Wallace; one of every five books sold in England in the 1920s, except for Bibles and classroom texts, was an Edgar Wallace title. And few have made a stronger impact on Greene. Note the reverberations in Greene's work from Wallace's first novel, *The Four Just Men* (1905): obscure private citizens working to prevent a national calamity (*This Gun for Hire, The Ministry of Fear*), the lonely, duty-ridden public servant (*The Name of Action, The Comedians*), the outlaw flying in the face of the law in order to do the law's work (*This Gun for Hire, The Confidential Agent, The Third Man, Our Man in Havana*), the inefficiency and disorder of normal governmental process (*It's a Battlefield, The Ministry of Fear, The Quiet American, Our Man in Havana*), the use of foreign settings and characters (*The Name of Action, Rumour at Nightfall, Orient Express, England Made Me, The Quiet American, Travels with My Aunt*), and moral ambiguity: Wallace says of the killers in *The Four Just Men* who protect the law by overriding it, "They are equally guilty or great according to the light in which you view their acts. The most lawless of us would hesitate to defend them, but the greatest humanitarian would scarcely condemn them." [22]

The flat voice, the chain of minor climaxes, the reliance upon far-flung coincidences to advance plot, and the trick of using characters from different social strata to create a mood of journalistic relevance are technical legacies from Wallace. Although it is hard to trace specific lines of influence, Greene's making Wallace the most widely read novelist in his fiction stands as more than a backhanded tribute. Also, the title character of Wallace's *Sanders of the River* (1930) might well have supplied the name of Greene's stammering detective in

This Gun for Hire. (Greene reviewed Alexander Korda's film version of *Sanders of the River* warmly in *Night and Day,* 29 July 1937, p. 30.) Greene wrote in 1964, "Wallace at the very beginning of his writing career had one great quality: he could create a legend. I read *The Four Just Men* for the first time when I was about ten years old, with enormous excitement, and when I read it the other day it was with almost the same emotion." Greene then salutes Wallace's ability to tell "an almost incredible story with very precise realistic details." This mingling of fantasy and realism is essential to adventure fiction. C. Day Lewis, writing as Nicholas Blake, says that the writer of thrillers "can put unreal characters into realistic situations, or he can put realistic characters into fantastic situations." Ralph Harper, who also labels the thriller a mixture of realism and fantasy, stresses the technical control needed to make the mixture go down: "It always takes a sure touch," Harper writes, "to prevent the melodramatic from dissolving into the ridiculous. Theoretically, there is no reason why the implausible should not occasionally happen." [23]

The thriller mode, then, is well geared to Greene. He has the craftsmanship to ground improbability in believability and get away with it; his low-keyed, conversational style both counterbalances and controls the violence and rapid tempo of the entertainments. Finally, his belief in the constant interplay of the natural and supernatural provides the imaginative soil in which miracles bloom. His fiction bristles with outlandish events that make sense theologically, and he has complained (in *Another Mexico*) that tradition has underplayed the magic and the miraculous in Christianity: "We are too apt to minimize the magic element in Christianity— the man raised from the dead, the devils cast out, the water turned to wine."

Improbability represents the chief difference between the novels and the entertainments for Allott and Farris:

In general the entertainment has to be distinguished from the novel by the comparative lack of development in the characters, by the wilful use of interesting background for its own sake, and, more particularly, perhaps, by the freedom Greene allows himself in linking up the various sections of his narrative by coincidences and improbabilities. . . . The pattern of the entertainments may be as subtle as that of the novels, but it is more easily achieved.[24]

The statement rings true on all counts. Greene's entertainments do achieve both the subtleties and depths of the novels and, moreover, achieve them with less toil. What shortens thematic distances and cuts dramatic corners for Greene is melodrama. Melodrama is what Allott and Farris are talking about.

But what is melodrama?

Melodrama is to tragedy what farce is to comedy—a vulgarization. Ignoring moral complexities, it simplifies reality into sharp-cut divisions of good and evil, and it aims at evoking a simple response—like horror, sympathy, or contempt. Its function is to entertain, and it entertains very well when the reader does not feel bullied or cheated. Stressing the masculine virtues of physical courage and decisiveness, it features threats of sudden death, hair-breadth escapes, coincidences, and surprises. It usually centers on an impending crisis, which, demanding action, often of a physical kind, limits the characters' range of movement and choice. The physical element promotes rapid story movement, which, in turn, quells skepticism. Speed is important: Besides getting off to a fast start, the narrative must move ahead so quickly that we never catch our breath and disbelieve.

Enriching story-flow in melodrama is suspense. Suspense stretches out an anticipation of fear, danger, and physical sensation. It has no place in the murder mystery, which, as an intellectual puzzle, rouses only a detached, emotionless curiosity. Even its place in the thriller, its proper domain, is limited; for, to work on the nerves, it cannot last too long. One way of generating suspense quickly is to shrink time and space. While time is running out on the hero, his range of physical movement also constricts. This close-in technique has a powerful sharpening effect, both narrowing the hero's freedom and increasing its importance. The best example of melodramatic suspense in Greene comes when Raven, in *This Gun for Hire*, prepares to escape from his hiding place in the teeth of the gathering dangers of daybreak and an encroaching cordon of police. The danger building around Raven both furnishes suspense and anchors it in the realistic motive of self-preservation.

Another staple of melodrama is the pursuit. Pursuit has many variations, and Greene seems to know them all. In *This Gun for Hire, The Confidential Agent*, and *Our Man in Havana*, the police chase the hero, while the hero chases the real evildoers. Chases sometimes reverse, with the hunter and the hunted man changing places; sometimes there are chases within chases. These are most exciting when registered through point of view. Arthur Rowe learns only at the end of *The Ministry of Fear* that he has been the target of a sustained bloodchase and brainwashing by a Nazi spy ring; Mr. K., in *The Confidential Agent*, does not find out that he has been followed through London until he is caught. A chase sequence at the end of *This Gun for Hire* resembles this one, but with a big difference: K.'s capture by D. was recorded through the point of view of D., the captor; when Raven, wearing a gas mask, catches Davis, his treacherous paymaster, the scene comes to life through Davis's point of view. Davis's false security creates a double irony that makes this scene richer than its counterpart in *The Confidential Agent*: not only do we enjoy seeing Davis, a most unsympathetic character, brought to boot; we get an extra fillip of fun out of learning before Davis does that he is going to die.

This richness gives both continuity and drive to the plot. But a slack tempo is not the only trap melodrama must avoid. Melodrama parts company with realistic art in its attempt to be larger than life. It fails when it calls attention to its purpose. Thus the florid phrase, the event thrown into too sharp relief, the oversimplified moral stance, and the sentimental plea to gain sympathy for the hero can turn melodrama sour. Greene's irony and his colorful prose lift the entertainments above this kind of escapism. But what accounts just as strongly for the realistic flavor of the entertainments is his omniscient technique.

Greene takes more authorial liberties in the entertainments than in the novels. An admirer of James and of Percy Lubbock's *The Craft of Fiction*, he nevertheless knows the uses of omniscience. In his essay on Mauriac, he bemoans the eradication of the author in the "dogmatically 'pure' " novels of Flaubert and James: "Even the author, poor devil, has a right to exist." Melodrama nearly makes this right a requirement. The entertainments lack both the sprawling largeness and the author-centered focus of Victorian fiction. But Greene does take a God's-eye view of the action and controls his characters with a firm Victorian hand. The technique allows Greene to strike in quickly with the telling detail, the revelatory shift in setting, and the sudden event that speeds up the plot. By moving freely from mind to mind and from setting to setting, he can pay out information suspensefully. The corollary is also true. Authorial mobility makes for the panoramic, a dimension that counts heavily in an art form which subordinates myth to journalism.

Flat characters—i.e., characters whose personalities

turn on a single governing passion are important in journalistic art, and Greene's precise diction can formulate character in a phrase or gesture. These formulations usually have an ironical humanizing edge. Mrs. Bellairs, the German spy and spiritualist of *The Ministry of Fear*, is called "wonderful" so often that the adjective reverses its meaning. Buddy Fergusson, the Fascist bully and thirdrate medical student in *This Gun for Hire*, becomes "the daredevil of the trenches" because he cannot distinguish himself in the arts of peace. And the sweet-toothed cheat Davis, reading an encouraging financial item in the newspaper, reacts in a way that both seats his personality and suggests a hierarchy of values. Moreover, Greene does this twofold job as economically and unpretentiously as you could wish: "He seemed satisfied: what he read there was as good as a lollipop."

Incidentals like this—so prosaic, yet so expressive of character—add iron and bounce. Greene's cinematic cutting from table to table in the dining car of the Orient Express is another plotting device that knits well with the omniscient journalistic novel: by reporting only selected scraps of conversations, Greene can advance his plot without worrying about the speakers' motives or personalities. And here is Greene breaking into *The Ministry of Fear* in order to propel the narrative forward in time, another privilege of the omniscient author. The break in chronology and the authorial intrusion have the sinister effect of conveying a calamity before its cause is known. Greene's periodic sentence jars us twice: first, by committing us imaginatively to its subject, the forlorn detective Jones, before releasing its meaning and, next, by releasing meaning outside its main clause: "The figure [i.e., Jones] slanted out of sight as the taxi wheeled away; he was lost among the buses and bicycles, absorbed among all the other loitering seedy London figures, never to be seen again by anyone who knew him."

Greene's exacting and exciting style brightens his dark ontology. Yes, God's mercy does look like punishment, and heaven remains a skimpy inference derived from the hell we all know firsthand. These facts, though, do not offset the truth that God's in his heaven ready to bestow grace upon the worst sinner. But are there any rewards here, in the human sphere, "that ravaged and disputed territory between the two eternities"? Tainted creatures, we can only hope for a mixed victory; Greene talks of "the sense of doom that lies over success" in "The Lost Childhood" and of "the defeat of something only partly bad by something only partly good" in *The Name of Action*. But even though the most selfless success is impure, the effort going into both success and failure compels Greene's admiration. James Hall is right when he says that Greene's heroes cause their own grief by setting themselves heroic goals: [25] by aiming too high, the loving acts of Arthur Rowe and those of Henry Scobie in *The Heart of the Matter* become the work of hate. But the very attempt at positive creative action in a stricken, soiled world constitutes heroism; even our failures shine forth. Greene admires cowardice because the coward has something he does not want smashed, if only his skin: " 'Envy me, envy me,' a character remarks in one of Stevenson's stories, 'I am a coward,' " writes Greene in *Another Mexico*. Affirmation also pulses through the form of Greene's entertainment-thrillers. The mood of danger and suspense the thriller generates implies that life has value and is worth saving.[26]

"Perhaps Kipling never wrote better than when he wrote out of hate," said Greene in 1956. Hate ignites action and also fuels it. But, he adds, Kipling's domination by hatred kept him from greatness: "Hatred confines, hatred is monotonous." Work inspired by hatred runs, finally, to waste. If the moment of greatest perception is also the moment of greatest pain, as Greene

believes, then only greatness can make vision serve
love. But any generous outgoing of self carries the seeds
of greatness. Gushing up from elemental sources,
passion, however destructive, always surpasses tepid good
conduct. Greene talks of the redemptive nature of commitment in his wise, beautifully tooled *The Comedians*:

> Catholics and Communists have committed great
> crimes, but at least they have not stood aside, like an
> established society, and been indifferent. I would
> rather have blood on my hands than water like Pilate.
> . . . If you have abandoned one faith, do not aban-
> don all faith. There is always an alternative to the
> faith we lose. Or is it the same faith under another
> mask?

In *The End of the Affair*, sin becomes a foundation of
grace; elsewhere, motives like revenge and sex bring
about needed changes in the dynamics of political power.
Sooner or later, Raven trusts another person; Pinkie
Brown, overcoming his satanic pride, has sex; the indifferent Fowler, in *The Quiet American*, acts on political conviction. Sooner or later, Christmas comes to
Nottwich. Sooner or later, the sun shines on the mean
streets and cheap lodgings of Greeneland.

2

Three Nights in a Train

Greene wrote *Orient Express* for money, as he says in *Journey without Maps*. But the book's real value for him was not immediate but long-range, and it was not financial but artistic. His first three novels, *The Man Within* (1929), *The Name of Action* (1930), and *Rumour at Nightfall* (1931), were brooding, cumbersome, and emotionally overcharged. *The Name of Action* and *Rumour at Nightfall*, which he has withdrawn from print, move very slowly. Weighted by psychological analysis, elaborate symbolism, and inflated language, they exude a lulling atmosphere rather than tell a story. Very derivative, they lack both action and drive. Greene says that they *"ont été écrites sous l'influence du Joseph Conrad dernière manière, du Conrad de* The arrow of gold, *après qu'il eut subi l'influence de Henry James."* [1] In a February 1959 entry in his African diary, *In Search of a Character* (1962), he said he stopped reading Conrad in 1932 because Conrad's "heavy hypnotic style" had "too great and too disastrous" an influence on him. The crisp story line, suspenseful plot, and sharp imagery of *Orient Express* form the happy result of this cessation.

Journey without Maps tells of Greene's seeing the film version of the book in Teneriffe, the Canary Islands. Greene is too self-critical when he says that the "cheap and banal" Hollywood film brought out the cheapness and banality of the book. While *Orient Express* avoids the Conradian opacities of the first three books, it retains Conrad's irony and drive toward tragedy. Also, Greene's distinctive voice begins emerging in *Orient Express*. The book's style, relaxed in both phrasing and rhythm, stands close to the language of contemporary speech. But it is neither hard-boiled nor journalistic, owing to its ironic edge, vivid color, and visual sharpness. Its carefully chosen images have the twin virtues of precision and evocative force. It is no accident that one of its characters muses about the impact of the film upon prose fiction. For the chief difference between *Orient Express* and its predecessor, *Rumour at Nightfall*, with its nineteenth-century Spanish setting, inheres in cinematic technique. The later book embodies a new clarity, speed, and economy; also, camera techniques like cutting, the tracking shot, the montage, and the dissolve begin to explain Greene's scenic method.

Greene reacts well to this new influence. *Orient Express* is rich and rhythmic, not jerky or staccato. Not only does it put contemporary materials to new use; its characters stand forward with a new freshness and vigor. Besides presenting them literally in transit, Greene plays them off well against each other. He introduces a new drama along with a new set of characters at each major train stop. These new data he then works into the developing action. Nor does he overlook changes in mood as the train speeds east from Ostend to Istanbul. Styles in dress and architecture are neatly touched in, as is a growing sense of danger as the train nears insurrection-torn Belgrade. Atkins has praised the book's geographical certainty and its power to evoke setting: "As frontier succeeds frontier and Teuton is replaced by Slav, the standard of living falls, uniforms become thicker and coarser, the position of women declines, and silk stockings give way to robust peasant legs." For comment upon the book's lively, well-documented action and technical control, let us turn to Philip Stratford's *Faith and Fiction*: "The action is full of suspense and invention. Closely observed detail replaces the former romantic vagueness. Dialogue is abundant and dramatic, revealing more of character through indirection than pages of brooding analysis." [2]

As Stratford suggests, action and incident abound. *Orient Express* probably has more movement than Greene's first three fictions combined. It contains a business merger, an engagement, the deflowering of a virgin, an insurgence, a court martial, two murders, and three arrests. It begins at dusk, with the passengers from the big transcontinental express crossing the gray wet quay of Ostend harbor. The mood is one of mixed hope. The season is Easter, and the train ride to Istanbul takes three days. Yet the forces of winter batter the April day: the sun cannot pierce the overcast sky, and the ice-edged wind drives so harshly that the passengers must wear their overcoats inside the coaches. Even the snow which drifts into the action in thinning and thickening layers is denied beauty: "If the flakes touched the glass at all, they were already gray like scraps of paper"; later, on the roof of the customs shed in Passau, the snow melts "into gray icy streams." This bleakness fits well with Greene's picture of European society in 1932. Business and trade, in particular, he sees as hard, bruising enterprises. The world of commerce is called a "rocky business," a merchant named Stein is spoken of several times as being "on the rocks," a business-woman's jaw has a "rocky outline"; another tradesman, who betrays both employer and wife, has sharp teeth which glint menacingly in a dream. And the character of Jacob Myatt, a cranky, white-bearded magnate who feeds his sharp, acquisitive mind with warm milk, foreshadows Sir Marcus, the evil munitions mogul in *This Gun for Hire*.

But business is not the only dangerous activity in the book. Ordinary social intercourse also has its snares. The riders on the Orient Express are a mixed lot: they have different jobs, nationalities, interests, and life-styles, and they are all traveling east for a different purpose. Riding a train, they have no home or work routine to stabilize their lives. Greene's device of portraying them outside their normal routines makes the trip a test of their humanness—their abilities both to deal with the unforeseen and to get along with strangers. And the ride changes their lives materially, mostly for the worst. As Pryce-Jones says, "one and all are being borne to a destiny as much as to a destination." [3]

As in many other short novels with many characters, *Orient Express* does not aim at psychological depth. Yet the book avoids flatness and obviousness by twisting its characters' governing drives into obsessions. As monomanics, most of the characters are closed to one another. The impact they do make on each other, although often jarring, is usually brief and superficial, as when the jouncing of the train flings them together. There is little free or penetrating interchange of selves. People try to own or annex others rather than responding to them openly. One character talks of having his business rival "in his pocket," and another voices an attitude just as loveless toward the woman she lives with: "I've made her, I'm responsible for her . . . I've paid for her. There's nothing she's wearing that I haven't paid for; sweated for." This second woman is used as an object again later in the book, when a businessman marries her in order to clinch a partnership with her uncle.

The theme of the novel thus weaves together human isolation and the thinness of human ties: people do not care about or even remember each other for long. The first character who appears in the book is suitably a man who sees hundreds of people every day and remembers hardly any of them—the purser of the boat-train at Ostend harbor. And one of the purser's first acts is to remark inwardly that he will not remember Coral Musker, a passenger aboard the Orient Express. He then turns to another passenger, Dr. Richard Czinner, and, after wondering briefly "whether something dramatic had passed close by him," forgets Dr. Czinner, too. Coral's ironic association with the doctor, which ends two nights later in an unlit railway shed, both starts and ends in darkness: "This was the first thing she shared with Richard [Czinner] . . . a darkness in the purser's mind."

In a book where human purposes miscarry and where noble motives quickly spoil, it is fitting that most of the reported action occurs in the hours of darkness. Although Coral's relationship with Dr. Czinner grows in importance, the two characters have little in common, say little to each other, and form no friendship. Coral observes, after Dr. Czinner examines her, "Never before had she the sensation of being so instantly forgotten." Accordingly, the chief character in a novel-in-progress by one of the passengers is a London tobacconist. The implied image of smoke, like the smoke disgorged by the big train's engine, suggests again the insubstantial nature of human action; that, sooner or later, our commitments and loyalties go up in smoke.

Yet this smoke casts a spell. James Joyce once said that, whereas the journalist writes about the exceptional, the novelist must write of the commonplace. As in his other works, Greene roots *Orient Express* in commonplace characters and settings. Carleton Myatt, a young Jewish entrepreneur, has "sharp, common features"; Quin C. Savory, the Cockney novelist, is "extraordinarily commonplace in appearance"; even Coral Musker, a professional dancer, looks plain except for her legs: "There was nothing remarkable about her," says the purser to himself before forgetting her forever. Yet, as we know, commonness contains fascinating possibilities. The first possession of Dr. Czinner's that Mabel Warren, a journalist on assignment, searches is Dr. Czinner's shabby overcoat. Greene portrays the common clay populating *Orient Express* with his usual engagement with human fallibility. The soldier who later arrests Coral, when the train crosses into Yugoslavia, has "simple unhappy eyes." Addressing her softly and "leading her gently," he conveys the deadly possibilities hiding behind easy-going, companionable conduct. And if success has a separating effect, as Greene's *A Burnt-Out Case* claims, then failure promotes sympathy and kindness. Greene's failures fend off easy mechanical responses; it is difficult to hate something as human as a failure or to subordinate a failure to our selfish needs.

Greene makes us care about his characters by presenting them to us as failures. One of the first passengers boarding the express at Ostend is Dr. Czinner. Posing as Richard John, an English schoolmaster on holiday, he is a political revolutionary secretly traveling to Belgrade. He hopes to overthrow the Yugoslavian government, and he has mounted his *coup* from Belgrade's slum quarter, where he grew up and worked as a doctor and legislator. Five years before the time of the novel, 1932, his political enemies failed in their plot to kill him but succeeded in driving him from the country. Now, "weary and hunted and the stuff of stories," he mixes memory and desire by assuming that his townsfolk will league behind him. Greene humanizes him by discreetly filling in his background as a Belgrade slum urchin, as a fallen-away Catholic, and as an educated son who eclipses his simple, pious parents.

To temper our emotional response to him Greene

presents him ironically. A political zealot whose initials, "R. C.," express his fervor, Dr. Czinner has two names and, as a teacher and physician as well as a Communist, more than one job. A political revolutionary, he is both a new man and, at age fifty-six, the book's oldest character. A theoretical disbeliever in private property, he is twice robbed on the train. Greene's irony hits home. Dr. Czinner sins by working to redistribute more equably the world's store of property and wealth. The political and economic arrangements of life are so disjointed that the lover of humanity must die. But not only does Dr. Czinner sin; robbery prone and the leader of an abortive *coup*, he also brings sin and death to others. Even his fellow passengers become his companions in sin. Greene eyes both moral and legal distinctions from new angles. In a sense, the satanic Pinkie is right when he denies there is "a pin to choose" between himself and his angelic bride in *Brighton Rock*; *The Power and the Glory* reaches a crescendo when it brings together the fugitive priest and the escaped Yankee gunman. Their violating an imperfect law makes the criminal and the idealist one. Dr. Czinner's inability to escape crime, even when the crime is done with clean hands, sharpens the distinction between justice and the law in a fallen world.

If the doctor boards the train as "the tired gray man in the mackintosh," Coral Musker also enters the book wearing a cheap mackintosh. The mackintosh in Greene stands for fatigue and futility; it is the uniform of the seedy, the lonely, the drifter. Coral has a job as a chorus girl in an Istanbul cabaret. Her freshness and her work make her, then, an atypical mackintosh-wearer. What Greene stresses is her candor. And the whiteness of her mackintosh suggests innocence, as does her first name, since Coral is a material often used in infants' teething rings. The following summary by Allott and Farris captures both the brightness and commonness of her personality:

> She works in a chorus. . . . She is used to "the innumerable necessary evils"—the long waits in an agent's office, the dreary journeys to fulfill provincial engagements, the knowing how far to let men go— but cherishes a secret dream of security, even of love. . . . Coral is shown as quick, matter-of-fact, capable of generous emotion.

Allott and Farris then mention her "pathos and courage" and her "frank easy friendliness." [4] Greene likes her well enough to make Nottingham, where he lived, her home town, and he also imparts to her the waiflike thinness so common to his heroines. At one point, she faints because of her weak heart. But she has more iron in her blood and a braver heart than anyone else in the book. Unimpressive at first glance, she grows progressively in moral stature as the action develops.

Like Carleton Myatt, the Jew, and Richard Czinner, the Communist traveling incognito, she is classless: "For years she had been hovering indecisively between the classes and belonged nowhere except the theater, with her native commonness lost and natural refinement impossible." Her candor converts this classlessness into freedom and growth. After she faints, Myatt, whom she meets in the train corridor, gives her his first-class stateroom. Myatt, a currant merchant, is going to Istanbul to find out whether his firm's agent there, a Mr. Eckman, has cheated the firm for personal gain. Hardened by her career as a dancer, Coral distrusts Myatt's generosity: "There's only one thing a man wants," she believes; "one never gets anything for nothing: a girl is expected to repay." But Myatt is not only a wealthy stranger offering gifts. He is also a Jew, and Coral cannot resist stereotyping him. He in turn, invites sterotyping. A dealer in currants, he is nearly totally defined by money, or currency. The object of anti-Semitic slurs, he wears a Savile Row suit and dines lavishly in a losing fight to overcome his Jewishness.

Myatt and Coral are an unromantic couple. His oily hair, sallow skin, and premature stoutness, like his vulgarity with money, make him an unlikely lover. Her plain looks and untrusting attitude make her just as bleak a prospect for the mistress's role. Twice, when asked how far she is traveling, she answers, "all the way." Her answer is both right and wrong. Although she never gets to dance in the Stamboul revue called Dunn's Babies, she is both done and undone: between England and Yugoslavia, she loses her virginity, gets arrested, and watches a man die. The psychic distance she travels is thus greater than the geographical. Out of a sense of indebtedness, she sleeps with Myatt, and the sex they have is both awkward and painful. But out of it comes excitement and love. That sex makes the lovers more human is seen in her changed view of him. Her humanity increases in direct ratio to the humanity she confers on him: "It was extraordinary to her, the transformation which the night had caused. His face no longer resembled that of all the Jewish boys she had known with half intimacy."

A character who lacks this freedom is the Cockney Genius, Quin Savory. "A little rat of a man" who travels second class, he is going to the Orient to get material for a novel. The undersized, overworked Savory is less unsavory than some critics, notably Kunkel and Atkins, believe. Greene's feelings about his future as a novelist were very complex in 1932. His two previous novels had won him little public favor or private satisfaction, and, as the head of a growing family, he felt his career threatened by financial worries. His complex attitude toward the writing of fiction he voices through the character of Savory. And, to date, Savory remains Greene's fullest portrait of the literary artist. A tradesman rather than an innovator, he nevertheless works with both control and awareness, as his ideas about writing suggest. The writer in Greene's story, "Chagrin in Three Parts," from *May We Borrow Your Husband?* (1967) describes himself as a spy ("like most writers I have the spirit of a *voyeur*"). Savory's concept of the novelist does not express the idea, implied by the word *voyeur*, that the writing of fiction is unwholesome. But it does describe the novelist as a spy who masquerades as a public person in order to serve the forces of imagination and artistic truth.

His view of the novelist as a man who wears a mask of fellowship and easy good cheer squares with Elizabeth Bowen's concept of the novelist as "God's spy" in *The Death of the Heart* and with John Osborne's view of the entertainer as a social psychologist in *The Entertainer*. Here are Savory's own words:

> I'm not a poet. A poet's an individualist. He can dress as he likes; he depends only on himself. A novelist depends on other men; he's an average man with the power of expression. 'E's a spy. . . . 'E 'as to see everything and pass unnoticed. If people recognized 'im they wouldn't talk, they'd pose before him; 'e wouldn't find things out.

Savory also puzzles over descriptive technique: "He wondered what terms he could use to describe the night. It is all a question of choice and arrangement; I must show not all that I see but a few selected sharp points of vision." Thus even commercial fiction requires selection and balance. And, like any good professional, Savory cannot overlook opportunities to select and weigh his materials more sensitively. It is fitting that, in a novel influenced by film technique, he should think about the film's influence on prose fiction: "One thing the film had taught the eye, Savory thought, the beauty of landscape in motion. . . . That sense of movement must be conveyed in prose."

The 1920s was an age of experiment in the novel: Joyce's *Ulysses*, Mann's *The Magic Mountain*, and Virginia Woolf's *To the Lighthouse* all belong to the decade, as to Gide's *The Counterfeiters* (1926) and Huxley's *Point Counter Point* (1928), which, with their straightforward discussions of narrative technique, nearly qualify as novels about novel-writing. Although *Orient Express* bears the influence of these works, it does not pretend to be a treatise on fiction. First, Greene would rather err in the direction of the gutter than in that of the literary coterie. Secondly, he dramatizes Savory's personality; Savory emerges less as an archetype of the novelist than as a person who writes novels for a living. He is not as fine-grained or theoretical as Stephen Dedalus. Yet, through him, Greene follows Joyce's example of describing the impact of literature upon the sensitive literary personality. Like Joyce, he both shows what it is like to be an artist among nonartists and describes his literary man's frustrated gropings toward a fictional ideal. Allott and Farris have praised Greene's masterly use of incidentals as a character-developing device: "Greene is a past-master in the art of conveying by means of epithet and gesture the anguish and futility of a whole existence." [5] Savory's personality has a pleasing balance and consistency. Our glimpses into Savory's stream of consciousness show that he is no crass public success but a former shop assistant who has risen painfully by dint of energy and cunning. His outward behavior, on the other hand, reveals raw nerve-endings. A simple act like accidentally dropping a pipe hits economically on his compulsiveness. Greene follows the act and Savory's flustered reaction

to it with a clinching summary: "He was a man overworked, harassed by a personality which was not his
own, by curiosities and lusts, a man on the edge of a
nervous breakdown."

Sexual love comes into the book in part 2, before
Coral meets Myatt. But the love is lesbian and seems
about to die. The roilsome, rough-handed, middle-aged
journalist Mabel Warren is seeing off her suitemate,
Janet Pardoe, at the Cologne Hauptbahnhof. Structur-
ally, Janet balances Coral Musker. Whereas Coral is
plain but piquant, Janet is "a beautiful vacancy, hardly
existing at all." And whereas Coral is going to Stamboul
to work, Janet is planning a week's loaf with her aunt
and uncle there. Jobless and helpless, she is always
treated as a toy by others. (She is the girl Myatt later
marries in order to become her uncle's partner.) Lacking
conviction, she always takes the easiest road. When
Mabel says she dislikes Jews, Janet, who has a Jewish
mother, agrees. This bisexual girl is both half-Jewish and
half-baked. That she prospers without any expense of
effort plays out one strand of the ironic tension running
through the book between appearance and reality.

There is nothing half-baked about Janet's friend,
Mabel Warren. A London newspaper correspondent who
lives in Cologne, Mabel is terrifying in both her loves
and her hates. She is, moreover, a crack reporter who,
even when drunk, can scent good journalistic copy. On
her way to the Orient Express, she spots and recognizes
Dr. Czinner, whom she had last seen five years before,
when the doctor, then head of Yugoslavia's Social Demo-
cratic Party, testified in Belgrade against a general
charged with raping a child. Mabel will not be bilked
of the biggest scoop of her career a front-page story
"which the *Times* correspondent himself would give a
year of life to know." So she risks concussion by jumping aboard the departing express in order to interview

Dr. Czinner. Mabel treats others with the s...
devil ferocity. She will play hell with anyone who...
in her way, and she uses every journalistic trick...
knows to get information from Dr. Czinner. Yet on t...
subject of Janet she loses her reason. Sexually insecure,
she fears everybody as a physical rival for Janet's love,
and she panics whenever she feels this love threatened.
Greene catches both her methodical toughness and
mawkishness in the scene where she is having an
allegedly last drink with Janet:

> There wasn't a suicide, a murdered woman, a raped
> child who had stirred her to the smallest emotion;
> she was an artist to examine critically, to watch, to
> listen. . . . But now she sat and wept with ugly
> grunts because Janet Pardoe was leaving her for a
> week.

Like part 2 ("Cologne"), part 3 ("Vienna") starts
with a distortion of normal sexual love, pits appearance
against reality, and introduces a highly skilled professional. In order to speed the narrative, Greene compresses professional expertise and the "seem-be" dualism
into one character. The action moves from the train to
a building overlooking Vienna's central station. Josef
Grünlich, a plump cat burglar, squats on the roof of the
stationmaster's office. But he is not waiting to make
love to Anna, the stationmaster's servant, as she thinks.
He is getting ready to loot her employer's safe. A macabre Santa Claus, this bobbing fat man gives no presents
but does take a life. He brings in the idea of sexual betrayal by shooting the stationmaster with a revolver sus-
pended between his legs. He had already betrayed Anna
sexually by staging his robbery as a lovers' tryst. Noting
"with distaste" her "uneven and discolored teeth," he
recoils from her "middle-aged coquetry" and "antique
lust." Although he never kisses her, he does press his lips

o the blow-pipe he uses to burn his way into her employer's safe. Staying with the implied sexual metaphor, Greene then shows him penetrating the safe, but never Anna.

First seen in the snow, his proper element, Grünlich stands for death. A police detective in *This Gun for Hire*, speaking of tracking fugitive criminals, says, "It's only spooks that don't leave any impression." Grünlich, using a false name, leaves no fingerprints at the office and, owing to the recent shoveling of the snow around the train station, no footprints, either. His only emotion, one more diabolic than human, however, is pride: "I . . . have killed a man. I am clever . . . I'll be too much for them." As his last name suggests, Grünlich thrives. And what enables him to thrive is his expertise. As a thief, he is professional in the best sense —careful, methodical, prepared for danger. He can do anything but be human: "It was only personal relationships that confused him." Greene compares him to steel instruments and machines. Like his tools, he is "highly polished, with a sharp edge." His calculating mind has "the reliability of a tested and oiled machine." A craftsman, he does not overreach himself. His cunning and control explain his continued success in eluding the police. Taking no chances, he leaves behind him both the stationmaster's money and, with more regret, his immaculate tools. He then uses the quickest and handiest means to escape Vienna and danger by boarding the Orient Express as it makes ready to continue its eastward course.

Part 4 opens at Subotica, a Yugoslavian border town near Hungary. The logic of the book decrees that its longest, most exciting, part take place in an obscure outpost. The Communists in Belgrade have launched their revolt prematurely; and, news of Dr. Czinner's part in it having leaked, the border guards at Subotica are waiting to arrest the doctor. The dingy row of sheds making up the station may not be a big glowing terminus, but it does become a termination. Hope fades quickly here, as Dr. Czinner's dream of freedom and the romance of Coral and Myatt both die. Two characters sleep during the trial where a rump court perfunctorily sentences Dr. Czinner to death. And when he is later killed trying to escape Subotica, his death is stripped of heroism: "Even in death . . . the face was remarkable for its lack of humor. . . . The long moustaches . . . were comic; they were pathetic; they could never let him seem tragic."

Wonder and joy, then, flare only briefly. Coral and Myatt might just as well never have met, let alone become lovers. Artistically, the handling of the death of their love lacks the naturalness of that of Dr. Czinner's last hours. Coral steps off the train for fresh air at the same moment Dr. Czinner sees the border guards closing in on him. Quickly, he gives her an envelope which he tells her to mail from Belgrade. But a guard, seeing the exchange, arrests them both. Meanwhile, Myatt, who has been smoking in the dining car, worries about Coral, and, when the train's engine breaks down half an hour later, drives back to Subotica for her in a hired car. Unable to find her, he goes back to the train with mixed feelings. Coral *is* rescued, but her rescuer turns out to be Mabel Warren. As has been mentioned, Coral is going to Istanbul to replace a girl in an English revue. Ironically, she does replace a British girl, Janet Pardoe, as Mabel's new friend. Yet, despite its unnaturalness, the getting together of Coral and Mabel has an odd appropriateness, for these two women are the book's only professionals not enslaved by their work. By bringing them together, Greene nearly says that a loving, balanced relationship cannot take place within normal sexuality.

The setting of part 4 is the heart of the matter.

Greene, it has been said, places human life on a border between two eternities. That the wreckage and distortion of part 4 occurs in a ragged border town makes the "Subotica" section emblematic of human life. A trait displayed by most of the characters here is that of selfishness. They prize their personal comfort above everything, and they welcome the end of their ordeals, however hopeless the outcome. Man lacks endurance, commits himself but feebly, and, preferring even death to hardship, acts suicidally. Self-destructiveness runs through Greene: " 'I won't live, I don't want to live, let them shoot. . . .' [Oliver] Chant flung himself with arms held out to clasp death and have done," in *The Name of Action*. The whisky priest, too, often courts capture and death as a release from his burdens.

Greene equates struggle with life: to be is to fight. Peace runs counter to the human lot, and any attempt to banish conflict constitutes death. The death-drift gets into *Orient Express* wearing the garb of self-dishonesty, a corollary of self-destruction. Characters serve death when they gauge their acts by the self-centered criterion of conscience rather than by the other-centered reality of other people. What goes wrong is that they twist the dictates of conscience to serve selfish needs. More pointedly, they only summon morality and reason to mask a failure. After he is shot by a guard, Dr. Czinner feels doubly comforted—that his ordeal is over and that he has put forth an honest effort: "He had done all that he could do; nothing more was expected of him." After Myatt loses Coral in Subotica, he too fails to rise above the letter of the law: "He wondered at his own persistence in the empty dangerous station; he told himself that he owed the girl nothing, and he knew that she would agree with him." Later, too, he takes comfort in squaring his conduct with his conscience: "He had done all that he could do." Coral also reacts defensively

when her efforts to revive the dying Dr. Czinner fail:
"I've done all I can, I'm sure," she remarks inwardly,
thus clearing herself morally. To drive home his argument concerning selfishness, conscience, and death,
Greene describes Dr. Czinner as turning increasingly
inward while he slips out of life: "He had no more
duties to anyone but himself."

Greene takes pains with the crucial Subotica section,
and his pains yield dividends. He deserves praise, first,
for developing the grim drama of the ice-rutted train
yards as a human reality rather than just as a philosophical argument. The police state of Yugoslavia pits
local police against government troops and nonmilitary
staff against militia. And while this bureaucratic infighting goes on, local peasants close in on the sheds to
find out what is happening. The officers presiding at the
Czinner trial, by virtue of differences in age, outlook, and
personality, add further variety. This small, frayed
margin of civilization, then, makes up in color and depth
what it lacks in scope. Greene more than justifies dramatically his presentation of it as a geographical
paradigm of human life.

Part 5 ("Constantinople") shows a sharp fall in
thematic tension. The drama of derailed loyalties plays
itself out within the sphere of money. Greene reintro-
duces the note of decadence early, as part 5 opens in a
"great garish hotel . . . sunk a little in the world."
Now the English title of *Orient Express* is *Stamboul
Train*; the specific mention of Stamboul counts heavily,
for Stamboul is the old sector of Constantinople, south
of the Golden Horn, across the Bosporus Strait, and
inside Asian Turkey. The land of the legendary infidel,
Turkey fought against England and the Allies in the
Great War. And, like the train that makes the long trip
from Ostend, Stamboul has been a setting for western
greed. Waves of Crusaders sacked the city in the Middle

Ages, stripping it of its treasures; although Greene's Europeans speak evasively, they are just as driven by self-interest.

Relieved that the nightmare of Subotica has ended, Myatt glides back into his proper milieu—the unfeeling world of business. His fears about his Stamboul agent, Mr. Eckman, are confirmed. But not only has Eckman betrayed the firm; he has also deserted his wife. The last event in the book reenacts this betrayal in a major key. As with Grünlich and now Eckman, love loses out again to money: Myatt marries Janet in order to become her uncle's business partner. His using her as an object is also the book's final outrage against the Holy Ghost. That it takes place in the city of the anti-Christ, besides creating artistic balance, adds metaphysical sting to Greene's social criticism. Ours is a fallen world: nobility dies or sours, while mercenary motives and heartless people like Mabel Warren, Janet Pardoe, Grünlich, and Eckman prosper. *Orient Express* has mass and, thanks to Greene's keen eye, also precision.

The novel's moral outlook permeates its tone. Greene's metaphor of the train tallies with his picture of a society railroading itself to death. Yet, never content with shadowy abstractions, Greene makes his metaphor live by showing what it is like to ride on a train. Visual and auditory data bombard us. Points groan, pistons grind, wheels thud, windows rattle. Sudden bursts of color shoot from the flaring blast furnaces, and the signal boxes seen in different visibilities form a dance of colors and shapes. The experience of riding a train also gains life through Greene's impressionistic technique. By describing data from the standpoint of a passenger on a moving train, Greene gives the impression that the passengers are still and that the landscape is moving. Thus trees and telegraph poles, fields and buildings, race past the stationary passengers. But they do not race past with an unrealistic evenness and regularity. The impressionistic technique accounts for the visual tricks played by distances: "The village was so far from the line that it remained still, to be stared at, while the trees and cottages on the near bank, the tethered boats, fled backwards." Noise and silence become confused, too. This confusion is just one example of the way the heaving and lurching of the train make the senses unreliable: "Noise was so regular that it was the equivalent of silence, movement was so continuous that after a while the mind accepted it as stillness."

For variety, Greene moves freely through the speeding train, describing activity in no regular order in the coaches, sleeping units, engine room, dining car, and lavatories. He includes some lithe, lively prose poems that describe the train passing through different locales at different times of the day. Like the book's plot, the lights darting from the train make the commonplace poetic, the familiar strange. The falling rhythm of the following sentence is perfect: "The sparks from the express became visible, like hordes of scarlet beetles tempted into the air by night; they fell and smoldered by the track, touched leaves and twigs and cabbage-stalks and turned to soot." Rhetorician, trick photographer, and scene painter, Greene also shows the train at rest, remaking itself by shunting back and forth, dropping and adding cars as an animal sheds and renews its coat. (There is an English businessman mentioned several times by the name of Moult, suggesting further the rhythm of decay and renewal.)

Variety characterizes *Orient Express*. Its breadth of characters and events offers something to delight everybody. For the lover of crime puzzles, it offers a sketch of intersecting circles and lines from Dr. Czinner's Baedeker. Mabel Warren, who steals the Baedeker, discovers that the semitransparent sketch, when laid over a map of Belgrade from a later page, describes the battle plan for the Czinner *coup*. But the developing drama unravels still more information: the sketch, the *coup's* failure, and Dr. Czinner's death at Subotica present Belgrade as a maze, as unreal, and also as a goal strived for but never reached. The economy with which Greene projects these different views of the modern city—from Baudelaire, Joyce, and Freud—argues remarkable sophistication in an apprentice writer.

The book's rich variety, like its technique of confounding sense perception, goes well with its strong antirational thrust. Avoiding one-to-one correspondences, Greene suggests exciting acausal dimensions and possibilities: Coral's white mackintosh and Quin Savory's characterization as "the white-faced man" channel into the book's innocence-experience dualism, as does Savory's calling himself a spy and then asking Grünlich if *he* is a police spy. Greene's practice of using dreams to enrich idea occurs several times. Mrs. Eckman, for instance, sews in Myatt's dream and sews again, Penelope-like, when Myatt meets her. A character named Joyce, who appears on the next page, fits into the Homeric joke, which started when Myatt's crimes, like those of Bloom in the "Circe" episode of *Ulysses*, vex his unconscious.

Greene's fascination with oral experience dates back to *Orient Express*. This fascination, it needs to be said, inheres in the fact that God enters the body through the mouth during Holy communion. Coral revives the wounded Dr. Czinner by putting snow on his tongue; later, he is shot in the mouth from close range by a soldier. If life and death both enter his body orally, several of his other experiences also confuse loss and gain. For instance, the bullet that nearly killed him five years before the time of the novel, when his enemies tried to murder him in a Belgrade beer-hall, affirms his political strength. And the poor timing of the Belgrade uprising, while spelling out failure for Dr. Czinner, its guiding force, protects him from the taunts of the headline-hungry Mabel Warren: "She had been bullied many times by the successful, never before by one who had failed."

Discussing the prevalence of failure in the book, Pryce-Jones sees most of the characters as dreamy innocents: in varying degrees, they entertain unrealistic hopes, they are strongly motivated, they are weak in self-knowledge.[6] Grünlich, Savory, Myatt, and Dr. Czinner are work-ridden. Work is their monomania; it throws their personalities out of balance, and it makes them incapable of dealing with human inconsistency. The monomaniac, we know, distorts reality; since his single-mindedness ignores so much, he is also an innocent, as Pryce-Jones says. The driven souls in *Orient Express* set the way for destructive innocents like Raven, Pinkie, and Alden Pyle in *The Quiet American*. Their obsession with work hits on a major idea in Greene— the dehumanization of work, especially work requiring great skill and dedication. Many of his characters find work an escape from life rather than a getting into it. Paul Demassener, dictator of Trier in *The Name of Action* (1930), and Luis Pineda, the career diplomat in *The Comedians* (1966), have had their sexual drives killed by work. A girl in *England Made Me* (1935), reading the palm of Erik Krogh, "the richest man in the world," tells him, "You don't care much for girls. You like work best." In *Carving a Statue*, work sinks to a dryness and a despair as the father uses it to shut out pain. He tells his son, "When your mother died I ran out of the room before the breathing stopped. I began to work. It was all I could do."

Allott and Farris object that, because *Orient Express* is so visual, it lacks depth: Yet later, they imply that the book does balance idea and appearance when they speak of "the vast amount of information we seem to have acquired . . . of everyone who makes even a fleeting appearance in the action." [7] Greene delivers this information through dialogue, imagery, dream, and interior monologue. There are many effective ways of telling a story, and the different techniques he uses to bring his characters to life in *Orient Express* suggest that by 1932 Greene knew most of them. Stylistically, too, he shows artistic seasoning. His highly graphic language sometimes unfurls with suggestiveness and power: "The great blast furnaces of Liège rose along the line like ancient castles burning in a border raid." And the following sentence has the precision and poise to frame pain, death, and joy within a sexual context: "Josef [Grünlich] laughed again happily, feeling the revolver rub gently against the sore on the inside of his knee: I'd have split his guts for him."

As Greene's first entertainment, *Orient Express* has intellectual and historical value. Its thematic variety and vivid style also give it artistic merit. Full of surge, it is worth reading for itself.

3

"Fancy a Thing Like That 'Appening 'Ere in Nottwich"

This Gun for Hire may be the critical anomoly of the Greene canon. Despite its suspense, social timeliness, and religious thrust, it has acquired neither supporters nor staunch foes. Viewing it more as a stepchild than as an anomoly, most critics merely note its melodramatic plot and then, owing to the similarity between its hero, James Raven, and Pinkie Brown, dismiss it as a rehearsal for *Brighton Rock*. Thus Atkins calls it "a very poor performance," and Walter Allen praises it as the best of Greene's early work, but neither critic defends his judgment at any length.

But even though Allen does not try to convince anybody of the high quality of the book, his description of the plot gives a good critical inlet: "the story of a political assassin and his pursuit by the police in a world on the verge of war." [1] *The Name of Action* revolved around a plan to smuggle arms into Trier; *Rumour at Nightfall*, like its model, Conrad's *The Arrow of Gold*, dealt with the smuggling of weapons into Carlist Spain; Greene's confidential agent is under orders to buy British coal in order to fuel a war effort. In keeping with these portrayals of western man edging dangerously the border of mass violence, *This Gun for Hire* depicts a nation arming itself for war. Its opening paragraph gives the reason for the mobilization in a blunt, low-key

Audenesque tone that balances the violence it describes. Since few novels open better than *This Gun for Hire,* the book's first paragraph is worth quoting in full:

> Murder didn't mean much to Raven. It was just a new job. You had to be careful. You had to use your brains. It was not a question of hatred. He had seen the minister only once: he had been pointed out to Raven as he walked down the new housing estate between the little lit Christmas trees—an old, rather grubby man without any friends, who was said to love humanity.

The murder that follows (part 1, chapter 1) is the most violent scene in the book until part 7, 2, where three people are shot to death. As the action unfolds, there is less violence because the memory of the first killing—more harrowing for its muted tone—carries over to the suspenseful scenes that follow. Besides murder, the opening episode also introduces the cinematic technique Greene uses throughout both to reveal character and to authenticate setting: Raven's eyes, "like little concealed cameras, photographed the room instantaneously." Panning from one object in the room to another—the desk, the easy chair, the map on the wall—Greene not only brings physical setting to life; he also roughs in a personality for the shabby minister. The next scene also has this economy, control, and vividness. Greene cuts from the Continent to London, from indoors to out, and from death to life. An engaged couple, Anne Crowder and Detective Sergeant James Mather, are riding a London bus. Greene shows quickly that the couple's loving world and the murderous one of Raven, the lonely harelipped killer, are one. Snow is falling; the time of day is still dusk; the Thames looks dark; Anne and Mather, whose shortage of money may stop their getting married, discuss the killing of the war minister. Then

Anne and Raven pass each other on a cold, dim street. *This Gun for Hire* takes place on a border where innocent and guilty walk together and where decisive victories and defeats do not occur.

Greene thus commits himself, both technically and philosophically, early in the book. And he makes good his dual commitment by working fuguelike variations on his underlying theme of the pursuit. In part 2, 2, the book's four main characters come together at London's Euston Station. Three take the midnight train to Nottwich, and the fourth, Mather, arrives there the next day. Starting with this scene, Greene shifts between the point of view of the hunter and that of the hunted; he devises chases within chases; he has chases reverse themselves; combining pursuit with self-discovery and expanding moral vision, he lays trails of red herrings, or sets false chases. The main chase is the same double one found in Hitchcock's *The Thirty-Nine Steps* (1935), *Young and Innocent* (1937), and *Saboteur* (1942) — while the police chase the hero, the hero is chasing the real criminals. Suspense follows automatically, for the hero must catch the criminals before the police catch *him*. What also follows from the double chase is reader sympathy. We sympathize with victims, and Raven, as the object of a blood chase, is victimized by both the police and his powerful paymasters. An underdog and a loner, he must sometimes take great risks to insure his safety. Pursuit, then, makes for excitement. G. S. Fraser shows how Greene shades reader involvement into moral statement. *This Gun for Hire*, Fraser argues, "uses the convention of the villain-hero, the bad man cheated by worse men, who comes out on the side of the good at the cost of his life." [2]

Physical danger runs higher and hotter in *This Gun for Hire* than anywhere else in Greene. The crime and the gunplay, the narrow escapes and the chain of minor climaxes, make the book his most melodramatic. Aggressive and full of attack, it is also his "purest" thriller. Character, as well as melodramatic technique, put the book squarely in the thriller tradition. Raven fits neatly Ralph Harper's pattern of the thriller-hero in *The World of the Thriller*: like Oedipus, the thriller-hero, as Harper sees him, is a hunter who discovers painful, but self-expanding, home-truths.[3] Harper is right. While lacking the cool detachment of detective fiction, the thriller has psychological drive. Tracing the movements of the outlaw rather than those of the detective, it can make psychic inwardness an anatomy of madness. *This Gun for Hire*, by dealing with a sick crime rather than a rational one, probes the mind of a murderer (Raven-raving). Raven lives in a different world from that of the methodical sleuth of detective fiction. C. Day Lewis, as Nicholas Blake, describes the aesthetic and social differences between the two literary modes (let us note that Anne Crowder, whose name labels her as one of the crowd, enjoys reading thrillers):

> The detective-novel proper is read almost exclusively by the upper and professional classes. The so-called "lower-middle" and "working" classes tend to read "bloods," thrillers. . . . The modern thriller is generally much below the detective story in sophistication and style. When we compare these two kinds of crime fiction, we cannot fail to notice that, whereas in the detective novel the criminal is almost invariably a squalid creature of irremediably flagitous tendencies, the criminal of the thriller is often its hero and nearly always a romantic figure.[4]

James Raven, the romantic hero-villain, resembles a Jacobean avenger. Like Pinkie Brown, he has a "starved intensity, a kind of hideous and unnatural pride." And like Iago, whom Pinkie both apes and quotes, Raven is twenty-eight years old. Before the book opens, he has already killed one man. The first chapter shows him killing two more. Killing, in fact, seems the only personal relationship he can have. Shrinking from human warmth, he has reached a dead end of trusting and loving. His inverted pride has made him a murdering machine. His mind works "with mechanical accuracy, like a ready reckoner," and, with his camera-shutter eyes, he seems "made for destruction." His father was hanged for a criminal; then his mother cut her throat, neglecting to lock the door between the kitchen where she killed herself and the room in which her small son was sleeping. Raven was then raised in an orphan's home which, with its poor food, floggings, and bouts of solitary confinement, rivals the workhouse in *Oliver Twist*.

A vivid sign of Greene's compassion for Raven is Raven's harelip. The harelip, by excluding him from society, leads him to crime and sin. He flashes his harelip angrily on people to punish them for excluding him. But besides expressing his social defiance and inner pain, the harelip also handicaps him as a criminal. The society that has driven him out does not even let him live comfortably outside its pale. Rather, it brings out his worst traits. It makes him cultivate technical cunning and murderousness out of a need to stay alive. Laced by cold winds as he walks alone through the mean streets of London and Nottwich, he is a sour, Satanic figure. Greene expresses his Satanic tendencies by giving him—the modern counterpart of the Prince of the Air—a bird's name and by associating him with darkness. Like the Prince of Darkness (another of Satan's names), he seems to fight light. He broods "darkly," his "dark overcoat" has a "clerical air," and the morning he arrives in Nottwich there is "no dawn. . . . Fog lay over the city like a night sky with no stars." A carrier of darkness, he is never seen in sunlight; even when he does appear during the hours of day, as on his first morning in Nottwich, the sky is dark. Three characters call him "poor devil."

Greene's characters do not usually interact vitally. Yet everybody in *This Gun for Hire* except Raven takes his identity from some force outside himself—like a job or a deeply felt human tie. Raven's upbringing and harelip cut him off from the world. They make him special. In line with his admiration for Mauriac, Greene confers great importance on the acts of obscure people. Twisted and bereft, the homeless Raven comes to matter a great deal to many people. He brings a squad of pursuers from Scotland Yard to Nottwich; he drives Sir Marcus, "one of the richest men in Europe," to the shabby home of Nottwich's chief of police; he purges corruption in industry and finance; he first sparks and then stifles a full-scale European war. Finally an angel of peace, he suggests, in his solitary vigil, Christ as vividly as he does Satan. His dark passage through London and Nottwich, culminating in a birth of sorts, resembles a night journey. The season is Christmas. Looking at a plaster model of the Christmas crib, he lights on "the swaddled child," calling him "the little bastard." An outcast himself, he then speaks of "this business of no room at the inn," and another character later thinks of him simultaneously with "the little lighted crib."

Raven moves, then, on the religious plane. His divine or demonic possession tallies with Greene's Manicheism —the belief that supernatural good and supernatural evil war continually for the soul of man. Related to this fascination with primitive Christianity is Raven's Judas complex. Although his moral code, sanctioning murder, may be warped, he does observe it honorably: "I don't go back on a fellow who treats me right," he says, adding later, "It's not the killings I mind, it's the double-crossing." Ironically, a book that mentions John

Galsworthy's play, *Loyalties*, has a protagonist who feels betrayed on all counts—by his parents, by the poverty that prevented proper surgery for his harelip, by the orphanage that raised him, and by his paymasters, who paid him with stolen marked bills for killing the old Czech minister. But what hurts him most is being betrayed by his own kind—the poor and the lawless. He tries to protect himself from treachery by avoiding other people. Treachery is so rife, though, that even his most fleeting relationships lead to betrayal. Nor is Raven, in spite of his moral code, always the betrayed party. By shooting the old minister, he leagues with the Judases; for not only did the minister cut military budgets to clear the slums; he, too, was reared in a government orphanage. The inevitability, or automatic nature, of treachery in human relations reaches a shrill note in the automatic revolver Raven uses to kill the minister.

Anne Crowder separates Raven's brain from his heart. He both fears and craves someone he can trust. Tired of guarding against treachery, he finally gives in to his feelings. He is reborn by trusting Anne, and his rebirth comes about as a combined cleansing and melting into life. He enters the book with a chip of ice in his breast instead of a loving heart. The pain he feels when the chip melts betokens real growth: "That dagger of ice was melting with great pain." Like the work-raddled perfectionists in *Orient Express*, he fears the ordinary and the normal. A "slow, sleepy tune" that voices the miraculous nature of the commonplace helps make him human: "It's only Kew/To you,/But to me,/It's Paradise." The tune, which Anne plays on her gramaphone, comes to Raven "as . . . something sharp and cold . . . breaking in his heart with great pain. He sat there . . . and began to cry." Music does not soothe Raven's savage breast, but it does activate the flow of warm human blood.

The song, twitching at Raven's mind during his dying moments, helps make the scene a compressed birth and death. Raven has shot the two men who hired him to kill the old minister, and he is shot in turn by a policeman. Yet these deaths, by easing international tension, let others live. More specifically, they give Mather the promotion and salary boost he needs to marry Anne. But for the gunman, his final moments are a dying-into-life. Chastened by the cleansing, healing waters of life, he feels "the ice melt at his heart with a sense of pain and strangeness as if he were passing the customs of a land he had never entered before and would never be able to leave." Like the crowning vision of the tragic hero in Shakespeare, Raven's illumination cannot be converted to deed. Both his privilege and punishment, it serves no practical use. As soon as he completes his mission of killing his treacherous paymasters, strange changes take place inside him. Thoughts throng his mind; he hears music; he becomes human, complex. This onrush of new life addles his coordination and keeps him from killing his pursuer, Mather, who has materialized—literally, a *deus ex machina*—on a painter's scaffold outside the window. His becoming human, then, cuts his effectiveness as a killer: being human and killing operate inversely.

Everything has turned out well. Even a policeman Raven shot while escaping a police ambush is recuperating in the book's only concession to a happy ending. Likewise, nothing has been wasted. As a timeless, or mythical, event occurring instantly in the eye of God or the Devil, the London-Nottwich drama can have no untrimmed edges. Life goes on and corruption is purged, but in violation of the law. Like the divine economy, man's law, however flawed, must be squared. Raven must pay for his crimes, even though they help the common cause; he must also pay for his prideful revenge, since vengeance and the power of giving and taking away life belong only to God. Raven's dying thoughts endorse these truths: "Death came to him in the form of unbearable pain. It was as if he had to deliver this pain as a woman delivers a child, and he sobbed and moaned in the effort. At last it came out of him, and he followed his only child into a vast desolation."

Raven's translation is genuine. His confusion with a woman in childbirth charts his spiritual growth by taking him, dying, into a realm of pure, supersexual being. An earlier thought registered by Mather—that Mather links "a certain kind of pain with the smell of fish"—gives Raven's spiritual growth a Christian slant. Yet even without Greene's veiled allusions to the Passion and to the fish as an emblem of Christ, Raven grows more spiritual as his soul-making ordeal unfolds. First described in a police broadcast as "a little above the middle height," he begins to shrink as soon as he loves Anne Crowder. In a scene deliberately staged to call attention to the process, Anne is "astonished at the smallness of his wrists; his hands had no more strength or substance than a delicate boy's." As the day wears on, he becomes progressively less physical and more spiritual, less mechanical and more human. He is seen as "thin and undersized," as "the small man," and as "the mean, thin, undernourished city rat." Continuing to shrink, he is then described as "a thin figure, little more than a boy's figure." This diminishing process goes on until his death, when, torn from his mortal frame, he becomes all spirit.

His Javert and love rival is the Scotland Yard detective, Sergeant James Mather. In contrast to Raven, Mather is an ordinary man who does ordinary things like work for a living and fall in love. The plight he shares with Anne—lacking the funds to marry—is also ordinary enough in a world just recovering from the 1929 crash. His ordinariness, in fact, is his chief virtue for Anne: "She lived too closely to thwarted genius . . . to admire difference. She wanted her man to be ordinary; she wanted to know what he'd say next." Bulky, prosaic, and anchored in a routine, Mather, too, craves the commonplace. His fiancée, once again, comes from the crowd, and she dances in a chorus line rather than as a solo artist. His preference for collective experience also governs his choice of career. He prefers working in an organization to working alone, and no drive of destiny or ambition impels him to leadership. Surprisingly, however, this conservative lawman has much in common with Raven, the desperate outlaw. Seeing the outlaw pick his way with Anne through a dark railyard, Mather likens himself to the criminal: "There was a kind of relationship between them." The relationship cuts more deeply than either man knows. A clue to their ironic kinship lies in their names. To begin with, they have the same first name. Next, they have the same *a-e* vowel pattern carrying over to their surnames. And where Mather's name begins with a nasal and ends with the letter *r*, Raven's, reversing the pattern, ends with a nasal and begins with R. Finally, the medial consonant in each bisyllabic surname (*th* and *v*) is a fricative.

The similarities linking the two men go on, both playfully and seriously. Some are richly suggestive. During a tense moment, Mather is "horrified at himself for losing grip." Later Raven censures himself in roughly the same way: "This is ruin . . . I'm losing grip." He literally relaxes his grip on his revolver on the next page and refers to Anne, Mather's fiancée, in the following paragraph as "his girl." Earlier, in London, Mather had to end his telephone conversation with Anne because he has no pennies ("I've no coppers": "He oughtn't to go out without coppers"). And at Euston Station, the same day, Raven fumes, "He hadn't even a copper to pass him into the lavatory." Anne, by contrast, dining in an elegant restaurant, takes three coppers from her purse to use in the ladies' room. Anne energizes the obscure tie yoking Raven to Mather. Both men are poor, penniless, and need her for self-enrichment. On another level, order and anarchy, or perhaps even good and evil are warring for Anne; she has these qualities within her and could respond strongly to an outward surge of any of them. At still another level, Greene is merely describing an inchoate, lopsided love triangle. Yet this everyday, prosaic level interests him deeply; this level he charges with vigor. As with Raven, a member of Mather's immediate family has committed suicide. Mather, then, inherits the same legacy of madness as the gangster. And when he sees a woman at a Nottwich church bazaar carrying Anne's handbag, this madness flares out. He becomes, in short, like Raven—an avenger with a private grudge: "Someone was going to die for this."

The scene at the jumble, or bazaar, encompasses a great deal. First, it features betrayal; whenever money comes into view in Greene, betrayal lies close by. Raven spots Anne's handbag just before Mather and, along with Mather, fears for Anne's safety. Both the handbag, a receptacle for money, and the particular woman carrying it, a member of Anne's own class, smack of betrayal. Raven, not Mather, follows the woman home, demanding information about Anne. In this scene and those immediately following, Greene departs from his suggestion that the lawman and the outlaw are identical. He swings the balance in Raven's favor. Raven acts more hastily, more decisively, on Anne's behalf because his love is purer. Although twisted, it is more urgent, it overcomes more obstacles, and it is based on a greater need.

Once again, primitive Christianity can be summoned

to explain Raven's superiority to Mather—or at least Greene's preference for the gangster over the detective. Mather, like his American namesakes, the Puritan Mathers, drips with original sin. Human failings are what his job is about, and he clings to the lawman's creed as to a religious creed. He fights crime because crime means doubt and uncertainty, which menace his stern absolutism. A literalist who wants life's colors flat and all the lines joined, he lacks the imagination fo face the half-tones. This archconservatism can cause little wonder. If his name suggests Puritan stiffness, it also invokes, phonetically, matter—sluggish, inert substance. The plain, heavy lawman, although able to enforce the law, cannot test or change it. Lacking originality, he instigates nothing new. Of the earth, he has no wings.

Raven does promote social change. His dark attire and deeds, his bent for the hours of darkness, and his cynical ravenlike croaking, "I'm educated"—all these things put him on the side of evil. Yet they also free him from the inertia of brute matter. The earthbound Mather lacks this airiness and freedom; his defying the law would undermine the things he lives by. The potential jailbird, Raven, who grows more than anyone else in the book, asserts his fluidity early. After shooting a minister of war who is actually a minister of peace, he does the minister's peacemaking work for him. Nor is this the only parallel between the two men. Both are killed by a bullet in the back. And, as if being shot from the rear does not symbolize treachery vividly enough, both men are betrayed by someone with whom they have a deep personal bond: Sir Marcus, the owner of Midland Steel, had once been the schoolmate of the minister whose death he orders; Anne, who tells the police where to find Raven, is the only person Raven ever trusted.

Nottwich, the setting for most of *This Gun for Hire*, is Greene's paradigm of the Midlands industrial town.

Like Brighton, Freetown (*The Heart of the Matter*), and Haiti (*The Comedians*), it is a seedy, low-slung place with corrupt politics. Its nastiness also resembles Dickens's murky portraits of London and the dark, evil-ridden California settings of Dashiell Hammett, Raymond Chandler, and Ross Macdonald. Set among scarred fields, mounds of torn iron, and deserted quarries, it comprises dingy Victorian office buildings, drafty restaurants, and cheap housing developments done in tacky pastel shades. Its Khyber Avenue, promising exotic romance, is merely a row of sooty apartments. Nor does the shabby gentility exuded by the apartments' coarse gray lace and serviceable furnishings insure safety. Khyber Avenue demonstrates Greene's power to infuse seediness with terror. Two of the book's main characters barely escape murder in Khyber Avenue; a third nearly dies of fright; a fourth, a defrocked priest who leases rooms as love nests, has already lost his mind.

Nottwich adds to the book's drive. Part of its personality stems from Midland Steel, its largest and most powerful business. The big armament factory with the innocuous-sounding name in turn takes much of its reality from its owner, Sir Marcus. To apply the logic that no effect can have more reality than its cause is to give the book's political satire a grim focus. Like Paul Demassener before him (*The Name of Action*) and "Papa Doc" Duvalier after him (*The Comedians*), Sir Marcus is a dictator who is more of a prisoner than a ruler. He enters the book in part 4, midway through Raven's seven-part pilgrimage and, like Raven, is called a devil several times.

The comparison can be extended. While Raven commits crimes outside the law, his counterpart's crimes take place with the law's approval. Sir Marcus lives at the top of the tallest building in town, where, like either Satan or Christ, he can survey his earthly domain. He leads a nearly static life. Hardly sleeping, expending little physical or nervous energy, and dining mostly on biscuits and warm water, he exists more as an idea than as a person. He even has a trained male nurse to help him through the day. But he cannot escape his bad health, his old age, and his greed. What causes terror in him, with his "old scaly eyes" and venomous whisper, is that a shriveled, miserly husk, unable to take care of his bodily needs, controls so many lives. Here is our first look at him:

> Sir Marcus entered on the tips of his toes. He was a very old and very sick man with a little wisp of beard on his chin like chicken fluff. He gave the effect of having withered inside his clothes like a kernel in a nut. He spoke with the faintest foreign accent, and it was difficult to determine whether he was Levantine or of an old English family. He gave the impression that very many cities had rubbed him smooth.

His decrepitude and his trans-European background make him a last descendant of Conrad's Mr. Kurtz, the dying gasp of the old imperialist-capitalist order. The modern fittings and appointments of his factory show his determination to stay alive. A tenacious realist, he adapts to changes outside the factory, as well. He trades profitably on the truth that his society's economy relies on the production of weapons to insure a balance of payments and a low unemployment rate. Greene voices through the business credo of his old munitions mogul his warning of an emerging military-industrial complex. Accepting the Marxist overtones of his warning, he shows western man unable to feed, clothe, and house himself adequately without gearing his economy to wartime production. (The book's typical middle-class couple, we repeat, lacks the money to marry.) By spearheading a war economy, Sir Marcus heightens the war hysteria sweeping Europe. A man nearing death who earns his living by serving the forces of death, he naturally opposes peace and love. Now several times in his career, Greene has used dogs to signal the budding-forth of these divine values. He gets the idea from Francis Thompson's *The Hound of Heaven* and from *The Waste Land,* where the dog whose nails claw the tired topsoil of modern life symbolizes religious terror. The implied metaphor of God as the sleeping dog who, refusing to lie still, dogs peoples' footsteps, plays a big role in *The Potting Shed.* Greene's 1957 play about rebirth mentions Lazarus, and its main character is brought back from death by the prayers of his priest-uncle. The recurring presence in the play of a barking dog and a toy spade suggest the unearthing of an awesome truth. Sir Marcus, the materialist enemy of Christian values, detests dogs.

A very modern protective measure that has helped him ward off a pursuing God, while also prospering, is that of facelessness. He engineers the death of a former schoolmate without remorse; he works through henchmen; his last name is never revealed:

> Everyone knew a lot about Sir Marcus. The trouble was, what they knew was contradictory. . . . His name did not appear at all in Who's Who, and an enterprising journalist who had once tried to write his life found extraordinary gaps in the register.

Sir Marcus is not the only person at Midland Steel who keeps his identity secret. His favorite lieutenant, Willy Davis, is just as faceless and impenetrable. Judging by these two men, impersonality goes hand-in-hand with business success. Davis, we remember, acts as Sir Marcus's agent, first by hiring Raven to kill the Czech minister and then by paying him in marked stolen bills. When we next see him, he is in a Nottwich variety theater, watching a musical revue he has sponsored. Then he has dinner with Anne Crowder, who has come up from London to dance in the revue. After dinner, he takes her to his Khyber Avenue *maisonette*. But instead of having sex with her, he panics at some remarks she lets drop about Raven and tries to kill her.

A hint of Davis's deathly impersonality lies in Greene's practice of always calling him "Mr." Davis; it is as if Davis, the only character in the book referred to in this way, has a shell of formality encasing him. Another hint lies in his practice of using aliases. Dr. Richard Czinner in *Orient Express*, despite his single-mindedness, has to hide behind an alias for five years before moving ahead with his life's work as a Communist. In the same book, the city of Istanbul, with its other names of Constantinople and Stamboul, is a likely setting for double-dealing and hypocrisy. Willy Davis may never get to Stamboul, but, as the enemy of love, eats Turkish Delight. And he has fewer qualms than Dr. Czinner about masking his identity. As has been mentioned, the mask serves him well. The sweet-toothed Davis is a force. And he exercises his power without responsibility. Despite his money and his influence, few people in Nottwich know how he supports himself. His favorite words, when asked to explain his conduct, are, "I'm just an agent." His actions with Anne show him just as impersonal about sex as about business. He demonstrates, with her, a mixture of prudery and excitement that constitutes, for Greene, a facet of British sexuality. He does not look at Anne during dinner ("Mr. Davis never looked at a face"), and he takes her to his *maisonette* as he would a client to his office. This impersonality shows its lethal edge quickly; for just as Davis's honeyed voice betrayed Raven, so do his sugary hands choke Anne.

Davis's emerald ring, with its cold glitter and resemblance to a snake's eye, symbolizes treachery. Curiously, the person he betrays most often is himself. Within three days, he blunders seriously several times: by paying Raven with nonnegotiable notes, by trying to kill Anne and then not killing her, and by forgetting his gas mask the day of Nottwich's air-raid drill. These blunders cost Davis dearly. They also help form Greene's satire on British business; for bunglers, mediocrities, and incompetents enjoy high places all over the power structure. Sir Marcus, who controls Nottwich's politics and police force, demands obedience from his subalterns rather than skill. Joseph Calkin, the police chief, shows how little merit and hard work count in local circles: "He remembered his appointment; it had been 'worked,' of course." The hen-pecked Calkin craves war, because, lacking the wit to flourish in peace, he needs the vividness of war both to give his life meaning and to take him out from under his wife's feet. Mr. Collier, the producer of the local variety theater, combines fascism with ineffectiveness. He is introduced thus into the book:

> "I want discipline," Mr. Collier said, "and I'm going to have discipline." He was rather undersized, with a fierce eye and straw-colored hair and a receding chin. . . . He wasn't a good producer: his appointment was due to more wheels within wheels than you could count.

Greene's point strikes home. This sleaziness could only achieve high status in a corrupt, involuted society. Like its foul weather, the corruption, labyrinthine complexity, and treachery that stream through all reaches of society make Nottwich an ugly place. Although capable of dishonesty and violence, its corps of seedy ineffectuals cannot apprehend Raven or halt the arms race sweeping Europe.

Whereas organized industry, the Nottwich police, and an ultimatum delivered by a foreign power all fail to quiet the war hysteria, Anne Crowder succeeds. Like many other Greene characters, Anne learns that she must take sides. In keeping with the costive spirit of her time, she defends the bad against the worst. In order to prevent war, she helps Raven find Davis before her fiancé, Mather, finds Raven. Raven, in turn, the avenger who destroys and creates simultaneously, seems driven by unseen powers. Such editorial intrusions as, "It was almost as if he were acting for someone else," strew his trail. Like Dickens, Greene often moves us most when either ancestral or supernatural forces shape the choices of his characters. Stratford's opinion, that "an unstated religious view infiltrates and colors" [5] *This Gun for Hire*, has already been proved correct. Greene continues to invite a religious interpretation for his narrative. He playfully suggests that his action takes place *sub specie aeternatatis*—under the aspect of eternity—by seating two characters under a statue of Jupiter, or Zeus, in the dining room of a Nottwich hotel. Kunkel has shown that the old minister's asking Raven in a dream to shoot him resembles Christ's consenting death; [6] Anne's flat in Nottwich is on All Saints Road; the very name of Nottwich suggests a naughting or routing of sorcery; all other doors in Nottwich closed to him, Raven sleeps one night in a Catholic church; the phrase, "Raven's head on a platter," recalls John the Baptist, another precursor. Then there is the number three, expressive of the Trinity: the midnight train that carries three of the book's chief characters from London to Nottwich boards on Platform Three; three people try to kill Anne; three people get shot to death on Christmas day in Nottwich; the time scheme of the book, after the murder of the war minister in 1, chapter 1, spans three days.

Nor has the harsh Midland winter dried the life germ.

Ice-clamped Nottwich clamors with suggestions of birth and renewal. Anne's lips, "as vividly stained as a winter berry," remind us, along with Christmas and a popular song about "a sunflower . . . from Greenland," that beauty can burst forth in winter. The various green appearances flickering over the narrative stress further the ideas of fertility and renewal. This vitality, no mere adornment, drives into the human drama. If Anne creates new life in Raven, Raven also revivifies her by pulling her out of the chimney where Davis had stuffed her. Shortly after her disinterment, Raven talks of "beginning life over again," and Anne speaks of babies.

Christian symbolism enriches the action from the time Raven arrives in Nottwich. The paragraph describing his arrival ends with the pealing of a church bell, as if to formalize his coming. Greene gives Raven's meeting with Anne at the train station a moment later the same ceremonial coloring. The hunted Raven uses Anne to get past the station guards. But Anne and Raven are not through with each other. Greene alerts us to the importance of their budding relationship by stating that she pushed him "finally into other people's lives, broke the world in which he walked alone." On the next page, she dashes coffee in his face when he turns his gun on her. Taking place both at daybreak and at the dawn of his new life, the coffee-throwing becomes a symbolic baptism. And like Jesus in the desert, Raven never weakens in his resolve as he wanders, homeless, through the dreary waste of Nottwich.

Critics have either neglected or misunderstood the importance of part 8 within the pattern of *This Gun for Hire*. Allott and Farris voice a typical view when they call Raven's death at the end of part 7 "the true ending of the story. Raven's death," they add, "completes the meaning of the book." [7] This attitude is curious, for it reflects an ignorance of Greene's fictional practice.

Greene never ends his books with the death of a main character; *Brighton Rock, The Power and the Glory, The Heart of the Matter, The End of the Affair,* and *A Burnt-Out Case,* to give some examples from his best work, all continue somewhere between ten and forty pages after their central figure dies. The tactic reaps gains: it gives a fuller picture of the central figure's impact on the lives around him, and it shifts the narrative focus away from the central figure and toward an encompassing—social and/or metaphysical—dimension. Part 8 builds this kind of ironic frame around Raven. Greene divides it into five chapters, thus registering the results of Raven's London-Nottwich adventure from five different angles. Nobody, it seems, knows that Raven has stopped a war except Anne and Mather, and *their* thoughts, now that they can marry, turn on themselves. Complexity and muddle are restored: Major Calkin sees "life . . . going on quite in the old way," and another character, following suit, says, "Well . . . life goes on." These reactions, and others like it, question the worth of Raven's sacrifice. The perpetuation of human life, though a victory, is a broken one. A great deal has been lost, and much of what has been saved may not be worth saving.

Evil has certainly not been driven out. A man who gives a speech at a local masonic hall looks like Davis, and a photograph above the speaker's platform reveals the master of the lodge as Sir Marcus. Yet Greene, always wary of simplified moralities, both refreshes and balances his picture of the treacherous arms merchant: Sir Marcus, we learn, in the days before the slump, gave his workers turkeys for Christmas. Life on the border permits no clear-cut distinctions. Like Eliot's *Murder in the Cathedral* (1935) and Auden and Isherwood's *The Accent of F6* (1936), which also treat the restoration of human life within a religious frame, Greene's 1936 entertainment gives its surviving characters the final say on the action. Yet their collective view is not definitive. The book ends on a moving train. The bells and twinkling lights of a London Christmas, by making Anne childlike, signal a new start for her as Mather's wife in a peaceful world. The train, however, has not reached its station. She remains a traveler until the end, with both her destiny and destination unreached.

Another way Greene expresses the predicament of living on a border between two eternities is by invoking the color mauve. Mauve gets into much of his work. The dining car of the Orient Express has mauve-shaded lamps; Erik Krogh wears a mauve-striped suit in *England Made Me*; an outsize lady at a gambling casino in *Loser Takes All* wears a mauve dress, and the narrator refers to "her massive mauve flank"; the frocks worn by some American women in "Cheap in August" are decorated with mauve flowers, and a man from St. Louis wears pajamas "with broad mauve stripes" in the same story, from *May We Borrow Your Husband?* Finally, the American edition of *Travels with My Aunt* (1970) has a mauve jacket and dustcover. But why? What do these patches of mauve mean? Thomas Beer defined mauve in the epigraph of his 1926 study of America's self-unfolding in the 1890s, *The Mauve Decade*. "Mauve? Mauve is just pink trying to be purple." Greene need not have read Beer's book. The struggle implied in Beer's tongue-in-check definition and the hybrid nature of mauve both go nicely with his metaphysics. A highly graphic writer, Greene likes bright settings, and mauve, by serving him both visually and thematically, has always been one of his favorite brighteners.

But why talk about his preference for mauve in connection with *This Gun for Hire*? First of all, the book is splashed with mauve; mauve appears three times in part 8 alone. Secondly, the book, with its observations on the dynamics of power, is the most political of Greene's entertainments. England's body politics coheres as a stubborn antidialectical flow. The crabwise rhythm of thin victories and losses describes the foggy, dual nature of things. Sooner or later, everything resembles its opposite: acts offset other acts, the work of hate and of love merge and dissolve while an ignorant public stands indifferently by. Change occurs in the eye of immobility. The narrative traces no progression, only a repetition. Western Europe has no engine other than material self-interest.

Mauve is just one example of how the book's concreteness makes ideas live. London stands forth as a physical reality; monuments, store fronts, and passers-by come into view as Raven walks from Soho Square to Oxford and Charlotte Streets and then takes a taxi to Euston Station via Tottenham Court and Charing Cross roads. The picaresque adventure also provides glimpses of the worlds of high finance, journalism, police work, the university, and the variety theater. We get a privileged inside view of the maneuvering underlying major public events. A relentless, severe book, *This Gun for Hire* gains much of its force from clear, sharp details. Yet it is no mere factual report. Greene's craftsmanship prevents congestion; rather than heaping up information, he channels his carefully selected data into a developing plot. As the horrors of mobilization emerge, the powers behind the war drive declare themselves Raven's enemies. Thus Raven, despite his motives, aligns with the forces of peace, and our hearts open to him.

Details often encourage our sympathy for Raven by creating nasty, sullen pictures of characters who cheat or betray him. Dr. Yogel, the London dentist who tries to betray Raven to the police, reveals dirty fingernails while inspecting Raven's lip. Acky, the mad defrocked priest

who keeps a rooming house on Nottwich's Khyber Avenue with his "old wicked wrinkled" wife, Tiny, materializes in hideous depth thanks to Greene's sure instinct for details: "A good school and a theological
college had formed his accent; something else had
broken his nose." Acky's Satanic descent from sanity to
madness and from the pulpit to a cheap rooming house
makes him a chilling character. Like Frederick Rolfe,
the self-styled Baron Corvo, about whom Greene wrote
three essays in 1934–35, he was defrocked because of
sexual misconduct. Greene, though, does not let his
obsession with spoiled priests cloud his artistry. Already
equipped with two diabolic figures in Raven and Sir
Marcus, he discretely limits Acky's appearances in the
book.

Discretion keeps the book from sagging under both
its documentary materials and grim overview. We want
to know what happens next in *This Gun for Hire*. The
suspense, the lively action, and the high proportion of
dialogue to narration maintain a high level of "story"
interest. Greene, moreover, manages his dialogue so
that speeches do not usually answer directly those pre-
ceding. If this technique rasps the nerves, it also keeps
the reader alert. And if the book suffuses evil, it also
suffuses a great deal of tenderness, as can be seen in
several private relationships. The book houses a wide
range of ideas, settings, and characters. Its smooth
assimilation of these data nearly makes it a handbook
on novel-writing.

Much of this economy can be traced to Greene's
omniscient technique. Instead of confining his narrative
to the scope of his characters, Greene steps in to summarize, to deliver the telling detail, or to give an event
social or historical resonance. His interrupting the scene
at the church jumble, where Mather and Raven both
spot Anne's purse, speeds narrative tempo and builds

suspense: "He [Raven] walked fast. He didn't notice in his hurry that he in turn was followed by a man whose clothes he would immediately have recognized, the soft hat and overcoat worn like a uniform."

It is odd that nobody has discussed the technical achievement of part 7, chapter 1, of *This Gun for Hire*. This chapter is a bright spot, not only in the book, but also in Greene's writing career, and it owes a good deal of its brilliance to the godlike mobility and control Greene arrogates to himself. Within ten pages, he translates the political temper of the 1930s into blood, muscle, and nerves. Here is the background for the episode: the war scare has moved Whitehall to order air-raid drills with gas masks for all British cities with a population of 50,000 or more. By chance, Nottwich's gas drill coincides with the ritual "rag" of the local medical college. Now Greene, in *Another Mexico*, says that rags are traditions in some universities. Community pranks by students, they represent to him a dangerous giving-in to infantilism, an expression of "cruel anarchic adolescence." In *This Gun for Hire*, the ragging students supervise the alleged casualties from the gas drill. Acting like storm troopers, they fly in the face of order, process, and reason. The rag smashes civilized values: "The very word 'rag' was powerful; it conferred complete freedom from control."

Buddy Fergusson, leader of the rag, embodies the fascist-militarist strain of Nottwich life. He is the ideal officer of the police state, and what fits him so well for the role is his weakness, not his strength. Greene brings him to life by projecting him against a moving background of time. Discussing the question of time shift in fiction in 1935, he pointed out the limitations imposed by a straight linear chronology: "The trouble in a novel which follows the chronological sequence is that your events are never history. You are condemned to write of a perpetual present and to convey the shrillness of its emotions." *This Gun for Hire* does not shift time as freely as either *The End of the Affair* or *The Comedians*. The rag episode, though, races back and forth in time to contrast Buddy's vivid present with his dreary, run-down future. The clash, besides describing the Nazi psyche, humanizes Buddy. A poor student, he welcomes the rag. Like Major Calkin, he needs the vulgar excitement of war and the simplified logic of rule by force. If a society based on reason and love withholds success from him, he must create one based on madness and hate: "Only war and death could save Buddy from the confinements, the provincial practice, the one dull wife." History and psychology merge as the power-drunk Buddy fights orderly civilized process:

> "Treat 'em rough," they shrieked at him, and "You're telling me," he said magnificently, keeping well at bay any thought of the future. . . . "Got your gas masks ready?" he called to them, the undisputed leader, daredevil Buddy. What the hell did examinations matter when you were a leader of men?

Greene anchors his subtle, inclusive portrait of Buddy in a key event. Seeing Raven without a gas mask, Buddy tries to arrest him as a "casualty." But Raven, whose deadly resolve clashes with the boyish anarchy of the students, turns his gun on Buddy, leads him to a garage, makes him take off his clothes, ties him up, and then goes away wearing his gas mask and clothes. The sharp visual picture of the well-fed Buddy shivering in his underwear imparts pathos and tenderness. The speed of the episode expresses the violence that the Mosley-prototype both craves and is done in by. Within minutes he loses more ground than he can ever recover. Greene conveys the depth of Buddy's humiliation by channelling it through an historical shaft:

It was a moment in his life that he never forgot; he was not allowed to forget it by friends who saw nothing wrong in what he did. All through his life the tale cropped up in print in the most unlikely places: serious histories, symposiums of famous crimes. It followed him from obscure practice to obscure practice.

Appropriately, Raven kills Davis while wearing Buddy's gas mask and clothes. The overweight, mediocre Buddy is a younger Davis. Their immaturity comes out in the mawkish view of sex they share: "He [Buddy] believed in love—something rather maternal with deep breasts": "When they sang, 'You have my mother's way,' he [Davis] really did think of his mother; he was the ideal audience." Dressed in Buddy's garb, Raven kills Davis with his own weapons—facelessness and impersonality. Anne Crowder's remark, "babies can't wear gas masks because there's not enough air for them," makes the gas mask a force for death. The gas mask, besides fronting Davis with his own deathly image ("I'm just an agent"), unifies Greene's satire. By making all people look alike, gas masks suit the police state perfectly. A dictatorship cannot tolerate human difference or individuality; if it did, it could never persuade its public that it had reached the zenith of political wisdom. But neither can it pitch the uniformity it encourages to a high civilized level. Thus the medical students leading the rag come into sight as "half-a-dozen masked monstrosities in white coats smutted with soot. It was impossible to tell one from another." The scorn for dialogue shown by Davis in his business dealings and by Buddy in his strong-arm politics stunts life. A few errand boys who pass by on their bicycles wearing gas masks look like "bears doing a trick cycle act in a circus." And while the mask flattens and distorts, it does not transform; Buddy is immediately recognized by two people in spite of his mask. The denial of freedom expressed by the mask leads logically to the denial of life expressed by the war fever already infecting British politics and business. The book's religious symbolism is redeemed; for only a miracle can pull western man out of the morass into which he has slid.

Unfortunately, though, the miracle does not join all the novel's loose ends. In spite of its many strengths, *This Gun for Hire* is not without flaws. Its rich, interweaving pattern is marred, first, by a coincidence-ridden plot. Just as Raven is about to kill Anne in a model home of a new housing development, a sales agent from the development comes into the home with a client. This staginess is excused in part by Greene's irony. The morning, we remember, is both Raven's first in Nottwich and the dawn of his rebirth. The real-estate man whose entry stops Raven from killing Anne is named Green, and his client is named Graves. Thus the new and gravelike companion each other, mirroring both the fusion of birth and death in Raven and the juxtaposition of the outsider with the girl from the crowd. Graves, moreover, carries the extremes of birth and death within himself. "A young-old man" funereally clad in a black suit, he emanates "the idea of babies." By thinking quickly and pressing two five-pound notes into Green's hand as a deposit on the home, Anne cheats the grave-Graves twice.

Unfortunately, Greene's impish humor does not smooth the harshness generated by the book's other coincidences. Just as a policeman shoots at Anne, masquerading as Raven in order to let the gunman escape, a startling whistle throws off the policeman's aim. Several hours before this coincidence, Mather and Raven see Anne's purse simultaneously at the jumble; several hours after it, Raven happens upon Davis, thereby repeating an earlier chance discovery of him in London. We have already mentioned the coincidence of the rag and the gas drill. More curious and unlikely is the fact that both these events take place on Christmas. And it can only be for the sake of the plot that Christmas is also a normal working day, not only at Midland Steel but all over Nottwich.

The book's use of gangster cant causes less worry. Raven tells Davis, "If you squeal I'll plug you so full of lead they'll be able to use you as a doorstop." But he is a professional criminal, and we cannot be surprised if he talks like one. The popularity of American hard-boiled detective fiction in the 1930s no doubt influenced Raven's speech, if not the conception and plan of the book itself. The influence, though, is not as strong as it might have been. Raven seldom lapses into gangster cant, and Greene keeps the book very British in spirit. A sordid thriller like James Hadley Chase's *No Orchids for Miss Blandish* (1939), shot through with sadistic crimes and told in an American gangster idiom, shows how another British novelist gave in to a popular trend Greene was strong enough to resist.

This Gun for Hire is exceptional both in its solidity and beauty of design. The most casual incidental can send out rays of meaning. Raven's hearing a scrap of Tennyson's *Maud* on the BBC, though capable of passing unnoticed, invites comparisons between *Maud* and *This Gun for Hire*. These comparisons bear out Greene's uncanny ability to turn his formal learning to the services of his art. Both works use as settings the yards, squares, and streets of an industrial town. Both attack capitalism. But whereas the poem rakes Britain's class system, the book shows members of the same class betraying each other. Raven and the narrator of *Maud* both have a parent who committed suicide; both have not only been spurned but also betrayed by the women they love. And like Raven, the poem's narrator is a hag-ridden figure ("Thro' the hubbub of the market/ I steal, a wasted frame" [2: 208–9]) who follows a single-minded course ("cleaved to a cause . . . pure and true" [3: 31]). Finally, hero and society are reborn in both works. But instead of explaining this rebirth rationally, Tennyson and Greene both ask, "Do we move ourselves, or are we moved by an unseen hand at a game . . . ?" (1: 127).

This Gun for Hire is the best book Greene wrote up to the time of its composition except, perhaps, for *England Made Me*. It also has a more cunning design and tighter organization than *Brighton Rock*, to which it is almost always unfavorably compared.

4

The Complicated Work of Half-Trust and Half-Deceit

The Confidential Agent both resembles and differs from *This Gun for Hire*. Greene again describes setting and character with drypoint sharpness; he also brings back the pursuit theme and carries it again into the leaden, frostbitten Midlands just before the Christmas season. And the web of trust, distrust, and betrayal stretched over the action creates the same tricky glow lighting the earlier book. Yet, even though attitude and technique coincide in both works, the later entertainment has a different outlook and emphasis. First, it is a smoother, more sober book. It does not try for the dazzling variety that marked both *This Gun for Hire* and *Orient Express*. Using fewer characters and confining itself to a narrower social range, it is a more digested, or "rendered," work, to use a term from Conrad. *The Confidential Agent* sets Greene new artistic challenges. Using less data and shifting its focus less freely, it generates excitement while maintaining a fixed point of view. Everything that happens reaches us through the mind of D., a university professor specializing in the *chanson de geste*, who, as has been said, has come to England to buy coal for his government's war. As an impressionistic fiction, *The Confidential Agent* stands closer to the life it describes than the two earlier books. Thus when D. is shot at, the misfire is a physical sensation; instead of saying that somebody shot D. and missed, Greene has us discover the shooting together with D.: "There was a small scraping sound behind him, and a piece of brick suddenly flew out of the wall and struck him sharply on the cheek. . . . He knew that somebody had fired at him with a silencer."

The fixed narrative focus delivers the virtues of economy, plausibility, and evenness of both voice and texture. *The Confidential Agent,* owing to its aim and design, works better from the finite perspective than it would have from the omniscient. D., the central intelligence, is a decent, sensitive man of forty-five, with most of his exciting moments apparently behind him. A former prisoner of war whose wife was killed by the rebels, he has a firsthand, as well as an historical, knowledge of violence. Like Conrad's *The Secret Agent, The Confidential Agent* studies civic freedom in England during a time of peace. By conveying its findings through D., who has not visited England for seventeen years, Greene sharpens his satire. He shows his English readers how they look to an intelligent non-Englishman accustomed to war. England does not hold up well when judged by D.'s standards. Officially at peace, it materializes as more stricken and war-raked than D.'s country. And the book's point-of-view technique makes this heartlessness live by showing D.'s shock and growing awareness as not only a rational protest but also as a skein of physical degradations. The book's sociology, then, gets translated into bone, nerves, and muscle, where it makes its shrillest impact.

Moving from technique to idea, we note an enlargement of political vision in *The Confidential Agent.* The book bears out Anthony Burgess's judgment, "British politics are too small for Greene."[1] Like Edgar Wallace's *The Four Just Men,* which Greene admires, it brings the civil war of a foreign power to British soil.

But it shows more vividly than Wallace's book the international character of politics, business, and war. Fabulist as well as raconteur, Greene ranges comfortably over this broadened social terrain. The international theme of *The Confidential Agent* both smoothes the transition and energizes the flow between his satire, ontology, and religious view. Also, it joins with the point-of-view technique to generate irony between life in a country at war and in one at peace. Greene's belief that life everywhere is a battlefield, channeled through the civilized, battle-weary mentality of D., creates surprises found neither in *The Four Just Men* nor *This Gun for Hire*.

Like John Le Carré's *The Spy Who Came in from The Cold* (1963) and Adam Hall's *The Quiller Memorandum* (1965), Greene's 1939 entertainment shows the growing aloneness of the secret agent who works alone. David Lodge links D.'s solitary mission both to Greene's Judas complex and to the title of the book: "The irony of the title is clear: D. is a confidential agent in whom no one has confidence, and who can have confidence in no one." [2] Treachery stalks D. as pitilessly as it did Raven. His leaders at home and his contacts in England both betray their government unflinchingly. The idea of betraying one's own kind comes back several times from *This Gun for Hire*. Besides the treason of D.'s fellows, a beggar lures D. into the mews where he is shot at with the following words: "I wouldn't have addressed you . . . if I hadn't felt that you were, well, of one's own kind." Also recurring from *This Gun for Hire* is Greene's description of life as a reversible flow; for, like Raven, D. unconsciously betrays people close to him into danger, even death.

Consequently, he mistrusts himself as much as he mistrusts others. Burgess, speaking of the paradoxes and enigmas in Greene, mentions "the sinner who is really

a saint, the philanthropist who is really a destroyer." [3]
D. fits Burgess's definition. He has no pat morality;
holding no brief with codes or credos, he weaves his
moral philosophy into his life style. He acts decently
and honestly because he cannot live otherwise: "All over
the world there were people like himself who didn't
believe in being corrupted—simply because it made life
impossible. It wasn't so much a question of morality,
but a question of simply existing." Nor is he disillu-
sioned about his country's war; he knows he is working
for unscrupulous men, supporting an impure cause, and
performing evil so that good may win out. Yet he is
called a fool, a bourgeois, and a sentimentalist by others
and, more scathingly, a carrier of violence by himself.
The scathing self-disclaimer is characteristic; Greene's
heroes usually scold themselves for their failings and
downgrade their virtues. Francis Andrews, hero of
Greene's first novel, *The Man Within*, is asked, "Why
do you always make so little of the good you do . . .
and make so much of the bad?" D. also follows Andrews
in being a coward. Nearly a burnt-out case, he claims
that fear is the only emotion he can feel. His emotions,
he says, have been smashed: his country has been at
war for two years; his wife of fifteen years is dead; he
is haunted by the memory of lying pinned under the
rubble of a bombed building for fifty-six hours with a
dead cat pressed to his mouth. In order to shield himself
from pain, he cringes from any threat. What he does not
understand is that his cringing, rather than denying life,
affirms it. Implying that his skin is worth saving, his
cowardice works as a declaration of faith.

The declaration is redeemed; for, according to
Greene's dramatic logic, D. comes through as the book's
most living person. First seen on a Channel ferry preparing to dock at Dover harbor, he emerges as "a middle-
aged man with a heavy moustache and a scarred chin

and worry like a habit on his forehead. . . . He carried
the war with him. Wherever D. was, there was the war."
The great stir this mild, tormented professor causes
affirms his aliveness. Referred to as a leper and a typhoid
carrier, he whips up trouble wherever he goes. During
his three-day stay in England, he is beaten and shot at
and robbed; his lodgings, wallet, and clothes are
searched; he is charged with using a forged passport,
inciting to violence, possessing a weapon illegally, stealing a car, and resisting arrest; he causes two deaths.
These ravages designate life. D.'s being dug out from
under the wreckage of a bombed building near the start
of his country's civil war stands as a birth—a birth into
pain and loss, the core realities of a world darkened by
treachery and original sin. No prisoner of a dead past, he
shapes a future both for himself and his countrymen. A
realist and not a savior, he creates this new life in the
world's own way:

> He wasn't certain that he wasn't watched at this
> moment. He wasn't certain that it wasn't right for
> him to be watched. . . . And the watcher—was he
> watched? He was haunted for a moment by the vision
> of an endless distrust.

D.'s birth as a suffering man in a sick, suffering world
turns the mind to Greene's obsession with dirt and
decay. Elizabeth Sewell first noted this obsession in
1954; [4] but by linking Greene with the Decadent poets
of the late nineteenth century, she overlooks his insistence on the life-renewing powers of decay and waste.
This insistence has expressed itself over the years in a
preoccupation with toilets and lavatories. *Babbling April*
(1925), a book of undergraduate verse, contains the
following lines: "Star of the evening,/Beautiful evening
star,/ Star of the evening,/Shining on the shithouse
door." The preoccupation has lasted. *Travels with My*

Aunt (1970) shows one character dying in a lavatory and another dying on the way to one; a CIA agent in the book tabulates the time he spends each day urinating. Raven had tried to kill Anne Crowder in a lavatory; one character does die in a lavatory in *The Ministry of Fear*, and others elude the police both in that book and in *Our Man in Havana* by climbing out of bathroom windows. Filth and ugliness, then, lead to freedom. In "Under the Garden" (1963), they even promote beauty and growth. The underground throne of Javitt, a roguish philosopher-gnome, is an old toilet seat, and Javitt's bowel movements certify his kingship: "I shit dead stuff every day, do I? How wrong you are. . . . Everything that comes out of me is alive, I tell you. It's squirming around there, germs and bacilli and the like, and it goes into the ground like a womb, and it comes out somewhere." Javitt's lovely daughter, at once the publicized "Ramsgate Beauty Queen" and the off-spring of malformed parents, makes good his boast. The sun does shine on the stranded chamber pot. A figure of fancy in a fantastic tale, the Ramsgate Beauty Queen nonetheless shows corruption working for renewal and vitality.

Decay and failure show their magnetism in *The Confidential Agent*. Two of the book's crucial scenes occur in bathrooms, and D.'s most dangerous foes are decidedly unheroic: a cross-eyed chauffeur, the bent, shabby beggar who decoys D. into the mews where he is shot at, and the ridiculously stiff butler who apparently steals D.'s credentials just before the official interview where D. must produce them. D.'s birth amid shards and rubble coincides with a sexual death, conveyed by the dead cat's fur pressing his mouth; he describes his first day in England, after being searched and beaten, as "on the whole a successful one"; he rediscovers sexual love and sees his English mission as "certainly half a victory" at the end of a parade of setbacks. These ambiguities symbolize the Manichean struggle of good and evil, light and dark, spirit and matter. Mani did not fret about light and dark existing side by side in the world; he complained that the light and dark had run together, producing hideous and baffling mixtures of vice and virtue, reason and brutishness. Life in *The Confidential Agent* maintains itself by mixing with death and decay. Loss and gain, heroism and diabolism, have grown so interlocked in our fallen world that rational systems of thought can only mislead.

D. earns relative success and happiness because he does not hold back from adding his measure of contamination to an already contaminated world. He thus faces the world realistically—as he finds it. He has the ability to commit himself unselfishly, and any warm outgoing of self in a fallen world is, to Greene, heroic. Besides implying courage, positive action endorses the worth of human endeavor. It has already been said that Greene's heroes, including D., underrate themselves. No bystander, D. risks his life for his political beliefs. An intellectual by profession and a skeptic by temperament, he has good reason to doubt his qualifications as a man with a mission. Yet he soon overcomes his skepticism, and his intellectual training prepares him for his ordeal.

Before we meet him, he has already edited the Berne manuscript of *The Song of Roland*. This text contrasts "the flashy courage of Roland" with "the humanity and common sense of Oliver," [5] one of Roland's warchiefs. In it, Roland sacrifices his troops for personal glory by refusing Charlemagne's help against the Saracens. Oliver, on the other hand, emerges as the *Song's* hero in the Berne manuscript. Whereas the standard Oxford version shows Oliver killing Roland by accident, the Berne text makes the deathblow intentional. The planned murder, by showing love doing the work of hate, paints a more realistic, more tragic, picture: "In the Berne version he [Oliver] strikes his friend down with full knowledge—because of what he has done to his men, all the wasted lives. He dies hating the man he loves." Adventure stories usually satisfy the reader's longing for decisive, successful action. The Berne version of *The Song of Roland* and *The Confidential Agent* withhold this satisfaction. More honestly, they show war creating a climate of unreality. Yet, D. learns, war is even redder today than in the Middle Ages. There are no more noble wars or warriors to follow with the Crusader's zeal. Today, one's confederates are wicked; both D.'s enemies and friends spy on him and are spied upon in turn.

D. quickly converts his theoretical knowledge of war to practical uses. A brief summary of his adventures reveal him as perhaps the outstanding male character in the Greene canon. For not only is he adaptable; despite recurring spells of fainting, he is also tough. He toils patiently against the grain. Even though everything he does seems to go wrong, he keeps his sense of humor and self-irony. His quick thinking and decisiveness win the day for him several times. He makes an impromptu speech to a crowd of jobless miners; he stuns a treacherous embassy official with a blow to the Adam's apple, steals his gun, and uses the gun to outwit the police. When finally caught, he holds his own in a police interrogation. One of the book's best scenes shows him outbargaining the directors of a colliery, although, representing a crippled government, he has little bargaining power. Negotiator, scholar, and man of action, he also appeals to women. Despite his blunted sexual drive, a London char loves him at first sight; while Rose Cullen, heroine and daughter of the peer whose coal he wants to buy, asks to spend the night with him the first two times they meet. These romantic awakenings speak highly for him, considering that Else, the char, is fourteen, Rose is twenty, and he is a battered widower of forty-five. And although he fails to buy British coal for his country's leaders, he keeps the coal out of the rebels' hands. His viewing his mission as "half a victory" is too modest an evaluation. Like *This Gun for Hire*, the book allows only broken victories and tentative gains. D. ends his holding action by holding Rose in his arms on the book's last page as their ship heaves and pitches in stormy waters.

D.'s powers do not make him self-sufficient. To his surprise, he needs Rose—both to escape the police and to restore his humanity. (Could Greene be hinting at her importance with the punning suggestion that D. comes to see life through Rose Cullen glasses?) He needs somebody to love in order to complete himself. Greene conveys his incompleteness by giving him an alter ego, or double, in the character of L. The two men, compatriots, have known each other for several years. The first chapter shows them taking the same Channel ferry to England for the same purpose; too, they have appointments the same morning with the same coal company. But whereas D. serves his government, L. is working for the rebels. Their first conversation is a mirror meeting at the rail dividing the first- and third-class decks of the fog-wrapped ferry. That D. is traveling third class suggests both the uphill nature of his mission and the disrepair of his government. His troubles in England trap him more tightly in the underdog's role. Yet, even though L. tries to bribe him, he never patronizes or despises him. The men treat each other respectfully, not only on the ship, but also during their three meetings on English soil. D. admires L. grudgingly and admits he could do his job better if he disliked him. The device of the double, or *doppelgänger*, had appeared in several earlier books by Greene. In none of them, though, either earlier or later, does it work better than in

The Confidential Agent. Not only do D. and L., who serve warring factions, meet during crucial moments; their actions offset each other. Both men have aristocratic ties; both are interested in scholarship and the arts. L., who has become Chancellor of the University where D. once taught, tells his counterpart, "You really belong to us."

What first comes to mind from the D.-L. pairing is that D., representing the underdogs in a civil war, stands for death and that L. serves the forces of life. D. says of L., "The man had an integrity of a kind: he gave an impression of truth." L., working with the same energy and devotion as D., deserves D.'s praise. And the praise is reciprocated. A mutual regard knits the two men, despite their conflicting missions. As it suggests, the difference between them is not so clear-cut as the life-death dualism first suggests. D. keeps alive under his burden of decay and destruction, and L., dyspeptic and effete, does not stand for vigorous, abounding life. The political theme of *The Confidential Agent* owes much to the Spanish Civil War (1936–38). As Orwell's *Homage to Catalonia* and Auden's "Spain 1937" say, England sympathized more with the Republicans than with Franco's rightist rebels. Although Greene specifies no ideologies—and Rose's complaint that D.'s language is gritty with consonants rules out Spain as an exact model—he aligns D. with communism and L. with totalitarianism. D. says of L., "His place was among dead things," and he calls him "an antique" and "a museum piece." He is right. The life L. represents is a poor show. A collector, he prizes his paintings, cabinets, and manuscripts above all else and, like all collectors, has no moral instinct—his possessions possess him. He maintains his cool elegance so effortlessly because he has turned his back on human inconsistency. To simplify the contrast between him and D., D. suffers because he rejects the formality of the museum in favor of the raw pungency of the zoo. The sterility and dryness of L.'s formalized life come through in L.'s person. Nervous, frail, and "thin as celery," he grasps life weakly.

War, then, both weakens and dehumanizes. It saps strength, destroys personal identity, and forces us to do evil. D. brings danger to everyone close to him; L. is sickly; K., a confederate of D.'s, dies of fright; Marie Mendrill, the British manageress of the Bloomsbury lodgings where D. stays, goes mad. What is more, the failures of D. and L. to buy British coal will probably extend their country's civil war. Atkins uses war to contrast D. and his nationals with the English characters in the book:

> In addition to D., we have a Mr. K., a teacher of the Entrenationo language and D.'s contact in London. The enemy agent is L. . . . It is also noteworthy that D. had previously been a lecturer at the University of Zed. It is only the foreign agents who possess this anonymity. The English characters, who exist in a less shadowy world, have substantial names.[6]

Atkins's argument has force. The cinematic tours of London Greene treats us to reveal colorful store windows, glowing lights, and trusting, well-fed faces. We meet several city types: a working-class mother, an Oxford Grouper, an intellectual Indian, and various fair-minded, easy-going London policemen. All seem to enjoy normal good health; all pursue orderly routines. Several Londoners swell with pleasure and national pride when they see Princesses Elizabeth and Margaret driving through Knightsbridge. On the other hand, London's air is often polluted, and the scarred Midlands throw up "hedgerows like steel needles." England, D. learns, is not the haven of safety and reason he believes.

The book both starts and ends literally at sea, thus setting forth insecurity as the norm for life everywhere.

Greene's satire on the English turns on a paradox from *Journey without Maps:* "I find myself always torn between two beliefs: the belief that life should be better than it is and the belief that when it appears better it is really worse." England turns out more deadly than D.'s country. Although violence thrives in both places, Britain's calm exterior seems so unlikely a setting for it that D. is caught offguard when it explodes. His moral outrage surpasses his sense of physical hurt when he is searched, beaten, and accused of stealing a car during his first two hours on British soil. Officially at peace, England seethes with private wars uglier than the public ones waged by paid militia. Whereas a bomb is impersonal, a physical injury inflicted on someone you know is appallingly personal: it makes him an enemy, and enemies in Greene are always closer than friends. And whereas life in D.'s land narrows to brute animal survival, England's brand of violence uncoils more subtly. Every loyalty has a price, and an enemy can materialize without warning.

Humanism and pacifism cannot cope with this contagion of distrust. Dr. Bellows's center for international peace, as well as the Oxford Group, with its commitment to interpersonal sharing, both fail because they misread reality. Dr. Bellows, the Center's founder and leader, even pads through the corridors of the Center on rubber-soled shoes to see if any of his staff have broken his rule of teaching Entrenationo by the direct method. But what drives home the warlike nature of England is English children: D. gasps to see British children exposed to fraud and crime, prostitution and adultery. At twenty, Rose Cullen drinks too much; what is worse, she accepts coolly the fact that her fiancé keeps a mistress. Her friendship with D., though, puts her beyond this jaded pseudosophistication. Like him, she becomes natural and human by accepting doubt and terror, loss and violence. Greene's characteristic dovetailing of love and war goes beyond making Rose the daughter of the British peer whose coal D. wants. At first pampered and cynical, she accuses D. of being melodramatic when he explains his job. Her growth, like his, depends on her admitting danger and death into her life. Violence gauges their love. Again in Greene, the moment of greatest perception is also the moment of greatest pain. D. first sees Rose as "lovely" when she tells him his war will never end. Then he embraces her and offers her his love in the presence of a corpse. On the last page, as she accompanies him to his stricken land, thus accepting his dangers as her own, her growth is unmistakable: "Her hair was lank with spray. She looked older than he had ever seen her yet—plain." Else, the "peaky, haggard" domestic of fourteen who falls in love with D., has less luck. She learns about vice even earlier in life than Rose in that she has a chance to work as a prostitute's maid. But even this relief from the ill treatment she gets from Marie Mendrell, her cruel employer, bypasses her, as she is pushed by the mad Marie out of a top-floor window.

Effects like this do not strain our credibility, because in no other work does Greene manipulate the reader more than in *The Confidential Agent*. With conscious craft, he both draws us into the action and then yanks us away, lest we get drawn in too deeply and relax. He will confide in us. He will establish a winking partnership with us by generating ironies between D.'s view of the action and ours. He will also flatter us by assuming great sophistication in us on matters like sex and crime. But no sooner does he build us up than he overturns us. We find ourselves no more clever than D. Apparently sinister situations turn out harmless, and danger breaks when least expected. Like Hitchcock, Greene has mastered the red-herring technique and its corollary, the technique of catching the reader offguard. Without warning, places of homey cheer or of prosaic business affairs become settings of danger, crime, and death. It has already been mentioned that the book's least threatening characters hurt D. most. It should also be said that these threats occur when he seems most safe—on a morning-lit London street, at a festive seaside resort, in his nation's embassy after he eludes a chase through London's streets. He says of Lord Benditch's conference room, "This wasn't the sort of place where you expected a war to be decided." Neither is it a place where credentials get stolen. But these expectations are reversed, and our smug detachment goes along with them. Like D., we can never feel on safe ground. Because appearance and reality do not square in peacetime England, we never know when danger will strike.

Further reader involvement comes from Greene's practice of fusing horror and humor. If these macabre pairings suggest Hitchcock again, they also summon Greene's early master, Conrad. Rose and D. embrace while Mr. K., D.'s treasonous confederate, lies dead on a nearby divan. Before, D. had given his credentials to Else and told her to hide them in her stocking. The irony of his act does not escape him: "In a way the whole future of what was left of his country lay in the stockings of an underpaid child." He then notes the suitability of his country's poor depending on another poor person. But the comic and the chilling can strike more immediately. Like Razumov in Conrad's *Under Western Eyes*, D. mixes malice and mirth in his talk. He is a master of the witty sarcasm whose import his interlocutor cannot grasp. These dramatic *non sequiturs*, besides serving as private jokes between Greene and the reader, expresses the psychology of danger. Through conversation, D. releases some of the pressure building from the constant danger he faces. His talk usually grows more reckless after he has weathered a nasty ordeal. The reckless talk mirrors a mind sensitized and set racing by the threat of death. Even when the threat goes away, D.'s mind continues to race, imagining wild, fantastic possibilities.

These wildly inventive moments occur with growing regularity as the book moves forward. Indeed, they make for the book's mock-grotesque tone. Tone is the stylistic equivalent of theme in literature. Unfortunately, criticism cannot recreate but only note or at best summarize the fun a book's tone generates. Tone lives. Permeating the narrative, it emerges as a vital process rather than an analyzable product. Let it suffice for us to show some of the ways the book builds its disarming comic mood and to note the harmony between this ambience and Greene's basic view of life as a battlefield.

Greene floods his views with dramatic force. *The Confidential Agent* is a very "built," or carefully assembled book, and its clear, firm details strengthen its impact. Lord Benditch's colliery has a structure, a personality, and a place in Britain's economy; and D.'s negotiations with the firm's executive board develop as an exciting duel of wits. Minor characters, both on Lord Benditch's staff and elsewhere, advance the action while bringing the English setting to life. These minor characters reflect Greene's economy. What makes them so vivid is their consistency: their outward appearance matches their inner, or psychic, reality. The dangerous jobs they undertake, the vividness with which their speech catches the contemporary mood, and the speed of the narrative acquit Greene of the charges of distorting and simplifying character. So smoothly are his minor characters built into the plot that his strategy only reveals itself as an afterthought. It is while writing about *The Confidential*

Agent that Allott and Farris, Greene's best critics, pay this compliment: "Greene is a past-master in the art of conveying by means of epithet or gesture the futility of a whole existence." [7] Greene does have a keen eye for the revealing incidental. Marie Mendrill's big thumbs and bad skin ("the impetigo was like the relic of some shameful act from which she had never recovered") capture her madness. Although the act occurs out of our view, Marie's shoving Else out of the window is foreshadowed dramatically.

Details also get the book off to its good start. The first paragraph, aboard a slow-moving Channel steamer, thrusts forward images of death whose sharpness and evocative force make death the condition of the book:

The gulls swept over Dover. They sailed out like flakes of the fog, and tacked back towards the hidden town, where the siren *mourned* with them; other ships replied, a whole *wake* lifted up their voices—for whose *death*? The ship moved at half-speed through the bitter autumn evening. It reminded D. of a *hearse*, rolling slowly and discreetly towards the "*Garden of peace*," the driver careful not to shake the *coffin*. . . . Hysterical women shrieked among the *shrouds* [italics added].

This funereal mood seems to clash with the violence D. carries inside himself. Only after he leaves the steamer, does it become clear that his violence cooperates rather than clashes with the deathlike aura thrown up around Dover harbor. This irony, sharpened by the appearance-reality interplay, carries into the book's structure. Part 1, called "The Hunted," shows D. searched, robbed, beaten, and fired at. Part 2, "The Hunter," reverses the pattern. Like Raven, D. becomes a fugitive from justice with a grudge. He had learned, at the end of part 1, of Else's death and vowed to avenge it. Spurred, then, by rage and not by love or patriotism, he first acts decisively in part 2: "Rage was like vitality in his veins." The last page of part 1 shows him looking ten years younger after shaving his moustache.

D.'s new strength only begins to pay dividends in part 3, "The Last Shot." But, in keeping with the book's negative spirit, his victory is but skimpy and shadowy. The title of part 3 refers to the bullet in the chamber of a pistol D. had stolen. Now Chekhov says somewhere that any gun shown early in a story must be fired before the story ends. Greene modifies Chekhov's dictum: part 3 ends with the sentence, "So even the last shot had failed." But "the last shot" does not refer to the cartridge in D.'s pistol. It refers instead to an explosion set off by a gang of youths near the village of Benditch, in the coal-mining Midlands. D. never finds out what happens either to the bullet or the revolver. The unfired revolver, by virtue of its mysterious disappearance, remains a strong presence, symbolizing aptly the disaster overhanging D.

Part 3 forms the thematic core of *The Confidential Agent,* and Greene hints at the importance of the issues set forth here by keeping Rose out of the action altogether. Although the book, with its atheist hero, has a more secular outlook than *This Gun for Hire,* its third part has a clear religious focus. It is hard to assess religion in *The Confidential Agent.* To stress it blunts the book's comic sting, but to omit it dwarfs the book's range of reference. Perhaps the sanest approach to the question is to describe some of the action of part 3 and then let the reader decide for himself. Action dominates part 3, which covers D.'s trip to Benditch, beginning before dawn at nearby Willing Junction and ending after dusk the same Sunday. Benditch and environs are ugly: D. notes the abandoned pits, the hunched homes of the miners, and the gored, shriveled landscape looming before him "like a gigantic rubbish heap." Yet hope shines through this land of the dead. An urgently crowing cock, the Sunday dawn setting, and the part's humble beginning at a "small unimportant junction" spells out the advent of something new. By the end of part 3, D. gains strength through contact with waste and ugliness: he feels "the tie weakening between him and the grave," and his efforts discourage Lord Benditch from selling his coal to L. Religion dogs D. through the frozen Midlands. The gang of youths that helps him escape from the police is led by a boy called "Crikey"; he hides near a garden; at day's end, he hears vespers celebrated at the local Baptist chapel.

This religious machinery does not give rise to the earthly paradise. The end of part 3 finds D. physically shattered and in the hands of the police. The new order that struggles to life thus emerges costively, and, as is characteristic, it sometimes looks more like a death than a birth. D. enjoins the colliers at one point not to work the mines: "This means a year's work to your people," he pleads, "but it's death to ours." At the end of part 3, the colliers are still jobless, and D.'s vanished gun still has a bullet in its chamber. Man's struggles will never end. Everything and nothing have been settled. The religious import of this paradox is both caught and criticized by the snakelike train D. takes from Willing Junction to Benditch: the rose, we remember, crowns Dante's Paradise: "At the end of a track a small blob of steam like a rose advanced, became an engine, a string of vibrating carriages." Greene deepens his transcendental-descendental ambiguity by calling a battered, scarred stretch of landscape in the vicinity Paradise.

Part 4, "The End," opens with D. in the dock. He is then freed, apprehended, and freed again in a chain of reversals worthy of Agatha Christie. Allott and Farris both summarize and criticize what goes on in this section:

No one could deny the legerdemain of the section "The End" where, in a matter of thirty pages, we follow "D" through a trial scene, a cross-country drive, a stay in a fantastic seaside hotel, a second arrest, and a quick get-away by boat to join a dingy Dutch coaster for the voyage to his own country. Here Greene resorts to every trick of melodramatic effect including the last-moment appearance, in the middle of the night and on the high seas, of the "heroine" herself.[8]

To censure Greene for slickness and melodramatic contrivance is unfair. As has been said, war, by undermining trust and reason, creates a climate where anything can happen. Speaking of the modern thriller, Zabel shows how mechanical gadgetry and a breakneck narrative tempo catch the temper of war in our machine age:

If the mechanics of the thriller—chases, coincidences, strokes of accident, and exploding surprises—can at times collapse into a kind of demented catastrophe, these were not too remotely at odds with the possibilities of modern terrorism, police action, international intrigue, and violence.[9]

The crowding of events at the end is also artistically valid. To speed narrative action to the point where events swarm into each other, confusing causes with their effects, is standard fictional practice in England. Ford and Conrad called it *progression d'effet* and used it widely. *Nostromo* has more raw event in its last hundred pages than in its first five hundred, and Ford introduces a telegram, a newspaper report, and a long-distance telephone call into the last part of *The Good Soldier* to promote inevitability. The stepped-up pace at the end of *The Confidential Agent* makes for the same inevitability and the same strong ending aimed at by Conrad and Ford.

Life's toughness has reasserted itself. War is everywhere, and there is no relaxing of the pain and distrust war breeds. D. is smuggled aboard a tramp steamer, but freedom for him means renewing his struggles: "He felt no elation; everything was starting all over again." Although reunited with Rose, whom he has not seen since part 2, he will enjoy neither a peaceful nor a long reunion. *The Confidential Agent* does not end on a cheap sentimental note. Its hero and heroine are adrift on an angry, battering sea, and their lurching ship may be bombed on its way to D.'s country: "It [the sea] smashed at them deliberately, like an enemy. It was not like an impersonal force . . . it was like a madman with a pickaxe, smashing at them now on this side, now on the other."

The Confidential Agent has a fine consistency—of mood, idea, and attitude. Its point-of-view technique, we can now say, keeps this consistency supple and vibrant. The differences between the book and *This Gun for Hire*, finally, outweigh the similarities. Whereas the earlier book accounts for everything, the later one bristles with unresolved mysteries: who is the down-and-outer who decoys D. into the mews where he is shot at? For whom is he working? What happens to him? Who shoots D.? Who steals his credentials? Who has the revolver he takes to Benditch? And why, finally, does Greene lace his book with so much indeterminacy? A possible answer to this question lies in a statement made by another leading Catholic novelist of our time, Flannery O'Connor. Miss O'Connor defines religion "broadly" as "an expression of man's ultimate concern," without reference to dogma or tradition.[10] According to this definition, *The Confidential Agent* is a religious work. Its unresolved mysteries, finite point of view, international theme, sudden reversals of expectation or fortune—these elements all point to a realm of meaning that both floods life and gives it its character. They anchor it, moreover, in a plot expressive of the uncertainty and rashness bred by the 1939–45 war.

Ministries of Fear

In 1961, Greene called *The Ministry of Fear* "an entertainment which I wrote in what spare time from work I could allow myself in Freetown," capital of Sierra Leone, in western Africa, where he served as an intelligence officer in 1942–43. Greene's throwaway tone does not do the book justice. Published between his two masterworks, *The Power and the Glory* (1940) and *The Heart of the Matter* (1948), it comes out of his most creative period. It is also his most personal, warmly perceived entertainment. Set in London and written in Africa while England was fighting Germany ("During the Blitz one loved London particularly"),[1] it deals with the things Greene lived by. Yet, resisting an outpouring of sentiment, he holds his homesickness and patriotism in check. *The Ministry of Fear* is a craftsmanly, well-distanced book. At the same time, its complexities surpass those found in the other entertainments. Any act, however noble its motives, can inflict pain. Lines break between real and imagined experience, between sleep and waking, and between madness and sanity. The symbolism is powerfully primitive, and the tensions are labyrinthine and deep-striking.

The critics have looked warmly on Greene's 1943 entertainment. Allott and Farris fault its construction but praise it as a total performance. The book, they claim, "is written with immense verve and non-chalance"; the "nearly impudent" liberties Greene takes riddle the plot with "incoherence." Yet, the "loosely knocked-up narrative" has a "fertility of invention" surprising that of the other entertainments. The approval of A. A. De Vitis and of R. W. B. Lewis is less qualified. De Vitis calls *The Ministry of Fear* "perhaps his [Greene's] best entertainment," and Lewis calls it "the most skillful of the entertainments and a very good story indeed." [2]

The book merits its high marks. Like John Buchan's *The Thirty-Nine Steps*, it describes an innocent bystander's involvement with a spy ring. The bystander is Arthur Rowe, and through him Greene portrays the psychology of wartime England. Atkins rightly calls the book "a nightmare that . . . tries to define the links between wake and dream." [3] Greene gets the action off to a fast start by yoking Arthur Rowe to his background, by embroiling him straightaway with danger, and by untethering him from job and family. A private income coupled with no responsibilities, as in *Orient Express*, frees a character, and Arthur Rowe's freedom creates opportunities unavailable to those pinned to a regular routine.

But Rowe's freedom is that of the outcast; nobody wants him and nobody helps him. Doors otherwise open have shut in his face because two years before the time of the book he murdered his wife. That the murder was a mercy killing does not soften anybody's harsh opinion of Rowe—even Rowe's opinion of himself. He stands condemned just as deeply in his own eyes as in those of others, and, when we meet him, he is more alone than ever.

His personality hinges on the childhood experience of seeing a rat with a broken back and then killing it because he could not watch it suffer. Pity is the mainspring of his character. It drives him to commit a mercy killing just as it drives Henry Scobie in *The Heart of the Matter* to adultery and suicide. Both men, gentle and peaceful by nature, are corrupted by pity, the dangers of which have been widely noted by Greene's critics. Lewis calls pity "a disguised form of contempt and a dangerous human weakness." Auden sees it bound up with self-pity and cruelty: "To feel compassion for someone is to make oneself their equal; to pity them is to regard oneself as their superior and from that eminence the step to the torture chamber and the corrective labor camp is shorter than one thinks." [4] Pity frets Rowe's nerves and addles his mind. He does not know whether he killed Jean because he loved her or because he could not face her suffering. If he killed her quickly by poison because he could not watch her die slowly by cancer, than his mercy killing sprang from selfishness. He regards himself, like D., another Greene hero with a dead wife, as a carrier of something deadly. But his disposition to downgrade his virtues and to stress his faults goes beyond D.'s. First, his guilt cuts deeper; although acquitted by the law, he feels condemned both by himself and by justice. Next, he learns that virtue can lead to evil: "It wasn't only evil men who did these things. Courage smashes a cathedral, endurance lets a city starve, pity kills . . . we are trapped and betrayed by our virtues." This knowledge immobilizes Rowe. His fear, that by moving he will cause pain, both sharpens his guilt and drives him further into himself. Several times he is called a lonely animal.

Rowe's mercy killing even makes him an anachronism. *The Ministry of Fear* stems from *The Confidential Agent* in its guilt-plagued widower-hero who cannot escape trouble. It also has a similar setting. But instead of going to D.'s country, Greene sets the book in a place like it—London during the Blitz. Rowe feels out of date here: a personal act, murder does not count in an age of impersonal massacres. Like the two entertainments that preceded it, *The Ministry of Fear* centers on rebirth. And like Raven and D., Rowe must overcome the hurdles that block the flow of new life. He cannot be reborn while separated from his time. His rebirth demands, specifically, accepting the dangers and privations of his countrymen as his own. Much of this immersion in violence is involuntary. In a political analogue to the doctrine of original sin, he learns that citizens of a warring country may be pressed into service as nonuniformed combatants at any time. He gives us both his private life and his safety in order to help the common cause. The Blitz conspires in his rebirth. A scene near the start of the book where a Nazi agent poisons him balances one near the end where another Nazi shoots himself. Both scenes take place during air raids; both heighten Rowe's sense of the danger surrounding him and his fellow Londoners. In the interim, several dreams in underground air-raid shelters give his painful past new tints and meanings. A ruin among ruins, he grows most dramatically when hemmed in by either destruction or danger.

Wartime London, where he lives, looks ghastly. The bombings have turned it into a rubble heap, and he contrasts it with the mellow peace of the Cambridgeshire village where he grew up: "London shops were reduced to a stone ground plan like those of Pompeii . . . he was part of this as he was no longer part of the past—the long week ends in the country, the laughter up lanes in the evening . . . peace. It was as if the ruins were part of his own mind." The war against Hitler has made a nightmare of humane civilized values. The two chapters where Rowe grows most significantly in self-knowledge are called "Between Sleeping and Waking" and "Bits and Pieces," and some of his new self-knowledge comes from the urgency of his nightmares. His growth amid chaos surpasses D.'s, which Greene limited dramatically to part 3 of *The Confidential Agent*. *The Ministry of Fear* exudes decay and terror: toilets, urine, bird-droppings, rotting teeth, smashed buildings, and the stench of unwashed people sleeping in bomb shelters keep the reader close to waste. The often-made comparison between Greene and John Webster rests most securely on the imagery of *The Ministry of Fear;* the mud, beetles, dead rats, and black stagnant pools, like the images of decay, convey a down-pulling terror akin to that of *The White Devil* and *The Duchess of Malfi*. "Tied to London," the seedy Rowe comes to life as soon as he begins to act like a character in a Jacobean revenge play.

He even makes sense of his bucolic past. At first, his contrast between his happy childhood and the adult terror of wartime London holds good. Modern life is out of joint. Good men who mean well do evil: people murder out of love; a madman runs a mental hospital; the hospital, apparently a haven of peace, is really a den of murder and treachery. Rowe starts the action when, despite his having no prospects, he has his fortune told at a charity bazaar where the charity workers act uncharitably. Before the bazaar, he is freed of a murder he committed; after it, he hides from the police for a murder that never happened. The hotel where an exploding bomb destroys his memory seems like an ocean liner: "It was like the corridor of a monstrous Cunarder." The numbering system the hotel uses for its room reflects the nightmarish reordering of life typical of wartime London: "It seemed to Rowe that one could be lost here for a lifetime. . . . He was touched by a forgotten sense of adventure, watching the numbers go backwards, 49, 48, 47: once they took a short cut which led them through the 60's to emerge suddenly among the 30's."

What can this madness have in common with the pastoral simplicity and peace of Rowe's boyhood?

Rowe's unconscious knits the two world. Now that life has become a walking nightmare, the logic of the times decrees that dreams resemble waking experience. And now that virtue and reason have failed peace, it follows that the irrational and the uncensored take man's measure. Wartime London and the tea-parties on the vicarage lawn fuse in an imaginary conversation between Rowe and his mother, who died before 1914. Rowe's early years were not as happy as he remembers. Just as his adult actions prove that life still has a place for positive, unselfish conduct, his dream exposes the falseness of the peace and easy heroism of his Cambridgeshire boyhood. First, his failure to talk logically with his mother squares with the breakdown characteristic of the Blitz. His boyhood killing of the broken-backed rat, furthermore, differs only in degree from his later mercy killing of his wife. The name of his Sunday School teacher, Miss Savage, and that of the woman who tended the general store and post office, Mrs. Troup, show Rowe's life as a battlefield from the start.

The proper contrast to the chaos of wartime London, then, is not English village life before 1914; as part of the fallen world, Rowe's bucolic past shares in the general guilt. To pit these two worlds against each other, Rowe learns, merely opposes two realms of reality. The book provides an unreal, escapist world in the rest home where Rowe goes after the explosion in the hotel blasts his memory. The mindless comfort and ease of the rest home both falsifies and denies reality. The treachery and death lurking under the home's pretty surface and Rowe's growing desire to leave once his memory returns spell out the life-denying nature of peace. No less than the whisky priest, Rowe certifies his humanity by choosing pain and doubt over comfort and serenity.

Charlotte M. Yonge's romance, *The Little Duke*

(1854), helps divide the twofold reality of Rowe's rural boyhood and urban adulthood from the unreality of his first three months at Dr. Forester's clinic. A boyhood favorite of Rowe's, the book tells of the early years of Richard the Fearless, Duke of Normandy, in the late tenth century. Richard is a Christian warrrior-chief, like his noble father, William of the Long Sword. Although beset by broken oaths, political trickery, and cruelty to both animals and children, he remains morally pure. Arthur Rowe can only muster this purity during his convalescence. The name given him in the rest home is Richard Digby, and, like the Richard of *The Little Duke*, he soon discovers himself a prisoner rather than a guest amid luxury and plenty. Whereas age, rank, and sorrow isolate young Richard at the intrigue-ridden court of King Louis, Richard Digby's three months at the rest clinic separate Digby from his name, his past, and his society. And though both Richards reintegrate themselves with their backgrounds, the terror and treachery of modern life prevent Digby-Rowe from sidestepping evil as gracefully as the young Norman duke. The difference between medieval and modern life is like that between story and fact and between innocence and experience:

> No books satisfy us like those which were read to us in childhood, for those promised a world of great simplicity of which we knew the rules, but the later books are complicated and contradictory with experience: they are formed out of our own disappointing memories. . . . The little duke is dead and betrayed and forgotten: we cannot recognize the villain and we suspect the hero and the world is a small cramped space.

The book's opening scene shades the innocence-experience dualism into Rowe's involvement with Nazi spies. *The Ministry of Fear* starts at a Bloomsbury church bazaar, or fête, on a drowsy summer Sunday afternoon. Ironically, the fête, with its church sponsorship and gay holiday mood, attracts attention while diverting suspicion. As in the Nottwich jumble in *This Gun for Hire* and the Entrenationo soirée in *The Confidential Agent*, danger suddenly intrudes. By chance, Rowe entwines himself in Fifth Column activities when he guesses the correct weight of a cake containing a film-strip of British security information. His impending danger is voiced indirectly in the book's opening sentence: "There was something about a fête which drew Arthur Rowe irresistibly, bound him a helpless victim." The next paragraph heightens this magnetism: "The fête called him like innocence: it was entangled in childhood, with vicarage gardens, and girls in white summer frocks, and the smell of herbaceous borders, and security. . . . It all seemed perfect in the late summer afternoon."

The opening simile explains the concrete by the abstract. The device, no verbal gewgaw, fits Greene's world view. Most of his characters are driven by intangibles, not wealth or property. The Fifth Columnists in *The Ministry of Fear* are idea-ridden, and Rowe gravitates to the fête, not to win prizes or enjoy the games, but to escape guilt and pain. The scene recalls Joyce's "Araby." Like the young boy in Joyce's story, Rowe comes late to a church bazaar. The festive spirit of both the Bloomsbury and the Dublin fête is broken by the fête's sparse attendance and by the crassness the late-arriving protagonist comes up against. The sharp imagery, the coordinated syntax, and the hope that first builds and then trails off create a Joycean ring:

> In adolescence the excitement had a different source; he might find at the vicarage some girl whom he had never seen before, and courage would touch his

tongue, and in the late evening there would be dancing on the lawn and the smell of stocks. But because
these dreams had never come true there remained the
sense of innocence. . . .

Joyce's and Greene's protagonists are both impelled
by a vision of sexual idealism. Yet, instead of longing
for romance and the rich flowing colors of the east,
Rowe wants to escape the terror of adult life. The much-
repeated fact that the cake Rowe wins contains eggs
signals his rebirth into new terror and danger. There is
no other way to become human (fate-fête). Book 1,
part 1, of *The Ministry of Fear* moves from fun to
collapse. Rowe's tea is poisoned by a Nazi agent who
has come to Rowe's flat for the cake, and then the
building is shelled by a German bomb. The episode
ends with an air-raid warden calling out, "Where are
you? Where are you? Where are you?" From this point,
the helplessness and uncertainty reflected by the question control the action. As has been said, nothing fits,
nothing is as it seems, nothing is where it ought to be,
nothing is used for its right purpose, and dream blurs
with waking reality.

The Nazis who first drive Rowe into hiding and then
plot to kill him are terrifying. Writing in 1942, Greene
did not underrate the enemy. Like Hitchcock in *Lifeboat*
(1944), he describes the enemy as methodical, cunning,
and imaginative. The book's title refers to the Nazis'
skill in undermining trust and confidence between people:

> The Germans are wonderfully thorough. . . .
> They did that in their own country. Card-indexed all
> the so-called leaders . . . and then presented the
> ultimatum. Everything forgiven and forgotten, or the
> public prosecutor. . . . They formed, you know, a
> kind of Ministry of Fear—with the most efficient

undersecretaries. It isn't only that they got a hold on certain people. It's the general atmosphere they spread, so that you feel you can't depend on a soul.

The harsh economy of Hitler's divide-and-conquer strategy is also described as "The maximum of terror for the minimum time directed against the fewest objects." The description, echoing Winston Churchill's summation of the Nazi terror, "Never in the history of mankind has so much been owed by so few to so many," stands as a warning. The Fifth Column is growing every day, attracting both nationalists, who want a strong leader, and Pan-Europeanists, who want to stabilize the Continent economically and politically. Nor are Hitler's followers harmless ineffectuals. One is a first-class photographer and entomologist; another, the majestic Dr. Forester, is a pioneering psychiatrist with a faithful following; the smuggling of military secrets out of England by a third reveals great ingenuity; a fourth, by stabbing himself in the neck with shears, shows more physical bravery than any British patriot in the book. Reverend Sinclair, who presides over the fête in the first chapter and later turns up at Dr. Forester's clinic, shows, along with the doctor, Nazism infecting Britain's clergy and medical profession. The psychiatrist and the minister are no mere agents of political prophecy. Their professions give an alarming picture of England's mental and spiritual health during the war.

The book's most sinister threat is the character called Poole. Possibly the most repulsive person in the Greene canon, Poole is the Nazi agent who comes to Rowe's flat for the cake containing British war secrets. Usually a master in creating moral ambiguity, Greene wastes no subtleties on Poole. Poole is shown no mercy. He combs his scruffy scalp with his fingers, he moves "like something on wheels," and he bears "steadily down on Rowe like something mechanized." It is as if his polio expresses an inner depravity. Either directly or through Rowe, Greene speaks of him as "dark and dwarfish and twisted" and as "that wretched little cripple." What makes Poole so sinister, though, is the character who resembles him most—Arthur Rowe. Rowe and Poole meet three times—at the fête, very briefly; at Rowe's flat; at Dr. Forester's clinic. Although they see each other only from a distance at the fête, both men arrive late and both go right to the fortuneteller's booth. If Rowe takes curious inverse pride out of being a murderer, Poole's intellectual snobbery is just as strong. Each man is twisted. Poole's "out-of-drawing shoulders" match Rowe's "tall stooping lean" frame and "nose a little twisted out of the straight." At the clinic Rowe steals into Poole's room partly as a gesture of "proving himself." On the next page, the room looks as if its owner "had something to prove."

Poole is like a contagious disease. He turns up everywhere, and his politics can blend with the common prose of ordinary life. The Nazis make the everyday the lurking-place of terror. At a meeting of Fifth Columnists arranged to frighten him, Rowe observes, "It was fantastic that Mrs. Bellairs could have anything to do with crime—or any of her group." And of a relief agency employing at least two Nazi spies, Rowe notes "the normality of everything . . . he was the only abnormal thing there." But revolvers do not only turn up in corner cupboards, to use Greene's metaphor for the compatibility of homeyness and danger. The drive to fascism goes deeper than our social and domestic arrangements. It is part of our ancestral heritage. Greene makes it a primordial force by reintroducing Poole in part 2 in a garden and by having Rowe tell him, "I don't know you from Adam."

Poole and his fellow Nazis lack a firm hold on life.

Besides pluming themselves on their intelligence, they see people as statistics and they sanction murder as means to an end. Theirs is an unreal, cruelly abstracted world. They work so well because, like machines, they have eliminated human error. But, also like machines, they have left out human warmth. "One can't love humanity. One can only love people," Greene warns. Slavery to an ideal, even humanity, inhibits life. Dr. Forester, who thinks of people as specimens under his microscope, is properly called "a victim." Armed only with abstract knowledge, he defeats himself. The upshot of his political theorizing is the murder and treachery that infect his clinic: he must be known and judged, finally, by his works. Ironically, like Raven, the error that humanizes him also dooms him. The carelessly erased pencil marks in the margins of his copy of Tolstoy's *What I Believe* cause Rowe to doubt the doctor's moral strength and prompt his secret visit to the restricted area of the clinic.

Spiritualism is the same kind of bloodless denial of life as fascism. Thus Rowe's first two encounters with the Fifth Column take place at a fortuneteller's booth and at a séance. Poole's first words, "One day . . . you'll see," convey the knowing smugness of a member of a secret society. Mrs. Bellairs dresses as a gipsy fortuneteller in chapter 1 and then conducts the seance at her home. Much of chapter 1, in fact, comes from the first chapter of *The Golden Bough*. Frazer's contrast between religion and both science and magic would impress the Roman Catholic convert, Greene. Whereas religion presumes faith, science and magic, by trying to shape the future, deny faith. Thus Poole and Dr. Forester are scientists, Fascists, and dabblers in spiritualism. Greene actually refers to the "unholy rites of Mrs. Bellairs" and then, on the next page, mentions "Mrs. Fraser—the Mrs. Fraser."

Greene's satire on the Fifth Column is usually more serious and straightforward. The Nazis, as haters of their own country and countrymen, are denatured. Like Greene's other work, *The Ministry of Fear* celebrates "dull shabby human mediocrity." Arthur Rowe says three times on one page, "I'm not important." The events of the book prove him wrong: "The Devil—and God too—had always used comic people, futile people, little suburban natures and the maimed and warped to serve His purposes." Rowe instigates action and then sees it through. His adventure involves luck, the help of other people, and a victory undercut by loss and pain. Yet his ordeal strengthens both him and his country's war effort. The Nazis he thwarts are more dramatic and colorful: Mrs. Bellairs is "wonderful"; Poole represents an extreme of ugliness and Dr. Forester a limit of lost idealism; the suicide of the Nazi agent who goes under the names, Cost, Travers, and Ford, takes monumental courage. But it is also unnatural. Anyone who kills himself so efficiently cannot value human life. Seen "leaning forward, his throat transfixed with the cutting shears held firmly upright between his knees," he emits a sexual sickness mirrored by Mrs. Bellairs's "deep powerful voice" and Poole's squalid room: "On the bed there were crumbs, as though Poole took food to bed with him."

Characters in Greene who use more than one name are usually evil. If Rowe, by taking the name Richard Digby, parallels Cost-Travers-Ford, just as his actions resemble Poole's, he falls short of both men in wickedness. In keeping with Greene's Manicheism, the Nazis in the book give off darkness, and darkness is their natural milieu. Poole is "dark and dwarfish and twisted," and the carious teeth of another Fifth Columnist, a Mr. Fullove, have black stumps. It is nearly dusk when Rowe chances upon the fête in chapter 1, and it is "very dark inside the tent" where Mrs. Bellairs tells his fortune. His first words upon seeing her, "a bulky figure shrouded in what looked like cast-off widow's weeds," are "It's so dark." Later, he is warned just before the séance, "They'll try to get you in the dark." The warning holds good. Soon after the lights go out, Rowe finds himself a suspected killer.

The book's structure traces a rough curve from dark to light. Book 1, "The Unhappy Man," includes the fête, the bombing of Rowe's flat, the séance, and the explosion that shatters Rowe's memory. His characteristic stance in book 1 is to be trapped in a dark, menacing place. At the end, he is trapped in the darkening steamship-like hotel with Anna Hilfe, a young Austrian refugee. Before he opens a suitcase holding the explosives that blast his memory, Anna talks to him about his wife's death. That she is the first person to broach the subject with him, that they are joined by danger, that a treacherous act brought him to the hotel, and that he has accepted the spirit of his time by acting like a character in a thriller—these carefully chosen elements prime him for rebirth.

His rebirth is gradual. The world into which he is reborn finds him as much at sea as before. Book 2, "The Happy Man," begins, "The sun came into the room like pale green underwater light." The paragraph is splashed with water imagery: "The light washed over the white clean walls of the room. . . . the only sounds were a fountain dripping." By not explaining that Richard Digby and Arthur Rowe are the same person, Greene makes us feel as unanchored as Rowe-Digby. The point-of-view technique, besides taking us inside a murderer's mind and disclosing gentle thoughts, captures Rowe's expanding consciousness. Selective amnesia has erased his life from age eighteen on. "I have a terrible lot to learn," he says. And despite his beard and gray hair, he looks younger. His amnesia has freed him from the wear of his private and public wars: "All this talk of a man called Hitler . . . the cruelty and meaninglessness—it's as if one had been sent on a journey with the wrong map."

Rested and rejuvenated, he wants to jump back into the lists. But his jump shatters his peace. The happiness of The Happy Man is built on lies. The dawn of his rebirth only breaks when he sees that the comfort he enjoys at the clinic denies reality. Happiness he learns to equate with mindlessness and escape. Scobie's view of happiness in *The Heart of the Matter* resembles Rowe's new knowledge: "Point me out the happy man and I will show you either egotism, selfishness, evil, or else an absolute ignorance." Rowe's ignorant bliss fades when he learns of the ugliness pervading the nursing home. Greene likens the reality of the home to the dank underside of a stone, and he strengthens his simile by having a Major Stone held prisoner and then murdered by Dr. Forester. Neither the clinic's garden nor its pond (nor the presence of an inmate named Still, for that matter) suggests new life. The garden lacks flowers, and the remains of a detective hired by Rowe and then killed by the Fifth Columnists lie under the stagnant pond. Rowe's visit to the sick bay, where the violent cases live, resembles an epic descent to the underworld. Enacted in a spirit of boyish adventure, the caper tests Rowe. He responds with a new force and maturity. Outraging his sense of human decency, the grisly realities underlying the earthly paradise send him to Scotland Yard.

Scotland Yard Inspector Prentice, a new character, dominates book 3. An Edwardian gentleman-sleuth, he speaks of breaking the Poole-Forester-Bellairs spy ring as "a beautiful problem," and he views his analytic job synthetically, as one of piecing the problem together. Yet, despite his intellectual tilt of personality, he is no cold logician-detective. He smashes Mrs. Bellairs's home unmercifully during a police search. "White and angry," he tears through the home "as destructively as a tornado." Also, Prentice is only a catalyst: Rowe catches the villain and recovers the film by himself. Prentice's job in the pattern of *The Ministry of Fear*, like that in the plot, is that of a piecer-together. The importance of this job is hinted at by the title of book 3, "Bits and Pieces." Prentice fills in gaps caused by Rowe's amnesia and also firms up the narrative by explaining the official aspects of the case. Artistically, he succeeds. He gives the narrative the solidity it needs to stay together during the *progression d'effet* of book 4. Furthermore, the efficient sleuth is always fun to watch at his work, and Greene, besides showing Prentice tracking down his quarry, discreetly limits the purview of the hunt to police business. There is plenty of drama left over for book 4.

Book 4, "The Whole Man," depicts Rowe's public and private reintegration. To sharpen the drama, the plot demands that he act alone. *The Name of Action* contains the phrase, "a mystery solved in a mean modern way." The phrase from Greene's 1931 novel applies to Rowe's recovery of the filmstrip, to his apprehension of Willi Hilfe, and to the sour aftertaste the drama leaves in Rowe's mouth: "He was no longer anxious for glory: the sense of adventure had leaked away and left only the sense of human pain." The climax of *The Ministry of Fear* is played down. Looking shabby and worn, Rowe traps Willi with lies, threats, and broken promises when he forces him off a train he had boarded in order to decamp to Ireland. Another Greene entertainment, then, features a scene in a train station. But this time the hunted man never leaves the station. Willi is caught while helping a deaf old woman wind wool. Now social decorum can run disproportionately high in

Greene; a character may literally prefer to die than to make a scene. Greene also enjoys creating images of helplessness. Willi Hilfe joins these two strands of his author's art. His hands swathed in a cat's cradle of wool, he is as helpless as Raven in the dentist's chair or Mr. K. at the Entrenationo soirée. The tired drama plays itself out in the men's room of the terminus, where Willi shoots himself rather than face a beating from the police.

Before Willi dies, he explains Rowe's mercy killing of his wife. Rowe, however, meets the test. It is a sign of his wholeness that Willi's disclosure does not shatter him. Anna, Willi's sister and the girl Rowe loves, wanted to spare her man the knowledge that he murdered his wife. Now Rowe must spare Anna the news of Willi's revelation. The book's title, then, applies to Anna and Rowe's future. Although their chances for happiness are good, their love is so bound up with fear and dishonesty that they can never relax. Yet the fear and dishonesty they pledge themselves to in order to stay together signify a strong love. The book closes with a summary that marks both an end and a beginning: "They [Anna and Rowe] had to tread carefully for a lifetime . . . they must watch each other like enemies because they loved each other so much." The paradox, though terrifying, affirms life. If love turns good men into killers, it can easily make them dissemblers. If endurance lets a city starve, distrust can serve love. With its fine Jamesian stroke, *The Ministry of Fear* ends well. Unable to confide in each other, Anna and Rowe face the mature human test of building a life on a mixed foundation of lies and love.

As poetically and psychologically right as this conclusion is, it does not grip the reader. The book lacks dramatic force because Anna and Willi Hilfe, the young Austrian relief workers, are too thinly conceived to carry their burden of the plot. Greene sketches them in crude simple colors as poles of a heart-head dualism: "Her brother had the ideas, but she felt them," Rowe observes of Anna and Willi, and the observation fairly exhausts them. With Anna reduced to feeling and Willi cut to the size of thought, it is no wonder that their relationship falls short of that of Kate and Anthony Farrant in *England Made Me*. In fact, the flatness of the Hilfes rule out exciting relationships altogether. Allott and Farris's complaint that "Greene the romantic theorist" portrays women badly applies to *The Ministry of Fear*. By making Anna, as a refugee of an occupied country, more experienced in danger than Rowe, Greene adds a fine effect: Anna is both older and younger than Rowe. Yet the effect does not dignify her role in the plot. She is, as Allott and Farris say, merely "an instrument of salvation." [5] She is Greene's ideal woman. While harpies like Mabel Warren (*Orient Express*), Marie Mendrill (*The Confidential Agent*), and Mrs. Bellairs are all middle-aged, thickly set, and masculine, Greene's dream girl is young, slight, and toughened by experience without being coarse. Greene usually gives his wispy heroines more pluck than Anna. Her love for Rowe, on which the plot turns, is hardly credible. It is not plausible for a girl in her early twenties to fall in love with a middle-aged mercy killer broken by his wife's death, frightened by finding himself a prospective murder victim, and then robbed of his memory. The reader cannot believe that Anna loves Rowe. The love affair not only upsets the balance of the book; it also undermines our faith in Greene.

Matching this psychological implausibility is the dramatic one centering on Willi's evil. Allott and Farris call Willi "an entirely selfish amoralist" but complain that his selfishness and amorality never develop.[6] They are right. His evil is asserted, not dramatized. Like his sister, he is too finished and fixed to rouse our interests: Greene does not create any room for growth in his personality. Most of Willi's villainy occurs out of view. To all appearances, Willi is a bright, friendly young man and a devoted brother. His only negative trait is an eagerness, common to young homosexual men, to be-friend older women. But he never makes homosexual overtures to anybody in the book, and, besides, Greene develops no link between homosexuality and Nazism. So thinly is Willi wrought that he cannot perform evil while in view. He does act swinishly at the end when he tells Rowe of the mercy killing, but no worse than most people faced with imminent arrest and death as an enemy spy.

Mechanical crudities also mar both Rowe's character and the plot. Whenever a painful truth or a key event from the past comes to Rowe's amnesiac mind, he grows dizzy with pain: "An odd medley of impressions fought at the gateway of his unconscious. . . . His head was racked with pain": "One doesn't necessarily kill because one hates; one may kill because one loves. . . . And again the old dizziness came back as though he had been struck on the heart." The plot stales when Greene smuggles in an idea and pretends it belongs to a character. Thus Prentice's lecture on pity, with its fine, flat tone, sounds too novelistic to be spoken by a policeman: "Pity is a terrible thing. People talk about the passion of love. Pity is the worst passion of all: we don't outlive it like sex." Rowe, too, often speaks with an irony and acuity out of keeping with his character. Although a journalist, Rowe, as Anna says, is not ob-servant; nor does his solitary, humdrum life challenge him: "A murderer is rather like a peer: he pays more because of his title"; "I suppose almost the only men they couldn't blackmail for something shabby would be saints—or outcasts with nothing to lose."

These speeches, though out of character, are memorable, and removing them would weaken the book. *The Ministry of Fear* is very quotable. It contains some of Greene's best insights, and its language is resonant, textured, and level in pitch. The clear, supple prose of the book gracefully accommodates Rowe's dreams, the melodramatic plot, and a range of physical settings. It also holds the book together, saving it from being a "loosely knocked-up narrative," and makes for some of its best surprises. The image that introduces Dr. Forester makes him capable of any horror: "His old noble face was bent above the body; one long sensitive delicate hand dabbled and came up stained, like a beautiful insect that feeds incongruously on carrion." This scene — the séance where Ford-Travers-Cost is supposedly killed — is just one of several exciting moments. Sometimes suspense will uncoil more subtly, mingling with either revulsion or pity. There is the memorable encounter with Mr. Fullove, the seedy book dealer and Nazi who feeds birds out of his mouth. (Greene has feared birds all his life.) Fullove plays on Rowe's pity to decoy Rowe to his presumed death in the Regal Court Hotel. His carious breath filling the taxi they take to the hotel, Fullove conveys again the power of failure and decay in Greene.

Greene's attitudes and values permeate *The Ministry of Fear*. The help Rowe gets from the police shows that Greene did not want to undermine public confidence in Scotland Yard in 1943. Yet Willi Hilfe kills himself to avoid a beating by the police, and Mrs. Bellairs, whose home is smashed by Scotland Yard men, learns that, although a woman, she can expect to hang for her crimes. War brings out the worst in everybody. As in John Le Carré, England is no better morally than its enemies. It distorts and withholds information from its newspapers, and its security chiefs act without honor. Treachery pollutes the highest reaches of Whitehall.

Though no formal inquiry is made—either by Parliament or the police—the photographing of military secrets denotes not indiscretion, but treason. This stealing of secret papers from the Ministry of Home Security looks ahead to the infiltration of British Intelligence by Russian spies like Burgess, Maclean, and Kim Philby in the 1950s. But Greene deserves credit not only for his timeliness and prophecy. He also dared to treat Whitehall harshly at a time when public opinion made harsh treatment unpopular.

Keeping a smooth, balanced tone and moving deftly between melodrama, psychology, and political prophecy, *The Ministry of Fear* has a surging orchestration. It is not as polished as *This Gun for Hire*, but most of its flaws can be explained by its broad scope. It is Greene's most ambitious entertainment. Its warmth, range, and colorful recreation of London during the Blitz have also made it his most praised entertainment.

6

"In These Days . . . Nobody Thinks in Terms of Human Beings"

The Third Man won the Grand Prix for the best feature film at the 1949 Cannes Film Festival. Greene dedicates the book version of *The Third Man* to the film's producer-director, Carol Reed, and speaks admiringly of Reed in the preface. The preface also says that the entertainment, *The Third Man*, was "never intended to be more than the raw material for a picture. . . . The film, in fact, is better than the story." Greene speaks home. But how useful is his comparison? If the film is better than the story, the story still merits a close look. For the differences in execution demanded by the different media make the book something other than "raw material." It contains scenes not in the film, makes different points, and generates its own reality.

The Third Man has strong credentials. Although nobody's favorite, it shares traits with Greene's other thrillers. It offers a vivid social and political background, a limber journalistic style, adroit cinematic cutting between scenes, and that staple of the thriller, the chase. Like two other works of the 1950s, *The End of the Affair* and *Our Man in Havana*, it discusses fictional technique on the wing. Like that of *The Ministry of Fear*, its chase sharpens just before the end to two men. Its world, though thin, is as dark as that of the other entertainments. Whereas the policeman wounded by

Raven in *This Gun for Hire* lives, the one shot by Harry Lime in *The Third Man* dies. Deepening this gloom is the book's setting—Vienna after World War II and during the four-power occupation. "Smashed" and "dreary," "a city of undignified ruins," postwar Vienna joins documentary and dramatic themes. Its hunger, black market, and political evil make danger a daily fact of life. The February snows wreathing the action add a macabre touch. Rejecting the humanistic notion of man as a worker and a reasoner, Greene also uses dreams, apparitions, and a crazy volley of echoes in the Vienna sewers to get past the drab prose of cause-and-effect materialism.

The action is simple. Harry Lime of the International Relief Agency in Vienna has offered his former school-mate Rollo Martins a job. When Martins arrives in town, he learns that Lime is dead. Rushing to the cemetery, he reaches Lime's grave site just in time for the funeral. One strange detail breaks the somber mood. The cold weather requires electric drills to break the frozen earth before Lime can be buried: "It was as if even nature were doing its best to reject Lime." Having no duties in Vienna, Martins visits some of Lime's associates after the funeral, and he grows suspicious when he hears different versions of his friend's death. Did Lime die instantly after being hit by a speeding car? Did two or did three men carry him from the accident? The search for the answers to these questions widens, as Martins hears with shock that Lime had been "about the worst racketeer who ever made a dirty living in this city." Denying Lime's guilt, Martins then vows to clear his former friend and hero.

When the untrained man of simple good will becomes a hunter, anything can happen. Greene assumes that an amateur detective can work more effectively than a professional. He follows no schedule, answers to nobody, and can take bizarre risks. Martins's career as a writer of cheap cowboy novelettes brings an added flare for detection, and Martins leads an exciting chase. To his shock, though, he finds not only that Lime sold black-market penicillin but that his partners staged Lime's death and funeral to hoodwink the police. These discoveries burst Lime's hero-image and give the ongoing chase a new object. But Martins is Greene's least interesting entertainment hero. Raven and D. each had the double job of vindicating the law while hiding from lawmen. Arthur Rowe, though not a fugitive, had a criminal record. Rollo Martins performs no crime and is not hunted. So even though he sets about righting a wrong for personal, not official, reasons, the chase flags in importance. Also, owing to Lime's crime and Martins's change in attitude, the avenger-savior figure splits and becomes two characters. This split disjoints the narrative. Because of it, Greene must use a third character to relate the story.

No disjuncture, though, mars the book's opening. Rollo Martins calls himself "a bad writer who drinks too much and falls in love with girls." He needs both seasoning and ballast. Drifting between mismanaged love affairs and boring jobs, he has not yet found himself. His "long gangly legs" and faintly homosexual hero-worship of Lime ("It's funny. I can't remember meeting any woman quite as well.") make him an ungainly cub of thirty-five. Another character notes the split in his nature: "There was always a conflict in Rollo Martins—between the absurd Christian name and the sturdy Dutch (four generations back) surname." Calm and lucid, rash and extravagant, Martins becomes the forked inconsistency God and the Devil both use in Greene to carry out their wills. And like other Greene heroes, he does his metaphysical job amid waste and wreckage.

Martins's search takes him to Lime's former sweetheart, Anna Schmidt, a Hungarian actress living in Vienna under a forged passport. Neihter beautiful nor talented, she is bound to Martins by their common love of Harry Lime. Lime returns this love shabbily. Just as he let Rollo take the blame for his schoolboy misdemeanors, so does he betray Anna to the Russians in exchange for asylum in their zone. Anna and Martins both learn the difficulty of loving people, that we often love our concepts of people rather than people in their own right. So long as Lime is a memory, Martins can love him. Up close, Martins hates him.

Rootlessness is a great threat in Greene. The discovery of Lime's crimes shatters Martins, and he resents Lime for leaving him so unprotected. (Not until 1970 and *Travels with My Aunt* does Greene accept insecurity as the norm of life.) Yet neither Anna nor Martins seek revenge. Martins only turns on Lime when he sees pictures of children destroyed by Lime's bad penicillin. As in *The Confidential Agent*, *The Heart of the Matter*, and *The Quiet American*, a child's death spurs a Greene hero to action. And again, the action is treacherous. Martins arranges to meet Lime in a café surrounded by British policemen. Lime is shot after an exciting chase through the Vienna sewers, and Martins goes off with the dead man's former sweetheart on the book's last page. Betrayal, then, is not only human. It is also a way to become human, promoting both civic justice and sexual love. It matures Martins. His getting the girl offsets the loss of both Lime and the schoolboy mentality connected with him. Unfortunately, Martin's new manhood is untested. Although Greene ends the book with a compression of events, he might have challenged Martins more deeply before pairing him off with Anna.

The romantic ending is also marred by the first-person narrative. *The Third Man* is told by Colonel Calloway, a Scotland Yard officer in charge of British military police in Vienna. Calloway's narration does not help the book, and, other than giving Greene practice for *The End of the Affair* (1951), serves no purpose in his 1950 entertainment. Audrey Nelson Slate has noted that Calloway stands outside the plot and that his tie with Lime is not personal but official. She continues:

> Calloway is never really characterized, and there is no compelling reason for his being the narrator other than the fact that the pattern of the detective or police story usually calls for the man with the greatest command of all the available information to reveal it at strategic times to the reader.[1]

But Calloway's narration does make up in clarity and judgment what it lacks in drama. Reasonable, professional, and fair, Calloway always looks for rational explanations and admits his mistake when he fails to find one. Although he gives a policeman's view of the action, he keeps reminding us that it is only *a* view. He never claims that his report is definitive. And as a policeman he subscribes to no political creeds and maintains professional self-control during the melodrama of the chase. Calloway is a reliable interpreter of the action.

Nor is his narration a cold compilation of facts. Although he reconstructs the story from official files, he also conveys some of the action through interviews with Martins. Like the book's shifting chronology, the directly reported speech makes the chase more vivid and natural. Martins's talks with Calloway both relax the tempo and let Martins take stock of his findings. When he digresses, Calloway sets him back on course. When he leaves the police station, Calloway summarizes the interview. He may even address the reader directly to drive home a point: "What happened later was a worse

shock to him than it would have been to you or me."
This warm, relaxed tone controls the melodrama. Martins's friendship with Lime and ignorance of Vienna
during the four-power occupation reduce Greene's range
of options in selecting a narrator. Yet Martins's
voice—which is that of a novelist—does not go unheard.
Although his background disqualifies Martins from
narrating *The Third Man*, his sharp observations of
both person and place, reported from conversations with
Calloway, add color to the action.

The trouble with all this is that it is unbelievable.
First, it is unlikely that Martins should talk as much as
Greene and Calloway say. He dislikes Calloway and,
as the man who gets the girl, has little reason to indulge
in postmortems. Next, Calloway's claim, "I haven't invented a line of dialogue," rings false. His report contains extended speeches accompanied by physical ges-
tures and psychological nuances which nobody but a
first-hand observer could have noted. Furthermore, not
even a first-hand observer could remember the long
stretches of dialogue included in Calloway's report.
The report also smacks of dishonesty elsewhere. Calloway reproduces notes and letters that Lime, due to
their incriminating contents, would have destroyed.
Finally, Calloway's admission near the end that his
men had been watching Martins ever since his arrival
in Vienna, belittles the drama. The reader feels cheated.

The foil of Calloway the lawman is Harry Lime the
outlaw. Artistically, Lime saves *The Third Man*. For
every problem caused by Calloway, Lime comes through
with a treat. At one time the sharp schoolboy who steals
the prize and lets someone else take the blame, he has
become the superspiv out to beat the system. Greene
said of him in 1964, "I wanted for my 'villain' a name
natural and yet disagreeable, and to me 'Lime' repre-
sented the quick-lime in which murderers are said to be

buried." ² The "villain," Lime, stimulates Greene more
than the hero, Martins, or the policeman, Calloway.
He does not appear until chapter 11, and he does not
speak until chapter 14 of this seventeen-chapter book.
But our imaginative commitment to him is so strong
that he dominates the action without being seen.

Harry Lime is fascinating. To deny him is to deny
life's surprise and suddenness. Anna and Martins, the
people who know him best, love him, and he has a cadre
of faithful helpers in his penicillin racket. Apparently
one of the world's privileged citizens, he seems destined
for riches and happiness. But ambitious, self-acting
characters usually make trouble in Greene. Misled by
egotism and pride, Lime overreaches himself. Mindless
of the law and other people, he is often likened to a
rabbit and called "bastard" by his pursuers. The terms,
rabbit and bastard, touch on his flashy wildness. He
undertakes rash acts because the repetitions and routines
of plain living bore him. But his rashness, although
dazzling, is the work of an amateur. It rarely merits the
effort that goes into it. Qualified as an M.D., he never
practices medicine. He needs a regimen more glamorous
than that offered by a steady practice. So, by perverting
both the doctor's healing mission and the healing proper-
ties of penicillin, he serves death. As in *The Quiet
American*, Greene portrays this evil as an outcropping
of immaturity. Martins is right when he tells Lime,
"You've never grown up."

Looking down from the Great Wheel in Vienna's
amusement park, the Prater, Lime feels no compassion
for the people dotting the landscape below:

> Would you really feel any pity if one of those dots
> stopped moving—for ever? If I said you can have
> twenty thousand pounds for every dot that stops,
> would you really, old man, tell me to keep my money
> —without hesitation? Or would you calculate how

many dots you could afford to spare? Free of income tax, old man. Free of income tax.

These same dots grow human as the Wheel swings to earth. Lime, reluctant to stand among them, must pay for his infantile pride. Soaring above his fellows, he must sink to mud and garbage. The medieval symbolism of the wheel holds good. Everything goes back to its proper station. Balancing the scene aboard the Prater Wheel is the one where Lime runs from the police through Vienna's sewers. The diabolic nature of his penicillin racket comes across in his mode of travel from the Russian zone—these same underground sewers. The would-be God lives like a sewer rat. Suitably, he dies scrabbling for the ordinary daylight he had previously spurned.

Lime had to be stopped. But if we do not sympathize with him, neither do we approve the society that stops him. Organized society has no moral right to butcher anybody. What Lime does illegally, the occupation troops in Vienna do with clean hands. Andrew Sinclair, viewing the 1939–45 war and its aftermath as a single epoch, interprets Lime's death fatalistically:

> Harry Lime scuttling across the bomb-sites, the small operator trying to get rich on the surface of a total waste, is the symbol of the futility of shrewdness in the face of devastation. . . . War and its aftermath crushes all individuals, however clever they may be.[3]

Hardship multiplies itself. It brings out the worst in people and punishes those who try to escape it. Lime's racket brings death both to Lime and his customers. Governments speed this death drift by failing to relieve hardship legally. They both encourage crime and destroy criminals. Life not only lacks dignity in wartime. War shrinks individual freedom to a choice between slow or sudden death.

As usual, Greene gives his public drama a religious twist. *The Third Man* takes place under the eye of God and its events have divine importance. The book's title refers to Luke 25, where two travelers to Emmaus are accompanied by a third, unknown, traveler who turns out to be Christ. By making Lime a Catholic, Greene invites a Catholic interpretation.[4] Specifically, he calls for a Jansenist reading. Cornelius Otto Jansen (1585–1638), bishop of Ypres and theology professor at the University of Louvain, wanted to reform the Church in line with Augustinian doctrine. Like Augustine, Jansen denied free choice. We can neither know nor save ourselves. Our lot is decided by God, not by our exertions. God chooses certain people for punishment; others He "converts." Only the converted receive divine grace. A Jansenist crucifix owned by a character in *The Third Man* shows Christ with arms raised to symbolize His having died for the converted alone.

Jansen's doctrine of conversion softens his determinism. God's grace is so powerful that even the worst sinner is eligible for conversion. The world of *The Third Man*, though wretched, is not God-forsaken. Our need for God exists in direct ratio to our suffering; the greater our suffering, the greater our need for divine mercy. Although nobody in *The Third Man* except Harry Lime has religion, the book moves toward salvation. It does this with its dualistic pairings. There is, first, the split in Rollo Martins's nature conveyed by "the absurd Christian name" and "the sturdy Dutch . . . surname." There is Martins's split view of Harry Lime as Harry the schoolmate and Lime the penicillin racketeer. Although Lime holds a high post in a relief agency, he sharpens pain instead of relieving it; in the wrong hands, a lifegiving drug like penicillin can kill. The chase through the sewers which ends with Lime's being shot confuses freshness and decay, rebirth and death: "The main stream [of the sewage network] smells sweet and fresh with a faint tang of ozone." Greene underscores this interplay of renewal and death by mentioning Susanna (A.D. 840–c.918), a saint associated with chastity and healing. When exhumed, "her body was found quite undecayed and giving off a sweet smell." [5] Harry Lime is also a healer, and his grave is also opened after his bogus death and funeral.

The tension between opposites found in *The Third Man* is the spring of all creativeness according to Heraclitus, Bruno, and Hegel. The ground thaws and the snow melts before Lime's funeral in the last chapter: "It was almost as warm as a spring day when Harry Lime had his second funeral." The readiness of the earth to receive Lime gives his death a rightness beyond man's justice. The hardships of postwar Vienna have, perhaps, served an end. *The Third Man* closes on a promising note. Evil has been scotched, and Anna takes Martins's arm on the book's last page.

Thin in inspiration, blurred in focus, and obvious in its emotions, *The Third Man* nevertheless has merit. Its trim, shapely design promotes both variety and drive. It alternates indoor and outdoor scenes; it takes us above ground on the Prater Wheel, and it goes below ground during the sewer chase. The short first and last chapters frame the action, which consists of the pursuit and capture of Harry Lime. The chase generates suspense. Although each chapter brings Martins closer to Lime, Greene reveals neither Lime's penicillin racket nor identity as the third man until the second half of the book. Chapter 9, the book's middle chapter, marks a crucial turn. Both the longest and most eventful chapter, it also speeds the action. Martins learns here of the murder of Koch, the porter of Lime's apartment building and Martins's chief informer as to the details of Lime's death. The murder both verifies the information Koch gave Martins and spells out Martins's imminent danger.

Chapter 9 also contains Martins's hilarious lecture to

the British Cultural Relations Society: as in Conrad, danger and hilarity fuse in *The Third Man*. The episode both relieves and intensifies the chase. Driven to the lecture hall in a speeding staff car. Martins fears he has been kidnapped. This fear stays with him in the lecture hall. His impromptu talk to the Society joins fact and fiction, and his answers to questions about his new book show a new understanding of Lime's alleged death. Incidentally, the whole episode turns on the similarity between Martins's pen name, Buck Dexter, and the name of a modern writer Greene compares to Henry James and E. M. Forster, Benjamin Dexter. Since no Benjamin Dexter appears in either the British Museum or Library of Congress catalog, he is one of Greene's pranks.[6] Prank or not, the confusion between the names fits smoothly into the action. Besides accounting for the book's funniest moment, it promotes Martins's growth. Things happen quickly after the meeting. In the next chapter, Martins learns of Lime's crimes. His reaction to the disclosure shows a new readiness to forgo schoolboy idolatry for adult responsibility. He outgrows his sense of boyish fair play and becomes the lime that catches the prospective jailbird.

Lime does not grow accordingly. His last words before he dies, "Bloody fool," refer to himself. Not satisfied to thrive as a racketeer, he must also enjoy Martins's friendship. His death has a ring of inevitability. After gainsaying those values that make friendship possible, he comes out of hiding to meet a friend. He deserves his death. Yet Greene does not let him die until he knits the book's political and religious themes. *The Third Man* makes its points without rushing to dramatic climaxes. Although its subject matter clashes with its form, it embodies timeliness, formal learning, and sound seasoned craftsmanship. For these strengths and for its place in Greene's development, it is worth reading.

7

Waiting for Gom

Loser Takes All is *sui generis*. It is Greene's only entertainment that does not feature crime. Although not
sunny in outlook, it bypasses the terror of the thriller in
favor of light romantic comedy. It uses many of the
stock trappings of commercial domestic comedy—the
middle-class couple who go to Monte Carlo to get
married, hire an expensive suite, and, never having slept
together, blush and blunder through their first evening;
the wedding and subsequent honeymoon quarrel; the
mutual pretense of taking a lover in order to make
the other jealous, followed by the chance meeting of the
two couples in a restaurant; the reconciliation of the
newlyweds.

These frayed narrative materials knit in a rich em-
broidery. Despite its speed and predictable plot, *Loser
Takes All* transcends slick magazine fiction. In 1933,
the year after *Orient Express*, Greene launched out
against commercial and escapist fiction: "Stories written
purely for entertainment are almost invariably dull . . .
are almost invariably deceitful." [1] *Loser Takes All*,
though called a "frivolity" on its dedication page, does
not ignore serious human problems. Atkins rightly sees
in it "hints of Greene's religious disquiet." And, as
usual, Greene plumbs religious depths by refusing to
portray man either as a worker or as a reasoner: in

1970, he called Patricia Highsmith's characters "irrational" and added that "they leap to life in their very lack of reason. . . . When we look back at them from Miss Highsmith's side of the frontier, we realize that our world was really not as rational as all that. Suddenly with a sense of fear we think, 'Perhaps I really belong *here*.' " [2] Greene might be talking of his own characters—their suddenness, their treacheries, their dream-ridden psyches.

Human need in *Loser Takes All* surfaces quickly and defies civilized arrangements. Human contact, again, makes for human growth, and the ratio between this growth and material success is sharply inverse. Money, property, even marriage, thwart love. Like Dickens, Joyce, and Lawrence, Greene knows that love is the best thing life offers. Yet he does not describe it as long-lasting, morally uplifting, or conducive to happiness. *Journey without Maps* describes his first sexual encounter at age twenty as a hideous ordeal: "I saw a man and woman copulating; they stood against each other under a street lamp, like two people . . . supporting and comforting each other in the pain of some sickness." The following description of two people kissing in *Brighton Rock* registers the same anguish: "They stood with lips glued together in an attitude of angry passion: they might have been inflicting on each other the greatest injury of which either was capable."

Like divine love, which usually looks like punishment in Greene, sexual love features pain. James Raven has never known it but gets infected by it anyway; the married Scobie, supposedly beyond sexual desire, has an affair at age fifty with a girl of nineteen in *The Heart of the Matter*. Now Greene does not argue, like Denis De Rougemont in *Love in the Western World*, that sexual love only reaches intensity outside of marriage and at the risk of death. Yet the pain and danger included in Greene's love ethic make De Rougemont a helpful analogy. Love cannot grow in rich, healthy soil in Greene; nor does it yield bumper harvests. (Greene's fiction abounds in childless marriages.) When it occurs, it is almost always adulterous, short-lived, and indulged in by sad, lost people. In "When Greek Meets Greek" (1941), it blooms amid poverty and fraud, and in both *This Gun for Hire* and *The Ministry of Fear*, fear, rather than sexual attraction, motorizes it.

Love's forceful nature is its reality. Love affirms itself by overcoming hurdles. Like religious faith, it requires a warm outgoing of self and the ability to forgo security. The god-figure in *Loser Takes All*, a great lover in his day, enjoys sailing and is often said to be "at sea." *A Burnt-Out Case* prizes any loving act in our wasted, stricken world as spiritually redemptive. *Loser Takes All* (1955) and *The Quiet American* (1955) also merge human and divine love by noting the self-transcendence and pain central to each activity. Greene has always said more about the miracles and mysteries of Christianity than about its logic and social gospel. This mystical bent informs the love story of the romantic *Loser Takes All*. Loss and gain oppose each other: if the loser takes all, then the winner gets nothing. The book's hero first wins and then loses a fortune at roulette and, in the process, loses and wins his bride's love. In human affairs, the shortest distance between two points is not a straight line. Though graced by love, the Bertrams' must lose love in order to know its worth. Their renewal of love through loss and rediscovery shows, along with the book's title, that, despite the inevitability of loss, life also has its happy winners.

This ironic shuttle of loss and gain pulses through the plot: Bertram (no first name) and his fiancée Cary (no last name) plan a small London wedding and a seaside honeymoon at Bournemouth. But about a week before the wedding, Bertram, an accountant, is sent for by the chief of Sitra, the large firm where he works. When Bertram mentions his upcoming wedding, his chief, Herbert Dreuther, insists that Bertram marry at Monte Carlo and then honeymoon on the company's executive yacht. Bertram agrees. He takes Cary to Monte Carlo, checks into an expensive suite, and gets married as planned. But Dreuther, or the Gom, short for Grand Old Man, does not turn up, and the Bertrams begin to worry about their soaring hotel bill. The Gom's non-arrival, it turns out, tests more than their patience. It also forces them to use their time and money wisely while keeping happy together. What happens to them proves that it takes faith in life to relax and enjoy oneself. Bertram grows testy and neglects Cary increasingly in favor of roulette. In a short time, he becomes obsessed by the wheel. After losing heavily, he invents a system to beat the wheel, and, so fixed is the obsession, he soon becomes one with his system: "I need the capital. The system needs the capital." Part 1 ends hopefully, though. He surprises us by announcing that he has won five million francs. This luck will let him do exactly what he wants, and his worries seem over. Greene, though, introduces a countercheck. Always distrustful of free will, he shows that freedom need not bring happiness and wisdom.

Bertram's luck tempts him anew. He feels driven to parlay his winnings into a still larger fortune. But the stakes of the game have changed. Unknown to him, his search for a system that will break the bank endangers both his job and his marriage. The active verbs in the first paragraph of part 2 point to a new strength and self-confidence. But by the end of the paragraph, his self-confidence has become overbearing, and his new strength has proved divisive:

> One adapts oneself to money. . . . I frequently *rang* the bell [at the hotel desk] for the pleasure of con-

fronting a uniform without shame. I *made* Cary have
an Elizabeth Arden treatment. . . . I *had* our things
moved to a suite and I *hired* a car to take us to the
beach. At the beach I *hired* one of the private bunga-
lows where we could sunbathe, *cut off* by bushes and
shrubs *from the eyes of the common people.* There
all day I *worked* in the sun . . . while Cary read
[italics added].

As the action swings ahead, Bertram goes on bullying
servants, flaunting his money, and neglecting Cary. His
world grows and shrinks simultaneously. But his losses
outweigh his gains. Cary asks him, "Don't you like me
to remember the days when we were poor and happy?"
Yet he keeps ignoring her: "I thought it best to ask her
to stay away. . . . 'I love you very much darling . . .
but work is work. . . . . We'll see each other for
meals.' " This rift widens. Stranded, Cary looks elsewhere for companionship, and Bertram, too, goes off
alone during off-duty hours. But his vision has shrunk
so much that even a ballet he watches exists only as an
offshoot of roulette: "The ballerina to me was hardly
a woman so much as a ball spinning on the wheel."
Then, coming back to the suite and frightened by the
rift in his marriage, he blames his chief, the absent
Dreuther, for his failure.

The next day brings a new development. He meets
A. N. Bowles, a senior partner in Sitra known to the
junior staff as A. N. Other. Bowles, who lives in Monte
Carlo, has made gambling his ruling passion. His addiction leads him to transfer his Sitra shares to Bertram
in a knotty business deal that makes Bertram Sitra's
owner. Bertram again fouls his good luck. Now he wants
to use his power and wealth to destroy Dreuther, or the
Gom. Cary condemns this vindictiveness and moves
further than ever from her new husband: "Darling,
you've been very lucky and you've won a lot of money,

but I don't like you any more." Then, when Bertram feels most alone, the Gom shows his face. Without being asked, he pays Bertram's hotel bill and invites Bertram aboard his yacht, where the two men review Bertram's wrecked marriage. The upshot of their review is the reconciliation of Cary and Bertram, a decision by Bertram not to seek revenge against the Gom, and, finally, a promotion and raise for Bertram. Everyone, after a few scares, gets what he wants. Everyone, too, knows the human value of his winnings: Bertram says of the Gom, "I owe him everything," and Cary tells Bertram, "I love you so much more [than before]."

But who is Everyone?

All the characters in *Loser Takes All* offer something special. Cary Bertram's chief gift is her freshness. Living in a timeless present tense, she sees everything as unique and special. And she charges this vividness of response with a good sudden healthy sense of terror:

> "Terrible" was her favorite adjective—it wasn't in her mouth a *cliche*; there *was* terror in her pleasures, her fears, her anxieties, her laughter, the terror of surprise, of seeing something for the first time. Most of us see only resemblances; every situation has been met before; but Cary saw only differences.

Cary, self-styled "the most superstitious woman in the world," believes in fate, omens, auguries. Her world has brighter colors and a broader scope than that of Bertram. She discourages his gambling because she knows that gambling inhibits love. She knows instinctively, in fact, what her husband has never learned. She views other people sympathetically, as units in personal relationships rather than as objects, and she does not weight these relationships with unfair demands. With her, the human comes first. She would rather take her chances with poverty than risk undermining love with money or rank, and she likes Monte Carlo because life there makes her marriage seem free and unofficial. Within her marriage, then, she represents the *spirit* of the law, while Bertram—with his penchant for formal systems and for revenge—stands for Old Testament retribution and accumulated sin. Her New Testament mercy and charity save Bertram from the sorrow he deserves. She is, in short, the interceding female of Christian romance.

She is also Greene's stock waiflike heroine. Both her parents were killed in the war; her frail frame and carelessness in crossing streets wreathe her in an aura of helplessness; she is fifteen years younger than Bertram. She need not cultivate learning or prudence because her inherent graciousness surpasses acquired virtues. Like other Greene heroines, she has been bruised but has healed well. She gives into no obsessions, harbors no grudges, and saves her man by good example rather than by preachment. But Greene works hard to present her as more than just a redeemer. Bertram says of her, "She was not too young to be wise, but she was too young to know that wisdom shouldn't be spoken aloud when you are happy." If she has a fresher view of life than Bertram, she is also more wild and impulsive. Each partner, in fact, by knowing things the other does not, complements his mate nicely. The marriage has a good healthy reversibility.

The marriage rounds her out as much as it does him. (Her lack of a maiden name and his lack of a first name express their mutual need.) When he scamps his duties as a husband, she turns to another man, thus introducing into her personality a realistic dash of rebelliousness. Her curious name also anchors the drama in the human, rather than the literary, sphere. By suggesting the words *care*, *carious*, and *carré* (the French word for gambling chip), her name frames her character within the human truths of burden, decay, and chance.

Bertram's personality has less sparkle. A divorced man of about forty, he lives prosily among numbers, accounts, and balance sheets. His is a sober, fact-ridden mind. He is not superstitious, and, like Colonel Calloway in *The Third Man*, he prizes reason and common sense. His remark about Cary, "She wasn't as good with figures as I was," is true but also misleading. Either he is not as apt with numbers as he claims or his aptness counts less than he admits. For he has worked at the same job for five years, and he calls himself both "an ageing assistant accountant" and "conspicuously unsuccessful."

What is missing from his life is a loving heart. Defensively, he equates professional success with death— the chilled immobility of statuary—when he ponders his failure to get ahead: "To be raised from the ground floor I would have to be a piece of sculpture." His chief, the Gom, shatters this self-apology by ascending the Sitra's executive offices on the top floor while staying alive. Human endeavor matters in *Loser Takes All*; the book's romantic plot and lavish vacation setting create a brighter tone than that of either *The Third Man* or *The End of the Affair*. And the endeavor matters most when prompted by love and generosity. Bertram does not invoke the letter of the law against the Gom. In return, as has been said, he regains his wife and gets both a promotion and a boost in salary. The promotion, in line with Greene's sermon on money and power, is not to a high executive post. In his wisdom, the Gom does not make the Bertrams rich and powerful all at once.

If this acquired wisdom puts the Gom thematically close to Cary, Greene's deployment of him recalls Harry Lime of *The Third Man*. Like Lime, he controls the action without appearing in it. Kunkel is rightly impressed with his social grace: "He is cultured, courteous, and fluent. He talks with easy familiarity to social inferiors and foreigners." [3] He seems to have done and forgiven everything: he has had four wives, made a fortune, studied poetry, and become accomplished in both sailing and languages. Neither obsessed nor driven, he enjoys relaxing as much as he enjoys the cut and thrust of business. He moves elegantly, but not showily, in a large, fully globed world—reading Baudelaire, going on pleasure cruises, and speaking of love and hope.

But it takes more than culture to control life the way Gom does. He thwarts life by failing to show up for the Bertrams' wedding and then gives life by uniting the Bertrams more powerfully than ever. His directorship of Sitra, a "huge office block" housing modern carvings "like statues in a Catholic church," gives him nearly godlike control over many lives. And who is a better god-figure in a society where money both decides a person's identity and shapes his decisions than an industrial magnate? Greene infuses Sitra with a good deal of religious symbolism. Its three-way partnership recalls both the Christian trinity and the Olympian triumvirate of Zeus, Poseidon, and Hades. Even though the book's comic mood jars with myth, the muted infighting between Sitra's three owners creates the singing tension that makes the business thrive. The name of the Gom's secretary, Miss Bullen, joins religious and domestic issues: it calls to mind both Mithraism (which has the bull as its focus) and the mazelike path the Bertrams must follow before finding peace together.

In keeping with the book's syncretism, the Gom salts his Olympian grandeur with Christian paradox. Described in large, loose-fitting terms, he exudes both infinity and humanity. His flowing white mane imparts majesty: although he speaks in a "deep guttural voice," his age, nationality, and religious outlook never surface. That he is an enigma makes all things possible with him. Bertram says of him: "Nothing was impossible with the Gom"; "He was like the weather—unpredictable"; and "He was of the Pentecostal type." His eyeglasses, "the thickest . . . ever seen on a human face," recall the eyes of Dr. T. J. Eckleburg, seen on a billboard in *The Great Gatsby* and called the eyes of God. He will fret over a small imbalance in Sitra's accounts but will neglect large sums. Inscrutably related to time, he gives his workers clocks as wedding gifts but misses Bertram's wedding. Although able to rescue Bertram's foundering marriage, he has failed in four marriages of his own. His office is "not like an office at all," and he makes Bertram feel like an Old Testament character in the presence of a king. There is no regal aloofness in his business dealings, though. No regressive force, "the wise old man with limitless ambitions" reorganizes his staff, phases out old office machinery, and headquarters his firm in a building of glass, marble, and gleaming steel.

But his real gift is his zest for life. Sufficient to himself, he does not need goals or competitors to stay sharp: "Where other men collected pictures to escape death duties, he collected for pleasure." As has been pointed out, Greene often uses the metaphor "at sea" to describe his private life. The metaphor is apt. The Gom has an intrinsic faith in life; he is content to live with the half-tones, with doubt. He does not need solid ground under him. This faith, like his favorite pastime of yachting, likens him to the legendary fertility god set out to sea in the spring of the year. He even "marries" Cary and Bertram by bringing them closer than ever before. They end the book, like him, "at sea," in a stateroom of his yacht.

The Gom makes Samuel Beckett's *Waiting for Godot* the book's most notable forerunner. Produced in France in 1952 and then in England in 1955, the same year *Loser Takes All* came out, Beckett's play features a god-figure who both takes away and restores hope. It also asks, like Greene's entertainment, whether life is chance or a closed system, and a meal Bertram has of *bresse à l'estragon* names Estragon, a character in the play. But the chain of resemblances breaks. Unlike Godot, the Gom appears personally, and his entry brings more hope than the waiting, the messenger, or the tree that buds bring to the play.

The dedication page of *Loser Takes All* denies that the book is meant to discourage gambling. Greene's statement is misleading. In a time-art, like prose narrative, gambling has artistic uses. It builds suspense as the stakes rise because of the correlation between rising stakes and psychological tension. Ralph Harper compares the mood of the thriller with the excitement generated by the gambling table: "The atmosphere of the thriller is feverish, with that airless, suffocating tenseness of the gambling table." [4] The epigraph of *The Spy's Bedside Book* (1957), which Greene edited with his brother Hugh, makes the same comparison. It follows that Greene, a writer of thrillers, should, once in his literary career, build a narrative around gambling. Like crime and war, the staples of the thriller, gambling traffics in impulse, daredevil courage, and nervous energy.

But when it tries to extend itself into a formal system, gambling leads to disaster. (In this respect, the thriller stands to the novel as gambling, with its short-lived melodrama, stands to reality.) The governing irony of *Loser Takes All* comes from the lag between the reader's and Bertram's knowledge that Bertram has risked more at roulette than just money. Other systems players come to worse grief. Like the opium smokers in *The Quiet American*, most of them have been dwarfed and debilitated by their addiction: A. N. Bowles, the senior partner in Sitra, uses a hearing aid and rides in a wheelchair. Philippe, the young roulette addict Cary drifts to when Bertram shuns her, shows that gambling blunts the passions: "The ball and not the bed was the focal point." In keeping with the idea that gambling thwarts love, Bertram wins Cary back by tempting Philippe with roulette chips.

Greene, as usual, gives his moral a religious reference. He calls the systems players "theologians, patiently trying to rationalize a mystery." They devise elaborate formulae that both deny chance and fail because of chance. At one point, Bertram hints at a link between the Casino and the local jail. But the depravity surrounding the wheel goes beyond civil law. The man who tries to sell Bertram a foolproof system with which to break the bank has already lost five million francs at roulette; he quotes scripture, and, just as diabolically, asks "the earth" as his selling price. Like his fellow theologians, the systems seller, or devil, as Bertram calls him, tries to foresee or alter the future. His attempts, faithless and freedom-denying in impulse, must fail.

Yet gambling has a brighter side. The metaphor of the wheel, carried over from *The Third Man*, denies fixed meanings: the ball can stop anywhere. "Pascal was a gambler—who staked his money on a divine system," Bertram notes. As with Pascal and Kierkegaard, religious faith is a commitment to God without the help of proofs and guarantees. The time spent by the Gom "at sea" signifies faith in the natural order. The Gom can enjoy life without trying to change or codify it. That two later Greene heroes, in *Our Man in Havana* and *The Comedians*, are born in Monte Carlo carries forward the idea of life as a network of chance and faith.

It is not easy to balance freedom and form. Though ours is still a fallen, stricken world, love makes it endurable. But love needs a catalyst. The Bertrams are not reunited by their own efforts alone. Bertram is especially lucky to have two redeemers in Cary and the

Gom. No *deus ex machina* helped the other systems players; none interceded to save any of the Gom's four broken marriages. The book's existential individualism is thus tempered. One's efforts do not always suffice, and one must not ask too much from life.

Greene makes these points naturalistically: *Loser Takes All* has a definable problem, a straightforward plot, and a set of characters who can be described. These characters, lacking complexity, live for the sake of the story. Yet the story generates depth, and the plot is inventive. Greene takes an overworked domestic situation and makes it exciting. He also reminds us that people need other people.

"All This Spying. Spying on What?"

Our Man in Havana has a fine reputation. Except for Harvey Curtis Webster, who, dismissing the three entertainments of the 1950s in a paragraph, calls it "barely consequential," everyone who has written about it has praised it. Most of the praise, furthermore, is intelligent. De Vitis calls it "a delightful satire with a serious edge, one of the funniest books to appear in many a day." Kunkel pays tribute to its range and flexibility when he speaks of its witchlike brew of "mirth and murder, pomposity and poison, satire and suspense." Atkins praises it as "one of the most professional pieces of writing Greene has given us; it moves with . . . speed and precision . . . and it manages to pass comments on life which are central to Greene's thinking." The salute ends with Atkins's calling the book "the best of the entertainments." [1]

These tributes are hard to gainsay. *Our Man in Havana* is freshly conceived and brilliantly executed. A warm, colorful work, it has all the absurd delicious trimmings of our technocratic age. It also maintains the difficult balance between comedy and terror. Greene builds to terrifying, even tragic, moments, but he always leaves a banana peel on the scene of the tragedy. This mixture of knockabout and terror cushions the suspense. But it restrains our laughter, too, lest we discover that the supports have gone out from under us and that we are laughing at ourselves.

The fragile balance between knockabout and terror makes itself felt in other ways. Although dealing with exiles, *Our Man in Havana* does not put forth a vision of homelessness and wreckage as sharp as that of *England Made Me, The Confidential Agent,* or *The Quiet American.* The book's comic spirit rules out the sharks, alligators, sick children, and mutilated beggars of Greene's two other Latin American novels, *The Power and the Glory* and *The Comedians.* Yet, for all the differences between *Our Man in Havana* and *The Comedians,* the two works stand as close as any other pair of Greene fictions. Both are set in Caribbean dictatorships. Both, while accepting murder and cruelty as facts of modern politics, make farce, not comedy, the true counterpole of tragedy. Finally, by describing the failure of internationalism and technocracy to tame man's savage drives, both uncover a primitive streak in our nature.

But *Our Man in Havana* owes more to fantasy than does *The Comedians.* Greene calls it "a fairy story . . . set at some indeterminate date in the future," and he begins it at Havana's Wonder Bar (*cf. wunderbar*) with a displaced German making a far-fetched comparison. The fantastic and the far-fetched irradiate the action. The Intelligence agent who recruits Jim Wormold, the title character, into Whitehall's Caribbean spy ring, has the same name as American literature's greatest master of the marvelous. The suggestiveness of Hawthorne's name reaches beyond plot and character. Like *The Scarlet Letter,* Greene's 1958 entertainment uses fantasy to heighten reality rather than to sidestep it.

It is also one of the timeliest books by a writer often praised for his timeliness. Boldly, it satirizes British security at a time when Soviet infiltrators like Otto

Fuchs and Kim Philby had thrown British security into worldwide disrepute. The atomic age imparts a different danger from that of the munitions buildup in *This Gun for Hire* or the four-power occupation of Vienna in *The Third Man.* Cold War politics—the feinting, jockeying, and countermaneuvering for power—are shadowy and puzzling. On the other hand, they use real people. The speed with which spying can crush a person shows through in the numerous references both to air travel and electronic communication. Wormold flies to Jamaica and later takes a plane with his daughter Milly to London; Hawthorne commutes by air between London and the Caribbean. A sketch will take shape on Wormold's drawing board and turn up in the next chapter in British security headquarters in London. A remark that people everywhere speak with accents suggests further a world both shrunken and demeaned by costly mechanized techniques of spying.

The city of Havana contributes to this unlovely trend. In 1970, Greene called Havana "an extraordinary city, where every vice was permissible and every trade possible." [2] As a troubled, corrupt place on the edge of war, it resembles many other Greene settings. Greene need not go into Cuba's swamps and jungles to implant his book with savagery; the streets of Havana are savage enough. Sullen, sordid, and watched over by a sadistic police chief, Havana does not worship science. In the late 1950s, it was one of the world's few busy international capitals more primitive than pragmatic in spirit. The night noises, the many animal images, and the violence bred by the civil war crush civilized values. Rational westernized man is lost in Havana. But technology cannot be escaped. If the jungle pervades Havana, so does the machine. And when the machine and the jungle collide, they induce a tropical madness from which nobody is immune.

It follows that a book centering on the idea that nature abhors a vacuum should also center on vacuum cleaners. Vacuum cleaners serve the plot of *Our Man in Havana* brilliantly. Early in the action Wormold asks, "What's the good of a vacuum cleaner if the power's cut off?" The question refers to both Wormold's faltering vacuum-cleaner business and the political turmoil brewing in Cuba. Guerrilla attacks have stopped service on all public utilities in Havana, and nobody wants a new electrical appliance when there is no electricity to run it. But Wormold's question also refers to the individual's relationship to his government. First, politics abhors a vacuum as much as nature does. Waste, corruption, and mismanagement have readied Cuba for insurrection. The political stalemate created there by the pull for power from different sides is unnatural, and any shift in strength will destroy it. Life and property will fall indiscriminately. Wormold may well ask, "What's the good of a vacuum cleaner if the power's cut off?" Can an effect have more reality than its cause? How much freedom can we have if our governments, by going under, stop protecting us?

And how much can a government ask of its citizens to prevent going under? Like the heroes of *The Ministry of Fear* and Hitchcock's *North by Northwest* (1959), Wormold is dragooned into his nation's security network. Unlike these men, he runs into waste, incompetence, and, despite new techniques in communications, communication failures between branches of government. Most vexing of all is his discovery that governments care so little about their citizens; the chief of the British Secret Service prizes military secrets over human life, and he does not quail at risking his agents' skin to get them. Nor does security work attract the best people. Spying appeals to drifters and misfits, to traitors and down-and-outers, and they are whipped into the maw of their countries' security as effortlessly as dust and dirt are drawn into a vacuum cleaner. Greene endorses the following disclaimers against spies and spying, from John Le Carré's *The Spy Who Came in from the Cold:*

> There's only one law in this game. . . . What do you think spies are: priests, saints and martyrs? They're a squalid procession of vain fools, traitors too; yes pansies, sadists and drunkards, people who play cowboys and Indians to brighten their rotten lives.
>
> .   .   .   .
>
> Everywhere's the same, people cheated and misled, whole lives thrown away, people shot and in prison, whole groups and classes of men written off for nothing.[3]

While sharing this dark view of espionage, Greene's satire brightens it. The book's technique of narrative selection slues the reported action away from violence and toward fun and frolic. Jim Wormold, an Englishman of forty-five, has been selling vacuum cleaners in Havana for fifteen years. Five years before the action begins, he was deserted by a wife he still loves. The intervening years have not lightened his load. The emotional strain of losing his wife has been matched by the financial strain imposed by his failing business; when we meet him, his finances have been squeezed tighter still by his spendthrift daughter. Just when the extravagance of the seventeen-year-old Milly has depleted his savings, Wormold gets his chance to spy for British Intelligence. This work he does in a unique way. He trumps up reports on nonexistent military installations, and he recruits a cadre of imaginary subagents. In the process, his bank account, his place in Havana's business community, and Milly's happiness all soar.

At the outset, he is cut off from more than his money

and a wife he loves. Disjointedness describes him. Living in a foreign land and speaking a foreign language, he feels like a permanent tourist in Havana. His ignorance of the mechanical details of his job puts him out of touch with his livelihood. Although he sells vacuum cleaners, he can neither fix nor build one: "I'm not much of a mechanic. When I touch one of these things it somehow seems to stop working." This apartness from the materials and techniques of his trade reflects an alienation that infects his home. Not only is he a Saxon in a Latin country; his atheism divides him from his daughter's (and his adopted country's) Catholicism: "He thought sadly, but I *am* a stranger. . . . Sometimes he felt that he had no child."

Like the whisky priest in *The Power and the Glory*, Wormold lets himself be led by a child when he decides to dabble in spying. He soon finds, though, that his new career limits rather than enlarges his freedom. Before he knows it, he is surrounded by outlaws ("this was a hotel of real spies, real police-informers, and real rebel agents"), arrested, and beaten up by the police. An act of will has joined him to the underworld of the gangster. A remorseless logic hems him in. He need not commit himself to British Intelligence to be treated like an outlaw; all he needs to do is accept their money. As the action builds, he grows less free, more implicated in danger, and less able to influence his daughter's choices. Unlike Chekhov's dreamers, whose hopes and prayers always go unanswered, Greene's characters get more than they can cope with when they try to enlarge their spheres.

The trouble constantly breaking around Wormold prompts British security to send him an aide—Beatrice Severn, a divorced cryptographer of about thirty. Beatrice's questions about his spy ring heighten both the intrigue and the fun. His answers show that she has also brought a romantic note into the book. Though not Dante's Beatrice, she does save Wormold, and, as her last name suggests, severs him from a severed state—both divorce and faction-riven Cuba. But her name tells still more about their relationship. In line with the book's many number games—for gambling and the number codes used by spies make numbers as strong a presence in Havana as in the Monte Carlo of *Loser Take All*—her last name indicates completeness. Though lacking a stay or support (her husband's name is Peter), she nonetheless fulfills Wormold: the number seven (*cf.* Severn) means an integration of spirit (three—the Christian trinity) and matter (four—the seasons, the humors, the elements, the points of the compass) to western man. Greene's play on the phonetic similarity between seven and Severn is the sort of name-prank or word-prank that comes more often in the entertainments than in the novels, and *Our Man in Havana* reflects this humorous practice as vividly as any of the lighter fictions. Beatrice Severn is not the only character whose situation bears on the plot. There is also a strip-tease dancer shanghaied from the Shanghai Bar, where she works; another evil character named Carter makes his way into the book, and Greene impishly has him ask Wormold about a Nottwich man named Davis; Hawthorne, the nasty Secret Service agent who recruits Wormold, has the first name Henry, a familiar badge of unsavoriness in Greene's work.[4]

Rounding out the roster of major characters are Captain Segura, Havana's chief of police, and Dr. Hasselbacher, a retired German M.D. who meets Wormold every morning for a daiquiri. Hasselbacher left Hitler's Germany for the tropics in the early 1930s in order to escape mechanized violence. Representing pre-1914 Europe, he cannot summon his wealth, wisdom, or historical sense to ward off pain. Although he prefers to be vague on the subject, he carries around with him an old hurt that has never healed. His favorite pastime, working crossword puzzles, shows his befuddlement with modern life. Good at his word games, he cannot shut out his painful past or make sense of the madness of the Cold War age. He takes up spying with a full understanding of its wastefulness, and his life, like Wormold's, soon becomes a vacuum into which interference rushes. His apartment is searched and gutted, his office and laboratory are smashed, and he is killed—all as a direct result of spying. His wise affability recalls the Gom in *Loser Takes All*. But spying is so cancerous in its evils that he cannot block the death drift engulfing him and several others in Havana.

Dr. Hasselbacher's foil—who also has a title in place of a first name—is Captain Segura. Practical rather than theoretical, small and tough rather than large and affable, Segura drips evil. Hasselbacher cannot bear being in the same room with him. Called "the Red Vulture," he is described as "a well-cared-for weapon" and as "a very small man in a very tight uniform." Said to torture his prisoners and to carry a cigarette case made of human skin, he represents a primordial evil. He rises from a chair "like a small tight green snake," and the tape recorder in his office gives off a snakelike hiss. Although his professional dedication recalls the lieutenant in *The Power and the Glory*, his police duties have not killed his sexual drive. The threat he poses to Wormold is dual: as a policeman and as an eager suitor to Milly. Both these threats dissolve, though, and Wormold's parting judgment of him is oddly charitable: "he wasn't a bad chap." But his smallness and the danger he exudes during Wormold's last months in Cuba mirror a general disconnectedness: the incipient revolution in Cuba has created a moral vacuum where everything is for sale and where nobody is safe from violence; Henry Hawthorne's elegant attire runs counter to his slangy speech; Milly Wormold has two selves—the pious Catholic and the pampered brat who set fire to a schoolmate at age thirteen; Beatrice Severn, fluent in English and French, is sent by her chiefs to a Spanish-speaking country.

This tangle of cross-purposes, subdivisions, puzzles, and games make reality elusive. Philip Stratford calls *Our Man in Havana* "a fiction about fiction-making," [5] in one of his many fine insights into Greene. Like Joyce's *A Portrait*, the book asks about the artist's pride, guilt, and dehumanization and also about the destructiveness of the creative instinct. The artist's imaginative reshaping of reality and his sacrifice of real to imagined life also get into two other works of Greene's late maturity, *A Burnt-Out Case* (1961) and *Carving a Statue* (1964). Like *Our Man in Havana*, these works turn on the obsessiveness of artistic creation. The novel counterpoints sexual drive and artistic activity, while the play shows a sculptor-father pridefully imitating God and Father and, in the process, killing life.

By inventing a corps of subagents, Wormold arrogates to himself the power to create life. And his imaginary world of spies rings of both tidiness and authenticity:

> The professor was the economic authority, and Engineer Cifuentes dealt with the mysterious constructions in the mountains of Oriente. . . . The chief engineer supplied descriptions of labor conditions. . . . As for the nude dancer, she supplied spicy details of the private lives and sexual eccentricities of the Defense Minister and the Director of Posts and Telegraphs.

Suddenly, this neat, lucrative world comes apart. Engineer Cifuentes, a real person unknowingly conscripted into Wormold's spy ring, is shot at. Then, a Cubana pilot named Raul Dominguez whom Wormold had invented to fly secret reconnaissance missions shocks everybody by turning up dead.

Spying stands closer to fiction than to architecture (*A Burnt-Out Case*) or sculpture (*Carving a Statue*). Dr. Hasselbacher says, "All you need is a little imagination" to become a spy. The chief of the Secret Service carries Wormold along "the tide of . . . [his] literary imagination" and turns him from a small dealer into a merchant king. Milly asks her father, "Are you becoming a writer?" and he answers, "Yes, an imaginative writer." He goes on to master the materials of his medium and to know his audience. He becomes a brilliant impersonator: he writes his official messages in the weary cadences, hollow voice, and self-important vocabulary of Intelligence officialese, and he supplements them with drawings of vacuum-cleaner parts meant to stand for the weapons in the Oriente province. At one point, he wonders, when his literary spy ring has suddenly edged into reality, "Can we write human beings into existence?" His spying has given him more power than he can handle—namely, the Godlike power to give and take away life. The Father, whose mediocre efforts as a sculptor parody God the Father in *Carving a Statue*, says "A man becomes his work," and several characters in *The Comedians* (1966) convey the same Pirandellian argument: we are what we imagine ourselves to be. The book's epigraph from Thomas Hardy, "aspects are within us, and who seems/Most kingly is the King," applies to Wormold's Intelligence work. And Wormold's limp recalls not only Murice Bendrix, the novelist-narrator of *The End of the Affair*, but also Hephaestus, or Vulcan, symbol of the maimed artist.

Wormold's troubles flare out when his fiction refuses to stay put. Art is insidious; unwatched, it burgeons into a full-time job from a weekend diversion. No green baize door intervening, an imaginative leap carries Wormold across the border from make-believe into fictional art. His standard of living, circle of friends, daily routine, and standing with the local police all change. At the same time, his characters, with whom, like any novelist, he gets more involved as his fiction unfolds, grow frighteningly real—leaping into life and plunging into death. Endangering Wormold further is the eagerness with which his paymasters await his messages: composing in code and sending his compositions by cablegram—the art form befitting an age modelled on adventure fiction—he does his job too well. He becomes lionized. And like any other literary lion, he finds his personal well-being running counter to his public favor. The enemies he makes and London's steady demands for news increase his danger.

Nor can he brake the danger. Dr. Hasselbacher tells him that facts are the enemy of espionage: "As long as you lie you do no harm" is his precept. The absence of facts gives full rein to the spy's literary imagination. Just as *Loser Takes All* rested on a groundplan of existentialism, idealism undergirds *Our Man in Havana*. To be is to be perceived is an axiom as vital to spying as to Bishop Berkeley. But Greene goes beyond the argument that reality is an activity of the mind. He shows our mental activities affecting other people. Wormold's creative instinct touches others without their knowing it or having a choice. Spying may be a ludicrous game played with codes and puzzles, surmise and guesswork; but it uses people. And like any other military operation, it produces casualties.

The book's comic spirit often makes these casualties funny. It glides from fun to seriousness and from safe detachment to life-and-death danger. It also creates for Greene the opportunity to comment further on the artist. One evening finds Wormold, like any other metaphysician, pondering the nature of being. And like any good novelist, he frames his speculations in contemporary terms: "That evening hour was real, but not . . . the cruelties of police-stations and governments, the scientists who tested the new H-Bomb on Christmas Island, Kruschev [sic] who wrote notes." His search for reality lifts him above fame and the dynamics of power. It takes him, surprisingly, to the figure of the clown:

> The cruel come and go. . . . But the clown whom he had seen last year with Milly at the circus—that clown was permanent, for his act never changed. That was the way to live; the clown was unaffected by the vagaries of public men and the enormous discoveries of the great.

Untouched by life around him, the clown leads a pure existence. What lasts is not spectacular but comic. The ability to make people laugh grows in importance in Greene's later fiction. Civilization, too, is not shaped by spectacular public events but by our need for fun and laughter. Like the figures of Keats's urn, the clown's buffoonery has a universality because it captures something timeless.

But what of the clown? As the Keatsian parallel suggests, Greene's belief in the clown's permanence makes the clown an artist as well as an actor. Wormold's personality has a clownish side. Someone tells him to open a practical-joke shop, and Carter, the enemy agent sent to Havana to kill him calls him "You—you clown." The book's epigraph, from George Herbert, "And the sad man is the cock of all his jests," hits on a facet of clowning beyond Carter's outburst. It refers to the clown as broken-hearted jester or sad buffoon. Victor Rhodes, the cuckold in *The Complaisant Lover*, enjoys puns and practical jokes. Yet like Wormold, he knows, first, that jokes sometimes recoil on the joker and, next, that his clown act is a shell, or routine, he cannot escape. Sanity, not choice, is at stake. Both men go on playing the fool in order to stay alive. Greene's use of the Musée Grimaldi in "May We Borrow Your Husband?" and of the Chateau Grimaldi in "Chagrin in Three Parts" recalls the famous story of the psychoanalyst who told a patient he could snap out of his depression by watching the clown Grimaldi. The patient answered, "But *I* am Grimaldi."

Besides the idea of the artist as a drooping harlequin, Greene gets from Joyce that of the clownlike artist as God. We have already touched on the idea. What remains is to channel it into Greene's fictional world. Wormold says to himself, "The clown had the comfort of not learning from experience." Milly tells him elsewhere, "God doesn't learn from experience, does He, or how could He hope anything of man?" Now a central idea in *Carving a Statue* is the artist's aloofness as a hallmark of godlike inspiration: God and the artist both view the passing moment with indifference. The sculptor-father's wife's death is no more than a "shocking inconvenience," and God, according to the play, sent His Son to earth because He, God, transcending human process, could not suffer. Querry, the world-famous architect in *A Burnt-Out Case*, chides himself for coldness and for making those who love him pay for his creativeness. If the artist, then, as a creator, stands close to God, he also cuts himself off from his kind. Doomed to apartness, the clown droops and weeps. His pride even turns him into an anti-God. Joyce compares Stephen Dedalus to both Satan and Prometheus in *A Portrait*; his powerful imagination, foraging into the heretofore unknown, makes the artist the natural enemy of the established order. The poet undermines Plato's ideal community; Stephen Dedalus cannot stay in Ireland; Wallace Stevens's "Esthétique du Mal" calls

Satan's death "a tragedy/For the imagination" (stanza 8) and refers to the artist as "A man of bitter appetite" (stanza 9).

Stevens's "The Comedian as the Letter C" and its main character, the "introspective voyager" and "ribboned stick" Crispin, bring to mind a theme in Greene that includes but goes beyond the clown. It is odd that nobody has noted how many names in the Greene canon start with the letter C. The recurrence of the name Carter we have already discussed in chapter 1, above. Yet the letter C need not label a character a villain, as it does with most of the Carters who pepper Greene's books. If some C-named characters are nasty, some are also sympathetic. In *Another Mexico*, a Mexican-born Briton designated as C is described as "the sort of person you avoid at a party." Earlier in the book, Green recalls among his schoolday acquaintances "Collifax, who practiced torments with dividers; Mr. Cranden with three grim chins, a dusty gown, a kind of demonic sensuality." Greene's early short stories include Colonel Crashaw, president of a psychical society in "Proof Positive" (1930), Chalfont, an ageing gigolo in "Jubilee" (1936), Calloway, a trapped millionaire in "Across the Bridge" (1938), and Craven, a surprised moviegoer in "A Little Place Off the Edgware Road" (1939). The first three pages of *Rumour at Nightfall* (1931) introduces the book's three main characters, Francis Chase, Ramon Caveda, and Michael Crane; the novel, moreover, revolves around Carlos, pretender to the Spanish throne in the late nineteenth century. Coral Musker, Carleton Myatt, Quin C. Savory, and Richard Czinner all appear in *Orient Express*; and *This Gun for Hire* includes Anne Crowder, Colonel Calkin, another Carter, and a Mrs. Cranbeim. Then, for about ten years, the flow of C-named characters in Greene thins. But in *The Third Man* (1950) we meet, besides

Crabbit and Colonels Calloway and Cooler (Greene's colonels almost always have last names starting with C), a "clean, controlled man creaking among the crucifixes." The "Congo Journal" in *In Search of a Character* (1961) gives the letter *C* a prominence it had not enjoyed since the 1930s. Greene is discussing the trouble he had naming his protagonist in *A Burnt-Out Case*:

> I don't know why X had so suddenly become C; if I was to avoid the national pinpointing which goes with surnames, C was the only initial that struck me as possible. . . . C somehow had the only quality possible.

Finally, most of the action of *Our Man in Havana* takes place in a land whose name begins with a *C*, and the chief of the British Secret Service is once called *C* by a colleague.

The meaning of this long scroll of Cs is an open question. But a clue is given by the figure of the clown —especially his lovable gentleness and his dedicated showmanship. Pagliacci-like, he boxes the compass of human emotions from broad jest to sorrow. He is like everybody else but more so in his range of feelings. The letter *C* stands as Greene's tribute to the common clay the clown both serves and typifies. Greene's worst villains always stop acting like partisans, profiteers, or love-rivals and reveal themselves as human. D. and Wormold both want to kill their persecutors quickly, before they become human. It takes less grit to kill an enemy than to kill somebody with fears, hopes, and perhaps a family. There is something special and sacred about everybody, if we only trouble to look. Murder denies this uniqueness; imagination and sympathy cherish it. The creative artist thrives on uniqueness. By enriching our perception of people, he makes our world more vital. Greene need not expound his themes with extraordinary people. His preference for C-named characters reflects a faith in the run-down and the third-rate. "Aspects are within us": at any time, greatness can flare out of anybody and change the surrounding human landscape. Life is a miracle when it seems least miraculous; art's great value is the ability to disclose the miracle energizing the commonplace.

Art's counterpole is espionage. Spying holds no brief with human decency or privacy, let alone sacredness. In scourging a practice that enjoys more prestige than it deserves, Greene's treatment of espionage is truly satirical. Scorning the reality of human flesh, the spy traffics in shadowy stuff. He is a mystic, inhabiting the unseen and the unspoken; he hears voices, has visions, denies the witness of his senses. Intelligence work makes the imagination run riot. It deals with surmise more than certainty, rumor more than fact, and the unsaid rather than the verified. Appearances count more for the spy than reality. Often, in fact, an appearance, or even the hint of one, becomes the reality. The spying profession has as its main business self-perpetuation. It discredits anything that threatens it and plays up anything that strengthens it. It cheats its paymasters. Because facts must be faced directly, it stays away from facts. It will sow distrust between nations if international tension nourishes it; it will kill if killing increases its prestige. Worst of all, it engenders an aura of nightmare and distrust. Wormold's mission as Agent 59200/5, for instance, is both vague and hideously precise. Without knowing what he defends or whom he represents, he lays his life on the line. His impressment into British Intelligence proves that everyone nowadays is a potential agent or victim.

Though imaginative, the spy is the opposite of the creative artist, taking away life and undermining human dignity. Spying, furthermore, violates the contractual duty of governments to protect their citizens. Governments today support massive security agencies which, by viewing everyone as a potential spy, endanger life and property. Whereas art tightens our hold on life, these agencies, despite their huge costs, do not make us healthier or happier, safer or wiser. At best they represent waste—wasted money, wasted talent, wasted effort. Whereas art dignifies our choices, spying demeans choice: the Cold War leaves little to choose between the morality of one side and that of another. Spying not only lacks positive value; it intensifies, rather than relieves, pain.

The book's animal imagery exposes the evils of espionage more subtly. The book code used in Wormold's bogus spying comes from Lamb's *Tales from Shakespeare*. Lamb's name summons up innocence and sacrifice, two realities of the spying trade. Ducks also suggest dispensability. Governmental indifference to human life makes us sitting ducks for enemy bullets, and our leaders play ducks and drakes with us because we can be replaced so easily. Now subtle, now bold, *Our Man in Havana* contains much solid good writing. In addition to its dramatically apt animal imagery, it exploits the simile to good effect. Two white suits hanging in Dr. Hasselbacher's closet look "like the last teeth in an old mouth," and the waiter who tries to poison Wormold runs "like a human being" when he sees that his dog, not Wormold, has drunk some poisoned whisky. The scene describing the business lunch where Wormold is to be murdered comes off brilliantly. Greene brings the dish of poisoned food to life by describing its progress as it keeps eluding the waiter who wants to serve it to Wormold. Wormold's after-dinner speech, made after the threat of murder has passed, shows new strength and confidence. Like Rollo Martins, in his impromptu speech to the British Cultural Relations

Society (*The Third Man*), Wormold mixes indirect statement, double meaning, and sarcasm into his talk to express his anger and command of the moment. Then, also like Martins, he stops being the hunted man and takes on, instead, the hunter's role.

Greene keeps the structure of the book loose, especially before Wormold becomes the hunter. Lacking the cold severity of *This Gun for Hire*, the book imparts no mood of tightening tension. Its loose design lets Greene exploit the comic possibilities of funny situations. It also adds a sinister note. Even though no urgency is generated, Wormold is playing a life-and-death game in which he cannot tell enemies from friends. The Interludes between the book's five parts, taking place in London, sharpen the satire. They balance the action geographically, provide a look into the infrastructure of British security, and anchor Wormold's vagaries into espionage in official government policy. They show us Whitehall remaking Wormold to suit its needs and self-image. More pointedly, the literary transfiguration shows how little Whitehall cares about him and how little it will do to help him out of danger.

This danger, as has been stated, comes to life at the end of part 3, when Raul Dominguez, a fictional reconnaissance pilot, suddenly dies. From this point, the net around Wormold tightens. The techniques Greene uses to step up narrative tension and to heighten the danger building around Wormold show great skill. First, he does not relax the urgency created by Raul Dominguez's death. Part 4 opens with the news that Dr. Cifuentes, an innocent conscript into Wormold's spy ring, has been shot at. While Wormold's Frankenstein becomes more real, it also becomes a public menace. Part 4 also includes the riotous scene where Wormold kidnaps a stripteaser, another of his unwitting spies, in order to protect her from the growing menace. Not only does the incident make for a good deal of fun and narrative heightening; it also uses repetition to limit further Wormold's freedom. This tightening is created by—the town of Cienfuengos. Teresa, the stripteaser, mentions Cienfuengos, where she has a sister and where Wormold went on his first spying mission. The chance recurrence of this little-known harbor town, whose local police first arrested Wormold and then handled him roughly, shrinks his range of choice and movement. The longer he stays a spy, the more often he will have to relive his prior hardships. Nor does he have lively options: Cuba is a small place; air travel and electronic communication have all but eliminated personal privacy; Whitehall's indifference to its agents force the spy to work without helps and aids.

Part 5 continues to delight and frighten us by turns. Wormold escapes the poison plot; then, after his obligatory confession to Beatrice that he invented his Cuban spy ring, he turns on Carter, his would-be killer, and shoots him dead. In keeping with the book's light tone, the murder is not shown. The difficult blend of the macabre and the frothy holds to the end. After Carter's death, Wormold is ordered to report to London immediately. When he gets there he is awarded an O.B.E. and a top-level job in the home office. The ludicrous finale obeys a curious logic. In order to save face, British Intelligence repeats the same unreason it has observed throughout as a rule of self-preservation. Wormold, too, deserves to be fêted; by cheating his superiors and by imagining danger into life so convincingly, he has kept faith with the two cardinal rules of spying.

Our Man in Havana uses the right modes and forms to develop its ideas. It issues a serious warning without losing cheer. One of Greene's best books, it balances vision, timeliness, and control. Here is no snobbery of pessimism: humanity has not worn thin, love is worth working for, and gadgets do not matter more than people. Nor is life futile. That existence is unreasonable does not cancel out its value. Greene always insists on a reality beyond causality. One of his outstanding gifts has been the ability to make this reality a force even when not in view. This ability—which accounts for much of the greatness of great art—is best summarized by Flannery O'Connor:

> The fiction writer presents mystery through manners, grace through nature, but when he finishes there always has to be left over that sense of Mystery which cannot be accounted for by any human formula.[6]

The mystery both energizes and transcends human activity. Greene's entertainments merit special praise for conveying it in everyday human terms and for affirming the importance of human acts because of its presence. The blend of journalism and metaphysics in the entertainments is unique. The affirmation ringing through them shows in another way their masterful use of the right forms and ideas to convey their ideas.

Any artist who generates serious, compelling ideas dramatically gives a new outlook on reality. What more can we ask of him? Graham Greene deserves to be viewed as one of the century's great writers in English.

Notes

1 – The Entertainer's Art

1. David Pryce-Jones, *Graham Greene* (Edinburgh, 1963), p. 1.

2. William Birmingham, "Graham Greene Criticism: A Bibliographical Study," *Thought* 27 (Spring 1952), 73.

3. John Atkins, *Graham Greene*, rev. ed. (London, 1966), p. 237; Philip Stratford, "Unlocking the Potting Shed," *Kenyon Review* 24 (Winter 1962), 132.

4. Morton D. Zabel, "Graham Greene: The Best and the Worst," in *Craft and Character in Modern Fiction* (New York, 1957), pp. 276–96; Sean O'Faolain, "Graham Greene: I Suffer, Therefore I Am," in *The Vanishing Hero* (Boston, 1957), pp. 45–72; Elizabeth Sewell, "Graham Greene," *Dublin Review* 108 (1954), 12–21; Ian Gregor, "The Greene Baize Door," *Blackfriars* 36 (September 1955), 327–33.

5. Atkins, pp. 31, 86; "Graham Greene Takes the Orient Express," *The Listener*, 21 November 1968, p. 676.

6. David Lodge, *Graham Greene* (London and New York, 1966), p. 23; Herbert Haber, "The End of the Catholic Cycle," in *Graham Greene: Some Critical Considerations*, ed. Robert O. Evans (Lexington, Kentucky, 1963), p. 149.

7. Graham Greene, "The Cinema," *The Spectator*, 1 September 1939, p. 325.

8. Harvey Curtis Webster, "The World of Graham Greene," in Evans, p. 8; Richard Boston, "Greene Being

Funny about Greene and Serious about Life," *New York Times Book Review*, 25 January 1970, p. 4; Wilfrid Sheed, "The Good Word: It All Depends on Your Genre," *New York Times Book Review*, 5 September 1971, p. 22; Anthony Burgess, *The Novel Now: A Guide to Contemporary Fiction* (New York, 1967), p. 63; Albert J. Guerard, *Conrad the Novelist* (Cambridge, Mass., 1958), p. 222.

9. Atkins, p. 30.

10. Graham Greene, radio interview with Walter Allen; cited in Pryce-Jones, p. 62.

11. Graham Greene, Preface, *Three Plays* (London, 1961), p. xiii.

12. Francis L. Kunkel, *The Labyrinthine Ways of Graham Greene* (New York, 1960), p. 111.

13. Steven Marcus, "Evelyn Waugh and the Art of Entertainment," *Partisan Review* 13 (Summer 1956), 348–49.

14. John Osborne, *The Entertainer* (New York, 1967), pp. 98–99.

15. Graham Greene, Introduction, in Ford Madox Ford, *The Bodley Head Ford Madox Ford* (London, 1962), 1:8.

16. Kunkel, p. 59.

17. Graham Greene, "The Catholic Temper in Poland," *Atlantic Monthly* (March 1956), p. 59.

18. Graham Greene, "The Cinema," *The Spectator*, 27 March 1936, p. 575; Greene, "Mr. Maugham's Pattern," *The Spectator*, 14 January 1938, p. 59.

19. G. S. Fraser, *The Modern Writer and His World* (Baltimore, 1964), p. 134; John Buchan, *The Three Hostages*, in *Four Adventures of Richard Hannay* (London, 1960), p. 930; Buchan, *The Thirty-Nine Steps*, in ibid., p. 99.

20. Atkins, p. 187.

21. A. A. De Vitis, *Graham Greene* (New York, 1964), p. 65.

22. Edgar Wallace, *The Four Just Men* (New York, 1920), p. 143.

23. Nicholas Blake, "The Detective Story-Why?" in *The Art of the Mystery Story*, ed. Howard Haycraft (New York, 1947), pp. 402–3; Ralph Harper, *The World of the Thriller* (Cleveland, 1969), p. 12.

24. Kenneth Allott and Miriam Farris, *The Art of Graham Greene* (London, 1951), pp. 78–79.

25. James Hall, "Efficient Saints and Civilians: Graham Greene," in *The Lunatic Giant in the Drawing Room: The British and American Novel since 1930* (Bloomington, Ind. and London, 1968), p. 117.

26. Harper, pp. 60–61.

2 – Three Nights in a Train

1. Ronald Matthews, *Mon Ami Graham Greene* (Paris, 1957), p. 150.

2. John Atkins, *Graham Greene*, rev. ed. (London, 1966), p. 37; Philip Stratford, *Faith and Fiction: Creative Process in Greene and Mauriac* (Notre Dame, Ind., 1964), p. 113.

3. David Pryce-Jones, *Graham Greene* (Edinburgh, 1963), p. 18.

4. Kenneth Allott and Miriam Farris, *The Art of Graham Greene* (London, 1951), p. 81.

5. Allott and Farris, p. 147.

6. Pryce-Jones, pp. 19–20.

7. Allott and Farris, pp. 44, 84.

3 – "Fancy a Thing Like That 'Appening 'Ere in Nottwich"

1. John Atkins, *Graham Greene*, rev. ed. (London, 1966), p. 75; Walter Allen, *The Modern Novel in Britain and the United States* (New York, 1964), p. 204.

2. G. S. Fraser, *The Modern Writer and His World* (Baltimore, 1964), p. 134.

3. Ralph Harper, *The World of the Thriller* (Cleveland, 1969), p. 26.

4. Nicholas Blake, "The Detective Story—Why?" in *The Art of the Mystery Story*, ed. Howard Haycraft (New York, 1947), p. 401.

5. Philip Stratford, *Faith and Fiction: Creative Process in Greene and Mauriac* (Notre Dame, Ind., 1964), pp. 188–89.

6. Francis L. Kunkel, *The Labyrinthine Ways of Graham Greene* (New York, 1960), p. 174.

7. Kenneth Allott and Miriam Farris, *The Art of Graham Greene* (London, 1951), p. 139.

4–The Complicated Work of Half-Trust and Half-Deceit

1. Anthony Burgess, "The Greene and the Red: Politics in the Novels of Graham Greene," *Urgent Copy: Literary Studies* (New York, 1969), p. 19.
2. David Lodge, *Graham Greene* (London and New York, 1966), p. 16.
3. Burgess, "The Greene and the Red," p. 20.
4. See chapter one, note 4, above.
5. Kenneth Allott and Miriam Farris, *The Art of Graham Greene* (London, 1951), p. 140.
6. John Atkins, *Graham Greene*, rev. ed. (London, 1966), p. 102.
7. Allott and Farris, p. 147.
8. Ibid., p. 145.
9. Morton D. Zabel, "Graham Greene: The Best and the Worst," in *Craft and Character in Modern Fiction* (New York, 1957), p. 287.
10. Flannery O'Connor, "Novelist and Believer," in *Mystery and Manners*, ed. Sally and Robert Fitzgerald (New York, 1970), p. 154.

5–Ministries of Fear

1. "'The Conspicuous Service of Graham Greene': A New Honor and a New Novel," *Life*, 4 February 1966, p. 44.
2. Kenneth Allott and Miriam Farris, *The Art of Graham Greene* (London, 1951), pp. 62, 194; A. A. DeVitis, *Graham Greene* (New York, 1964), p. 61; R. W. B. Lewis, "Graham Greene: The Religious Affair," *The Picaresque Saint* (Philadelphia, 1959), p. 240.
3. John Atkins, *Graham Greene*, rev. ed. (London, 1966), p. 149.
4. Lewis, p. 226; W. H. Auden, "The Heresy of Our Time," *Renascence* 1 (Spring 1949), 24.
5. Allott and Farris, p. 46.
6. Ibid., p. 210.

6–"In These Days . . . Nobody Thinks in Terms of Human Beings

1. Audrey Nelson Slate, "Technique and Form in the Novels of Graham Greene," Ph.D. diss., University of Wisconsin, 1960, p. 74.

2. Graham Greene, "Epitaph for a Play," *Carving a Statue* (London, 1964), pp. 7–8.

3. Andrew Sinclair, Introduction, in Graham Greene and Carol Reed, *The Third Man* (New York, 1968), p. 5.

4. For a study of Christian and pagan themes, see Lawrence Alloway, "Symbolism in *The Third Man*," *World Review* 13 (March 1950), pp. 57–60.

5. Herbert Thurston, S. J., and Donald Attwater, *Butler's Lives of the Saints* (New York, 1963), 3:171.

6. See Philip Stratford, "Unlocking the Potting Shed," *Kenyon Review* 24 (Winter 1962), 129–31.

7–Waiting for Gom

1. Graham Greene, "Creative Reading," *The Spectator*, 22 September 1933, p. 380.

2. John Atkins, *Graham Greene*, rev. ed. (London, 1966), p. 236; Graham Greene, foreword in Patricia Highsmith, *Eleven* (London, 1970), p. x.

3. Francis L. Kunkel, *The Labyrinthine Ways of Graham Greene* (New York, 1960), p. 96.

4. Ralph Harper, *The World of the Thriller* (Cleveland, 1969), p. 61.

8–"All This Spying. Spying on What?"

1. Harvey Curtis Webster, *After the Trauma: Representative British Novelists Since 1920* (Lexington, Kentucky, 1970), p. 114; A. A. DeVitis, *Graham Greene* (New York, 1964), p. 68; Francis L. Kunkel, *The Labyrinthine Ways of Graham Greene* (New York, 1960), p. 97; John Atkins, *Graham Greene* (London, 1957, rev. ed., 1966), pp. 241–42.

2. Graham Greene, "The Lowdown from Our Man in Havana," *Vogue*, 15 April 1970, p. 94.

3. John Le Carré, *The Spy Who Came in from the Cold* (New York, 1964), pp. 246, 248.

4. Philip Stratford, "Unlocking the Potting Shed," *Kenyon Review* 24 (Winter 1962), 133.

5. Philip Stratford, *Faith and Fiction: Creative Process in Greene and Mauriac* (Notre Dame, Ind., 1964), p. 322.

6. Flannery O'Connor, "The Church and the Fiction Writer," in *Mystery and Manners,* ed. Sally and Robert Fitzgerald (New York, 1970), p. 153.

Selected Bibliography

Main Works by Graham Greene

Note: I am only listing the first English and American editions, except in cases where later editions have different titles. Most of Mr. Greene's work is published in a uniform format by Heinemann, London; a second uniform edition, with each volume introduced by Mr. Greene, is being prepared by the Bodley Head, London.

The Man Within. London: Heinemann, 1929; Garden City, New York: Doubleday, Doran, 1929.

The Name of Action. London: Heinemann, 1930; Garden City: Doubleday, 1931.

Rumour at Nightfall. London: Heinemann, 1931; Garden City: Doubleday, 1932.

Stamboul Train. London: Heinemann, 1932; Garden City: Doubleday, 1933 (as *Orient Express*).

It's a Battlefield. London: Heinemann, 1934; Garden City: Doubleday, 1934.

England Made Me. London: Heinemann, 1935; Garden City: Doubleday, 1935; New York: Viking, 1953 (as *The Shipwrecked*).

Journey without Maps. London: Heinemann, 1936; Garden City: Doubleday, 1936.

A Gun for Sale. London: Heinemann, 1936; Garden City: Doubleday, 1936 (*as This Gun for Hire*).

Brighton Rock. London: Heinemann, 1938; New York: Viking 1938.

The Lawless Roads. London: Longmans, Green, 1939; New York: Viking, 1939 (as *Another Mexico*).

The Confidential Agent. London: Heinemann, 1939; New York: Viking, 1939.

The Power and the Glory. London: Heinemann, 1940; New York: Viking, 1940 (as *The Labyrinthine Ways*); New York: Viking, 1946 (under the original British title).

The Ministry of Fear. London: Heinemann, 1943; New York: Viking, 1943.

Nineteen Stories. London: Heinemann, 1947; New York: Viking, 1949 (reset and with one story changed). *Twenty-one Stories* (with one story omitted and three added). London: Heinemann, 1954; New York: Viking, 1962.

The Heart of the Matter. London: Heinemann, 1948; New York: Viking, 1948.

The Third Man, by Graham Greene and Carol Reed. London: Heinemann, 1950; New York: Viking, 1950.

The Lost Childhood and Other Essays. London: Eyre & Spottiswood, 1951; New York: Viking, 1952.

The End of the Affair. London: Heinemann, 1951; New York: Viking, 1951.

The Living Room. London: Heinemann, 1953; New York: Viking, 1954.

Loser Takes All. London: Heinemann, 1955; New York: Viking, 1957.

The Quiet American. London: Heinemann, 1955; New York: Viking, 1956.

The Potting Shed. New York: Viking, 1957; London: Heinemann, 1958.

Our Man in Havana. London: Heinemann, 1958; New York: Viking, 1958.

The Complaisant Lover. London: Heinemann, 1959; New York: Viking, 1960.

A Burnt-Out Case. London: Heinemann, 1961; New York: Viking, 1961.

In Search of a Character: Two African Journals ["Congo Journal" and "Convoy to West Africa"]. London: Bodley Head, 1961; New York: Viking, 1962.

A Sense of Reality. London: Bodley Head, 1963; New York: Viking, 1963.

Carving a Statue. London: Bodley Head, 1964.

The Comedians. London: Bodley Head, 1966; New York: Viking, 1966.

May We Borrow Your Husband? and Other Comedies of the Sexual Life. London: Bodley Head, 1967; New York: Viking, 1967.

Collected Essays. London: Bodley Head, 1969; New York: Viking, 1969.

Travels with My Aunt. London: Bodley Head, 1970; New York: Viking, 1970.

A Sort of Life. London: Bodley Head, 1971; New York: Simon and Schuster, 1971.

Studies of Graham Greene

Allott, Kenneth, and Miriam Farris. *The Art of Graham Greene*. London: Hamish Hamilton, 1951; New York: Russell and Russell, 1963.

Atkins, John. *Graham Greene*. Rev. ed. London: Calder, 1966.

Cargas, H. J., ed. *Graham Greene*. Herder Christian Critic Series. St. Louis: B. Herder, 1969.

De Pange, Victor, *Graham Greene*. Paris: Éditions Universitaire, 1953.

De Vitis, A. A. *Graham Greene*. New York: Twayne, 1964.

Evans, Robert O., ed. *Graham Greene: Some Critical Considerations*. Lexington, Kentucky: University of Kentucky Press, 1963.

Gregor, Ian. "The Greene Baize Door." *Blackfriars* 37 (September 1955), 327–33.

Hall, James. "Efficient Saints and Civilians: Graham Greene." *The Lunatic Giant in the Drawing Room: The British and American Novel since 1930*. Bloomington, Indiana: 1968, pp. 111–23.

Kohn, Lynette. *Graham Greene: The Major Novels*. Stanford Honors Essays in Humanities No. 4, 1961.

Kunkel, Francis L. *The Labyrinthine Ways of Graham Greene*. New York: Sheed and Ward, 1960.

Lewis, R. W. B. "Graham Greene: The Religious Affair." *The Picaresque Saint*. Philadelphia: Lippincott, 1959, pp. 220–74.

Lodge, David. *Graham Greene*. Essays on Modern Writers. New York and London: Columbia University Press, 1966.

Madaule, Jacques. *Graham Greene*. Paris: Éditions de Temps Present, 1949.

Matthews, Ronald. *Mon Ami Graham Greene*. Paris: Desclée de Brouwer, 1957.

Mesnet, Marie-Beatrice. *Graham Greene and the Heart of the Matter*. London: Cresset, 1954.

Modern Fiction Studies. Graham Greene Special Number 3 (Autumn 1957).

O'Donnell, Donat. "Graham Greene: The Anatomy of Pity." *Maria Cross: Imaginative Patterns in a Group of Catholic Writers*. New York: Oxford University Press, 1952, pp. 63–94.

O'Faolain, Sean. "Graham Greene: I Suffer, Therefore I Am." *The Vanishing Hero*. Boston: Little, Brown, 1957.

Renascence. Special Graham Greene Number 12 (Autumn 1959).

Rostenne, Paul. *Graham Greene, Témoin des Temps Tragiques*. Paris: Julliard, 1949.

Sewell, Elizabeth. "Graham Greene." *Dublin Review* 108 (1954), 12–21.

Shuttleworth, Martin and Simon Raven. "The Art of Fiction III: Graham Greene," *Paris Review* 3 (Autumn 1953), 24–41.

Slate, Audrey Nelson. "Technique and Form in the Novels of Graham Greene. Ph.D. dissertation, University of Wisconsin, 1960.

Stine, Norma Contryman. "As it is and As it Ought to Be: Graham Greene on the Cinema," Master's Thesis, University of Nebraska, c. 1969.

Stratford, Philip. *Faith and Fiction: Creative Process in Greene and Mauriac*. Notre Dame, Indiana: Notre Dame University Press, 1964.

———. "Unlocking the Potting Shed." *Kenyon Review* 24 (Winter 1962), 129–43.

Turnell, Martin. *Graham Greene: A Critical Essay*. Grand Rapids, Michigan: Eerdmans, 1967.

Webster, Harvey Curtis. "Graham Greene: Stoical Catholic." *After the Trauma: Representative British Novelists since 1920*. Lexington, Kentucky: University of Kentucky Press, 1970, pp. 97–123.

Wyndham, Francis. *Graham Greene*. London: Longmans, Green, 1955.

Zabel, Morton D. "Graham Greene: The Best and the Worst." *Craft and Character in Modern Fiction*. New York: Viking, 1957, pp. 276–96.

Index

AND MISTRESS MAKES

AND MISTRESS MAKES

Three

Francis Ray

ST. MARTIN'S GRIFFIN

New York

This is a work of fiction. All of the characters, organizations, and events portrayed in this novel are either products of the author's imagination or are used fictitiously.

ISBN-13: 978-1-61523-151-5

Once again to my daughter, Michelle.
I don't know what I would have done without you.
May God continue to bless and keep you.

A LETTER TO MY READERS

Thank you so much for your support of the Invincible Women series. I truly enjoy writing about women who, when faced with adversity, find it within themselves to overcome the problems and succeed.

In the fifth book, *And Mistress Makes Three*, we meet Gina Rawlings on what she feels is the worst day of her life, the day her divorce is finalized. No one likes to admit they've failed, especially in a marriage with two children. Gina has to reach deep within and find the courage and the faith to stand on her own two feet. I hope you'll enjoy her journey.

Those of you who have read my romance novels are aware that I write another series called Grayson Friends. I really didn't want to leave the popular Graysons of New Mexico series, so I created Grayson Friends.

Because of your tremendous support the second book in the Grayson Friends series, *Nobody But You,* made the *New York Times* and *USA Today* bestselling lists. I can't thank you enough. The third book, *One Night with You*, is scheduled for release November 3, 2009.

I wish you every happiness. Please remember to kiss those you love and tell them daily.

Warmest regards,
Francis Ray

ONE

Not even in Gina Rawlings' worst nightmare had she ever envi-
sioned this day would come. Last night, in the vain and foolish
hope that she could somehow forestall what would take place
at the stroke of midnight, she'd gone to bed before ten for the
first time in years.

It hadn't worked.

Curled in a fetal position in her king-sized bed, Gina finally
faced the gut-wrenching reality of what this day meant to her,
to her two children. Robert, her husband of fourteen years, no
longer wanted her. Today, the State of South Carolina, the City
of Charleston, had granted him his divorce request. Clamping
her eyes shut, Gina curled tighter under the bedcovers.

Fourteen years tossed away as if they were nothing. Her
husband didn't love her anymore. The only thing that kept
them remotely connected since he'd walked out eight months

ago was their two children, Gabrielle and Ashton. Gina bit her lower lip.

Gabrielle, their thirteen-year-old daughter, blamed Gina for the divorce and wasn't shy about showing her displeasure with her mother. To Gabrielle's way of thinking, Robert was the best father in the world. It was easy to understand why their daughter thought that way. While Robert lived there he always let her have her way, overruling Gina's decisions—unless it dealt with money, and then it was a different story. Gabrielle was too young to realize it was easier to give in than set parameters.

On the other hand, Gina couldn't have asked for a sweeter, more loving child than six-year-old Ashton. Sadly, he seemed to have figured out that his father's fitness gym, Bodies by Robert, came before any of them.

In the months since Robert left, he'd canceled numerous weekend visitations with the children. They'd spent only one night in his new apartment. He always gave the excuse that the gym was short of staff or extremely busy. He tried to placate all of them by saying it was for Gabrielle and Ashton's benefit that he worked so hard.

Gina snorted, flinging the bedcovers from her body. Robert was habitually late with his child support payments. More galling was that when the money did come, it was never the correct amount. She'd stopped asking him about the discrepancies. When she did, he always made her feel small and like a failure.

Robert was always quick to point out that it was he, not she, who'd taken care of the family for fourteen years while she wasted money on one penny-ante home business venture after the other.

In the months since he'd left, he'd put a dent in her pride

big enough to drive a semitruck through—because he was right, she had failed. What scared her and kept her awake most nights was that she was failing again.

She had countless failures in her life. Her attempts at home businesses so she could stay at home and be available if her children needed her were all disastrous. She'd spent more than she'd earned, and both she and Robert knew it.

Like Gabrielle, Gina blamed herself for the ruined marriage. The morning Robert told her he was filing for divorce he'd said she didn't excite him anymore. Stunned, she hadn't known what to say as he'd picked up his gym bag to leave. She'd recovered enough to ask him to stay so they could tell the children together. She'd never forget his response.

You tell them. At least you can do that much.

Gina shrank inside again as she had then. His carelessly tossed words had wounded her deeply and slapped her in the face. He didn't value her, thought her worthless.

To her undying shame, Gina had gone to the gym later on that day, determined to get Robert to change his mind, determined to do whatever it took to save her marriage. The children needed a father, and she didn't want to add another failure to a long list.

She'd dressed carefully in her prettiest yellow sweater and black pants, even worn makeup, only to find a slimmer, prettier woman wearing a midriff-baring top in her husband's arms. Robert had been annoyed, the woman smug.

You don't excite me anymore, and I can do better, he'd told Gina, not releasing the other woman.

Gina had quickly left, fighting tears and shame. Finally, she accepted what she had been trying to deny for months— Robert's all-nighters at the twenty-four-hour gym weren't all business. During their separation, so-called friends and acquaintances seemed happy to keep her informed about seeing her health-conscious husband around Charleston with slimmer, prettier women.

Gina did her best to act indifferent, but the gleeful or pitying looks on the persons' faces always made her aware she was unsuccessful. Since Ashton's birth, she'd gained more and more weight. Her weight last Christmas was 177 pounds. Forty-seven pounds more than what she weighed before her first pregnancy. Since then, she'd put the scale in the back of her closet.

On the other hand, Robert worked hard to maintain his muscular, toned body. In his eyes, it made up for the premature balding he hated with a passion. He'd let his sandy brown hair grow longer in a useless attempt to hide the hair loss at the top of his head.

While he lived his dream with the fitness gym he'd always wanted, Gina's dreams of a husband and family were shattered.

Aware she couldn't spend the entire day in bed, Gina sat up and slid her legs off the side just as the doorbell rang. Her heart thumped hard in her chest. *Robert.* Before the chime ended, she knew it wasn't her husband. Her ex-husband. He wasn't coming back.

The ringing phone on the night table startled her. She reached for the receiver. "Hello."

"Morning, time to get up. You have a guest at the front door."

Gina somehow felt worse at the cheerful voice of her best friend, Celeste de la Vega. Celeste never met a stranger and was perpetually happy.

"Celeste—"

"No excuses. Come on; we have an appointment."

Before Gina could ask where, the line went dead. Sighing, Gina stood and shoved her arms into her robe. It was almost ten and past time for her to get up. The children would be up soon and want breakfast. She'd told them last night that they could sleep in instead of going to church. They didn't know she was avoiding the inevitable.

Leaving the bedroom on the first floor of the two-story home, Gina opened the front door and almost sighed. As usual, Celeste was stunning in a magenta-colored sheath that stopped mid-thigh. As an interior designer Celeste wore pants at work, so when off-duty she always wore skirts to show off her great legs. Gina felt every ounce of the weight she'd gained in her butt and thighs.

"Good morning, and stop frowning," Celeste said as she entered the house.

Gina closed the door. "If you weren't my best friend and I loved you, I'd be irritated at how good you look."

Dimples winked in Celeste's olive-toned face. "I could say the same thing, since I've always wanted to be tall instead of a midget."

It was an old argument. Celeste, at barely five feet, two inches, was perfectly proportioned, with sparkling black eyes, a generous mouth, and enough sex appeal for ten women. Her three engagements proved men found her attraction and elusive. "What's that in your hand?"

Celeste lifted the mid-sized shopping bag with *Serendipity*, the name of her interior design firm, emblazed on it. "Color charts, samples of cloth, tile, and carpet in tones of yellow and green, your favorite colors. It's a new beginning for you. You can redecorate the house the way you always wanted." Celeste wrinkled her pretty nose as she glanced around the paneled den with black leather furnishings and ugly black-and-brown plaid curtains. "Since I can get you fabulous discounts and help, we can have this place redone in no time."

Gina couldn't afford to spend any money at the moment. The home travel agency business she'd started shortly before Robert left was barely keeping her afloat financially. It was a delicate balancing act. And as close as she and Celeste were, Gina didn't want her to know how shaky she was financially.

Celeste succeeded at everything she tried and had no difficulty getting what she wanted out of life or men. Gina was the exact opposite. At thirty, two years younger than Gina, Celeste owned her own successful interior design firm, Serendipity. Men adored her. The men she had been engaged to were wealthy, successful, and wild about Celeste. Yet each time, Celeste had called it off. Any one of the men would take her back in a heartbeat.

"I'll think about it," Gina finally answered.

Celeste stared at Gina for a long moment, then said, "I'm not letting you out of this, so be warned." She set the bag on the black leather sofa on her way to the kitchen. "Gabrielle and Ashton still asleep?"

"Yes." Gina followed. Each woman knew the other's house as well as her own and felt comfortable in it.

Taking a tall glass from the cabinet, Celeste filled it with orange juice she took from the refrigerator. "You'd better wake them up if we're going to arrive on time."

Gina frowned. "What are you talking about?"

Celeste shook her head, causing her thick black unbound hair that stopped in the middle of her slim back to sway. "The pre–grand opening of Journey's End is today."

Gina held up her hand before Celeste finished. She didn't want to go anyplace . . . unless it was back to bed to pull the covers over her head. "No, I don't feel like going."

The glass in Celeste's hand hit the counter. Her eyes glared. "And that is exactly why you *are* going."

"The children—"

"Will enjoy themselves." Celeste came to stand in front of Gina. "It's over. You hurt now, but you know it was for the best."

"Best that my husband divorced me?" she asked incredulously.

Celeste kept her gaze level. "You were roommates more than husband and wife. You didn't sleep together and the last time you made love was more than a year before he left. You said neither of you enjoyed it."

Gina looked back over her shoulder to ensure the children hadn't wakened and wandered into the kitchen. "The children might hear you."

"I notice you didn't correct me." Picking up her glass, Celeste took a sip of juice, her gaze direct once again.

Gina glanced away. Another failure. "Perhaps that was why—"

"Stop it!" Celeste snapped. Setting the glass down, she went to Gina. "It isn't your fault, so stop beating yourself over the head about Robert's inability to stick. He hadn't been here for you or Gabrielle or Ashton long before he took his sorry behind off."

"But I'm supposed to keep the marriage together!" Gina came back.

"And what book did you read that in?" Celeste asked impatiently. "Marriage takes two people for it to work. Stop laying the blame at your feet; heap some on Robert's thick neck he's so proud of."

Gina finally looked at her best friend. Celeste looked ready to fight, and it was for her. "I'm glad you're my friend."

"Same here." Celeste threw her arm around Gina's shoulder. "We deserve men who will cherish us, make us feel safe and naughty at the same time."

Gina had to admit that Robert never had. She'd been crazy about him in college. He was BMOC and co-captain of the football team. She'd thought she was the luckiest woman in the world when they started going together. Five months later she was pregnant with Gabrielle. "Is that why you broke each of your engagements?"

Celeste's face grew serious. "It wasn't fair to them or me. Thank goodness I realized it before it was too late. I was just trying to get Mama off my back."

Gina had met Ramona de la Vega on several occasions. The petite and elegant woman exuded charm and graciousness. Second-generation Puerto Rican, she had definite ideas about marriage and family. "She loves you and wants you happily married."

"I know, and that's why I haven't moved to Greenland or gotten an unlisted phone number. It helps that I can vent to you and Yolanda."

Yolanda, Celeste's older sister, had been a nun for twelve years, until five years ago when she renounced her vows to work with troubled teens as a high school counselor in Houston, where their parents lived. Yolanda was one of the calmest persons Gina knew and, if possible, more outgoing than her little sister. However, Yolanda hadn't the faintest interest in a relationship with a man, which left Celeste the sole target of her mother's matrimonial quest.

"Since I vent to you, that sort of makes us even," Gina finally replied. "You'll find the man you're looking for."

"And you'll find one who'll appreciate you."

Shock widened Gina's eyes. "My divorce was just finalized."

Celeste placed her hand gently on Gina's arm. "I love you. We both know this was only a formality. The marriage was over long ago."

Gina's hands clenched. "It's hard. I never saw it coming."

"I told you, I'm ready when you say the word to do a number on that convertible he's so proud of," Celeste said, dead serious. "We'll have an airtight alibi and two lawyers ready to defend us." Two of Gina's ex-fiancés were lawyers.

"It sounds tempting, but with my bad luck we'd get caught," Gina said. "Besides, I'm trying to listen to Pastor Carter's message and not do evil for evil."

Celeste made a face. They belonged to the same church. "The man does have a tendency to make you want to do better. So how about we just spray paint those fancy car rims?"

Gina almost smiled. Robert would have a conniption fit and come straight to her door. Her smile faded. "He's moved on. I have to do the same."

"And that's what you're going to do, starting now." Celeste gently pushed Gina toward her bedroom. "Get dressed while I get the kids up. We're going to kick your independent travel agency into high gear."

Gina let herself be pushed, hoping, praying, Celeste was right, that this time she wouldn't fall flat on her face. Again.

. . .

Today was a new beginning, Max Broussard thought as he stood on the wraparound front porch of Journey's End, the newest bed-and-breakfast in Charleston. And he was the proud proprietor. His once soft hands, now lined with calluses, clasped the top railing. With joy came a deep sadness because Sharon wasn't standing beside him, her beautiful face shining with love and happiness.

"God, I miss you."

He felt the soft brush of wind on his face and could almost imagine it was her sweet lips. It had been seven years since he lost her, three years since he'd stopped feeling sorry for himself, not caring about anything—he'd been at the top of the list of self-pitying people. It hadn't been easy finding his way back.

He'd blamed himself for not being with her when she needed him, hated all the time he'd wasted running after the corner office in the insurance firm he worked for and all that an executive position entailed. He'd always thought there would be time to start the family he'd insisted they put off, to take the vacation to Hawaii she had wanted.

None of those things had happened. He'd lost her after five short, pitiful years of marriage.

Tears no longer stung his eyes; the lump didn't form in his throat. He'd brought her dream of a bed-and-breakfast to life. There was a satisfaction in that.

He stepped off the porch and glanced around the lush green lawn. The three-story white Victorian sat one hundred feet from the street and gleamed in the mid-morning sun. The newly repaired concrete walkway led to the driveway that circled to the back of the house where the unattached garage was located.

To his eyes, the place looked restful. He'd tried to envision what Sharon would have wanted, tried to remember their many conversations of one day retiring and buying a B and B near the water just to keep busy and have a place for their children and grandchildren to visit.

There were no children, but the three-story house backed up to the Ashley River. It was as painful as it was pleasurable to be here, but Max felt a strange peace that he'd found in no other place since the day he'd rushed back from the airport after being unable to get Sharon on the phone to find her unconscious on the den floor. She'd never awakened.

"The caterers are almost finished setting things up."

Max turned at the sound of his aunt's soft voice. Sophia Durand was a tall, slender woman with strong features, and Max's favorite aunt of his mother's three sisters. She'd never been married or engaged.

She'd retired from being a principal at an elementary school in Memphis at the end of the last school term and had accepted Max's invitation to come live with him and help run the inn. It was she who had tracked him down and made him realize that he was dishonoring Sharon's memory by turning his back on life.

"How does it look?" Max asked as he came back up the wooden steps that no longer swayed with his weight.

Sophia shrugged. "It's pretty and tastes as good as the samples. They want to know if you want the trays set out or for them to serve."

Max opened the screen door for them to enter the house. A cool breeze from the ceiling fan and central air he'd installed greeted them. "What do you think?"

"You know I don't have a clue, but I'm guessing it would be

better if the caterers served. You don't want people bunched up around the food. They're here to see what a great B and B this is," she answered.

"Good answer." He threw his arm around her shoulder. "I'm glad you decided to come and help me."

She wrinkled her nose. "I'm not sure how much I helped. I can't cook, can't decorate, and I kill a plant just by looking at it."

"You're here for me, and that's enough."

Her face softened and she palmed his cheek with her wrinkled hand. "I'm proud of you."

He smiled back. "It feels good to say I'm proud myself. Now let's go talk to the caterers. The first guests should be arriving soon."

"We're here," Celeste said as she parked her BMW convertible at the end of a long line of cars leading to a pristine white three-story Victorian.

"Whoop-de-do," intoned Gabrielle from the backseat, her slim arms folded across her chest, her expression belligerent.

Gina barely kept from sighing as she opened the door of Celeste's metallic silver convertible and pulled her seat forward for her daughter to get out. She honestly didn't know how to handle Gabrielle anymore. She often wondered where her sweet, lovable daughter had gone and who was the surly teenager in her place.

"Wow! The yard is as big as a soccer field," Ashton said as soon as his feet hit the ground.

"All you think about is soccer," Gabrielle said.

"It's better than talking about silly stuff like eye-shadow colors."

Gabrielle rounded on her brother. "How dare you listen to my phone conversations!"

"If you don't want me to listen, you shouldn't talk so loud," he promptly came back.

"Stop it, both of you," Gina ordered, well aware that the heated exchange could go on for several minutes. Lately Ashton had been going word for word with his older sister. "I'm here on business, so please be on your best behavior."

"He started it," Gabrielle said.

"Did not," Ashton said, copying her pose with his hands on his hips.

"I don't care who started it, but I'm going to finish it if I hear another word out of either of you," Gina said, staring at Gabrielle first, then Ashton.

Gina could hear her mother's voice as clearly as if she were standing beside her. Her mother had raised four children with love and a strong hand. None of them would have dared talk back as Gabrielle did.

"Come on; let's look at the grounds so your mother can tell her clients about this place," Celeste said into the silence. "Then we can go inside."

Throwing Celeste a thankful look, Gina placed her hand on Ashton's head to get him moving. He and his sister were developing the habit of seeing who could outstare the other.

"The backyard is beautiful, but there's not even a walkway to get you to the edge of the water," Gina said as they started around to the back of the house. She didn't think the owner would mind, as other people were walking on the grass as well.

"I don't see a boat, but at least he should have built steps on the uneven incline for the guests to get to the water, and a short pier so the guests could fish or simply walk out to the water's edge."

"You're right." Celeste glanced around. "There are only a couple of unattractive stone benches behind the house. They're not even under the trees."

"Let's go see what the inside looks like," Gina said, going up the slight incline.

"I can't wait," murmured Gabrielle sarcastically.

Gina paused, then continued around to the front of the house. Reprimanding Gabrielle or reminding her that this was business, which paid for the new tennis shoes she wore, wouldn't help. She'd bring up her usual reply that started with, *If Daddy was here . . .*

Not up for an argument, Gina kept walking and tried to remember that Gabrielle had a right to be angry and miss her father. Besides the divorce, she was having a difficult time dealing with the changes in her body and wanting to fit in.

She'd missed the coveted spot of a cheerleader but snagged the position of captain of the booster squad, which meant she had, in her words, "to be cooler than cool." There was also a boy she liked who hadn't noticed her, which added to her problems. Ashton was right. Gabrielle didn't talk softly.

People in casual attire for the warm September afternoon spilled out onto the wide front porch and sat on the heavy black cast-iron furniture. Two huge baskets of ferns swung gently in the breeze. Opening the screen door, they went inside.

Directly in front of them was a staircase. Instead of a picture or plant at the top of the stairs that arrested the eye, there was nothing. The foyer contained an uninspired wooden bench.

Nothing invited or enticed or compelled a visitor to want to stay or see more of the establishment.

"The place needs work," Gina said quietly.

"That's an understatement," Celeste said in an aside.

Gina walked into the separate dining room to the left. A sideboard, an enormous china cabinet with four fret grilles and Gothic cathedral window tracery, and a double pedestal table with eight ladder-back arm- and side chairs were crowded into the room. Two other straight-back chairs with twisted-ribbon carvings were on either side of the lit china cabinet. The furnishings were dark, antique, heavy. Simple and uninspiring red velvet curtains draped the windows and made the room even more oppressive and uninviting.

"Welcome to Journey's End," greeted a slender woman with stylishly cut gray hair, a lived-in face, and one of the warmest smiles Gina had ever received. The woman looked cool and poised in a celery green linen pantsuit.

Gina had never been able to wear linen. She looked as if she'd slept in the outfit thirty minutes after putting it on.

"I'm Sophia Durand. Max Broussard, the owner, is my nephew."

"Nice to meet you," Gina greeted. Giving the woman her business card, Gina introduced herself, Celeste, Gabrielle, and Ashton. "I'm an independent travel agent. I wanted to evaluate Journey's End for my clients."

Sophia's brown eyes brightened even more. "Wonderful. I'm sure you'll agree that Journey's End is the perfect place to come and de-stress, or just have a quiet place to vacation. There is nothing like being near the water to calm a tired soul, and we're less than ten minutes from downtown."

"Your location is wonderful," Gina said, wishing there was

something about the interior that set it apart from every other B and B she'd seen. Unfortunately, there wasn't. "Can we look around?"

"Of course," Sophia said. "I'll let Max know you're here."

Gina didn't speak until the friendly woman had moved away. "Let's see what the living room and kitchen look like."

"We're right behind you," Celeste said.

Gina was pleased to see the living room's furnishings were kept to a minimum, leaving room to move around. The spacious kitchen had a vegetable sink in the large island, and Viking appliances, a Sub-Zero refrigerator, a double oven, and a microwave.

On the screened-in porch was more black wrought-iron furniture with flowered seat upholstery. The large room cried out for something softer, like white wicker with plump seat coverings that would match the window treatment in the connecting kitchen. Instead of dark green, she'd paint the walls white. At least he hadn't painted the wooden beams in the ceiling green. "It's pretty, but it needs work."

"Exactly." Celeste leaned in closer. "I don't see one thing that will make a person book here instead of another B and B. On second thought . . ." Her voice dropped even lower and she said, "Unless it came with the gorgeous hunk coming up the back steps with Sophia."

Gina didn't even look around. Celeste was like a homing device when it came to attractive men. If one was within a hundred-foot radius, he found his way to her with one lame pickup line or another. Gina was more interested in the one-hundred-year-old house. There was something reassuring about a house that old.

She had grown up in a seventy-five-year-old house and had

always wanted to live in an older home when she married. That hadn't happened. After Gabrielle's birth, Robert began complaining about their one-bedroom apartment being too small. Almost every morning, he'd grumble that they needed more space, that the baby kept him up so much he couldn't work.

To make him happy, Gina had asked her parents for a loan for a down payment on the house she now lived in. She'd given up her dream of an older house because Robert had wanted a new one.

Then, as when they were dating in college and throughout their marriage, she'd given in to please him, and in the end it hadn't mattered. He'd walked away from her without a backward glance.

The nostalgic creak of the screen door opening behind her caused her to turn and see Sophia entering the house. Behind her were two couples and the man Gina knew immediately Celeste had been talking about.

He was tall, at least six feet two, with wide shoulders and an impressive chest in a sky blue polo shirt, and tan slacks. He had the kind of handsomeness that would turn heads and make hearts flutter. It popped into her mind that Robert would envy the man as much for his muscular build he carried so easily as for the full head of thick wavy black hair.

"Max, this is Mrs. Rawlings, the independent travel agent I was telling you about," Sophia said, and then went on to introduce those with Gina. "I thought you could give her a personal tour."

He smiled, warm and welcoming, then extended his large hand. Dimples winked in his toffee-colored face. Gina absently wondered why he wasn't still looking at Celeste. Men tended to ignore Gina when she and Celeste were together.

"Pleased to meet you, Mrs. Rawlings, and thanks for coming." His voice, a rich baritone, stroked and soothed. His handshake was gentle and self-assured.

Celeste was right. Customers, females at least, would enjoy being the center of attention of such a gorgeous, attentive man. "It's my pleasure. I want to be able to advise my clients." Gina handed him her card.

"A conscientious travel agent." He smiled. He glanced at the card, then slipped it into the pocket of his pants. "Then let me help. I can give you a personal tour if you'd like."

"Oh, bro—"

Gina's stern look at Gabrielle stopped whatever she had been about to say. Hoping she didn't flush with embarrassment, Gina said to the owner, "I'd like that very much. Thank you."

"It will be my pleasure. This way," he said, extending his arm for her to proceed ahead of him.

Gina turned toward the open doorway, hoping Gabrielle would behave, but somehow she doubted it.

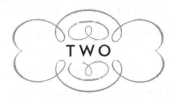

TWO

Max kept the pleasant smile on his face as he led the travel agent and her party through the kitchen, the separate living room, and then up the polished oak stairs, pointing out as they went the various improvements to update the house that he had completed in the past two years.

It was in the best interests of Journey's End for him to be cordial, even when it wasn't deserved. Besides, he had been around his friends' teenagers and knew their brains often lagged behind their mouths.

"This place was in pretty bad shape when first I saw it. It took a lot of hard work to bring it back to its former glory, but it was worth it," Max said as he walked down the hallway with Gina. "The pine flooring beneath our feet is original. This is the first of four guest bedrooms." He paused to let them enter the open door, watching Gina's face closely.

Neither he nor his aunt was a decorator, but they had both decided that all the guest rooms should have a complete suite of furniture. He tried to see it from an outsider's point of view. The queen-sized bed was covered with a bedspread splashed with small pink and red roses. The topper over the single window—at least that was the name he thought was on the package—was in solid pink. It wasn't so overly feminine that a man would go "yuck" if he had to spend the night there.

Gina went in, looked around, glanced at the friend beside her, then, wearing the same placid smile on her face, came back out. The teenager, Gabrielle, didn't bother going inside. She just kept the bored expression on her face.

He'd expected more of a reaction from the women and began to worry. He led them to the next room. "This is the largest of the rooms. As you can see, all have antique furniture and adjoining baths," he said, hoping to get some reaction out of the two women as he opened the door to the bathroom.

Gina peered into the rectangular mirror over the new, upright basin and ran her hand over the stack of freshly laundered white towels on a shelf next to the white commode. "The claw-foot tub is nice. Does the other bathroom have a shower?"

"Yes. It even has a bench." *Finally, some interest,* Max thought. Perhaps he should have hired a decorator, but he had wanted to do it himself. It had been important to Sharon's memory that he do this on his own, just as they planned. But Sharon had been great with colors and design.

Worry creeping through him, he followed Gina and her friend and children back into the hallway and watched them enter the next bedroom. He hung back a bit to let them have a better view of the room.

"Do you have your first booking?" Celeste asked, looking at him over her shoulder.

"Yes," Max answered, watching Gina out of the corner of his eye as she opened the armoire, her son stepping in front of her to peer inside. The space for the television contained an extra pillow and a down comforter. Max figured people on vacation would want to be out sightseeing and not watching television. He had put a small alarm clock radio on each nightstand. "Some of my friends from Memphis are coming up."

Gina closed the doors. "What is your official opening date?"

"October second," he answered. "A month from now. I wanted to give travel agents, such as yourself, and potential clients a chance to see Journey's End and book."

"You must be excited," Gina said, her hand on her son's shoulder.

"A bit." Max was buoyed by the warm smile on her face. "There's another bedroom, and then you can tell me what you think," he said, watching Gina's eyes widen, her gaze dart toward Celeste. Max knew that look couldn't be good. "Or perhaps you'd like to tell me now."

"I, er—"

"Mama thinks it needs work," the little boy blurted.

Gina gasped, her eyes widened with embarrassment. "Ashton!"

"Can we go home now?" Gabrielle asked with a loud sigh. "This is boring."

Gina whirled on her daughter, then took her arm. "I—" She turned, her gaze stopping in the middle of Max's chest. "Forgive me. I'm sorry." With her daughter's arm clasped tightly, she hurried from the room with her son close behind them.

"Thank you for the tour, and good luck," Celeste said, then followed.

"Well, that went dismally," Max muttered.

Gina didn't release Gabrielle's arm until they were by Celeste's car. "What is wrong with you? How could you be so rude?"

Gabrielle absently rubbed her hand over the upper forearm where her mother had held her. "It was boring."

"The world does not revolve around you, Gabrielle Evette Rawlings. This was business, and you knew it."

"If Daddy—"

Gina held up her hand. "No. Do not go there. I've tried being patient with you, but today is it. When we get home, there'll be no phone for a week and you're grounded."

"But I'm supposed to go with the gang for pizza Friday night!" Gabrielle wailed.

"You should have thought of that before you embarrassed all of us by your thoughtlessness."

Flouncing around, Gabrielle opened the car door and got into the backseat. Gina glanced at her son slowly making his way toward her. He had his head down as if he knew he was next to be reprimanded. Ashton was a loving, giving child. He wouldn't hurt anyone's feelings intentionally. Besides, he'd only been repeating what he'd heard her say, so Gina shared the blame.

"You mad at me, too?" he asked as he reached her, his head still down.

Her hand on his shoulder, Gina squatted down to eye level with him and lifted his head. "No, but I wish you hadn't repeated what I'd said in confidence to Celeste. It made Mr.

Broussard sad. How would you feel if no one liked one of your drawings you worked so hard to complete?"

Next to soccer, Ashton loved drawing with crayons best. Her refrigerator was covered with his "masterpieces."

Ashton momentarily tucked his head again, then glanced up and said, "It would make me sad, too. I'm sorry."

She smiled at him. "I know. Now, let's go to lunch."

Ashton looked back at the house. "Maybe I should go tell Mr. Broussard I'm sorry."

"Your mother apologized to him, Ashton," Celeste opened the driver's door. "Now, what do you say we go get some food, with apple cobbler and ice cream for dessert? My treat."

As she knew it would, that got Ashton moving. Happily he climbed into the backseat next to a sulking Gabrielle, who had her arms crossed tightly across her chest, her gaze fixed pointedly out of the window.

Shaking her head, Gina slid inside and buckled her seat belt. Not only had she failed in her marriage; she also had failed one of her children. Gabrielle was too big to turn over her knee, as Celeste advised. Gina just wished she knew what to do.

Closing the back door after the caterers left, Max looked around the kitchen. Had he missed the mark?

"Everything went well, so why do you have that worried look on your face?" Aunt Sophia asked in her usual straightforward way.

Max walked over to the island, leaned his hip against it, and folded his arms. "Probably half the people here came for the free food and had absolutely no intention of staying here; the other half were supportive friends."

"The newspaper sent a reporter and that travel agent came," Aunt Sophia pointed out.

"She thought the place needed work." His arms came to his sides. "At least that's what her little boy blurted out when I asked her what she thought of the place."

"Some children," Sophia said, and the way she said it wasn't a compliment. "Most of them are a joy to teach. Seeing students blossom when they suddenly get it is one of the greatest joys of teaching. However, the day they took prayer out of the school system was a sad day for the country and the schools."

Max had heard the sentiment before. "I thought the place looked pretty good."

Lines radiated across Sophia's broad forehead. "I don't guess she said what concerned her?"

"Nope, she didn't," Max told his aunt. "She had barely turned to her son before the daughter said she was bored. She apologized and hustled her children out of the room. You could tell she was embarrassed."

"As well she should have been," Sophia said. "Children need a strong hand."

Max smiled. His aunt might love all of her nieces and nephews, but they had never been able to get over on her as they had with their parents. But she was fair and loving, as she'd proven by hunting him down in Chicago and getting him to turn his life around. "Everyone should be blessed to have someone like you in their lives."

A pleased smile crossed her plain face. "The same goes for you. You rescued me from a monotonous life in Memphis. With helping you, there is something new each day." Her smile faded. "Although, if the travel agent was right, I wasn't that much help."

He went to her. "Nonsense. You helped me bring Sharon's dream to fruition. Kept me strong when I wanted to give up. Without you, there would be no Journey's End."

"Sharon loved you so much and would be so proud that you didn't forget the dream you shared together," Sophia said.

"I loved her, too," he said, his voice hoarse. "I'll do whatever it takes to make this place a success."

"I haven't a doubt in the world."

His aunt always believed in him, just as Sharon had. "That means a lot." He turned toward the back stairs leading up to the second floor, where the guest quarters were located. His and Sophia's bedrooms and two other bedrooms were on the third floor. "I'm going upstairs to see if I can visualize what's missing."

"You do that. I'm going to call your mother and the rest of the family to tell them how it went."

Nodding, Max took the stairs two at a time. He'd worried about his aunt climbing the stairs, but they'd actually been good for both her and Max to keep in shape. He recalled the first time. They'd both been out of breath when they reached the top. They had looked at each other and laughed. It had been good to laugh again, to share it with someone you cared about.

A few minutes later, Max stood in the middle of the fourth and last bedroom. He couldn't see anything missing. All the furniture pieces made the room a little tight to maneuver in, but it couldn't be helped. The antique store wouldn't break up the sets.

Sharon had wanted the B and B to have period pieces and to be as comfortable and as charming as possible. But was it?

Frowning, he pulled the travel agent's card from his pants pocket. He'd failed Sharon in life; he didn't want to fail her in

this as well. If Gina Rawlings could help him, he'd find a way
to convince her to do so. Perhaps when they met again, her two
rude children would be nowhere around.

Celeste was barely through the door of her home Sunday evening when the phone rang. Her head fell. She didn't need the
caller ID to identify who was on the other end of the line.
Tossing her handbag onto the slate gray counter in the kitchen,
she continued to the built-in refrigerator for a Pepsi to fortify
herself. After taking a long swallow, she eyed the ringing blue
phone. Another ring and it would go into voice mail, but the
caller would call back every thirty minutes.

Celeste picked up the phone. Ramona de la Vega might be
only five feet—two inches shorter than Celeste—but she was
tenacious when she wanted something. "Hello, Mother."

"Hello, Celeste. How are you doing?" her mother asked.

Translation: Are you getting any closer to picking out a husband? "Just fine, Mother. I just came home."

"Oh."

Celeste heard the speculative excitement in her mother's
voice and finished off the soda. *Sorry, Mother, no man was involved.* "I was with Gina and her children."

"Such a tragedy," Celeste's mother murmured. "A woman
and children need a man."

Celeste rolled her eyes as she rinsed out the can and put it in
the recycle bin. Her mother might be second-generation Puerto
Rican, but she still believed in the old tradition that a woman
wasn't complete unless she had a husband and children.

Celeste's three aunts thought the same way. They considered

her abnormal for still being single at thirty. All of her cousins were married and had children.

"Women don't need men to validate them these days, Mother." *Especially cheating bastards like Robert,* she thought to herself as she went to the counter to retrieve her purse before heading down the hall.

"Nonsense," her mother scoffed. "No matter the time, a woman always needs a man. What would I do without your father?"

They both knew the answer: She'd be lost. Celeste's father pampered her mother, catered to her, despite his busy schedule as a cardiologist. She had never written a check, but she had no equal when it came to shopping with her platinum credit cards.

"Father is an exception," Celeste said, meaning it, and stepped out of her stiletto heels in her bedroom.

As in the living and dining room, her passion for intense colors was shown here in the coral walls trimmed in white. She'd designed the gray-silk scalloped headboard and draped yards of lush gray silk damask behind the headboard and on the side of the bed in a short canopy. The reupholstered bench at the foot of the bed in striped coral, white, and gray fabric once belonged to her great-grandmother. Although some thought it a sign of status never to buy new furniture, just update with textiles, to the de la Vega family it meant a sign of love.

"By the way, where is he?" Jorge de la Vega was a wonderful father who spoiled his two daughters as much as he did his wife.

"On his way back from the hospital," Celeste's mother said. "One of his patients was having some problems, and he wanted to go in to check for himself."

Celeste stuck the phone between her shoulder and her ear and wiggled out of her dress. "Dad is a dying breed and a heck of a doctor."

"I wish— Never mind."

On the way to her walk-in closet, Celeste paused. She knew what her mother had been about to say and it triggered a wave of pain that after nine years remained as fresh as ever.

"How is the business coming?" Celeste's mother asked in the thick silence.

"Fine," Celeste managed, and continued undressing. Her mother might stay on Celeste's case to get married, but Ramona would never hurt her intentionally. "In fact, I start a new job tomorrow. I'm redoing the master suite of a longtime client while she is on her honeymoon in Europe."

"Honeymooning in Europe. How romantic. Are you seeing anyone?" Celeste's mother asked, apparently tired of hinting.

"No, Mother. I don't have time." Celeste reached for a padded hanger and hung up her dress. No one ever called her mother subtle. "This job will require the full three weeks the couple will be away to complete. I'm even papering the walls and retiling the bathroom floor."

"Why don't you hire more help?" her mother asked. She'd grown up with servants who catered to her, just as everyone still did.

"Because, as I keep telling you, I like seeing projects unfold." Celeste slipped out of her demi lace bra and thong, then pulled on a short aqua silk robe. "This way takes longer, but it makes my clients and me happy."

"People still rave about our house," her mother said with unmistakable pride. "The spread in *Southern Accents* magazine practically made us celebrities."

"And you enjoyed every second," Celeste teased. Her mother wasn't above showing off, but she never did it maliciously. Many of her friends had been green with envy.

"Why shouldn't I be proud of the home my husband has provided for me, and that my youngest daughter decorated for us?"

"Point taken. How is my big sister?" In the bathroom, the blue walls trimmed in gray offered a cool counterpoint to the warm-toned coral in the bedroom. Celeste placed her undergarments in the hamper, turned on the faucet of the sunken Jacuzzi tub, then poured Rouge Hermès bubble bath into the swirling water.

"You know Yolanda; she's always happy. School hasn't been in session a month and she's already planning activities for the students to keep them and their parents involved," her mother told Celeste, and there was love and pride in her voice.

"That's my sis, happiest when she's the busiest." Celeste shut off the water when the bubbles almost reached the top. "Tell Father I love him and give him a kiss for me. I'll call him tomorrow afternoon when I get in from the job."

"All right, Celeste. But try to get out a bit more, or you could come home for the weekend," her mother suggested.

And be met with a constant barrage of men. No thanks. "I won't be able to come down for a while. I have other projects lined up as soon as I finish the job I mentioned."

Her mother's sigh of defeat drifted through the receiver. "I guess I understand, but try to take time out to meet other young people."

"I have lots of friends." Untying the robe, she hung it on a garment rack and stepped into the tub.

"Isn't there one who is special?" her mother asked hopefully.

"Yes." Celeste waited a beat. "Gina. I couldn't ask for a better friend and now she's hurting and there's not a thing I can do to help her."

"You know that's not what I meant, but since I like Gina, I'll let you sidestep the issue this time," her mother admonished. "And don't think you aren't doing anything. You're there if she needs you. You're a good girl."

"Thanks, Mother. You're pretty terrific yourself." *When you're not trying to marry me off.*

"Then make me happy and find some nice religious young man with good potential from a good family to settle down with."

Celeste stared up at the mural of angels in the clouds on the ceiling. "In time, Mother, I will, but no one interests me now."

"Perhaps if you didn't work so much, hired someone to help you, you'd have more time to find a man who does," her mother told her.

"Yes, Mother. I'm in the tub and the water is getting cold. We'll talk later, all right?"

Her mother emitted another long-suffering sigh. "All of my friends' daughters your age are married."

"And many of them are not happy," Celeste said, her voice carrying a hint of irritation. "When I do marry, I want it to be forever. I want what you and Father have."

"I want that, too," her mother said.

"I know. Good night, Mother."

"Good night, Celeste."

Pushing "end" on the phone, Celeste placed it on the lip of the tub and tried to relax. Her mother's phone calls usually left Celeste's shoulders tense and her head pounding with a raging headache. Picking up the sponge, she rubbed it down her arm.

She wasn't getting engaged again for all the wrong reasons. The three men she'd been engaged to were all wonderful, successful, and seemingly crazy about her. But there had been no spark, no craving to be in any of their arms. Her eyes didn't light up when she saw them. More important, her body didn't, either.

Celeste moaned and closed her eyes. Pastor Carter would admonish her if he knew she was thinking such wicked thoughts. Or perhaps he'd understand, since he had done a series on sex. She giggled. Some of the older members of her church had been outraged by his first topic, "Sex Is Good." But, with his usual boyish charm, he'd brought them around.

Her sponge paused on her stomach. That was what she wanted, the hot, sizzling attraction that made you want to be a little, all right, a whole lot wicked. She wanted her body to burn with desire. She'd decided when she'd attempted to return the two-karat diamond ring back to her last fiancé that she wasn't settling for anything less.

Standing, she reached for her oversized bath towel and wrapped it around her body. Sliding her feet into her bath slippers, she picked up the phone to return it to the kitchen. It rang. "Hello."

"Hello yourself," Yolanda chirped.

Celeste smiled. Yolanda was the sweetest person in the world. "How do you always know when Mother has called and I'm fighting a headache?"

"She loves you," came her sister's bright answer.

"So perhaps she should love me less." Unwrapping the towel, Celeste anchored the phone again and slipped a white silk gown over her head that stopped at her ankles.

"Impossible, and you know it."

Tossing back the imported duvet in grays and blues, Celeste sat on the bed. "I don't suppose some guy has caught your eye."

Mischievous laughter twinkled through the receiver. "I think love is beautiful and wonderful, but my heart and mind aren't thinking that way."

"Thought so." After two years of prayers and contemplation, Yolanda had renounced her vows. She felt she could help more people by working in the urban school district than by writing grants. She had friends around the world, she could talk openly about sex and relationships, but for her, the desire to have a man in her life wasn't there.

"If there was another way to help you, you know I would," Yolanda told her.

"I know." Celeste pulled her legs under her. Yolanda had helped her through one of the roughest times in her life. "I'm glad you're my sister."

"You know I feel the same about you. So when are you coming for a visit? I'll do my best to help you steer clear of the men Mother will line up," Yolanda told her with soft laughter.

"Not for a while. I have a big project that I start tomorrow," Celeste explained. "Mrs. Gilmore's husband died four years ago. She recently celebrated her sixtieth birthday, but she looks fifteen years younger. Her new younger husband adores her."

"There is nothing like love to lift the spirit and gladden the heart," Yolanda said with feeling.

"So I'm told."

"You'll know it one day. The man is waiting for you."

"Now you're beginning to sound like Mother," Celeste admonished.

"You're beautiful, intelligent, successful, and full of life and good humor. It would be a travesty not to share that with a husband and children," her sister said.

"Don't you start," Celeste said. "I thought you were on my side."

"I'm on the side of you being happy."

Celeste wrinkled her nose. "Cryptic as usual."

Yolanda laughed. "I'd better let you get some sleep. We both have to go to work in the morning."

"Mother told me you already have programs lined up for your students." Celeste pulled the duvet up to her shoulders. "They're lucky to have you."

"I feel blessed. They give so much, are so impatient for life and yet so afraid. How many people get a chance to touch so many lives in their lifetime? The children are a blessing to me as I hope to be to them."

No matter how many times she heard her sister speak that way, it always touched Celeste deeply. Yolanda might not have any biological children, but she had hundreds who loved her as much as any mother. "You are. Just as you are to everyone you meet."

Her sister chuckled. "I'd better get off this phone before you make my head swell. Good night, *niña,* and sleep well."

"Good night, Yolanda."

Celeste snuggled under the covers. If a man was out there, he'd better find her, because she sure wasn't going looking for him.

THREE

Alec Dunlap was a man who never second-guessed himself. He knew what he wanted and went after it with everything within him. Then one faithful night, it all went to shit.

Leaning against the island counter in the spacious kitchen of the home of his new sister-in-law and brother, Alec's hand clenched the coffee mug he held. Four months ago, he'd killed a twenty-nine-year-old repeat drug offender. Every minute of that night would forever remain indelibly etched in Alec's mind.

He and his partner, Tony Durant, had been returning to the station after interrogating a suspect in a double homicide when the call came in for any car near the scene of a robbery to respond. Shots had been fired and a security guard wounded.

Alec and Tony had arrived less than two minutes later and found the security guard unconscious and bleeding from a chest wound. A white panel van with the motor running and the back door open was backed up to the dock. Alec had guessed the security guard must have surprised the thief.

"My turn." Tony drew his 9mm. "Call for backup. I'm going in."

Knowing Tony could be as stubborn as he and that they alternated taking the lead, Alec came to his feet. "Be careful, Tony. If he went back inside he's either a fool or high. Either way, he's dangerous."

"Noted." Tony stepped inside the warehouse.

Alec radioed for backup, checked on the wounded guard, then followed Tony inside. He hadn't gone thirty feet inside the building before he heard a shot followed by a grunt of pain. From the sound, he knew it was a .38 instead of Tony's 9mm.

Adrenaline rushing though his body, Alec ran. Seconds later he rounded a stack of boxes to see a slim black man in jeans and a hooded sweatshirt, an evil grin on his face, standing over Tony with a gun aimed at his head.

"Drop it!" Alec yelled, his arm straight and braced.

The suspect swung the gun toward Alec. He squeezed off one round of his 9mm, hitting the man in the chest. The man fell and didn't move.

Alec spared a glance at his downed partner on his way to make sure the criminal was out of commission and disarmed. He kicked the gun away and leaned down to find the suspect's eyes wide and fixed. Blood blossomed from his chest, staining his gray sweatshirt. Alec felt his carotid anyway. Nothing.

Alec had received accommodation, praise, and thanks from his partner and his parents, a call from the mayor. Everyone congratulated him on doing his job.

He'd been almost embarrassed by the praise and attention.

He'd just been doing his job. His brother Patrick had been shot in the line of duty and they'd almost lost him. At the end of the day, you wanted to go home to your family. Alec and Tony had been able to do that. He was just happy he'd been there and went about doing his job as always—until he had to draw his gun three months later.

But he froze when the perp got a shot off at him. This time, the perp had taken the lead. The bullet had missed Alec by mere inches. The man had pulled the trigger again, and all Alec could do was stand there and wait to die. He would have if the man's gun hadn't been empty. Throwing the gun at Alec, the man had fled. Alec overtook and cuffed the suspect.

The men at the station had praised Alec for getting another criminal off the streets of Myrtle Beach. Tony had been just as effusive with his praise. Alec had just nodded, too aware that by a miracle he'd missed death, that if he'd been with anyone else his inability to act might have gotten them killed.

Being a policeman was all he'd ever wanted to do. His father had proudly served in the police department. Alec and his four brothers were extremely close. All were on the police force, until Patrick retired after he was wounded.

Simon recently had transferred to Charleston, where his new wife lived, but his older and younger brother remained on the Myrtle Beach police force in different units. In the past they openly went to one another with their problems, but Alec couldn't tell them about this. He was too ashamed of his cowardice.

The only thing he could figure out was to take some time off to work through his problem. Telling his commander would be a death knell to Alec's job. He'd be assigned a desk job, have more mandatory psych counseling, and have it put in his permanent record. No one would want to stand shoulder to shoulder with him or have him watch their backs if they knew he hadn't been brave.

Alec's hand flexed on the handle of the coffee mug. "You have three weeks to get your act together, Dunlap," he told himself.

Alone in the spacious kitchen, Alec took a sip of coffee, glad Maureen had an automatic timer. He was probably the world's worst coffee maker, but his body needed at least one cup in the morning to function properly. Too bad, he thought, that it couldn't heal his other problem. Neither could the dollop of whiskey he'd added, but perhaps it would chase away the face of the dead man that haunted him in his dreams.

Laced coffee in his hand, he headed for the stairs. He had a job to do. Build the surprise wedding present for Simon and his new bride, Maureen. The corners of Alec's mouth lifted as he thought of the happy couple during their wedding on Saturday, their happiness yesterday when he, Patrick, and his wife, Brianna, had seen them off at the airport to Europe for a combined honeymoon and buying trip for Maureen's antique shop.

Thankfully, none of Alec's brothers realized his true reasons for taking a leave of absence. His oldest brother, Sam, might have his suspicions, but thankfully he'd kept them to himself. If he hadn't, all of Alec's brothers would have been in his face, trying to help. He wasn't so sure about Sam's wife. They didn't keep secrets from each other, but since she hadn't hovered over him, Alec thought he was safe on that front.

The pensive look his oldest brother had given Alec the day before the wedding, when he'd told Sam that he wanted to build a gazebo for the newlyweds, warned him that his story wasn't holding up.

Alec might like to do woodwork, have a workshop in his garage, but he loved being a policeman. He'd gone to the police academy straight out of college and quickly climbed in the force. His keen eye, interrogation skills, and attention to detail made him a natural.

A natural that no longer can find it in himself to pull the trigger of his gun.

He was worthless and potentially dangerous to his fellow police officers. Until he conquered the demon, he couldn't return to the work he'd always wanted to do.

Resolve swept through him. He'd find a way. His sanity and career depended on it.

Monday morning Celeste was in a buoyant mood as she climbed out of her van and went to the front door of Maureen Gilmore-Dunlap's beautiful Georgian home. It was a little past eight, and all was quiet in the upscale residential neighborhood.

Celeste smiled and glanced toward the house next door, wondering if Maureen's son and his new wife, Traci, were up. They'd been married two weeks before in a lavish ceremony, then honeymooned in Paris for a week before returning so Ryan could give his mother away to Simon, his friend and frat brother.

Love had come to Maureen and Traci, close friends, widows, and neighbors, at the same time. *Just goes to show,* Celeste thought as she inserted her key into the heavy oak door, *that it is never too late to find love, and that there are those lucky ones who find it twice.* Celeste's smile deteriorated.

Gina was such a wonderful, loving woman. She deserved a second shot at the kind of happiness that Traci and Maureen had found.

The rat Robert played the field while Gina worked hard to make a success out of her travel agency business. Through Celeste's prodding, Gina had contacted Traci and Maureen and had been able to book both their honeymoons and Maureen and Simon's extended stay in Europe. Gina, always trying to please others, hadn't wanted to trade on her friendship with Maureen. Celeste had to remind Gina that who you knew was often as important as what you knew.

After so many attempts at a career, Gina had finally found something she enjoyed. She'd make it this time. Celeste was a living witness that if you enjoyed what you did and worked hard, success followed.

Celeste was always excited to begin a new project. Being given free rein in design was a challenge she eagerly looked forward to. She planned on turning Maureen's bedroom into a luxurious retreat without making it too frilly for Simon to relax in.

Willie, Celeste's assistant, had tried without success to find matching material to redo the duvet and shams Maureen hadn't wanted to keep after a burglar had broken into her house and slept on her bed. Unfortunately, the silk material from a French manufacturer wasn't available.

Maureen, in her typical calm and assertive manner, had decided to redo the master suite after her engagement to Simon, and she'd asked his opinion. Being an astute and loving man, Simon had suggested she keep the blue and beige colors that were throughout the house.

Celeste grinned and twisted the key. She'd bet her van that Simon also knew the same colors were in the master suite. Maureen was certainly a blessed and lucky woman. She probably woke up with a huge smile on her face every morning.

Chuckling softly to herself, Celeste stepped inside the spacious foyer and stopped dead in her tracks.

A man wearing only jeans stood less than twenty feet in front of her, his fingers wrapped around a blue mug. Faded denim molded to his muscular thighs. His long feet were bare as well. Even with him half-dressed, she recognized Alec Dunlap, Simon's younger brother, immediately.

It would be difficult for a female over twelve years of age to forget the five Dunlap brothers. Even the oldest, with gray at the temples of his thick black hair, was gorgeous. Only the two youngest, Alec and Rafael, were single. The women at Simon and Maureen's wedding reception hadn't been shy about trying to hook up with the mouthwatering, tempting Dunlap brothers.

"Good morning, I'm Alec Dunlap. You must be Celeste de la Vega, the interior decorator Maureen said was coming this morning."

Alec's voice, a seductive mixture of deep midnight and velvet, vibrated across every one of Celeste's nerve endings. No wonder there had been such a crush of women around him. Lethal. His dark head twisted to one side. "You are Celeste, aren't you?"

"Yes, sorry," Celeste managed, stepping forward to extend her hand and finding her legs a bit unsteady. Alec Dunlap certainly packed a wallop. "Hello, Alec. Maureen didn't mention anyone would be here."

Her smile wasn't returned. Odd. She was known to be able to charm the grouchiest person. Apparently Alec hadn't heard. The handshake was brief. She tried her best to keep her eyes on his face and not on the impressive chest—which fortunately wasn't difficult.

"It was sort of last-minute. Sorry about the way I'm dressed," Alec said. "Maureen said you probably wouldn't get here until around nine."

"I thought I'd get an early start," she explained, and was glad of her decision. Seeing a well-built man like Alec with every muscle delineated was definitely worth getting up early for.

His long-fingered hand speared though jet-black hair. "Me, too. I'm building them a gazebo as a wedding present."

Celeste's gaze dropped to his other hand, which was curled around the mug. It was large, competent looking, with long fingers. *Bet that isn't all they are good at,* she mused. Aloud she said, "What a fabulous idea. Maureen has a beautiful garden. Have you decided where you're going to put it?"

"Not yet," he said slowly.

"Would you like a suggestion?" she asked, watching his beautiful black eyes narrow as if he wasn't sure of the type of suggestion she meant. Celeste's smile widened. It was sort of nice to have a handsome man like Alec a bit unsure of her.

"Maureen said you were great at what you did," he finally said.

Celeste decided to take his comment as a "yes." "Maureen loves calla lilies. They're her favorite. They've finished blooming for the year, but there's a great area near their bed that I could show you. It would be perfect for her and Simon to sit and enjoy the flowers surrounding it anytime."

He frowned. His dark eyes crinkled sexily at the corners. Was there anything about the man that wasn't an enticement?

"Was that the flower she carried at the wedding?"

"Yes. I'd be happy to show you where the area is." *And keep on looking at you.*

"Thanks. I'll get a shirt and hurry back."

Watching him pass, her gaze dropped to his butt. Prime. "Don't bother on my account."

He turned, his dark brow arched. "What?"

Oops. She'd forgotten that he was a policeman and could probably hear a pin drop on cotton or, like her mother, could understand hushed whispers at thirty feet. And wouldn't her mother just love it if Celeste brought Alec home.

She'd heard Simon mention that his maternal grandmother was Puerto Rican. Celeste's parents were intelligent enough to realize that although heritage was important, it wasn't the only consideration in finding someone to care for. "Take your time."

He stared at her a long time as if trying to figure out if that was what she'd said. Celeste's smile widened. Flirting could be fun. A new experience for her, since men always tried to come on to her. Yet there was something about Alec that excited and drew her.

"No problem. We both have jobs to do," he told her. "After this morning, you won't be seeing much of me."

A pity, Celeste thought. Fortunately, she didn't voice her opinion. However, she wasn't able to keep her appreciative gaze from running back over him. A real pity. After one last puzzled look at her, Alec continued up the stairs.

Alec had been a policeman too long not to know when he was being watched. He could actually "feel" Celeste's hot gaze on him. He kept going. This was no time to get mixed up with a woman. His first and only priority had to be getting his head on straight. Thinking about the way Celeste ran her tongue over her lips when he'd mentioned she wouldn't be seeing much of him, imagining it gliding over his body, was definitely off-limits.

Opening his bedroom door, Alec snatched up the shirt from the foot of the bed and shoved his arms into the long sleeves. Sitting on the bed, he put on his socks and heavy work shoes. A woman was the last thing he needed right now—even if he'd noticed her Saturday at the wedding reception. Sexy and drop-dead gorgeous with a figure that would make a monk weep for mercy, she had been hard to miss.

And no one could call Alec a monk. It was just as well. His only focus had to be on getting his head on straight. Like he'd told Celeste, he planned to stay out of her way.

Opening the door, he headed back down the stairs, buttoning his shirt as he went. He'd only gone a short distance when he saw Celeste at the bottom, a warm smile on her face. She smiled a lot. Each time he'd been able to find her in the crowd Saturday afternoon, she'd had a smile on her face. A man could get used to that smile.

He stepped off the bottom stair. "I can probably find the spot you're talking about."

"With me showing you, you'll find it that much quicker and be able to start on your project." She started toward the living room, which led to the terrace. "What type of material and design do you plan?"

So perhaps he had misjudged the way she was looking at him, he decided as he followed, trying and failing to keep his gaze from dropping to the enticing sway of her hips. Just his bad luck to have been sleeping single for the past year. "I plan to match the brick on the house."

"That's a good idea, but you might consider unfinished cedar. It would give a softer look and blend in more naturally as the wood ages." She tossed her suggestion over her shoulder before opening the terrace doors and going outside.

She looked even better in daylight. She came to the middle of his chest. He thought of her resting against him after they made love while he stroked her unbound long black hair, now worn in a ponytail, and gritted his teeth. "You seem to know your way around here pretty well."

"Maureen is more than a client; she's a good friend as well."

Celeste took a path bordered by alternating bursts of purple and white flowers. Alec thought they were pansies.

"She has exquisite taste, as you can see. She just needed someone to bring it all together." Stopping, Celeste bent to cup a blossom almost as large as her hand.

"That's not the flower," he said, marveling at how gently her fingers touched the pink blossom. Would she touch a man's body the same way?

"No." She tilted her head, causing her thick, silky hair to slide sensuously across her shoulders and back. "It's a camellia. My favorite." She straightened. "And would you believe I can't get them to grow in my own flower garden, so I have to admire them when I see them."

"Maybe it's your soil," he said before he thought; then he frowned. Why had he felt the need to help her and see her smile again?

"Tested several times." She continued on the paved path. "Nettie believes it has something to do with the exposure."

He knew that name. He pulled his gaze from the enticing sway of her hips and tried to think. "Nettie. She's one of the women in the Invincible Sisterhood."

She turned, the smile he was becoming to associate with her

on her lips. "Yes, and another woman who might prove that love has been working overtime around here. In any case, a lot of Maureen's friends and associates teased her about not being able to be a member of the Sisterhood any longer because all of the five members were widows." Celeste folded her arms. "Maureen nixed that by saying her finding a wonderful man to marry just showed how invincible the Sisterhood really was."

"She and Simon are crazy about each other," Alec admitted, trying not to stare at Celeste's tempting mouth.

"Just as it should be when a man and woman fall in love."

He felt a strange sensation in his chest. He stared at her; she stared back. "The calla lily."

"There." She pointed to an area covered with cedar bark and surrounded by smooth river stones. Nearby was a flat patch of green grass. "Do you plan to build a bench, or a fire pit if you use brick and have a cement floor?"

He hadn't thought that far. His hesitation must have shown.

"If your brother likes to grill I'd say a fireplace to double as a romantic refuge where they could enjoy each other's company while he cooks," she said.

"Simon and Sam each try to outdo the other on the grill," he remarked, trying to stay focused. Celeste had folded her arms under her generous breasts, pushing them distractingly upward in the thin yellow T-shirt.

"Sam?"

"The oldest. There are five of us." *Thank goodness,* he told himself when she let her arms fall to her sides. He tried to make himself believe he really felt that way.

"Maureen said you're a policeman, too."

A policeman who didn't have the nerve to fire his gun.

Her words effectively reminded him of why he was here and

why she was off-limits. "Thank you for showing me, but I don't want to keep you from your work."

Was that disappointment on her face? "You're welcome."

She started back toward the house, then stopped. "I brought lunch since Maureen said the maid and housekeeper would be on vacation while she's gone. I have more than enough to share."

"Thank you, but once I start, I plan to work straight through," he said.

"I see," she murmured. This time he clearly saw the disappointment. "If you change your mind the offer stands." Continuing on, she stopped at the camellia bush again and smelled the flower before continuing on to the house.

Alec turned away. He didn't need the additional headache, and that's exactly where having any thought about Celeste would lead. He had enough problems in his life already.

He just hoped he could remember that when he saw her again.

FOUR

Half past eight Monday morning Gina scrolled through the hun-
dred or so new e-mails since last night, hoping, praying, there
was an e-mail from someone wanting to buy rather than sell to
her. There wasn't.

Trying to remain optimistic, thinking perhaps she had been
too anxious the first time, she patiently went through the e-mails
a second time, no matter that they didn't have the subject header
that indicated the person was inquiring about information to
book a trip.

A fourth of the way through she tried to keep the creeping
desperation at bay. But she was unable to stop herself from
throwing a glance at the stack of bills on her desk in her home
office. Bills that were due soon. Bills that unless Robert stopped
making empty promises and paid the child support on time
she wouldn't be able to pay.

By the time she finished the last e-mails, her hands were shaking, her stomach in knots. Absently she pressed the flat of her hand to her stomach, felt the slight roll of fat, and jerked her hand away.

Out of nowhere Robert's words, *You don't excite me anymore,* came like a slap in the face. Tears didn't come this time as they had so many times in the past. They were useless and another sign of her failure to her children. Because of a lack in her, their father had walked out.

Too restless to sit, she stood, shoving her hands into the pockets of her sweats, and thought of the toned woman she'd seen Robert with the day she went to his office at the gym. They were as different as night and day. Gina was older, weighed fifty pounds more, and even with makeup and her most flattering outfit, she wasn't as vibrant or as pretty as the other woman Robert had kept his arm around.

Aware that looking back on the past wasn't going to pay the bills, Gina went back to the computer. Opening a drawer, she reached way in the back and pulled out a miniature Baby Ruth candy bar. Perhaps the many flyers she and the children had passed out at a street event in downtown Charleston would eventually pay off.

Ashton thought it was fun. Gabrielle, of course, thought it was another form of begging. Gina had bribed her by promising her the new pair of tennis shoes she wanted. The shoes were in Gabrielle's closet. The water bill was due in two days. Gina peeled away the wrapper and ate the candy in two bites.

And, as was becoming his habit, Robert was late with the child support payment. She needed that money. She no longer watered the yard and subsequently had the worst-looking yard on the block. Paint was chipping on the eaves and shutters that should have been painted last year, but Robert had purchased a Cadillac convertible. She'd ridden in it exactly once. He played, and she and the children paid the price. That had to stop.

Gina snatched up the phone and dialed his cell phone number, which had taken threats for him to give to her. He was crazy if he thought he could take the children off with no way for her to reach them.

"Hello."

Her grip on the phone tightened at the happy greeting. He wasn't fighting bills; his back wasn't against the wall. "Hello, Robert. Where is this month's child support check?"

"Wait a minute," he said brusquely.

Gina paced. He had probably been in one of the exercise areas. The gym was open 24/7.

"What are you worrying me for? I told you I had to replace some equipment," he snapped a few moments later.

Gina flinched at the whiplash in his voice. No greeting, just accusations. "The water bill is due in two days and I can't pay it. The yard—"

"Nobody told you to plant those stupid flowers or those red-tips around the house. What kind of woman are you that you can't take care of things for a month?" he asked, then rushed on before she could answer. "I took care of all the bills while I was there. You did squat. We would have had more if you'd managed the household money better instead of those stupid home businesses you kept sinking my money in, just like you're doing now. Get a real job, be a woman, and stop bothering me while *I* work." The line went dead.

Gina held the phone in her hand, her entire body trembling. Slowly she returned it to the base. Had she ever known Robert? Was the hateful, accusatory man there all along? Probably. He'd become more and more distant as his fitness center prospered. Why hadn't she seen it? Robert didn't respect her, thought she was worthless. Gina reached for another candy bar.

The phone ringing on her desk snapped her upright. With greedy desperation, Gina picked it up. "Rawlings Travel Agency, carefree travel for a carefree vacation," she answered.

"Good morning, Gina."

Gina didn't feel disappointment as much as she felt disappointed at the sound of her mother's voice. Her parents had wanted her to accomplish so much and she had failed time and time again. "Good morning, Mother; how are you?"

"Wonderful," she said. "How are Gabrielle and Ashton? I guess they've already gone to school."

"Ashton is fine, but a surly teenager is still invading Gabrielle's body," Gina told her mother, trying to forget the hurtful phone call with Robert.

Light laughter filtered through the line. Nothing ever got the best of Lois Malone, the youngest daughter of Horace and Matilda Hempstead of Columbia, South Carolina. Too bad that trait hadn't filtered down to Lois's youngest child. "She's there, Gina. Young people these days just like to test their parents. I'm just thankful I'm a grandmother and can send them back home."

"You dote on all your grandchildren, and they know it," Gina said. All of them were doing well in school and were happy, except Gabrielle. But none of them were going through what Gabrielle was. Their parents remained in love, a united team. They hadn't had to get married.

Gina winced, recalling her wedding anniversary two years ago when Gabrielle had added up the dates and learned she'd been born weighing a hefty eight pounds only five months after her parents were married.

"I'm not as bad as your father," Gina's mother said. "September is barely here and he's already talking about everyone coming for Thanksgiving."

Ashton and Gabrielle's first without their father. What would Christmas be like? Her fault and another failure to add to her long list.

"Honey?" her mother queried.

"Just thinking."

"I won't profess to know what you're going through, but I do know you made a wonderful home for Robert and the children. It's not your fault that he was too stupid to realize it."

Her mother didn't pull punches. "Stupid" was one of the nicest words she'd called Robert. Gina's father hadn't been shy, either.

"We love you, Gina," her mother said softly.

Gina had never doubted her parents' love. It had helped Gina get through the darkest days of her life, but that love had been a burden as well. Her two older brothers and younger sister sailed through life without a blip. Honor students in high school, graduated in the top of their college classes, had gone on to have wonderful careers, married, and had happy, polite, successful children. She, on the other hand, was an average student in high school, dropped out of college her senior year because she was pregnant, had divorced, and her older child was a pain in the rear.

"Gina?"

"I know, Mama." But this time she wouldn't let her parents bail her out again. They hadn't crucified her as she was afraid they would when she'd confessed she was pregnant. When she'd told them, her father wanted to know why Robert hadn't been there with her to help shoulder the responsibility.

She'd explained that Robert had thought it would be best if she told them alone. She didn't dare admit to them that she'd begged Robert to come with her, but he had football practice. It was then her father had asked for Robert's phone number. She'd given it to him and he'd left the room. She never knew what the conversation was, but she had her suspicions, because the next day Robert asked her to marry him. Before then, marriage hadn't been mentioned.

She'd married at home instead of the church as her brothers and sister had. Her mother was cordial, but her father was cool toward Robert, and so were her brothers. It was obvious they thought Robert less than a man for not going with her to tell her parents.

But whatever her father thought of her new husband, that hadn't stopped him from helping them get an apartment, pay her medical bills, or come up with the down payment of their first and only home two years later. Gina hadn't wanted to ask for any more money, but Robert had been tired of living in an apartment. His parents were barely making ends meet in St. Louis, where they lived.

Gina, desperately wanting to please him, had asked her parents for help once again. She'd always been afraid that Robert had married her because her father had somehow pressured him into it and not because he loved her.

Apparently she'd been right.

"You know you can always count on us, or your brothers and sister for that matter," her mother went on to say.

"I know." Another subtle reminder that if Gina's finances weren't good, they'd help her out. Not this time. "I suppose Dad is on the golf course this morning."

"And every morning," her mother said, love and happiness

in her voice. "He should be home in a couple of hours. This afternoon I'm dragging him to a tea."

Gina smiled. "He'll grumble, but he'll enjoy himself because he's with you."

"We do have fun together," her mother said. "I'm glad he took early retirement so we can do some of the things we always planned. Speaking of, we wanted you to look into booking us and two other couples to Las Vegas within the next six weeks. It should be cooler by then."

Gina's hand flexed on the phone. This would be the third trip her parents and friends had taken in three months. "You and Dad are sure traveling a lot."

"None of us have been there and we decided why not when I had friends over Saturday night for a bid whist party," she said. "All of us are retired, so there's nothing to stop us."

It sounded legitimate, but Gina wasn't fooled. Once again her parents were bailing out their daughter who couldn't get her life on track. "I'll look into some packages and e-mail them to you. Any hotel preference?"

"You know what we like," came her mother's answer.

"Luxurious with a spa for the women, excellent restaurants, and easy access to a golf course for the men," Gina said. Her mother had always stayed at home, but Gina's father had retired from a Fortune 500 company. Both enjoyed being pampered a bit and both deserved it.

Gina's mother laughed. "I'd say that covers it. It's nice having a travel agent in the family."

"It's better having great parents," Gina said. No matter what, they supported her, loved her.

"Thank you. Now I'd better get off the phone and let you get back to work."

Because of her parents, she now could do just that. "Good-bye, Mother. Give Daddy a hug for me and have fun at the tea."

"You know he sends his love as well. Bye, Gina."

Gina replaced the phone. She had a job. Once again her parents had stepped in and averted financial disaster. Although she was grateful, she wished there hadn't been a need. When would she come into her own and make her life a success for her and her children?

She honestly didn't know, and that scared her most of all.

"Celeste, will you come away from that window?"

"In a minute," Celeste said, watching Alec slowly peel his perspiration-soaked shirt from his magnificent body and toss it over his shoulder. Squatting, he picked up a piece of lumber and placed it over the shoulder where the shirt was, then stood and started back to his work site. Celeste's watchful gaze followed his every step.

"Never known you to be so distracted by a man," Willie said, joining her at the window, "but I have to admit he's easy on the eyes."

"That he is." Celeste straightened when a tall tree obscured Alec from her sight. Willie might be sixty-two and happily married, but she also had an observant eye, as many of Celeste's clients could attest to. "He also works hard. He didn't even want to stop for the lunch I offered him."

Willie's thin brows arched over sharp brown eyes. "I still can't believe it. Men drool when they see you."

Celeste rolled her eyes, then tossed her ponytail over her shoulder and arched her chin in the air. "As well they should," she said, then broke into laughter. "Come on; let's finish taking the curtains down."

Walking over to the twelve-foot ladder in front of the curtains, Willie wrapped her hands around the aluminum frame as Celeste climbed back up. "That's what I like about you, Celeste: You never take yourself too seriously."

"That and I sign your paycheck," Celeste said, unhooking the voluminous material from the rod. "It's a good thing Maureen agreed to swag curtains on rods instead of a cornice board. That will make things easier."

"But it still will take almost the entire three weeks to redo this suite," Willie said. "I really like this material and hate that I couldn't find any more to remake the bedcoverings."

Celeste stopped and smiled down at Willie, who was considered a bit of a miracle worker by those who knew her. She had a knack for finding just the right fabric and accessories. "But you have to admit the new fabric is scrumptious and will look beautiful in here. And redoing Ryan's free clinic for unwed mothers with the fabric we're taking down will make it the swankiest clinic in Charleston."

"He and Traci are so much in love. Love has certainly been working overtime."

Celeste paused. "Just what I told Alec."

"Oh, mercy, why did I have to mention anything that would remind you of him?" Willie asked with a shake of her graying head. "Why does this man interest you so much?"

Celeste didn't have to think long. "Isn't that magnificent body enough?"

"It would be if you were that shallow. You're not, so stop stalling," Willie told her.

"He has sad eyes," Celeste said, reaching for another hook.

"You were always a sucker for anyone in need," Willie said, but there was no condemnation in her voice. "You can't pass a beggar without opening your handbag."

Celeste shrugged. "I've always been blessed, so why shouldn't I help others less fortunate?"

"Because most of them are just preying on an easy mark, like in that undercover story the reporter did last month. It's all an act."

Celeste didn't say anything else, just continued to work. She knew what it was for your life to spin out of control. She had a strong feeling she knew why dark shadows lurked in Alec's eyes. She'd seen them in her own mirror.

Alec didn't come inside until he heard Celeste's van pull out of the driveway. Hot, sweaty, he opened the refrigerator for a cold beer and shook his head. Directly in front of him was a plate covered with plastic wrap with a note attached.

In case you get hungry later.
Celeste

She didn't give up easily, but she was wasting her time. He wasn't interested. But there was no reason to let the food go to waste. Maureen had apologized over and over because she'd cleaned out the refrigerator in preparation for being gone a month. Alec had assured her he was used to fending for himself.

He had a list of take-out places by the kitchen phone in his home in Myrtle Beach for emergencies, but he could cook if pressed to do so. However, he hadn't had a chance to go to the store. Traci and Ryan had called and invited Alec to dinner, but he had no intention on imposing on the newlyweds.

Picking up the plate with one hand, he grabbed the beer with the other and shouldered the refrigerator door closed. When he was halfway to the large kitchen table, the phone rang. He never paused. He'd told Maureen he'd let her answering machine pick up her messages. All her friends knew she was out of town.

Taking a seat by the window, he unwrapped the food, a mound of potato salad, coleslaw, and a sandwich stuffed with vegetables and smoked chicken. No fork. Sliding his chair back, he reached the cabinet just as the answering machine clicked on.

"Alec, hope you hear this, since your cell phone is off. We're having grilled salmon tonight. You're invited. Call me."

Blowing out a breath, Alec pulled open the drawer and picked up a fork. He'd left his cell phone off for that very reason. He and his brother Patrick were very close. All of the brothers loved one another, looked out for one another, helped one another. This time Alec needed to work his problem out on his own. Knowing he was going through a difficult time would worry them.

The phone rang again. Alec looked at the caller ID and saw Patrick's name. Alec knew before the answering machine message stopped he'd hear Patrick's wife, Brianna.

"Hi, Alec, it's Brianna. In case you don't know it, I love you and you're always welcome. Your fabulous cook of a brother made bread pudding with vanilla cream sauce although I can only have a small portion. My darling husband watches my caloric intake like a hawk."

"I watch you," Patrick said; then there was a giggle. Alec smiled without being aware of it.

"You're kind of easy on the eye yourself," Brianna whispered, then said aloud, "We expect to see a lot of you while you're here. The door is always open. Sister-in-law number two signing off."

The line went dead. Alec shook his head, a bemused smile on his face. Five months pregnant, Brianna was something else. His brother had his hands full married to such an outspoken, beautiful woman and he enjoyed every moment of it. He was happier than any of them had ever seen him.

Alec's smile died as he recalled the night Patrick had been shot and critically wounded by a drug dealer. It had been touch and go for a while, but Patrick had survived to find a woman he loved more than anything. Their child would be lucky.

Out of nowhere Alec recalled that the man he'd killed had a wife who had been pregnant. Alec's actions had taken the unborn child's father away and widowed the young mother. That the drug dealer had shot a security guard and Alec's partner, was about to shoot Tony again when Alec arrived, no longer seemed to matter. Nor did it matter that Alec, with the help of a friend in banking, had set up an anonymous trust for the mother and child.

He'd taken a life.

Retracing his steps, Alec went to the table, rewrapped the food, and placed the plate in the refrigerator. He wasn't hungry. Grabbing the beer by the long neck, he drained the contents, then put the empty bottle in the trash. It was still light enough to work on the gazebo.

If he worked hard enough, perhaps he could get the look of

surprise on the man's face, the hatred, out of his mind. He prayed so hard, but so far his prayers had gone unanswered.

"You won't believe who's living at Maureen's house," Celeste said the moment Gina answered the front door that evening.

Despite her own worry, Gina smiled at the excitement in Celeste's voice. Besides Gina's mother, there hadn't been one inquiry about travel plans. "I don't suppose it was Pierce Brosnan?" Gina asked as she stepped aside to let Celeste enter.

"Better, because Pierce, although a fine specimen, is married," came Celeste's reply.

Shutting the door, Gina studied Celeste's animated face. "You're beaming."

Celeste's smile broadened. "Where are the kids?"

"Gabrielle is still on punishment in her room. Ashton is outside kicking the soccer ball around," Gina answered. "The coast is clear for adult conversation."

"Perfect." Taking Gina's arm, Celeste headed for the kitchen. "This is strictly for adults."

"I take it, it was a man."

Celeste paused in the entryway of the kitchen. "In spades."

Gina had never seen her friend so giddy about a man. "Will you tell me who it is that has you so excited?"

"Alec Dunlap," Celeste confessed, and continued to the kitchen. She took a seat on one of the high stools at the island. "I couldn't believe it when I saw him again. I thought after I didn't get a chance to meet him at the reception I wouldn't get another opportunity."

Gina chuckled, pulled a bottle of water and a Pepsi from the refrigerator, offering Celeste a choice. "As I remember, you were quite taken with him."

"So were a lot of other women, but I now have him all to myself." Celeste selected the water and unscrewed the top.

"Is he house-sitting?" Gina popped the cap of the soda and took a swallow, then slipped into the seat beside Celeste.

"He's building a gazebo as a wedding present for Maureen and Simon," Celeste told her. "When I let myself into Maureen's house, he was standing there with his shirt off. I didn't realize my legs had turned to jelly until I went to shake his hand. The man is gorgeous and sexy as hell." Hastily she chugged water.

Gina stared at her best friend. "I don't recall you ever saying anything like that about any of the three men you were engaged to."

"Because none of them moved me the way Alec does. The reason, you'll recall, that I broke off the engagements." Celeste took another long swallow of water. "Alec packs a punch. I've found a man who finally makes me want to throw caution to the wind and be a little wicked."

"Wait a minute, Celeste," Gina cautioned, swerving her chair toward her. "You've just met the man."

"I know it, but something about him just tugs at me."

Gina didn't know what to say. Celeste wasn't the kind of woman to go after a man just because he had a great body. "Can you tell if he feels the same way?"

Celeste stared off into space. "No. In fact, I don't think it would be an exaggeration to say that he wished I wasn't there. He hasn't smiled at me once. He even refused to eat the lunch I took him."

"I'm sorry." Gina knew how horrible it felt to be dismissed.

Robert did it while they were married and continued to do so after their divorce.

"I'm not giving up." Celeste tilted the bottle to her lips.

Gina frowned with worry. "Do you think that's a good idea?"

Celeste blew out a breath. "It's not in my nature to sit back and let things happen. Besides, you know how persistent I can be when I want something."

"I also know how much it hurts when you're the only one in love," Gina said quietly, her voice unsteady.

Anger flashed in Celeste's black eyes. "Robert's a pri—" She broke off hastily and glanced around, then leaned closer. "Some men are fools."

"Maybe it wasn't all hi—"

"Don't you dare put this at your doorstep," Celeste snapped. "You always put your family first, did everything you could to be the best wife and mother possible. I don't ever want to hear you say anything differently."

But she'd failed, Gina thought, keeping the words unspoken. "I'm glad you're my friend."

"Same here." Celeste finished her water and stood. "How did it go today?"

Gina's smile faltered for a moment. "My mother called this morning and asked me to book a trip to Las Vegas for her and my dad and two other couples."

"Your parents certainly know how to enjoy themselves. My mother can't wait until Father retires from his medical practice next year." Celeste wrinkled her nose. "The only thing is that she'll have more time to badger me about getting married and having a baby."

"You can handle Mrs. de la Vega," Gina said.

"Yeah, I know, but it still gives me a headache." Celeste went to the door. "I almost forgot, have you given any more thought to going ahead and redoing your bedroom at least?"

"I think I'll wait awhile," Gina said. Every penny counted.

"I don't guess you'd let me do it as an early Christmas gift," Celeste asked.

"You guessed right, but thanks for the offer." No more handouts. Her parents would learn the same thing.

"All right. Take care of yourself. I'll keep you posted on my progress with Alec." Celeste grinned. "It's kind of fun flirting with him. I don't remember having this much fun with other men."

"Robert wasn't much fun, either," Gina blurted. Her eyes widened at the admission.

"He certainly wasn't, but the next guy will be."

Gina shook her head. "I keep telling you, there will never be a next time."

"I learned long ago never say never. Bye."

Gina waited until Celeste got in her van and pulled off before closing the door. She hoped things turned out for the best for Celeste, but for her a man wasn't in her future.

Never again would she subject herself to another failure. The pain that resulted when it went sour wasn't worth it.

FIVE

Max stopped his Pathfinder at the edge of Gina Rawlings' prop-
erty line and shut off the motor. He wasn't impressed by what
he saw of the two-story house and yard.

Patches of Saint Augustine grass were dead or needed cutting, the red-tip shrubs were overgrown, the flowers wilted, and
the house and gray shutters begged for a coat of paint.

On closer inspection, he could actually see something green
sprouting from the gutter that ran along the front of the house.
In no way did it look as if the owner had any decorative acumen
or style. She had the worst-kept house and yard on the block.

He'd wasted his time by coming here. Gina Rawlings didn't
know any more than he and his aunt did about making the inn
the charming place of refuge he wanted. Instead of wasting his
time here, he should be making contact with other travel agencies to let them know he was ready for business.

Friends had booked Journey's End for the first two weekends of the opening and had scattered weekends until the end of the year, but Max wanted solid bookings and had hoped Gina might help him accomplish his goal by making the place more inviting.

Starting the motor, Max took one last look at the house. He hadn't realized how much he had counted on her helping him. He was about to reach for the gearshift when the screen on the front door opened, then banged shut. With his head down, her outspoken little boy came out of the house carrying a soccer ball. The small child plopped down on the porch, put the soccer ball in his lap, and rested his forehead on top.

In trouble again, Max thought. His hand curled around the gearshift lever. The kid wasn't his problem, but he couldn't make himself shift the SUV into drive. Sharon had wanted a dozen children.

Hoping he wasn't going to regret this, Max shut off the motor and got out. Going up the sidewalk lined with wilting and dead pansies, he stopped a couple of feet in front of the dejected-looking little boy. "Hi, Ashton, remember me?"

Ashton raised his head. Tears glistened in his big brown eyes. The sight tugged at Max's heart. He'd wanted children as well. Forgetting his annoyance with Ashton, Max took out his handkerchief from the back pocket of his jeans and hunkered down in front of Ashton.

"It can't be that bad," Max said, gently wiping away the tears.

"It is, too," Ashton said, his lower lip trembling. "No one will play with me. My mother is sad and my sister yelled at me to get out of her room. She's mad because I told Mama that she talked on the phone when she wasn't supposed to. You're probably mad at me, too. I'm sorry. Mama explained to me it wasn't nice to tell someone you didn't like something they were proud of, like my crayon drawings she always puts on the refrigerator. She said it's not nice to repeat what grown-ups say. I got into trouble, too, but not as much as Gabrielle."

Max was totally captivated by Ashton's nonstop talking and his honesty. "You play soccer?"

He nodded. "I'm the goalie. We have a game Saturday against a really good team and I wanted to practice. I already did my homework because we had early release today so the teachers could have a meeting."

So that's why the children were home at barely past two. "I'm here to see your mother."

Ashton shook his head. "Against the rules. We can't bother her unless we're hurt or the house is on fire. She's working on travel plans for Grandpa and Grandma Malone."

Max felt a smile tug his mouth upward. Ashton was a wealth of information. "How about your father?"

Sadness entered the little boy's face. "We're divorced. He's busy working, so he doesn't come around much."

Max's heart went out to Ashton. There were too many absent fathers in the world. "If you'd like, we can kick a few balls around."

Ashton's face lit up. He jumped to his feet. "Really?"

Grinning, Max stood. "Really."

"Come on." Grabbing his hand, Ashton took off around the side of the house with a laughing Max following.

Gina checked and double-checked the travel itinerary for her parents and the two couples going with them. Nothing could go wrong. She didn't want her parents making excuses for a mix-up in their flights or hotel rooms. She'd been the same obsessive way when she'd scheduled the honeymoons for Traci and Maureen. Not only was Gina a friend of Maureen's, but her aunt Ophelia was an Invincible and one of Maureen's closest friends. Gina never wanted to let her friends or her clients down.

Gina's hand flexed. There weren't many clients as it was. She'd only booked two vacations on cold calls and one from her pitiful Web site. She massaged her forehead that had begun to throb. Maybe she needed sugar. She got up from her desk for a miniature Snicker bar. Unwrapping and eating the candy, she tossed the wrapper in the trash and retook her seat.

Charleston was a popular vacation destination. The potential was there; she just had to be able to tap into it. She'd studied the market, studied those agents who were successful. One thing all of them had in common was a dynamic Web site and a high listing on search engines. Gina had built her own site because she hadn't been able to afford to hire someone . . . and it showed.

Rawlingstravel.com was plain, with pictures of Charleston and Europe. Nothing was there to impress the viewers with what they saw, nothing interactive to draw them back or make them want to book a trip with her.

For some odd reason she thought of the Web site for Journey's End. The site was gorgeous, but once Gina was inside the beautiful house, it looked crowded and stiff. It wasn't lost on her that she and the owner of Journey's End had exactly the opposite problems.

Gina blew out a breath. There was a picture of Max and his aunt on the main page. Single women would book if only to see Max. Gina had purposefully left her picture off her site. She wanted to drive business to her, not away. Yet unlike Max's site, where you could move your cursor and another delightful page would pop up, hers remained stationary.

She was positive that if she had a more interactive Web site she might stand a chance in the competitive travel market. Unfortunately, she didn't have the money to hire someone. Ashton and Gabrielle were fantastic on the computer, but they couldn't do the graphics she need—

Her head came up sharply. Cocking her head, she listened. She thought she heard a man's laughter. Gabrielle was barred from watching television, and Ashton would rather play soccer than watch. He'd come into her office earlier and asked her to practice with him, but she'd been too busy.

She turned her attention back to the monitor. Once she finished, she'd go outside and play with him. Her lips pressed together. Robert didn't spend enough time with him. Ashton needed a father. She'd seriously considered putting him in a mentoring program, but had made the mistake of mentioning it to Robert. Predictably, he'd pitched a hissy fit.

"I'm man enough to bring up my own son. Too bad I can't say the same thing about you bringing up Gabrielle."

Gina's head lowered; then she heard the sound again, this time intermingled with that of a child's laughter. *Ashton.*

Gina shot up from her chair. A cold chill ran through her. All the men who lived on the block were at work. Through the window in her home office in the back bedroom, she saw the broad shoulders of a man as he slowly maneuvered a soccer ball toward Ashton, who grinned from ear to ear at the net she'd helped him erect. Gina grabbed the nearest heavy object and rushed outside.

"Run, Ashton!"

The man stopped, whirled. She stumbled to a halt on recognizing Max Broussard.

"Mama, you know I'm supposed to stay here and defend the goal," Ashton said, coming to stand by Max.

Max's speculative gaze dropped to the heart-shaped paperweight in her hand, then went back up to her face. A dark brow lifted in query. Embarrassed, Gina didn't know if she should drop the paperweight or hide it behind her back.

"Good evening, Mrs. Rawlings. I owe you an apology for luring Ashton to play without consulting you first," Max said, then glanced down at Ashton. "You have a first-rate player here."

"He only got two balls past me," Ashton said proudly.

Gina fished for something to say and came up with nothing. Max probably thought she was a bit off.

"I came to ask you about your decorating ideas but changed my mind." Max extended his hand to Ashton. "Thank you for a good game, but I think I could have tied the score that time."

Ashton's expression fell. "You don't have to leave. We can play some more."

Max's large hand rested on her son's shoulder. "Perhaps some other time. I have to get back to the inn."

Seeing the gentle way Max treated a little boy he hardly knew helped Gina make a quick decision. She wasn't sure why he'd changed his mind, but she had a good idea. Her house needed work, but everything involved money, including watering the yard. "If you'll wait a minute I'll get you the list of my suggestions. I've written everything down."

"I don't want to bother you," he said, clearly anxious to leave.

"You're not. Besides, I owe you for helping Ashton practice." She smiled down at her son. If only his father were as attentive. "If you'll follow me, I'll get them for you."

Without giving him a chance to reply, Gina went inside. As she passed a wicker plant stand by the back door, she placed the paperweight on the edge. Reaching her desk, she picked up a manila folder marked "Journey's End" and gave it to Max. "I hope you find it useful."

Max glanced around her office. It was bright and inviting with pictures of her children on the bookshelf, healthy plants, and a collection of childlike crayon drawings in wooden dollar-store frames. Through the open door on the other side of the room, he saw what he assumed was the den. The paneled room with black leather furniture looked gloomy. It was hard to believe the same woman lived in the house.

He nodded toward a crayon drawing of a couple sitting on a porch swing on the wall. "Ashton, is that one of your drawings you were telling me about?"

"Yes," the little boy said proudly. "Grandpa and Grandma Malone like to sit on the porch swing at their house."

"Open it," Gina urged. "I admit to being a little anxious about what you'd think. My best friend, Celeste, is the interior designer."

Max opened the folder. The first thing he saw was a wisteria arbor. His eyes briefly shut.

"What's the matter?" Gina asked, her tone worried.

As he opened his eyes, his head lifted. "The arbor. I just remember that my late wife wanted one."

Sympathy shone in her expressive brown eyes. "I'm sorry if I've made you sad."

He shook his dark head. "On the contrary."

Quickly he flipped through the folder. There were more pictures of flower gardens but also furniture placements, decorative accessories. This hadn't been done lightly, and what was so amazing was that she hadn't even known he'd drop by. There was more to Gina Rawlings than he had first thought.

"Thank you. This took effort and a lot of thought."

Her tense shoulders relaxed. "At one time I wanted to own a B and B, but things didn't work out." She pulled Ashton in front of her.

Max wondered if the ex-husband was the reason. "How about helping me make mine as inviting and warm as you envisioned yours to be?"

She frowned. "I don't understand."

"I want to hire you to help bring these plans to fruition," he told her, lifting the folder again.

"Would that mean we could play soccer some more?" Ashton asked.

"Ashton, you know better than to interrupt adults when they are talking," Gina admonished.

"Sorry." His head fell.

Turning him to her, she smiled down at him. "I know you were just excited. Why don't you go tell Gabrielle to help you set the table for dinner."

"She'll yell—"

"Ashton," Gina said firmly.

"Yes, ma'am." The little boy faced Max. "I had fun. Thank you for playing with me."

"So did I, Ashton," he said, and meant it.

"Maybe, maybe you could come watch me play Saturday at the park . . . if you're not too busy," Ashton quickly tacked on.

Out of the corner of his eye, Max saw anger flash in Gina's eyes. Definitely an absent father. "I can't promise anything, but if I can make it, I will."

"I hope you can," Ashton said; then with the soccer ball under his arm he walked away.

Gina waited until Ashton was out of sight. "Thank you for taking time with him."

"He's a good kid." *And hungry for a man in his life,* Max thought.

"He is." Gina stared fondly after her son.

"I could really use your help," Max said.

She faced him. "As I said earlier, my best friend, Celeste, is the interior designer. She was with me Sunday."

"Which one of you did this room?" Max asked.

Gina looked startled. "I did."

"That's what I thought." He lifted the folder. "I'll make you a trade. You help me in my business and I'll help you in any way I can with yours, plus I'll pay you."

"Pay me?" Gina echoed.

"Of course. I'd be taking you away from your business. It's only right that you should be compensated." Max had another sneaky suspicion that, besides not being around, her ex wasn't helping out financially as much as he should. The woman who took pride in her office would take pride in the outside as well.

"Could you help me with my Web site?" she asked, her brown eyes anxious. "I looked up yours and liked it."

She certainly didn't ask for much. "I could. I designed mine."

"The pictures of the house were beautiful, but. . . ."

"But what?" he asked, a bit anxious.

Gina thought of all the times she'd suggested changes in the house to Robert, but he'd disliked every one. Perhaps Max wouldn't like any of her suggestions.

"Gina, your children are waiting, and I have to get back to the inn," Max prompted.

She recalled Ashton's happy laughter earlier with Max and took a small leap of faith. "You have too much furniture in the rooms, causing them to look crowded and uninviting."

He frowned. Gina held her breath. "My aunt and I thought people would enjoy the antiques, the feel of stepping back in time. Besides, the bedroom furnishings were sold as sets."

Gina couldn't believe he was actually listening. She forgot to be afraid. "But you didn't have to put it all in the same room. Perhaps the pieces could function in another part of the house or be stored. Even in the largest bedroom there was hardly room to move around. If you added other amenities, you'd increase people's desire to stay there."

"Add? Like what?" he questioned.

"A small refrigerator," she said softly, then rushed on. "It would be just another touch that set Journey's End apart. A good carpenter could build a cabinet around it so it wouldn't distract from the look of the room."

"You're amazing."

Gina blinked. She'd been called a lot of things in her life but nothing close to amazing, and certainly not by a man.

"Mama, make Ashton stop."

"I'm not doing anything."

Gina's buoyant mood didn't plummet as far as usual. An amazing woman could handle her children.

"Mama," Gabrielle wailed.

"I'll let you go. Can I call you later, and we'll discuss this more?" Max asked.

"Yes," Gina said. There was no telling what Gabrielle and Ashton were doing.

"Good." Max smiled. Gina wanted to smile back. He was certainly a handsome man and easy to talk to. "Good-bye. I'll go out the way I came in."

Gina didn't try to dissuade him. The moment she closed the back door she headed for the kitchen. It was a good thing she loved her children.

"Looking good."

Alec straightened, knowing he'd see his brother Patrick. He schooled his expression. "Hey, man."

"Hey yourself." Patrick caught the extended hand, clapped his brother on the back.

"You playing hooky?" Alec asked. To be able to help Brianna and her father in their law practice, Patrick was working on a paralegal degree at the local college.

"Finished for the day." He squatted in front of one of the erected posts beside Alec. "I could help after class."

That was what Alec had been afraid of. "This is my wedding present, but thanks. Besides, aren't you already helping Brianna and her father out?"

"Yeah. She's some kind of lawyer." Patrick frowned. "But she gets busy at times and forgets to rest and eat properly. She works hard."

"And you're there to make sure she takes care of herself," Alec said.

Patrick chuckled. "She says I'm worse than her mother. Although the trip to the emergency room a couple of months back proved to be nothing, I still worry about her and the baby."

Alec slapped his brother on the back and tried not to think of another pregnant woman who now had no one to watch over her. "She's fine, and so is my niece or nephew."

"How about you?"

The question had come out of nowhere and caught Alec completely off-guard. "What are you talking about?"

"It's not like you to take off from the force for three months. You love what you do better than any of us," Patrick said, watching his brother closely. "And your cell phone is almost an extension of you, yet you stopped wearing it. This is the third day you've been here by yourself, yet you haven't been by or called."

Alec hoped his smile seemed natural instead of forced. "I decided if I was going to take a vacation, I should really take one. Besides, I don't have time to answer the thing. And by the time I finish here in the evenings I'm too tired to go anyplace."

"It's just not like you," Patrick said, a frown pleating his brow.

"If it will make you feel better, from now on my cell will be hooked to my belt," Alec said, meeting Patrick's probing gaze head-on.

"It would." Patrick glanced around the beautiful but deserted backyard. "You're here by yourself. If you got hurt, there would be no one to help you."

"That's where you're wrong," Alec said; then he explained about Celeste working there. "She brings me lunch every day."

Patrick cocked a brow. "How old is Celeste, and what does she look like?"

Alec opened his mouth to say he wasn't interested, but since at one time he'd dated almost as much as their baby brother, Rafael, who on occasions had two dates in one day, he said instead, "Mid-twenties and hot."

Patrick grinned and slapped Alec on the back. "I see your luck with women is holding."

Alec smiled as was expected of him. "So if I don't see you and Brianna much, don't worry about me."

"We wanted you over for dinner tonight."

"Can't make it," Alec said. "But I'll be here for a while."

"I've never known you to move so fast. She must be something." Patrick glanced toward the house.

"Yeah, so don't mention her to Rafael," Alec said. "You know how he is."

"I won't."

"Good. Now get out of here, and let me get back to work." Alec picked up his hammer. "Give Brianna a hug and a kiss for me."

"Will do. Bye."

A bitter taste in his mouth, Alec watched Patrick disappear around a flowering crape myrtle. He'd had to lie to his brother. It was another reason to feel guilty. There had always been trust between them. That Alec could no longer be that way tore at him.

His hand clenched on the hammer; then he tossed it to the ground and headed for the house. If having the cell would help alleviate his brother's suspicion and worry, he'd just have to deal with it.

Inside, he bounded up the stairs, marveling again that his brother would be living in such a beautiful house. More than the house, he'd found a woman he deeply cared for. At the top of the stairs, Alec glanced toward the other wing where the master suite was located.

Celeste was a puzzle. This morning she'd brought him donuts. She'd worn her usual grin and said she didn't want him doing without while he was away from home. He was positive she hadn't meant the comment as sexual, but that hadn't stopped his body from being aroused. He'd muttered thanks and turned away to hide his response.

He owed her an apology. It wasn't her fault that his life had taken a detour into hell. His mother would be ashamed of him if she knew he'd treated a woman rudely, especially one who was only trying to be nice.

Before he changed his mind, he strode into the bedroom, then rushed to steady the ladder leaning precariously on one leg. "What the hell are you doing?"

Celeste shoved her hand through her long black unbound hair and licked her lips before answering. "Hanging wallpaper."

The fit of his pants got tighter. "You shouldn't be doing it alone."

"Can't be helped. Willie broke the cap off her tooth and is at the dentist." She climbed back down the rungs. "I have to stay on schedule."

"Can't you do something that isn't dangerous?" he asked, trying to keep his gaze from lowering to the jutted fullness of her breasts.

He lost the battle when she took something out of her pocket, gathered her hair on top of her head, and slid it over her hair to make a ponytail. He saw a smooth patch of olive-toned skin and the indentation of her navel. "I've done this before. I just miscalculated."

She prepared another length of paper and climbed the ladder.

Alec grabbed the ladder, his gaze naturally looking upward. She stretched upward, causing her white knit top to rise. His eyes bugged on seeing a small flower at the base of her spine, and the blue elastic of her thong. "Mercy."

"Did you say something?" she asked, smoothing out the paper.

"No." Gritting his teeth, he stared straight ahead. *Think of something else.* "I'm sorry about this morning and the donuts."

Smiling, she glanced down. "Did you enjoy them?"

"I did." After missing dinner last night and breakfast this morning, he was hungry. The beer had only left him thirsty.

"Good." She smoothed the paper out with a long-handled brush as she came down the ladder. "Simon made a good choice with this wallpaper."

Alec's head jerked back up. He stared at the subtle blue-on-blue striped paper. "Simon picked this out?"

Laughter floated over his head. He worked his shoulders. It was easy imagining the same playful laughter in a bed draped with moonlight and Celeste draped over him. "He did. Most men hate wallpaper, but he saw that Maureen liked it and opted for wallpaper instead of paint."

"That sounds like Simon. He'd do anything to make Maureen happy. Just as my other brothers will do for their wives."

"How about you? Would you do anything to make the woman you love happy?"

"Since I haven't met her yet, I couldn't say," he told her, keeping his voice emotionless. He might be doing a little fantasizing about Celeste, but that was as far as he planned to go.

Without a word, Celeste went back to working with the brush. The silence seemed oppressive. For some foolish reason he thought he might have hurt her feelings. Again. Deep in thought, he didn't realize she had come down a step on the ladder until he caught a motion out of the corner of his eye, glanced up, and gulped. Celeste's firm little butt was inches from his face. He stared at the small flower, the blue elastic.

"Alec, you can let go now."

His head jerked up. She stared down at him with a puzzled frown. "Are you all right?"

"Yeah." His fingers uncurled. He stepped back. "If I leave, are you going to work on something else that's safer?"

"This is safe." She came completely down the ladder. "Unfortunately, I'm a creature of habit. I do things in sequences, so the room unfolds. If I get the wallpaper up, I have a good visual as to how the room is going to work or if I need to make adjustments."

"I like knowing where I'm going when I do woodwork, too," he said. "It's a waste of time and money otherwise."

She beamed at him. "Exactly."

He glanced around to break eye contact. *Be careful, Alec.* "All right. Grab a sheet and let's get going."

"You're going to stay?"

"I wouldn't get much work done wondering if you're going to fall."

"I don't want to take you away from what you're doing," she said.

Her reluctance surprised him. He thought she was trying to make him more aware of her. "I'm almost finished with the work for the foundation, so I'm making good time."

"You work fast," she said.

There it was again, subtle words that could be taken entirely differently. "On some things, but in others I'm cautious."

"Since you're a policeman, I'm not surprised." Her arm brushed his as she passed. Tingles ran up his arm. His eyes narrowed. He wasn't certain she hadn't done it on purpose.

Squatting by her supplies, she quickly prepared the next length of paper. "Me, I believe in going all out."

"That could be dangerous," he warned.

She waited until she stood in front of him, her stance as flirtatious as it was challenging. "It could also be very rewarding." Smiling, she moved toward the ladder.

Alec gripped the ladder, more to control his reaction to the tempting woman climbing it than to steady it. This time he watched her every step. She couldn't have made it any plainer; she was coming after him.

All he could think of was that he hoped the good Lord helped them both.

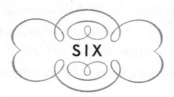

SIX

They were at an impasse, but Celeste had no intention of losing.

"I mean it, Alec."

"So do I."

Celeste stared at Alec. He stared right back.

He wasn't used to being pushed. Tough. She'd seen the hungry, intense way he'd looked at her. He was interested, but he had no intention of giving in to those feelings—which elevated him in Celeste's opinion. Who wanted to spend time with a man who took just for the sake of taking, or one who couldn't control his emotions?

"Ms. de la Vega—"

"Celeste." Before this was over, he'd purr her name. "The only way I'm letting you help me any longer is if we both take a break and eat lunch."

His beautiful black eyes narrowed. "That's a form of blackmail. Did you forget I'm a policeman?"

"Nope." She wasn't about to forget one glorious thing about the very annoyed man standing in front of her, his wide hands on his hips, his sensual mouth compressed in a narrow line. "I'll meet you in the kitchen. I made gumbo."

"You're stubborn."

"So I've heard a few times." Smiling to herself, Celeste left the room and quickly went downstairs to the kitchen. The table was already set for two. She'd thought a great deal about Alec Dunlap last night. He was a man worth getting to know better.

First thing was getting him to eat. When she'd put the things for lunch into the refrigerator, she'd seen the uneaten sandwich she'd left him on Monday, the fish on Tuesday. She had a sneaky suspicion that he wasn't taking care of himself.

Opening the refrigerator, she took out the gumbo and popped it into the microwave, then went back and took out the salad and bottled lemonade. She shook her head on seeing the only things left inside were three bottles of beer. She'd snooped that morning and found nine empty bottles in the trash beneath the sink. Alec was definitely having problems, but drinking wouldn't help. It only caused more problems.

Her eyes briefly shut as a painful memory tugged at her.

"What's the matter?" Alec asked, joining her in the kitchen.

"Nothing. Please have a seat." Going to the cabinets, she took down two glasses and filled them with ice before turning to the table. The timer on the microwave sounded.

"I'll get it."

Surprised but pleased, Celeste said, "Thanks, and don't forget to use pot holders. Please put it here."

Alec placed the Corning Ware dish on the stainless-steel tray, then reached over to hold Celeste's chair. She smiled her thanks and took her seat. As soon as he did the same she bowed her head and blessed the food. Reaching for his bowl, she filled it to the brim. "I hope it's not too spicy. I learned the recipe from Gina, then added my own touch."

"I'm sure it's fine." Alec reached for his spoon.

Aware that a lot of men didn't like to talk while they were eating, Celeste decided to wait until Alec had eaten a bit before she picked up the conversation. Which was a good thing because Alec was hunched over the table, his head down as he ignored her. Celeste couldn't remember a man ever ignoring her.

"How is it?"

"Fine."

Her delicate brow arched. The three men she'd been engaged to had raved about every dish she put in front of them. Alec was definitely a challenge, but one she was up to. "How did you come up with the idea to build the gazebo?"

"Maureen admired Sam and Helen's when she and Simon visited," Alec answered without lifting his head. He kept eating.

"Did you build theirs?" she inquired.

"Yes."

"What else have you built?"

His head slowly came up. It was all Celeste could do to keep from squirming under his intense gaze. "Perhaps you should eat so we could get back to work."

So, he wasn't going to be easy. She picked up her spoon. "How long do you think it will take to finish?"

"Too long." He stood, taking his bowl to the sink. He rinsed it out and placed the earthenware in the dishwasher. "I'll be back in ten minutes. You should be finished by then."

Celeste leaned back in her seat. It seemed Alec couldn't be prodded. He was a harder nut to crack than she had anticipated. Perhaps she should let it go. Then she thought of the nine empty beer bottles, the desolation in his dark eyes.

No way.

Standing, she cleaned up the table and put the food away. Upstairs, she prepared the next length of wallpaper. She was three rungs up when Alec walked into the room. His face was closed. She knew without saying a word that there would be no more talking. He'd been pushed as far as he was going to be pushed.

Continuing up the ladder, she began working. Alec held the ladder, moving back as she came down. She'd never known someone who could remain so still while such turmoil was in their eyes.

Alec obviously wanted to be alone, but he'd put aside his own wants to make sure she was safe. Even after she'd pushed, he'd stayed to ensure her safety. Very few people would be that unselfish. Alec was a man worth saving.

She'd let him have today, she thought as she stepped off the ladder for the last time and found the room empty. But she wouldn't stop trying to get him to open up. She hadn't healed until she'd finally stopped running from her demons and instead confronted them.

Alec needed her, whether he knew it or not.

Finished for the day, she loaded her van and climbed inside. Before pulling away, she took one last look at the house and envisioned Alec's face when he opened the refrigerator.

Tomorrow would be very interesting, she thought as she drove down the quiet street.

The tension didn't finally start to leave Alec until he heard Celeste's van start up. She got to him. There was both sympathy and challenge in her beautiful dark eyes. His hands clenched. She probably knew what had happened to him. The shooting had made national news, thrusting him into an unwanted spotlight.

He'd saved his own life and that of his partner, but he'd taken a life in the process. Sitting on the ground in front of the base of the gazebo, he looked at his hands, saw the fine tremor, felt perspiration dampen his skin.

Closing his eyes, he tried to think of anything except the startled face of the man he'd killed. Celeste's face appeared. Only she wasn't smiling as usual. Her small chin jutted in challenge, her eyes seeing too much.

Alec scrambled to his feet, raking his hand through his hair. Thinking of a woman was the last thing he needed to be doing. Annoyed with himself and Celeste, he went inside the house.

He didn't stop until he stood in front of the refrigerator. He jerked open the door, his hand already reaching for a beer. His long necks weren't there. Even knowing he'd put them on the top shelf, he opened every bin. Empty. He straightened, seeing the gumbo and salad. His eyes narrowed.

Celeste.

He slammed the door shut. She didn't know who she was messing with, but come tomorrow she would!

· · ·

With every rotation of her wheels, Celeste's trepidation grew. No one liked being manipulated. She should know that better than anyone. Yet that was what she had done.

At the next stoplight, instead of pulling through, she took a right, then a left, and headed back to Maureen's house. Her hands flexed on the steering wheel. Alec wasn't going to be happy with her, and she had brought it all on herself.

Pulling into the driveway, she grabbed the key to the front door and quickly went inside. She had barely gone five feet before she saw Alec, his eyes narrowed with anger.

"Who the hell do you think you are?"

"I'm sorry. I thought—"

She almost shrieked as he quickly closed the distance between them, towering over her. "Stay out of my life."

"The beer is in the cabinet over the refrigerator."

"Don't interfere in my life again."

Her knees trembled, but she stood her ground. "I left the rest of the gumbo."

He leaned closer until she could see her reflection in his eyes. "I poured it out."

"Poured it out! You imbecile! Do you know how hard I worked, how long it took, to make that gumbo?"

"No one asked you," he said.

"My mistake. If you want to wallow—" She bit off the words she'd been about to say. If he had been angry at first, he was livid now. His lips flattened into a forbidding line.

Stalking over to the door, he yanked it open. "Leave!"

Her temper abated as quickly as it blew. She had overstepped. "Alec—"

"Now!"

When she messed up, she really did a bang-up job of it. "I'm sorry. I won't bother you again." As soon as she stepped over the threshold, the door slammed behind her. Her bungling attempts to help him through a rough time had made things worse, not better.

Why hadn't she listened to Gina?

Alec cursed a blue streak all the way to the kitchen. Who in the hell did she think she was? His life was his own.

Picking up the small step stool in the kitchen, he placed it in front of the refrigerator, climbed on, and lifted the cabinet door overhead. Muttering, he grabbed two bottles with one hand and one bottle in the other. They were still cold. She must have hidden them just before she left.

Stepping off the stool, he carefully placed the two bottles on the counter when what he really wanted to do was slam them down. One irritated twist of the cap of the third bottle and it came free. He took a long swallow. He wasn't some drunk you had to hide the booze from.

He tilted the bottle to his lips again and again. He'd been drinking beer since he was sixteen.

So he'd had a couple every night since he'd arrived, so what? So he might have one in the morning. He could hold his liquor. Only pansies got drunk off a beer. He tilted the bottle and frowned when he discovered it was empty.

He spat out an expletive, reached for another bottle, and unscrewed the top. He was entitled to a beer with all the stuff he was going through. The worst thing that had probably happened to Little Miss Sunshine was a broken nail.

She might think she knew, but she didn't know squat. The

stark terror he lived with daily. The fear that he'd never be able to return to a job he loved. The guilt that he couldn't assuage. The knot in his gut that he let his family down. The inescapable knowledge that because of him a child would never know its father.

He took a swallow, then another. No woman, especially one he'd just met, was going to stick her nose in his business. It wasn't the hard stuff. She'd better stay—

The phone rang behind him. He spun sharply toward the sound. The room tilted. He reached for the counter to steady himself and hit a beer bottle. He heard the click of the bottle hitting the granite top, reached for the bottle . . .

And missed. He watched helplessly as the bottle seemingly in slow motion hit the granite floor, shattering. Alec stared as the foaming liquid spread out on the floor, the shards of brown glass scattered in every direction. Behind him, the phone clicked on.

"I doubt if you'll get this, since you didn't get the message we left Monday night, but if you happen to be in the kitchen and listening, turn on your bleeping cell phone," Patrick said.

Brianna's happy laughter sounded in the background. "He's practicing so he won't say any bad words around our baby."

"I'm glad you're here. Night," Patrick bade.

"Me, too. You're going to make a wonderful uncle," Brianna said. "Good night."

The machine clicked off. Alec lifted his head and stared from the machine to the mess on the floor. *You're going to make a wonderful uncle.* His eyes shut.

Would a wonderful uncle guzzle two bottles of beer in less than a minute? Blame someone else for his shortcomings? He stared at the bottle still clutched in his hand.

In the past, a six-pack of beer would last a month unless friends came over to his house. He enjoyed a cold beer after a day of working in the yard or when he was out with his friends, but one had been his limit.

"I'm certainly going to try, starting now." Putting the empty bottles in the trash, he went in search of cleaning supplies.

"I should have listened to you," Celeste said when Gina opened the door. Celeste had driven straight there from the confrontation with Alec.

"Come on in and tell me what happened." Gina curved her arm around Celeste's trembling shoulders. "We can talk in the den. The children are in their rooms."

Celeste sat down on the sofa and told Gina everything. "I thought I was helping. He was furious."

"Celeste."

"I know." She clasped her hands in her lap. "I stuck my nose in someone else's very personal business and made things worse."

"You were trying to help," Gina consoled.

"That's of little comfort. I was so sure I had all the answers, that he'd come around to my way of thinking just as others have."

Gina rubbed her hand up and down Celeste's arm. "What are you going to do now?"

"Mind my own business and focus on renovating Maureen's suite," Celeste said. "What I should have done in the first place."

Wanting to take Celeste's mind off what had happened with Alec, Gina said, "Guess who stopped by today?"

"Since you're smiling, it wasn't Robert, I take it."

"Max Broussard," Gina told her, then said, "I showed him the things I thought should be changed at his inn and he wants to hire me. He's supposed to call tonight."

Celeste's eyes widened. "Gina, that's wonderful. You have a good eye."

"But I'm not trained. What if I make a mistake?" Gina said, voicing her concern.

"Even the best get it wrong at times," Celeste said. "But apparently Max liked your ideas."

"He did." Gina's smile returned. "If I'm not sure of something, can I call you?"

Celeste frowned at her. "I ought to hit you for even asking."

Gina laughed. "I guess I'm just nervous. He's offered to pay me."

"Shows he's a fair man. Interior designers charge by the job or the hour. Once you've seen what needs to be done you can decide how you want to do it." Celeste took her friend's arms. "Don't falter. Be firm. You have a service he wants."

"I'll try, but I'm not as assertive as you are," Gina said softly.

"And look what happened," Celeste said. "Alec was so angry, but beneath the anger was the sadness."

"Men don't like being told what to do." Gina wrapped her arms tightly around her waist. "Robert never listened."

"Looks like Max is the exception." Celeste stood. "Let me know how the conversation goes. I'll probably be up."

Gina walked her to the door. "Don't be so hard on yourself."

"I can't help thinking I made things worse." Celeste shook her dark head. "He helped me today, was concerned for my safety, and I repay him this way."

"You don't know that you made it worse."

Celeste shook her head. "You didn't see his face. I've never seen anyone that furious."

"Do you want me to go with you tomorrow?" Gina asked, concerned.

Celeste smiled in reassurance. "Even furious with me, he controlled his anger. Alec Dunlap is not the type of man to abuse a woman."

"Men change," Gina whispered, then hastened to explain as Celeste's eyes narrowed. "I meant about their feelings. Robert never hit me. He just stopped loving me."

"His loss," Celeste said fiercely. "One day he'll see it, but you will have moved on to a better life."

"You don't know how much I want that."

"Start by believing in yourself as much as others do. Take the job Max offered."

She tucked her head for a moment. "You think I'm a coward, don't you?"

"I don't have cowards for friends. You try so hard to please everyone; from tonight on please yourself. You deserve happiness, but sometimes you have to fight for it," Celeste whispered.

"Like you did before you came to Charleston."

A shadow moved in Celeste's eyes. "Yes."

"You wanted Alec to fight, didn't you?"

"Yes, but I handled it the wrong way. Get back inside. I don't want you to miss that call. Night."

"Why don't you come by for breakfast in the morning? I can tell you about the conversation with Max."

"You can also check on me," Celeste said, with a lift of her brow.

Since it was the truth, Gina didn't deny it. "I'll expect you around eight. You know you love my biscuits."

"All right. See you in the morning. Night."

"Good night." When Celeste pulled away from the curb, Gina closed the door, then headed for the stairs. She wanted to check on Gabrielle and Ashton.

In front of Gabrielle's closed door, Gina said a swift prayer to find the right words, then knocked. "Gabrielle."

Silence.

Gina lifted her head, praying for guidance. After Gina settled the squabble earlier, Gabrielle had given her the silent treatment. Ashton had taken advantage of it and talked almost nonstop about how "neat" Mr. Broussard was, how Ashton hoped he could come to his game Saturday.

"He won't," Gabrielle said with entirely too much malice.

"He said he would if he could, didn't he, Mama?" Ashton said, his face filled with a mixture of hope and fear.

Gina frowned at Gabrielle before turning to Ashton. "He said he'd try, but remember, he has to run his inn."

Ashton's head fell forward. "He's busy, just like Daddy."

At that moment Gina could have gladly strangled Robert. He'd been even worse at missing games and practices once he walked out and filed for divorce. He'd been to two games all year and left both times before they were over. He had yet to attend a practice.

It was bad enough that Robert didn't pick the children up every other weekend as he was supposed to; he showed no interest in their extracurricular activities, in them. His response to Gabrielle being the captain of her booster squad was, *That's nice.* Her school team had already performed at two football games and, again, Robert was a no-show.

"I'll be there," Gina said, watching Ashton's head slowly rise. "I'll be yelling for you and your teammates."

He'd smiled and the crisis was averted—for the moment.

Now standing in front of Gabrielle's door, Gina faced another crisis. She felt as if she were doing a delicate balancing act. One wrong move and she'd lose Gabrielle. There were too many bad influences out there, just waiting for troubled teens.

"Gabrielle, honey. Can I come in?" Gina's mother would have had the door open the moment one of her children thought to ignore her, and when she finished with them their backside would have been sore and their father would have been waiting for his turn.

Gina's paternal grandmother had a saying: "Spare the rod and ruin the child." Her parents had taken the saying to heart. Gina had taken the new approach—talking and reasoning— and it wasn't working. Gabrielle wasn't listening or talking.

Gina opened the door. At her desk Gabrielle quickly closed a small pink leather-bound book and swung around in her chair. Her lids were puffy. Gina felt her own eyes sting. It wasn't easy growing up.

"You're supposed to wait until I give you permission to come in," Gabrielle accused.

Gina accepted the reprimand. She'd accidentally found the diary months ago while cleaning Gabrielle's room. Gina hadn't read it, hadn't wanted to invade her daughter's privacy. "You didn't answer, and I was concerned. Are you all right?"

Her arms folded across her chest, which only months ago had been flat; now she needed a training bra. "Just fine. I can't watch TV, talk on the phone to my friends, go out."

Gina closed the door. Ashton wouldn't eavesdrop on purpose, but he wasn't above listening and using what he'd heard to aggravate his sister, his new favorite pastime. "You were deliberately rude. Be glad it was only for a week."

Her chin jutted. "So was Ashton and you didn't do anything to him. You always take his side over mine."

"He only repeated what I said. You were deliberately rude." Gina walked farther into the room. "I love you both equally. You're older, and I expect more from you."

"If Daddy were here, he wouldn't let you punish me this way," she tossed, shooting Gina a belligerent look.

She would have been searching for her head if she'd spoken to her mother that way. But Gina had grown up with supportive, loving parents who still went out of their way to help her. "Your father isn't here. I know it's difficult for you at times, and you're angry, but you can't take it out on other people."

Gabrielle's arms unfolded. "If he was happy, he wouldn't have left us."

Gina didn't recoil or flinch at the accusation. It was the truth. Even a thirteen-year-old could figure that out, but Gina was still the mother. "Gabrielle, if you want to make it two weeks, just keep being rude and disrespectful and I'll see that it happens."

Her daughter folded her arms again and looked away.

"If I could make things the way they used to be, I would," Gina said, not sure if it was the truth anymore. "I can't. So we have to make the best of things."

Silence.

Gina walked over to her. Enough was enough. "Please give me the respect to look at me when I talk to you."

After a moment, Gabrielle slowly brought her gaze to her mother.

"I love you, Gabrielle, but there is only one adult in this house and you're looking at her. I make the rules. Keep pushing me and you aren't going to like the consequences."

A moment of unease flickered in her daughter's eyes. "I could go live with Daddy."

Your father doesn't want you. Want any of us. "I have custody of you except for every other weekend with your father. You're staying here, and you're going to mind and stop lashing out at people because your father isn't here."

"I could ask him," she said.

"Ask all you want, but you're staying here. And you're going to start considering other people and not just yourself," Gina said. "Do I make myself clear?"

Another pause, then, "Yes, ma'am."

"Good." Gina glanced at her watch. "Lights out at nine."

"Yes, ma'am."

Gina's eyes narrowed at her daughter, unable to tell if there had been a bit of bite in the words. "Remember, Gabrielle, it's all up to you. This is just as difficult for me. I don't want us to be at odds."

"Yes, ma'am."

This time Gina was sure there was mockery in her daughter's tone. Gina recalled her grandmother's saying, but she also recalled a Bible scripture, "Do not provoke your children to anger." The strain between her and her daughter wouldn't be solved tonight, and to push it would potentially make things worse between them.

"Good night, Gabrielle." Gina quietly left the room, too achingly aware that Gabrielle had not wished her a good night.

Robert had a lot to answer for.

SEVEN

Max wasn't going to call.

Sitting on the side of her bed later that night, her hands clasped together in her lap, Gina stared at the silent phone on her nightstand. The clock radio read 9:07. A short while ago she'd checked on Ashton and Gabrielle to make sure they were asleep, then come to her room to wait.

There was an extension in her office, but being there was too big a reminder of how slow business was. So she'd come to her room and put off taking her bath for fear she'd miss the call.

She hadn't been aware of how much she wanted to work on the project until now. The money would certainly help, but also important was the opportunity to be of assistance to Max. She knew how it felt when your dream didn't come true. How it made you feel inept, a failure, useless, stupid.

Unfortunately, she was somewhat of an expert on the subject. Robert was always ready to say, *I told you so.*

Was it so bad that she wanted to work from home so that she could be there if her children needed her? Being at home allowed her to volunteer at the school, go on field trips with Ashton. Yet she wasn't sure how she'd manage if her travel agency business failed.

She had to admit Max Broussard didn't appear the type to give up if his plans didn't work out. He'd proven that by his visit to her. Whatever he wanted, he probably went all out to get, just like Celeste. Gina, on the other hand, wasn't a risk taker. She'd tried too many times and ended up falling on her face.

Gina glanced at the silent phone again. What if he'd decided to hire a licensed interior designer? What if he'd decided he didn't need her once he had the list of ideas? What if—

The ringing phone interrupted her thoughts. She jumped. Could it be Max? She'd had caller ID taken off to cut down on the phone bill. With a shaky hand she picked up the receiver. "Hello."

"Hello, Mrs. Rawlings, it's Max Broussard."

Her eyes closed briefly in relief. "Hello, Mr. Broussard," she said, moistening her lips.

He chuckled. " 'Max,' since we're going to be working together."

"Max." *He still wants her.*

"I hope it isn't too late to call," he said. "I knew you'd have to get Ashton and Gabrielle to bed and ready for school tomorrow."

"That was considerate of you," she said. "They're in bed, and we can talk."

"Good. I showed everything to Aunt Sophia and she liked

your ideas as well. If possible, we'd like for you to come over tomorrow for lunch and we can do another walk-through."

Her schedule for the next day was completely blank, since she'd finished with the travel itinerary for her parents and their friends. But should she talk money now or tomorrow?

"Mrs. Rawlings?"

"I was just thinking about my schedule," she said, which wasn't exactly a lie.

"About your salary," he went on to say. "My aunt went on-line and called several interior design firms since we know this is not your chosen field. We can go over that tomorrow and settle on a fee."

"Celeste told me, depending on the project, designers are paid by the job or the hour, but I'm not a designer, of course," she felt compelled to say. If she wanted him to be fair, she had to be the same way.

"In my opinion, you don't have to have the initials behind your name to be a designer. Let's talk about it tomorrow if you can come for lunch," he said. "Of course, I'm prepared to give you a consultation fee at the very least."

"Consultation fee." She stood to her feet.

"Yes. It's standard procedure, my aunt learned. You get what I want the B and B to be," he told her. "Another designer might not."

"Southern gentility and down-home charm. Understated elegance."

"Exactly," Max said, a smile in his deep baritone voice. "You're the one I want."

Unexpectantly the softly spoken words sent a warm tingle through her. She felt a bit overheated.

"Do we have a deal?"

Go on, Gina. Take a chance on life, a small voice whispered. "Yes."

"Great. Would eleven thirty be all right?"

"Yes, and thank you," she said.

"I'm the one who should be thanking you. Good night, Mrs. Rawlings."

" 'Gina,' since we're going to be working together," she said, smiling.

"Good night, Gina. Sleep well."

"I will. Good night, Max." Sitting on the bed, she hung up the phone, aware that there was a huge grin on her face. She'd done it. Picking up the phone, she punched in Celeste's home phone number.

"Hello," Celeste said.

"I took the job. I'm going over there tomorrow for lunch and he's paying me a consultation fee," she blurted out.

"Way to go," Celeste said, excitement in her voice. "You can do this."

"I'm going to try," Gina said before her smile faded. "Are you all right?"

"I feel like crap."

"Celeste, you don't know that he's still upset," Gina told her. Celeste might be impulsive, but she was also a kind and generous woman. "Good night. I'll see you in the morning. I can tell you more then."

"Wonderful. I can't wait to hear it. Good night."

Gina sat smiling for a minute longer, then got up to take a bath and get ready for bed. Thanks to Max, life had taken a definite upward swing.

· · ·

It was good to have a friend to share things with, Gina thought as she talked with Celeste the next morning at the small breakfast table in the kitchen. For the first time in months Gina was the one with exciting news. As they ate breakfast, Gina went over Max's visit.

"Max is becoming more interesting by the moment. Tell me more about him," Celeste said as she forked in a bite of honey-cured ham.

Seated across from Celeste, Gina frowned, lowering her coffee cup. "Max?"

Celeste rolled her eyes. "Gina, I don't know what I'm going to do with you. Max Broussard is a gorgeous hunk with the body of a Greek god."

Gina didn't know why she flushed again. "Celeste, this is just business."

"Who said you can't mix business with pleasure?" she said. "You won't make the mistake I did. You aren't pushy."

Gina wished she could do or say something to help. "I envy you your assertiveness. I'm a pushover and everyone knows it."

"Tell you what," Celeste said with a hint of her old self as she lifted her coffee cup. "Let's make a pact this morning that I'll try to be less pushy if you try to be more assertive. We'll compare notes, and the one who does the best wins lunch."

Gina lifted her cup. "Deal."

"Deal." Celeste touched her cup to Gina's, then drank her coffee. "Today will test our new resolve." She placed her cup in her saucer and picked up her fork. "I know, but at least I won't have to face him on an empty stomach." She picked up her biscuit, fluffy and light. "I still can't believe he threw out my gumbo. At least he didn't throw me out of the hou—" Her eyes widened.

"What is it?" Gina asked.

"What if he called Maureen and Simon and told them what happened?" Celeste asked, worry in her voice.

"From what you've said, I don't think he wants his family knowing he's having post-traumatic stress," Gina said, her fork poised over her scrambled eggs.

"You're right." Celeste bit into her biscuit. "He wouldn't have called them."

"Exactly." Gina placed her fork on her plate. "Are you sure you don't want me to go with you this morning?"

"I am. If he wants to chew on me, which is his right, then he'll have his chance." Celeste finished her coffee.

"If you change your mind, call."

"It won't be necessary, but I'd better get to it." Celeste stood and pushed her chair beneath the table. "Both of us are going to have an eventful day."

"That we will."

Celeste pulled into the driveway of Maureen's house and switched off the motor. Instead of getting out, she slumped back against the leather seat. Usually she wasn't afraid of confrontation. Speaking her mind had often landed her at odds with people. She'd never minded before or considered pulling back. So why did she hesitate this time?

The answer was simple: She'd hoped that she and Alec could be friends. Well, a bit more than friends, but it would start with friendship. She had ruined any chance of them growing closer. Worse, she'd stuck her nose into his personal affairs, a definite no-no. Some men's egos were the size of Alaska and bruised easily.

She should have stopped to think before she hid the beer. An assertive, take-charge man like Alec wouldn't want anyone pointing out that he might be drinking too much. But she knew better than anyone how alcohol destroyed lives.

"You can't sit here all day," Celeste muttered to herself, then climbed out of the van and went to the front door. Cautiously she opened it and peered inside, listened. Her shoulders sagged in relief when she didn't see Alec. She didn't have a doubt that she'd see him before too long, but she wasn't ready to face his anger again and know she was to blame.

Leaving the heavy door slightly ajar, she went to the van and opened the back door. Today she planned on covering the walls surrounding the window bench with a silk fabric that matched the wallpaper. The same silk fabric would be used to upholster the window bench as well, the elaborate swags and jabots covering the fourteen-foot windows, the duvet and drapes around the bed, and at least five custom pillows of the fifteen in varying designs on the bed.

A custom-printed silk linen stripe on the bed pillows, shams, and bed skirt would introduce butter yellow and soft peach to the blue and beige palates that meandered throughout the house. Two Venetian rococo armchairs in cream chenille that dated back to the eighteenth century placed in front of the fireplace would offer a spot for Maureen and Simon to curl up with a book or each other. The suite with its upholstered furniture, relaxed yet elegant fabrics, and period antiques would be the height of luxury without squandering comfort when finished.

Picking up two rolls of batting and her toolbox, Celeste locked the van's back door and went back inside. And came face-to-face with Alec. It was all she could do not to drop the things in her hands and run back to the van.

His face was hard, his eyes harder. She searched her mind for something to say that might make him understand she was sorry, but nothing came.

"You have no right to interfere in my life, but maybe it was a good thing that you did."

She couldn't have been more surprised if he'd kissed her. "What?"

"However, I think it's best that we stay out of each other's way from now on," Alec said, his gaze intent. "I don't need anything from you, not food, not advice, not anything. Understand?"

Ouch, but she'd brought it on herself. "All right."

Nodding, he walked past her. She couldn't help but turn and follow his progress through the living room and out the terrace doors. He couldn't have made it any clearer. He wanted no part of her. She'd known he'd feel that way before she arrived, so why did hearing him say the words wound her so deeply?

It's done, Alec thought as he set another post in concrete for the gazebo. He'd thanked Celeste and asked her to leave him alone. Not in the most gracious fashion, but it had to be that way.

He'd have to be blind to not see the signals she was sending. Now wasn't the time to get mixed up with a woman, especially one as beautiful, perceptive, and intelligent as Celeste. She saw too much, made him feel too much.

It was best for her, as much as for him. What would any woman, especially one who probably had her pick of men, want with a cop who didn't have his head on straight? Nothing.

He picked up the next post. She didn't impress him as a

good-time woman. If she was, she probably would have brought him another twelve-pack instead of donuts and coffee.

Lifting his head, Alec started toward the house. If the wind was just right, the breeze swayed the tall oak tree just enough for him to see one of the windows of the master suite. Annoyed with himself, he abruptly turned away to pick up another post. He was here to build a gazebo and nothing else. It was none of his business if she was putting herself in danger again. She was a professional.

He put in a third post, unable to keep from glancing upward. Now that he'd started thinking of her putting herself at risk again, he couldn't seem to get it out of his mind. She'd had a toolbox and a roll of something that looked like cotton beneath her arm—which didn't give him a clue what she planned today.

Grumbling to himself, he set the last post. After this morning she certainly wouldn't ask him to help. He had a sneaking suspicion that even if they were on speaking terms, she was the self-reliant type. Women! Whoever said you couldn't live with them and couldn't live without them had certainly hit the nail on the head.

Finished, Alec jerked off his work gloves and admitted defeat. Stuffing them in the back pocket of his jeans, he went inside the house. Stopping at the terrace door, he took off his work shoes, then went up the stairs. He'd just take a quick peek. If she was on that ladder again, he had no idea what he'd do. Perhaps he should have taken that fishing trip instead of building the gazebo. But he hadn't wanted his family worried about him, had wanted to do something constructive with his time that he could look back on as worthwhile.

Showing Simon and Maureen he wished them every

happiness had seemed the right move. It still did. If he didn't have to worry about Little Miss Sunshine.

Alec's steps slowed on the runner in the hallway. She hadn't been smiling this morning and it was because of him, because she had tried to help him and, instead of being grateful, he'd acted like an ass.

His long-fingered hand shoved its way through his hair. He'd taken his bad behavior out on her.

Finding no way around it, he entered the master suite. Across the room, Celeste stood on the bare window seat, stapling the roll he'd seen to the area around the window above the window seat. He frowned, then took an involuntary step into the room. He thought he'd heard his name.

"Take that, Alec Dunlap. And that."

He silently shook his head. Celeste wasn't the type of woman to let a man throw her for long. She'd give as good as she got.

"Pour out my gumbo, shout at me. Well, this one is right between the eyes, this one farther south."

"Ouch."

Celeste whirled, almost toppling off the seat. Alec quickly crossed the room, but by the time he reached her she had righted herself. "Are you trying to get me killed?"

"Hardly," he said. With her back to the window and the sun pouring over her, she looked magnificent and sensuously beautiful enough to make any man beg.

"You come to take another shot at me?"

He stopped inches from her, his gaze direct. "I wanted to see what was on the agenda for today."

Celeste's brow lifted in surprise. "Why?"

She didn't take things at face value. He liked that. "You

have a tendency to take chances without thinking of the consequences."

She stared at him a long time, then gracefully came down from the window seat. "Which incidents are you referring to?"

"You like to push, don't you?" he asked.

She shrugged her elegant shoulders. "Sometimes."

What do you do with a woman who refuses to back down? Alec didn't have a clue and he was afraid Celeste knew it when a smile spread across her enchanting face. Today she wore a pink T-shirt that cupped her high, firm breasts and tempted him to do the same. He slid his hands into the pockets of his jeans.

"We both have deadlines," he said reasonably. "Maureen said you were in high demand. You probably have another job already scheduled. If you're injured, you won't be able to work."

"So why should that concern you?"

"I don't want you hurt if I could prevent it," he rasped.

The smile left her face instantly. She touched his shoulder briefly before lowering her hand. "You'd never allow that to happen."

He stiffened, knowing she was no longer talking about her. He saw the concern in her eyes and looked away. He wasn't sure he deserved it, but at least it wasn't pity.

"I'm padding the walls over the window seat, then faux painting the walls in the bathroom. I'll be perfectly safe," she said. "Thank you for watching out for me."

"This doesn't mean anything. I'd do it for anyone," he told her, as much for his benefit as hers.

"I never doubted it," Celeste said, smiling up at him.

He didn't want to admit how much the smile, the caring that came with it, meant to him. "I'll be going."

"Thanks for checking on me, Alec."

"Yeah." Turning, he left the room before he did something stupid like brushing a loose curl from her forehead, kissing her trembling lips. He had made sure she was safe, but he wasn't sure about himself any longer where she was concerned.

EIGHT

Max came out of the front door of Journey's End as soon as Gina pulled onto the driveway even with the house. Her heart thumped. She honestly couldn't have said if it was from fear or excitement.

What was she doing here? She wasn't a decorator. She wasn't much of anything. *But wasn't that just what I wanted to change?* a small voice whispered. Grabbing her shoulder bag, she opened the door of her seven-year-old Ford sedan.

"Good morning, Gina. Welcome again to Journey's End." Curling his fingers around the door frame, he reached out to give her a hand to help her out. It struck her again how courteous he was.

"Thank you." She stood, drawing her hand back and looking around. "It's so beautiful and peaceful here."

"I was lucky enough that the house sat on two acres, and

able to pay the hefty asking price," Max told her. "I know that it was worth it. Journey's End can be what we envisioned."

Another moment of unease slithered down her spine. "I'm not a professional decorator."

His dark gaze settled gently on her face. "But you have the vision of what I want to accomplish. You can help me make this work. Come on, and let's go inside."

Gina allowed him to lead her into the house. Strangely, once she was inside, her fears began to recede. Her steps slowed. Max paused and glanced down at her. She flushed and tucked her head. "I'm sorry. I was just thinking that if we took the large armoire out of the first bedroom it could go against the wall facing the entry as a focal point."

He stared at her so long she became nervous. "You're amazing."

Gina blinked. First "fantastic," then "amazing," and all compliments from the same man.

"You've been here once and you can already visualize what to do," he said, awe in his voice.

"I wanted to live in an older home, so I pored over a lot of magazines," she explained. "I probably saw the idea there."

"I still think it's amazing that you can remember the room." He started walking again. "Let's eat first and then get started. By the way, the clock started ticking the moment you pulled up in the driveway."

She paused. She didn't like taking money to help someone.

"What is it?" His hold on her arm gentled. "I don't think it's furnishings this time."

Her hand clenched on the strap of her handbag. "It's just that— I don't like taking money to help someone."

His other hand lifted to take her arm. He stared down at

her. "You're offering a service just as you do to your other clients. You're going to help those who come here enjoy it all the more. For that you deserve to be paid."

"Thank you." She could do this.

"You're helping me." He entered the dining room. His aunt held a pitcher of tea in her hand. "Gina, you remember my aunt Sophia, don't you?"

"Yes. Hello, Ms. Durand."

"Hello, Gina, and please call me Sophia. I try to forget my age and single status," she said, filling the last glass on the table.

Gina didn't know if she meant it or was joking. Max still wore his jovial expression.

"Please have a seat." He pulled out a chair. "Aunt Sophia, please sit down. I'll finish everything else."

Gina had started to sit, straightened. "Is there anything I can do to help?"

Max chuckled and winked at his aunt, who smiled back. "Since we're both lost in the kitchen, I ordered our lunch. I just have to put it in serving dishes."

Gina barely kept the shock from her face. She'd been cooking since she was a little girl. Even Celeste, who usually ate out, was a fantastic cook. "Then who cooks?"

"Max was smart enough to buy a freezer and a microwave," Sophia quipped. "We get by."

"Why don't I help you with everything?" Gina said. "I want to see your kitchen again."

"Why?" Max asked with a frown.

She looked between the two. "Because one of my suggestions to make Journey's End stand out is a signature dish and drink made from products grown in Charleston."

. . .

His instincts were right. It did Max good to know that contacting Gina Rawlings had been on target. She had a grasp of what he was trying to do, and a shy way about her that was endearing. She was also a hard worker. They'd finished lunch two hours ago and they were still coming up with ideas to enhance Journey's End.

"A friend of mine, Maureen Gilmore-Dunlap, owns an antique shop, Forever Yours. She might be able to take two of the bedroom sets. She is on her honeymoon in Europe, but her assistant should have a way of reaching her," Gina said, inspecting the chest on chest in a brown cherry finish.

"She's going to take time for business on her honeymoon?" Sophia asked incredulously.

Gina threw an embarrassed glance at Max and tucked her head. But Max had seen the flush that stained her cheeks. He hadn't seen a woman blush in years.

"The second part of her honeymoon is a buying trip," Gina explained, finally lifting her head. "I should be able to contact her after next week."

"That leaves the other two crowded rooms," Max said. Looking at it with new eyes, he could see what Gina meant.

Gina's fingers trailed along the dresser; then she looked up and smiled. For some odd reason, Max felt a ripple of response in a place that had no business responding. "We can put this chest in the living room, the armoire in the hallway. Is there any room on the third floor for furniture pieces?"

"The halls are wide. Besides our bedrooms, the other two are empty," Max answered.

"Good. I'd like to move out the dresser and put in a chair

and a small writing table. The armoire can stay. In the next bedroom, I think the bench in the living room would look great under the window. The seat padded, of course, with the same fabric on the window above. It would allow your guests to have a great view of the river," she said.

"You certainly can pick 'em, Max," Sophia said with jubilance.

Max didn't know how to respond. He wondered if his aunt recalled she'd said the same thing about Sharon.

Gina glanced at her watch. "I'm afraid I have to leave. I need to pick the children up from school. Ashton has soccer practice immediately afterward."

"We understand. Thank you, Gina," Sophia said. "I'm going to my room. Max can show you out."

"Of course," Max said, taking Gina's arm.

"I hope I didn't tire her out," Gina said as they walked into the hall and watched his aunt head for the stairs.

"Hardly," he said truthfully. "She does calisthenics for an hour each day." He checked to make sure the coast was clear and leaned over. "She's hooked on soap operas. The two things she insisted we have were cable and a minimum thirty-two-inch flat screen in her room."

Gina laughed. Max smiled down at her. "You should do that more often."

She flushed and continued down the hallway. "There haven't been too many things to laugh about lately."

"Hopefully that's going to change now," he said.

She regarded him solemnly but said nothing. Max's brow furrowed. Had that been a come-on or was he simply being compassionate? He honestly didn't know; all he knew was that she looked as if she hadn't had it easy, yet she went out of her way to help others. A compassionate woman like that deserved to be happy. He didn't think she was.

He'd studied her Web site, checked the dismal stats. He doubted she'd gotten very much business from the site. If he didn't miss his guess, her business wasn't doing well, yet she had taken time to help him and was a bit embarrassed about taking the check he'd given her after they finished lunch. He'd paid for ten hours up front to ensure that she returned. If they went over that time, they'd look at paying her by the job.

He opened the front door for her. She walked past him and turned. "I think we're off to a good start."

"So do I," Max said, meaning it. "Can you come by tomorrow?"

He thought he saw something flicker in her eyes but couldn't be sure. "Why don't I come around the same time? This time I'll bring lunch."

"I probably should protest about lunch, but thanks."

She smiled. "I like to cook, and after lunch we can walk over the grounds."

"To see where the wisteria arbor will go," he said.

"Yes, it will be a focal point, but there's more," she said. "If you're agreeable to a cottage garden, you can place stone pavers on the sloping backyard leading to the pier."

"I don't—" He stopped and smiled. "I suppose you're thinking of a pier?"

"It would be wonderful for your guests to be able to meander through the flowers, then down to the pier to fish or just relax," she said wistfully.

"Did you grow up near the water?"

She looked startled. "Yes."

"And you were happy," he said, already knowing the answer.

"Yes," she repeated softly. Turning abruptly, she went to her Ford and got in. "Good-bye, Max. Thanks for the check."

"Good-bye, Gina." He placed his hand on top of the car, then stepped back. "Drive carefully, and tell Ashton I said hello."

"I will."

Max stood in the yard as she backed up into the street, his eyes on the tires. They looked all right, but he planned to inspect them better the next time she came over. Getting to know her better was proving to be an unexpected pleasure.

If Alec had a wish at the moment, it would be that the cell phone had never been invented. He'd received five calls in the last hour. Three of his brothers had called, then an old girlfriend who wanted to hook up and a telemarketer. Alec hadn't wanted to talk to any of them.

He ignored Patrick's ring tone, an old Otis Redding tune, and pondered his present problem. He'd forgotten he'd had his brother's help when he'd built the gazebo. He couldn't hold the beam and nail it at the same time.

Alec wasn't about to ask Patrick to help. He could only keep up the "everything is fine in my life" for so long before his nerves began to fray. He could hire someone, but that would take time, and besides, he didn't want to bring anyone he didn't completely trust to work here. Thieves often used jobs as covers to case the place.

Case in point, Maureen's house had been burglarized by one of the workers who had been redoing her kitchen. Hands on his hips, Alec pondered his dilemma.

"Problem?"

He whirled around to see Celeste with a pitcher of iced tea. "You don't listen, do you?"

" 'Why, thank you, Celeste, for thinking of me while I worked outside.' " She set the pitcher and a glass on a stack of lumber with a clunk. "How you could be related to a nice guy like Simon heaven only knows."

Whirling, she stalked back down the path. *Hell,* Alec thought, and chased after her, catching her by the arm, then had to duck a right swing. His foot wasn't so lucky.

"Ouch," she said, grabbing the heel of her tennis shoe–shod foot.

Alec smiled despite the situation. "Steel-toed work shoes."

"I know one thing that isn't steel, so I suggest you release me," she said sweetly—too sweetly.

With his arms around her, her back to him, he felt her alluring softness. He thought it might be worth it.

"Now."

His arms loosened. He stepped back as she turned around and glared at him. "I'm usually a nice guy. People like me."

"You could have fooled me."

He couldn't very well tell her he acted stupid because she tempted him more than he thought possible. "The past few days haven't been my best."

She folded her arms. "Tell me something I don't already know."

I wish I had met you months ago, he thought. "I'm not used to not being in control."

Her face softened, her arms unfolded. "I'm a good listener."

He shook his head, surprised he had confessed that much. His life was private. "I'll work it out."

"The invitation still stands." She stepped around him. "It's coming along. Who is coming to help you attach the beams to the posts?"

Quickly he went to her. "You know about construction?"

"In my business, it pays to know as much as possible." She gave him one of those special smiles that twisted his insides. "Since you're a policeman, you wouldn't be surprised at how dishonest some people are. Shoddy work, inferior supplies, double billing. The list goes on and on."

"I don't suppose you'd have time to give me a hand?"

Her dark eyes twinkled. "I think you'll need two."

He stood there staring down at her, feeling himself being pulled into those mesmerizing eyes, the beguiling smile. "My gloves are too large for you, but they should protect your hands."

She was slow in taking the gloves he handed her. "What about you?"

"I might be many things, but I'd never let you be hurt while trying to protect myself," he said.

"I never thought you would." She slipped on the gloves, wiggled her fingers. "Let's get this show on the road."

Alec jerked the phone from his belt. It was either that or throw the thing as far as he could. "Yeah."

"Who pulled your chain?"

"Patrick, I'm kind of busy," Alec said, attaching another board at the base of the gazebo.

"You're invited to dinner tonight at six P.M."

"No can do, thanks. I'm too busy." He hammered in a nail,

wishing he had a nail gun. He always thought the same thing in the midst of a project, but after seeing the damage one could do to a person and the deep indentation in wood he'd decided to continue the old-fashioned way.

"No excuses. You need to eat. You're going to hurt Brianna's feelings if you don't come."

Damn. He came to his feet, wiping sweat from his brow with the sleeve of his shirt. He'd do anything for Brianna. Love had given Patrick all he wanted in life. Love. They'd understand that. "Can't. I have a date."

"The interior decorator you mentioned?" Patrick asked, then continued at Alec's silence, "Like I said, you work fast."

"Not at this rate. Bye, Patrick." Alec disconnected the call, then went back to work, this time ignoring Patrick's ring tone, "(Sittin' On) The Dock of the Bay."

Alec glanced at his watch. Five fifty-five. Celeste usually left around six. Adjusting the utility belt, he went inside. He didn't think she'd tell him if her hands were sore, but he wanted to see for himself.

Celeste was something, caring and seductive, with an inner strength that called to him. On the terrace, he removed his boots. In his stocking feet, he continued through the living room. At the bottom of the stairs, the doorbell rang.

He glanced around and barely kept from cursing on seeing Patrick's truck through the windows by the door. No wonder they'd nicknamed him Bloodhound at the station. Once he had something in his head, it stayed.

The chime came again.

"Aren't you going to see who it is?" Celeste asked from the top of the stairs.

Alec's lie about a date came back to bite him on the rear. "I'll get it. You can go back to work."

She sent him a strange look, then went back down the hall. Alec waited until he couldn't see her, then went to the door. "Hello, Patrick. I was just about to get cleaned up."

"Glad I caught you." He stepped forward. Alec had to move to the side. "I don't want you to be late for your date."

It was all he could do to keep from looking over his shoulder. "Can't have that, so let's talk later." He stepped around his brother and reached for the door.

"If I didn't know better, I'd think you were trying to get rid of me." Patrick smiled. "You want her all to yourself, huh?"

"Yes," Alec answered, disturbed when the words felt so right.

Patrick looked behind his brother and smiled. "Too late, and all I have to say is that you're right, you'd better not let Rafael see her."

Slowly Alec turned to see Celeste coming down the stairs. He gritted his teeth. His lie was about to take a bite out of his backside all right.

Patrick stepped forward to take the toolbox from Celeste with one hand and extend his other. "Patrick Dunlap. Alec's older brother. You must be the woman he mentioned."

"Celeste de la Vega," she said, her gaze going to Alec. "And what exactly did he say?"

Patrick chuckled. "Nothing bad, I assure you. Just that you two had a date tonight. I just wanted to see the woman that has been tying up all of my brother's time," Patrick said, a grin on his face.

Celeste's gaze again flickered to Alec, his tightly drawn mouth. He was angry—so what else was new? "He did, did he? What else did Alec say?"

"Not much, except you're the reason he hadn't been around much since he's been here." Patrick turned to slap Alec playfully on the back. "I can see why."

"That's very kind of you to say," Celeste said. At least his brothers liked her.

"No more than the truth," Patrick said. "I'll get out of here. You two have fun tonight. I expect both of you Sunday around eleven for brunch. Afterward we're going to take the boat out."

Alec's eyes darted to Celeste. "She might have plans."

She smiled sweetly. "As a matter of fact, I don't. Thank you for the invitation. Should I bring anything?"

"Just a hearty appetite." Patrick clasped Alec on the shoulder again. "You had me worried."

Exactly what he had wanted to avoid. "I've just been busy."

"But you've been here almost a week and you haven't been by the house once or to see Brooke. That's not like you."

To the Dunlaps, family was important and came first. Brooke was their favorite niece and lived in Charleston. "I wanted to get as much work done as possible. You never know when it might rain," Alec said.

Since Patrick didn't look as if he were buying Alec's explanation, Celeste said, "I threw him off-schedule. He helped me when my assistant was ill. We both want to have things finished when Simon and Maureen return."

"Another reason to be there Sunday. Simon called last night and said he'd call me Sunday. He and Maureen are having a great time and he's learning about antiques."

The tension around Alec's mouth eased. "You're taking para-legal courses to help Brianna. Now Simon is learning about antiques, but I can't see him in her store."

"When you find that special woman, you want to do every-thing you can to make life easy for her, to show her you care, to be with her." Patrick glanced at his watch. "I'd better get going. I'm picking Brianna up after work."

"Her car in the shop?"

Patrick momentarily tucked his head. "She has a hard time getting in and out of her Benz, plus I worry about what might happen if she has to stop suddenly with her stomach so close to the steering wheel."

"I'd say Brianna is one lucky woman," Celeste said.

"I'd like to think so." Patrick opened the door. "Bye, Alec, Celeste. See you both on Sunday."

Alec closed the door and faced Celeste. He didn't like the smile on her face. "Celeste, I appreciate you helping me out. I had no idea that Patrick would come over here."

"So we're not going out?"

It was all he could do not to shift nervously under her steady gaze. "You know we don't have a date. I just said that so he'd let me have some space."

Folding her arms, she tilted her head to study him. "Are you in the habit of lying to your brother?"

He knew where she was heading and didn't like it one bit. "Of course not."

"I didn't think so." She headed for the stairs. "I'll leave my address on the island in the kitchen."

"Celeste—"

"I think Sticky Fingers. Neither one of us will have to worry about dressing up." She looked back over her shoulder. "Plus I love their ribs. I'll be ready at seven thirty."

"You aren't going to let me out of this, are you?"

"I might if . . ." Her voice trailed off.

"If what?" he prompted.

Her smile was slow, sexy and entirely too tempting. "Since you're the detective, I'll let you figure it out. Now I have to finish cleaning up. And by the way, I don't like to be kept waiting."

Alec watched her climb the stairs, his gaze unerringly settling on the enticing sway of her hips. He was afraid he already knew the answer. He wanted to take her out. If his life hadn't been in such turmoil, he'd have asked her out when he'd seen her at the wedding reception.

Rubbing the back of his neck, Alec headed outside. He could handle tonight, and Sunday she'd probably be with the other women.

All he had to do was get through tonight.

NINE

"*I wanted to stop by to see how things went today, but from the* smile on your face I already know," Celeste teased as she stepped into Gina's foyer.

Gina's smile widened. "It was wonderful. Max liked everything. He's fantastic."

Celeste tilted her head to one side. "You like him."

"Of course. He's courteous, thoughtful—" Gina abruptly stopped when she saw the teasing grin widen on Celeste's face. "What is it?"

Not wanting to make Gina aware of how animated she was when talking about Max, Celeste said, "Nothing. I'm just glad you see what I've always told you."

Gina's smile dimmed. "I always wanted to please Robert, and failed so many times."

"He failed you and your children," Celeste said hotly. She

detested him for leaving Gina, for making her doubt herself. Celeste had never told Gina, but she'd never liked Robert and thought Gina could do better if she could just get her confidence up. "Never forget that he was the one who couldn't stick."

"You don't know how hard I'm trying, but after doing everything to please a man for almost fourteen years, it isn't easy to move on and be my own woman," Gina confessed.

"You'll do it," Celeste told her firmly. "You have so many people pulling for you."

"I have to." Gina looked into the backyard, where Gabrielle kicked soccer balls to Ashton. "I have to for their sakes."

"Gabrielle still acting like the world revolves around her?" Celeste asked, narrowing her eyes as Gabrielle, probably intentionally, kicked the soccer ball ten feet wide of the net Ashton guarded. The smile on her face as Ashton, hands on his hips, said something to her proved it.

"I don't know what to do with her," Gina said. "I didn't want her holed up in her room like a prisoner, so I let her kick balls to Ashton." Gina shook her head. "She keeps taunting him. I was about to go out and send her to her room when you rang the doorbell."

"And when you do it, add all of Ashton's chores for the week," Celeste advised. "My neighbor has seven children and they all walk a straight line."

Gina folded her arms. "The children probably have both parents."

"No, they don't. He walked when the youngest was two." Celeste started from the kitchen. "She said since they outnumbered her, she had to be meaner and smarter. She loves her children and they love her back." Celeste stopped at the front door. "You let Gabrielle be stronger and meaner because you hurt for her, but *chica,* it's not working. She's making everyone miserable."

"I guess it's time for tough love," Gina said slowly.

"Way past due." Celeste opened the door. "Talk to you tomorrow."

"I almost forgot; how did things go with Alec today?" Gina asked when Celeste was midway down the walk.

Celeste tossed her a saucy grin. "We have a dinner date tonight."

"What? You're kidding?" Gina rushed down the sidewalk. "What happened to change things?"

"Long story. Suffice is to say he's taking me out under duress, but I'm hoping before the night is over he'll have warmed up to me," Celeste said, determination in her eyes.

"Alec is a goner," Gina said with a laugh.

Celeste's laughter mixed with hers. "Hope so." She hooked her thumb over her shoulder. "Go rescue Ashton and show Gabrielle who is meaner and smarter."

"I'm on it. Have fun." Gina spun on her heels and went back inside, closing the door after her.

Gabrielle, you're in for it now. In the past Gina had never closed the door, no matter what time of day or night it was, until Celeste was safely in her car, the motor running. Her leaving now said a lot. Gina was taking control of her life. *About time,* Celeste thought, and climbed into her van. Starting the motor, she pulled out onto the street and headed for the freeway.

She and Alec were each fighting for control of whatever it was that was happening between them. Alec wanted to ignore the sexual sparks flaring; she wanted to fan them. Dangerous and a first for her, but there was no way she was backing down or turning her back on what she felt in her soul was going to be important to her.

"Watch out, Alec. I'm coming for you."

Alec considered not going, but that would have meant standing Celeste up. He didn't have a doubt that she expected him. He'd gotten himself into this mess, and he had no idea how to get himself out.

Climbing out of his truck in front of her house on a quiet street, he shut the door. Business must be good. The single-story Mediterranean-style stucco home with a red clay barrel roof sat on at least a quarter acre. Celeste might have trouble with camellias but not, it seemed, with other flowers. They were everywhere. Peeking out from beneath the boxwoods surrounding the house, in pots on either side of the step, and anchoring the house.

He stepped on the sidewalk leading to the eight-foot arched door and paused. This was a mistake.

The front door opened. Celeste stepped onto the porch and propped one hand on the door frame. His breath stalled in his lungs.

She might be a tiny thing, but the woman had knockout legs. He'd always seen her in pants. Tonight she had on a little black skirt that stopped five inches above her knees, a white blouse, high-heeled sandals. He knew this was a bad idea.

Lowering her hand, she came down the steps and didn't stop until she stood directly in front of him. "You're five minutes late."

"This is a bad idea," he said. There was no sense beating around the bush.

"We're just going out to dinner, just as you told your brother."

His gaze flickered over her face, exquisite and unforgettable. "This is not going to work."

"I'll get my purse and lock the door." Turning, she walked back up the steps. His gaze was again drawn to the enticing sway of her hips. Why couldn't she have buck teeth and a rail-thin body?

Celeste disappeared inside the house, then came back almost instantly. Clearly she had been waiting for him.

Alec joined her on the small porch. "Did you lock both locks?"

She smiled and hooked her arm through his, undisturbed when he jumped. "Yes, and the timer for the landscape lights comes on at nine and goes off at five."

Alec started toward the truck at a fast clip. If Celeste's tempting body weren't enough, the tantalizing fragrance she wore made him want to tear off her clothes with his teeth. He opened the door and helped her in, then bit back a groan as the skirt slid up farther. He slammed the door and rounded the truck. Inside, he started the motor and pulled away from the curve, his gaze straight ahead.

"How are things going with the gazebo?" she asked.

"Good." He threw a quick glance in her direction. "Thanks again for your help today."

"No problem. If you need to hire someone to help out, I know a couple of reliable men," she told him. "Both are retired, and helping at odd jobs gives them purpose and extra income."

"I'll keep that in mind." He eased to a signal light. "How about you?"

"I'm making good progress. I can't wait to see Maureen's and Simon's reaction when they see the master suite."

"How long have you been a decorator?" he asked. There was such excitement in her voice when she talked of her work. Once he had been the same way.

A haughty brow rose. "Interior designer," she said, then laughed. "Right out of college. A loan from my father got me started."

The light changed and he pulled off. "And the rest was up to you."

Clearly pleased, she smiled. "Charleston, like many of the cities in the Old South, has a short list of designers who have set the standard, so I had to work harder, smarter. I hung out at the design studios, antique shops, getting to know the people there. It was tough going, but it was worth it."

"You're living your dream, then?" He pulled into the restaurant's parking lot.

A shadow flashed across her face. "Almost."

He frowned. "What's missing?"

She leaned closer. "Perhaps one day I'll tell you. Now, I'm starved." She opened her door and met him at the front of the truck, once again hooking her arm through his.

He studied her face. The shadow he'd seen moments ago was gone. It disturbed him to think life might have treated her unkindly. "You're also evading."

She leaned against him. He felt the soft impression of her breast, and his mind fuzzed when all his blood rushed south. "I'm hungry. Come on."

Somehow Alec got his feet moving. He knew about secrets. "You eat here often?"

The door opened. "Welcome back, Celeste," greeted a slender brunette.

"I guess I have my answer."

She gave him a quick grin. "Hi, Bette. Table for two, please."

"This way."

Releasing his arm, Celeste stepped ahead of Alec and followed the hostess. Even if he hadn't been a cop, he would have noticed the hungry gazes of men following Celeste's progress. He'd already figured out she wasn't hurting for a date, so why him?

The hostess stopped by a table in a quiet corner of the room. Alec reached for the chair. Giving him another smile, Celeste sat, hanging the strap of her small purse on the back of the ladder-back chair. Alec took the seat next to her, figuring this way she wouldn't be in his direct line of vision.

He accepted the menu. Celeste placed hers on the table. "I thought you were hungry."

"I know what I want."

She gazed at him in that direct way of hers, and his entire body came to attention. Why couldn't he just ignore the signals? Ignore the woman?

"Have you decided?" she asked.

Since his menu remained closed, he knew they weren't talking about food. "You know the answer to that."

"Pity."

He was used to women who went after what they wanted, but not one he was having trouble resisting.

"Are you ready to order?" asked a fresh-faced waitress.

"Celeste?" Alec said, studying the menu; he heard Celeste order ribs and sweetened iced tea. Lowering the menu, he eyed her white blouse and handed the waitress the menus. "I'll have the same. It's a good thing they have bibs."

"So you've eaten here before?" Celeste asked.

"It's one of Brianna and Patrick's favorite restaurants," he said.

Propping her chin on her palm, she leaned toward him. "Do you have a favorite back in Myrtle Beach?"

The waitress arrived and placed their drinks on the table, then withdrew. Alec didn't like to think about home. "Not really. I work long hours and, when I have free time, I like to work in my woodshop."

"How did you get into woodwork?"

"My father liked making things. I guess I took after him."

"Was he a policeman as well?"

"Here is your order." The server placed the platters on the table and withdrew.

"Yes," Alec answered, fast losing his appetite.

Celeste put on a bib and picked up a rib. "I hope this doesn't embarrass you, but I'm from Texas and this is the only way to eat ribs."

Alec watched her white teeth bite into the meat, watched her eyes close, then heard a little moan. Celeste could drive a man crazy.

Her eyes opened as she chewed. "Every time my family visits, we come here."

"Where exactly in Texas are you from?" Alec asked, glad she was no longer asking questions about him.

"Houston. My parents and older sister still live there."

Celeste put the small end of the bone into her mouth and sucked. Alec stared at the ribs, his imagination going where it shouldn't.

"Ah— Is your sister an interior designer?" he asked, reaching for his tea and taking a huge swallow.

"A high school counselor." Celeste cleaned her fingers with a wet nap, then picked up her fork. "She loves her students and they love her."

"You sound close." He picked up a rib. "What made you decide to leave Houston?"

"It was time," she said, placing her fork on the plate without using it.

If he hadn't been looking he might have missed the almost imperceptible tensing of her body. "Did your mother teach you how to cook?"

She laughed, a bright, happy sound. *Good.*

"Hardly. Gina and her aunt taught me."

"Gina?"

"My best friend." Celeste picked up her fork. "She's a travel agent. We were freshman roommates at the College of Charleston. Her parents live in Columbia, so her mother's sister Ophelia, who lives in Charleston, made sure we weren't starving." She dug into her coleslaw. "They considered it a travesty that I couldn't cook and proceeded to teach me."

He thought of the food he'd thrown out. "I'm sorry about the gumbo."

"As well you should be," she told him. "If Aunt Ophelia knew about it, she'd have a few words for you."

"Ophelia, isn't that one of Maureen's friends?"

"And one of the Invincibles." Celeste sipped her tea. "One

or all of them will probably drop by next week. They said they'd give me a week or so."

"They're checking on you?"

"In a way, but that's all right," Celeste said easily. "All of us want the redesign to go well. You start with the basic elements of floor, ceiling, and walls, but a lot can go wrong in between." She was certainly self-assured. "I thought I'd see Maureen's son and his new wife by now."

"Ryan and Traci called to see if I wanted to come over for dinner. They're leaving Sunday for a medical symposium in Hawaii. Ryan is one of the speakers," he said.

Celeste leaned closer. "Traci's grandfather is sweet on Nettie. They're so cute together."

She tempted him to close the distance between them, taste her tempting lips. He resisted. Barely. "Isn't she in her mid- to late sixties?"

"So? Love is love," Celeste said adamantly.

"I guess. What do you do when you're not working?"

"Garden, or at least try to. Then I love a good suspense novel." She dug into her baked beans. "Edgar Gunn is my favorite author. His real name is Dalton Ramsey. He lives in Charleston."

"I know. Dalton is a friend of mine," Alec said casually.

Her fork clattered to the plate. "You know Dalton?"

Alec looked at her excited face and decided it wasn't jealousy he felt. "He recently married."

She waved her hand. "Everyone knows that. He married Justine Crandall, the owner of It's a Mystery bookstore. I missed both of his signings there. How do you know him?"

Since she hadn't mentioned the scandal surrounding Justine and her adulterous ex-husband, Alec figured she didn't gossip. She couldn't have missed it or the subsequent scandal of her ex-husband being caught with a married woman in California a month later. He was persona non grata in the religious community.

"Come on, Alec; give."

"Dalton is an ex-policeman. His wife and Patrick's are best friends," he explained.

"Please tell him I enjoy his books," she said, and went back to her food.

Alec caught himself before asking if she wanted him to arrange a meeting. Tonight and Sunday was it as far as he was concerned, their first and last dates. "Would you care for dessert?"

"I love their double fudge sundae."

He signaled for their waitress and ordered. "What's on the agenda for tomorrow?"

"Finish painting the bathroom, then start on retiling the bathroom floor. We've already taken up the old tile."

"Will your assistant be there?" he asked as the waitress placed the dessert with two spoons on the table.

"Yes." She picked up her spoon. "But you can still come to check on me."

"Celeste."

She handed him his spoon. "Let's share or I'll eat the whole thing and gain weight in all the wrong places."

His gaze swept slowly over her. He took the spoon. "You look perfect to me."

Her head came up.

"I—"

"No." She held up her hand. "Please don't take it back."

There was such a softness in her face, in her eyes, that he would have done anything to please her. *Damn.* He dug into the dessert. "We'd better finish. We both have a lot of work to do tomorrow."

"More than you know," she murmured.

Alec kept eating. Somehow he had to figure out what it was about Celeste that pulled at him. He happened to glance up. She looked straight at him. Down went his head again, but not before he had the answer to his question. *Everything.*

He was definitely in over his head. Signaling the waitress, he paid the bill, then hustled Celeste to his truck. Strangely, she was silent on the drive to her house. Parking, he walked her up the walk, and then he waited until she opened the door. Light shone from the house and the double brass lanterns on either side of the door.

"Thank you, Alec. You might have been forced into tonight, but I had a good time."

"I did, too."

"Good night." Lifting on her tiptoes, she brushed her lips across his cheek, then slipped inside. He heard the locks click.

The kiss had been sweet, chaste, and left him wanting more. "Celeste, what are you doing to me?"

Turning away, he walked slowly to his car.

Celeste almost hated to see Willie's small truck parked in Maureen's driveway the next morning. Alec wouldn't come to check on her once he knew Willie was there. Celeste still felt a small thrill knowing he'd worried about her even after she'd overstepped. He was a great guy, one she was determined to know better.

Parking behind Willie, Celeste picked up the shopping bag and went inside and straight to the kitchen. It was spotless as usual. Since most men hated washing dishes, it looked like Alec had skipped breakfast again. In her heart, she knew, without opening the refrigerator door to store the food in her shopping bag, there would be no beer. But neither was there milk or juice or any staples.

"You're not taking care of yourself, Alec, but that's going to change." Unloading the bag except for a few items, she closed the refrigerator door and stopped at the bottom of the stairs. "Good morning, Willie. I'm going out back for a minute," Celeste called, then waited for her friend to appear.

Willie peered over the balustrade. "To get a closer look, no doubt."

"I'll have you know I got that last night," Celeste said, and walked away. She might have worked hard, but Willie had helped build the business as well. Some customers trusted someone they deemed had more experience, someone seasoned.

Stepping onto the terrace, Celeste followed the paved path to Alec. He had his back to her, hunkered down measuring a length of wood. He had his shirt on, but it was tucked, giving her a very nice view of his butt. She'd always wanted to know the big deal about a man's backside. It just took the right man for her to learn the answer.

Alec spun. His eyes narrowed, tracked her from her tennis shoe–shod feet to her face.

She barely bit back a sigh. She'd hoped after last night that they'd progressed further. Seemed not. She lifted the bag. "Homemade breakfast, organic carrot juice, utensils, napkin, and wet nap. Too many donuts are bad for you." Walking over, she set the bag on a stack of lumber.

"There's also lunch in the fridge with your name on it since I prepared lunch for Willie and me. I also picked up bread, milk, eggs, cooked sausage patties, cold cuts, a bag of salad, and juice for you. The receipt is taped to the egg carton for those items. The cooked food is on me. Have a nice day." She started to turn.

"Thank you."

"You're welcome."

"Your assistant arrived about fifteen minutes ago."

She wanted to believe she heard disappointment in his voice. "Yes, but as I said, feel free to check on me."

The corners of his mouth lifted slightly. He picked up the bag. "Thanks for everything."

"My pleasure," she said, and watched his gaze drop to her lips. She felt a small fission of heat. She moistened her lips. His hungry gaze followed.

"Your assistant is waiting on you."

"Yes." She started to leave, then turned back. "I put the names of the two men on a sheet of paper in your bag. Just mention my name. Unfortunately, they've done work for people and once it was finished, they weren't paid what they'd been promised."

Alec's face harshened. "Did they report it?

Celeste shook her head. "They didn't get it in writing, so it couldn't be proven."

"I bet you saw to it that they don't get taken again."

"I had a friend of mine draw up a simple one-page contract," Celeste said. "That way, both parties are covered."

"You care about people," he said.

"Yes. It's the only way to really live a happy life."

"Celeste, daylight is burning," called a high, thin voice.

Alec lifted a brow. "Your assistant?"

"Afraid so, and a Western fanatic. As you probably noted, Willie likes to use Western slang when we're working. Enjoy your breakfast." Celeste walked away wondering if Alec was doing a little backside watching of his own.

She was almost to the terrace doors when her phone rang; she jerked it up immediately at Shakira's "Whenever, Wherever" ring tone of her sister. "*Hola,* Yolanda. Are you playing hooky?" she teased, knowing her older sister would never dream of doing such a thing now. However, before her call to the church, there hadn't been a dare she wouldn't meet.

"I'm at a counseling workshop," came the laughing answer. "Registration is going on, and I thought I'd call."

Opening the terrace doors, Celeste stepped inside. "Work is going fabulous on the current project."

"I hear a 'but' in there."

Celeste didn't even hesitate. "A man I'm interested in is fighting being interested in me."

"We have ten minutes before I have to go back inside. Talk."

Celeste climbed the stairs and talked. Yolanda had a true feel for solving problems. "I think he's having a difficult time because of what happened." She told her sister about the shooting.

"His burden of guilt is easy to understand. However, he has to get to the point of knowing the other man chose his fate. He didn't put the gun in his hand or set him on a path of crime," Yolanda said, regret and sadness in her voice. "We can't be responsible for the poor judgment of others."

Celeste leaned against the banister at the top of the stairs. She'd heard those same words directed to her countless times. "I have a strong feeling that Alec knows that on one level, but not on a deeper, emotional level. Until he does, he's doing his best to keep me at arm's length. He's hurting, and I wish I could help."

"If you weren't interested in him, would you still want to help?"

"Yes."

"Good. And since a male has never ignored you, I can just imagine you're doing your best to impress upon him what he's missing."

It was scary how well her sister knew her. "True, but he doesn't take care of himself."

"Celeste, you ever notice how you take certain things for granted, like your car, for instance? You never think about it until it has a flat or won't start," Yolanda said. "Or more to the point, how do you feel about the men vying for your attention?"

"Flattered, but more often than not, I just wish they'd go away," she said honestly, then groaned. "I see your point."

"This work won't get done by itself," Willie said, her hands on her hips.

Celeste held up one finger. With an indulgent shake of her head, the older woman went back inside the master suite. "How did you get so smart?"

"By observing people. They're asking everyone to come inside. I have to hang up."

"*Gracias*, Sis."

"*De nada.*"

Replacing her cell, Celeste entered the bedroom, her mind formulating a new plan to attract Alec's attention.

TEN

Gina was a good person. She respected her parents, loved her children. She went to church, volunteered. She didn't gossip or harbor ill will against anyone—which was difficult to do considering the way Robert had treated her—so why, Gina asked for the umpteenth time since last night's confrontation with Gabrielle and her silent treatment this morning, couldn't she get through the wall her older child had erected?

Gina shuddered as much as the old Taurus when Gabrielle slammed the car door. It flashed through Gina's mind to get out of the car and give Gabrielle something to really be angry about.

"Breathe. You're an adult. You have more sense and more control," Gina repeated until her grip on the steering wheel eased. Chastising Gabrielle in front of half the school as the students loitered outside, waiting until the last possible moment to go inside, would only cause more problems. It could wait until this afternoon when they were home.

Gabrielle didn't know it, but she'd just added another week to washing the dinner dishes. If she protested, she'd find herself scrubbing the bathroom. Gina had to get control of Gabrielle, and fast.

Shifting the car into gear, Gina pulled away from the school and into the slow-moving traffic in the school zone. The moment the bumper of her car cleared the zone, Gina stepped on the gas.

She was looking forward to helping Max with Journey's End. It felt good knowing you were appreciated.

Ashton never failed to say he loved her each morning, always did his homework and chores with the first gentle reminder. Gabrielle— Gina pulled her thoughts away as she arrived home. She was thinking good thoughts only and enjoying her day.

Later that morning Gina put on her signal to turn onto the street for Journey's End. She slowed, admiring the different architecture of the homes on the street but also studying the landscaping. Many had gone for shrubbery, others a combination of flowing shrubs and evergreens, another one had thick beds of rosebushes. There seemed to be no central theme, and since all of the homes were on at least a half acre it gave the owner of the house a great deal of leeway. It also helped solidify Gina's ideas on how to make Journey's End stand out.

Slowing down, she turned into the long paved driveway. Once again, Max came out almost immediately. His welcoming smile warmed her. Smiling, she opened the door and stepped out. "Good morning, Max."

"Good morning, Gina. How are you doing today?"

Her shoulders slumped. "Only another person with a teen-ager would understand. On second thought, maybe you would," she said, thinking of how bratty Gabrielle had been the first time they visited here.

"I have lots of friends with children. I've heard more than once one of them comment that they'd strangle one if they didn't love them," Max commented.

"Exactly. She's angry because of the div—" She stopped abruptly, flushed. "I'm sorry. This isn't your problem."

"No, but I'd like to help," he said. "It can't be easy for you."

"No, it hasn't been, but it's nothing that countless other women haven't gone through." Her shoulders snapped upright. "If you'll take the bowl covered by the yellow dish towel, I'll get the other things."

He didn't move. "If you change your mind, I'm here." Stepping around her, he reached for the bowl. "It smells good. I'm starved."

Gina grabbed a shopping bag and hurried after him. She wasn't about to discuss her problems.

"Come on in," Sophia said, holding the door open for them. "What did you cook, Gina?"

"Spinach salad with grilled shrimp," she said. "My aunt always said the secret to a really good salad is fresh ingredients, simply prepared and well seasoned." Gina might be hesitant about other things, but she knew she cooked well.

"I can't wait," Max said, placing the chilled bowl on the kitchen counter. "Can I help?"

"No, thanks. Please have a seat. I need to add the fresh peaches and feta." She pulled two plastic containers from the bag she carried. "This is easy to prepare and so is the raspberry vinaigrette dressing."

"If you say so," Sophia said, deadpan.

Gina found herself laughing at the older woman. She handed her the containers. "Open, dump, mix."

Sophia stared at the containers for a full five seconds, then did as told. "I hope I didn't ruin it."

Since Sophia and Max both were frowning at the salad, Gina didn't laugh this time. Instead she took the bread sticks from the foil and placed them on the table. Next came a bowl of cheese tortellini tossed with fresh basil and grape tomatoes. "You can use Italian dressing or the vinaigrette."

"Let's dig in," Max said, holding her chair.

"Thank you." Gina quickly took her seat, then bowed her head when Max this time blessed the food. She couldn't remember a time Robert had thanked anyone for anything. She lifted her head and found Max, a smile on his face, patiently holding the salad out to her.

She flushed and quickly served herself, then handed the crystal bowl, one of her best and a wedding present from her sister, to his aunt. "If I had time I would have made a serving bowl from bread stick dough."

Max and Sophia both just stared at her. She could feel herself start to withdraw inside. Until Max said, "Aunt Sophia, I've discovered a national treasure."

He said it with such awe and respect that Gina didn't know how to respond.

"I'll say." Sophia bit into her salad. "I couldn't even ruin this delicious salad, and the pasta is scrumptious."

"I told you," Gina said.

"You've made a believer out of both of us." Max chewed, savored. "You've ruined me for frozen dinners."

Gina preened. "I love cooking, but Gabrielle and Ashton both are at picky stages. They'd turn their noses up at this."

Max and his aunt shared a look. "If we add cooking to your duties, well paid of course, would you run from here screaming that we're overworking you?"

More money, yes, but being valued was priceless. Gina picked up her bread stick. "Let's finish lunch and talk."

Max hadn't been kidding when he'd said he'd discovered a national treasure. Gina might have been shy at first, but the more they worked together, the more her confidence seemed to grow. He'd noticed that she no longer got that weary look in her eyes as if waiting for him to tear her idea apart when she made a suggestion.

It took time to become that weary. It was a learned response from either her parents, the husband, or both. Pity, when she smiled she made you glad to be in her presence, just as she did now.

"The main lawn can hold everything together if you plan the gardens well. When they come out of the back door they'll view an arbor gate. Going through it will lead them down to the pier. It will be breathtaking in the spring and, with seasonal planting, remain inviting in the fall and winter." She turned to him, a wistful smile on her lips.

"I've been thinking about the screened-in porch. Since the living room is so formal, there's no place for your guests to relax. If you'd whitewash the wood floors, add white wicker furniture with cushions covered with outdoor fabric, a colorful rug, and possibly an inexpensive painting on the back wall, plants, and a small game table, they could relax there and view the river. What do you think?"

"I can see it," he said. Gina had the ability to paint her vision so that you could see what she talked about. He recalled her lifeless flowers, the yard turning brown. "You like flowers."

"I love them. I—" She glanced toward the river. A sailboat slowly drifted by.

He stepped closer. "What?"

She turned. "Nothing. I'd better go see what you have so I'll know what to purchase when we go to the grocery store Saturday evening. I'll call once the game is over."

He frowned. "Did you forget that I told Ashton that I'd try to make it?"

Her hands linked together in front of her. "He and I both know that, when you own your own business, your time is not your own."

The absent father. Once Max might have been the same way. Life had taught him to live for today, because tomorrow wasn't promised. "I'll be there if I can. My cousin and his wife are on vacation and might drop by Saturday. They aren't sure what time."

"I understand. I'd better go inside and start on my list."

Max almost reached out to stop her. She didn't believe him. Once he might have been insulted. Now he knew how easily he'd once made promises and how easily he broke them.

He was a better man now, but he'd paid a hell of a price to be so. He looked up at the bright sky. "I'm learning, Sharon." His eyes shut. He had too many regrets to count. If he thought about them too often, he knew melancholy would overtake him as it had before.

You made mistakes, hopefully learned from them, picked

yourself up, and went on. Opening his eyes, he saw Gina open the back screen door and go inside.

If he didn't miss his guess, they were both learning lessons. Her marriage hadn't held the happiness his had. Nobody had to tell him that life had dealt him a sucker punch, but it had also given him one of those rare loves that most people can only dream about.

He hadn't been smart enough to appreciate the precious gift until it was too late. He didn't hold out any hope or even think that he'd be blessed a second time.

His life now revolved around Journey's End and fulfilling a shared dream. That was enough—or had been.

His brow creased in a frown, he stared toward the inn.

What do you do with a woman who is beautiful, won't take no for an answer, has your best interests at heart, and cooks like a five-star chef? Alec scraped the plate, searching for another taste of the free-form plum pie. The crust had been flaky, the fruit just sweet enough. The herb-crusted chicken with wild rice and a fresh salad had been just as delicious.

Was there anything that threw Celeste? He didn't have to think long of the evening when he'd torn into her for helping him before he realized he was headed for trouble. She was definitely an interesting combination of compassion and fire, but she wasn't for him.

No woman was at the moment.

He turned to put the dish in the sink and saw her standing there. She was the most exquisite thing he'd ever seen. She wore a smile that made his gut tighten and had a body a man would plead for.

"Don't let me disturb you. I just came to get us a bottle of water." Crossing the kitchen, she pulled two bottles from the refrigerator and headed back the way she came. She was almost out of the room before he realized she really intended to leave.

"You could give the cooks at Sticky Fingers a run for their money."

She paused and looked at him.

He lifted the empty container. "That's the best pie and probably the best meal I've had in a long time. Thank you."

"You're welcome. I'm glad you enjoyed it." With that she was gone.

Alex frowned as he watched her leave. She hadn't stayed to entice him, to draw him into a conversation. Had she suddenly decided he wasn't worth her time? Had he finally pushed her away? He tried to be glad about that but couldn't.

Going to the sink, he rinsed his plate, bowl, and utensils. Time to go back outside. Looked like he'd have some peace and quiet. His steps slowed when he reached the bottom of the stairs. His hand on the newel cap, he looked up, trying to figure out why she'd given him the cold shoulder.

He should get back to work but found himself climbing the stairs. He needed to pay her for picking up the groceries for him. It might as well be now. He removed thirty dollars from his billfold in his room and headed back out.

He wandered into the master suite to see both women strapping on knee pads. Celeste saw him first. "Yes, Alec?"

The saucy smile he'd come to associate with her wasn't there. "I brought you the money. Thanks. I appreciate you taking the time."

"No bother. I had to pick up some other things for myself."

Bending, she finished buckling the last knee pad. "Just leave it on the table."

He looked at her; she looked back. "All right." He placed the money on the small table in between the two side chairs in the sitting area. He turned and saw her pick up a trowel.

"Ready, pardner?" she asked the other woman.

"Let's do it."

They entered the bathroom without a backward glance. Alec had been dismissed, and he didn't like it one bit.

Celeste slowly spread the tile adhesive on the floor, her ears alert. Finally she heard Alec's feet going down the stairs. She'd noticed he didn't wear his work shoes in the house. She breathed a sigh of relief. She hadn't put it past him to come into the bathroom to try to figure out why she was acting differently toward him.

On the other side of the spacious room, Willie chuckled. "You certainly took him off-guard and gave him something to think about."

"Thanks to Yolanda," Celeste said as she seriously got to work. She wanted the tile laid today. She planned to come early in the morning and grout.

"She's right. Two husbands and two engagements taught me a thing or two about catching a man." Willie paused and straightened. "That young man is probably wondering what happened to the woman in hot pursuit."

Celeste groaned. "I was so obvious."

"Nothing wrong with going after what you want; just don't make it easy for them to catch you," Willie cackled.

Celeste laughed so hard she almost lost her balance. "No

wonder every time I see Joe he has a smile on his face," she said, referring to Willie's husband of thirty years.

"Just because there's no smoke in the chimney doesn't mean a fire isn't burning." She went back to work spreading the adhesive. "Maureen and the Invincibles have the right idea about life. Live every day to the fullest with no regrets, love deeply, and help someone along the way."

"And it's a much better life living with someone you care deeply about," Celeste said a bit wistfully.

"You sound serious this time."

Each of the three times Celeste had become engaged, Willie had asked if she was sure, and when it was over, she and Gina were the only people who never seemed surprised. Each time Celeste's mother cried for a week.

"I don't know, Willie. He's different from any man I've dated," Celeste said slowly. Working together, they had a lot of time to talk about their personal lives. Willie probably knew her almost as well as her sister, Yolanda, and Gina. "I just know something about him calls to me, invokes emotions I've never had before."

"Easy and charming is boring," Willie said with feeling. "Go after him until he catches you."

"What if that doesn't happen?" Celeste asked, unable to keep the worry to herself. Alec wouldn't succumb easily.

"From the obscene way he was looking at you, I'd say it's in the bag. Now, enough jabbering, let's do this so I can get home to my man."

Gina waited until she'd picked up Gabrielle and Ashton from school and they came into the house. On the way home, Ashton as usual told Gina about his day and the new girl in his class, the planned field trip to the aquarium. All the time Gabrielle, sitting in the front passenger seat, stared out the side window, ignoring them.

Once in the kitchen, Gabrielle started to push past her mother. She caught Gabrielle's arm. The start of surprise in her eyes was priceless. "Gabrielle, I want to talk to you. Please wait."

Not giving her daughter a chance to say anything, Gina opened the refrigerator, took out a carton of apple juice and a small package of cut apples, and handed them to Ashton. "Please go to your room and stay there until I call you."

Ashton looked from his mother to his sister and headed for the stairs. Gina waited a few minutes, then waved Gabrielle to a seat. "Please sit down."

"I have homework."

"Sit down," Gina repeated, clearly enunciating each word.

Uneasiness flickered in her daughter's eyes, so much like her own; then the surly expression returned. Shrugging off her backpack, Gabrielle let it fall to the floor and plopped in the chair.

Gina took a seat next to her daughter. Twelve inches of space separated them, but it might as well have been miles. "As long as you live in this house, you'll respect me."

Silence.

"That means you'll give me the respect and courtesy to look at me when I speak to you," Gina said, fully aware that they'd already had this conversation once this week, but she didn't plan to have it again after tonight.

Gabrielle turned to face her mother. Her lips were pressed together in mounting anger.

"I've tried to understand you, be lenient with you, but all it has done is let you think you call the shots in this house. That stops today, do you understand?"

More silence.

Gina leaned back in her chair. "If you don't want to talk to me, I can't make you. I refuse to take a belt to you."

Gabrielle's eyes flared, and she shrank back in her chair. Finally a reaction.

"But there are other ways to get through to you that you're the child and I'm the adult and your mother."

She could almost see Gabrielle relaxing back in the chair, the wheels turning in her head, as she thought that once again she'd emerge the victor.

Not this time.

"Each time you're rude, snotty, discourteous, and a general pain, more household duties will be allotted to you. If they're not done in a timely manner and to my satisfaction, you'll have to do them over no matter what time it is or what your other plans might be. If after the second time they are still unsatisfactory, I'll deduct two dollars from your monthly allowance for every hour it takes you to do them right."

"That's not fair!" she wailed. "You can't take my money. That's what Daddy sends to me."

Gina knew that argument was coming and had prepared in advance. Getting up from her chair, she opened a drawer in the kitchen, took out copies of all the checks Gabrielle's father had sent since he left.

"Look at these." Gina held the copies out to her daughter, but she made no move to take them. "I said look at them. The court ordered your father to send ten percent of his net income for you and Ashton each month. I asked for no alimony and received none, just the house. He agreed to that if I relinquished any claim to the gym. I agreed."

Gina nodded toward the copies of the checks. "There have been times your father had difficulties, for whatever reason, in sending the checks, yet your allowance has never stopped."

She waited and let that sink in. Gabrielle finally took the copies, clutching them instead of looking at them.

"I don't want to hear any more about your money," Gina told her. "You have more new clothes than anyone. Your booster team outfit cost a month of child support, and that didn't include the boots, the practice gear," Gina said. "And if you spend every penny, how do you expect to go to college?"

"Daddy said I could go to whatever college I wanted," Gabrielle said. "He said he'd pay for it."

Your father is a liar and a cheat. "As you can see by those checks, your father's business is not doing well at the moment," Gina said. Not for anything did she want Gabrielle to know her father didn't care about any of them. She retook her seat and stared at her daughter. "My house, my rules."

"What if I went to live with Daddy?" she asked.

Her disloyalty was a stab in the heart. Gina leaned back in her chair. Threats again. "You'd have to change schools. You would have to make new friends. I'm sure that the booster squad has already been selected." Gina took a big gamble. "If that's what you want, I'll call your father, but I wish you wouldn't leave. Ashton and I would miss you. We love you."

"Ashton. It's always Ashton!" Gabrielle shot to her feet. "He can never do any wrong. You let him get away with murder."

This time Gina was taken by surprise. She stood as well. "That's not true."

Moisture glistened in Gabrielle's eyes. "It is, too. It's always been that way."

Gina didn't even have to think about it. If anything, Gabrielle was the one she was too lenient with. "No, you don't, Gabrielle. You won't blame your poor behavior on me. Was he rude to the B and B owner? Did he deliberately kick the ball wide? Did he call you a snot? No. His crime is that he stands up to you and tries to get your attention because he's a little boy in the house with two females. Stop picking on him and you'll see."

Gabrielle brushed the heel of her hand across both eyes and looked away. "I might have known you'd take his side."

Gina wanted so badly to take her daughter in her arms, but if there was ever a time she had to be strong it was now. "Gabrielle, open your eyes and see that you bring all of this on yourself."

Silence, then, "Yes, ma'am. May I go to my room now?"

Gina's heart clenched. She wasn't listening. "All right, Gabrielle, if that's the way you want it. For being disrespectful this morning and slamming the car door you have another week of doing the dinner dishes."

Her lips pursed. "Can I go now?"

"Yes."

Jerking up her backpack, Gabrielle left the room.

Gina felt drained. She wasn't meaner or badder; what she was, was in danger of losing her daughter.

ELEVEN

Celeste made sure she left with Willie, so even if Alec had wanted to talk to her, he wouldn't have been able to. Pulling away from Maureen's house, Celeste couldn't resist the temptation of looking in her rearview mirror.

No Alec. She looked again just before she took a left at the end of the street. *Nada*. Wrinkling her nose, Celeste continued on. She hadn't thought he would be easy, but as Willie said, easy was boring.

In twenty minutes Celeste pulled into her garage and activated the door. She didn't move until the door closed. It was half past six, still daylight, but that didn't stop crazy people from trying to rob you. She had missed Simon's first lesson on home safety at Maureen's house but not the next one.

Climbing out, Celeste shut the door and went to the back of the van. Opening the door, she took out the toolbox and carried it to the sink she'd installed in the garage. She kept her tools clean, her van neat. If she wanted something, she didn't want to waste time looking for it.

Finished, she set the toolbox back in the van and went inside. The alarm blared. She punched in the code, then turned Kenny G down on the intercom radio.

Sitting on a small bench in the mudroom, she took off her tennis shoes, stripped down to nothing, throwing all of her clothes into the hamper. If she did any remodeling, she always undressed in the utility room. She didn't want to track dirt through her house.

Slipping on a short robe, she belted it at her waist and continued to the kitchen. She wasn't hungry, so a small salad would do. Opening the Sub-Zero refrigerator, she thought of Alec. At least he'd eaten today. If he didn't continue to eat properly and take care of himself, he'd start to burn muscle, and that would be a true pity.

"Get your mind off the man's great bod." Closing the door, she continued through the one-story house, her sanctuary, to her spacious bedroom, a generous twenty by twenty-four with a sitting area and a small curved sofa in front of the fireplace.

Getting fresh panties, she used a scrunchie on her hair to pull it off her shoulders and stepped into the open shower tiles in pale blue and gray. Ten minutes later, she shut off the water, dried, then liberally used her favorite Hermès lotion.

Her mother might nag, but she had taught both daughters to pamper themselves, not to wait for anyone to do it for you. Slipping on her panties, she pulled on a strapless sundress that stopped midway up her thighs. In front of the mirror, she let her hair down and brushed it until it fell thick and silky to the middle of her back.

She stared into the mirror, trying to see what others saw. She guessed she looked all right, but she couldn't take any credit for her looks. Besides, life had taught her that no matter how beautiful you were, life could still bring you to your knees.

Turning away, she went to the kitchen. Opening the refrigerator, she pulled out Bibb lettuce, grape tomatoes, scallions, slivers of almonds, and cubed chicken. In a matter of minutes she had a salad and green iced tea ready.

The phone rang as she passed the end of the counter. Setting the plate down, she picked up the receiver. "Hello."

"I'm not meaner or smarter," Gina said, her voice weary.

"What happened?" Celeste asked, putting her plate and glass of green tea on the table. She listened as Gina told her about her confrontation with Gabrielle. "Give it time. I'd say you're off to a good start."

"I just pray you're right. I don't want to lose her because I'm too strict," Gina said, worry echoing in her voice.

"Being too lenient will be just as bad." Celeste took her seat and sipped her tea. "Hang tight."

"I suppose. On the bright side, I have another job with Max." She explained about her deal to cook for Max and his aunt.

"You're a fabulous cook. They're lucky to have you." Celeste leaned back in her cushioned chair. "I'm lucky you and your aunt taught me."

"I almost believe my life is turning around when I'm at Journey's End with Max, who couldn't be nicer, and then I have to come home and fight with Gabrielle." Weariness laced each word. "It's becoming more and more difficult not to hate Robert for what he's put this family through."

"I already told you I'm up for doing a number on that precious convertible of his," Celeste said. "Need I remind you that I have friends who'll give us an airtight alibi?"

"Evil for evil never works. Besides, you're interested in a policeman, working in the home of another. How would it look if you were arrested?"

"We won't get caught, so that's not an issue," Celeste said with every confidence.

"So you say, but I'm still against it."

"Life can turn on you in the blink of an eye," Celeste said, recalling her three public breakups.

"I just wish Gabrielle would revert back to her old loving self."

"She will. It just takes time."

"Hope so. Good night."

"Night." Celeste hung up the phone. "Now if someone would just give me a pep talk about Alec," she said with a sigh.

Picking up her fork, she knew it would take a lot more than talk. "But I'm not giving up."

The doorbell chimed. Frowning, Celeste went to the intercom. She wasn't expecting anyone and hoped it wasn't a salesperson. "Hello."

"Er, Celeste. It's, er, Alec."

Speechless, she stared at the intercom.

"I— we forgot to set a time for me to pick you up on Sunday."

Thank you, Yolanda. "Hold on." Releasing the lever, Celeste went to the front door and opened it.

Alec stood on the porch, his hands stuffed deep in his pockets, his wide shoulders hunched. He looked like a man with a problem. "I don't have your phone number."

"No, you don't." She stepped back. "Please come in."

He hesitated, then brushed past her. He'd showered and put on cologne as well. A tantalizing mixture of orange and spice. He smelled good enough to eat. She shut the door. "I was about to eat, would you like to join me?"

She thought she saw the corners of his sensual mouth tilt upward. "You know, you're always trying to feed me."

"Imagine that." Hoping he'd follow, she went to the cabinet in the kitchen and set another place setting, then prepared his plate. "Is iced tea all right or would you like bottled water or a Pepsi?"

"Tea is fine."

Celeste grabbed a glass, filled it with ice, then tea. "Please have a seat." She set the glass on the table and started to sit. "You were saying?"

Alec jumped to hold her chair, then took his seat next to hers at the small round table. He looked at the salad, then back up to her. "You made this?"

She picked up a fork before answering, "Yes."

He briefly bowed his head to bless his food, picked up his fork, and took a bite, chewed. "You really can cook."

"Thank you," she said, trying to be casual when he looked absolutely scrumptious. His thick hair was damp. She could just imagine water sliding down his muscled chest, his flat stomach, farther still.

"Like I said, I don't have your phone number."

Flushing, she dragged her mind back to the conversation. Did he want it for himself? "I'll give it to you before you leave. Would you like crackers or bread?"

"This is fine, actually better than fine." He lifted his gaze to hers. "Patrick is the cook. I usually pick up take-out."

Be careful, Celeste. Don't be too anxious. "Charleston is full of fine restaurants. Several are not far from Maureen's house. I can give you a list if you'd like."

Alec studied her a long time, then returned to eating his salad. "I might need the names of the men you recommended next week. I guess I didn't see the numbers you left."

"No problem. I'll get that, too, before you leave. Would you like more salad?"

Alec looked down at his empty plate. "No, thank you."

"I'll get you the numbers." Rising from the table, she went to a small desk in the kitchen and wrote the information on a piece of business letterhead. "Here you are."

Alec rose, taking the paper. "I'll pick you up around ten forty."

"Or I can meet you there?" Celeste suggested. "I might not be able to stay to go sailing."

His beautiful black eyes narrowed. "I thought you said you didn't have plans."

"It now seems as if I was wrong." She smiled innocently. "I'll show you out." At the door, she pulled it open. "I'll expect you Sunday at ten forty unless you have to cancel."

"Patrick and Brianna expect us."

"Then I wouldn't like to disappoint them. Good night, Alec."

Frowning, he stared at her, not moving.

"Was there something else?"

"I—" He glanced down at his feet, then up again. "My family is not going to believe that we're dating if you keep acting the way you are now."

Folding her arms, she lifted a brow. "And how is that?"

"Like you could care less if you ever saw me again," he answered.

The bite in his voice let Celeste know he wasn't thrilled about the idea. "Isn't that what you wanted?" she asked.

His gaze captured hers. "Yes, I guess."

Unfolding her arms, she stepped closer. "Make up your mind, Alec; what do you want from me?"

"I already know what I want from you," he rasped. His nostrils flared, his gaze narrowed on her lips, his hand lifted to slide around her neck.

"So, what's the problem?" she asked.

His hand fell. "I'm trying to sort through a lot of things. A woman like you could complicate matters."

She took another step until her unbound nipples brushed his shirt. "What kind of woman is that?"

"A woman that fulfills a man's every fantasy."

Bolder than she ever believed possible, she slid one finger down the curve of his cheek to his tempting lips. "What's your fantasy, Alec?"

He jerked her into his arms, his hot mouth fusing on hers. Sensations pummeled her. Their tongues met, fed on each other. She heard a groan. She wasn't sure who emitted the sound and didn't care. She feasted on him and he returned the erotic pleasure.

She felt herself being lifted, faintly heard the door slam. His hand cupped her breast, causing her knees to tremble. His thumb grazed the sensitive nipple, causing it to bud to hardness.

Lifting his head, his breathing as rough and as labored as hers, he rasped, "This shouldn't have happened."

"But it did, and we both enjoyed it."

"Still pushing, Celeste."

Withdrawing her arms from around his neck, she took an unsteady step backward. "Habit. Good night, Alec."

His expression changed, his eyes narrowing as if he were trying to figure her out. "Night. Celeste." Turning, he opened the door and left.

Celeste plopped in the nearest chair, her heart still thumping out of control, her legs unsteady. Kissing Alec was like catching the tail of a comet, wild, exhilarating, dangerous. Playing it cool toward him was going to require all of her willpower.

Alec got to her in the best possible way. During dinner tonight she'd caught him looking at her a couple of times like he wanted to pull the top of her dress down over her breasts and put his mouth there.

Her legs quivered. She wasn't sure how much longer she could remain cool when all she wanted was to give free rein to the sensual attraction arching like an electric current between them. She wanted to find out where all those hot looks of his would lead. But more than that, she wanted him to find the peace he sought.

Could she accomplish both, or was she doomed to finally find a man who made her heart glad, her body hum, only to lose him?

Gabrielle was taking a chance, but it had to be done. She huddled beneath the bedcovers waiting for her mother to check on her. None of her friends had to go to bed by nine; some of them could stay up as late as they liked. Not wanting to be called a baby, she'd told her friends she had an 11:00 P.M. bedtime. All cell phones, however, were discontinued at nine, but there were always ways around that.

A brief knock sounded on her door. With the covers pulled up to her neck, she pretended to be asleep. Moments later she felt the brush of her mother's lips on her forehead.

"Sleep well, Gabrielle. I love you," her mother whispered.

No, you don't, but that's all right because my father loves me. After slowly counting to two hundred, Gabrielle opened her eyes. Not taking any chances, she pulled the covers over her head, activated her girlfriend's cell phone, and called her father.

Parents didn't know anything. They might take your cell phone, but all you had to do was borrow a friend's, a friend who you would do the same for when theirs was taken away.

"Yeah?"

"Daddy," she said, her voice shaky.

"Gabby, is that you?" he asked.

Hearing her father use his affectionate pet name for her, Gabrielle felt better already. "Yes, sir. I want to come live with you." She had thought about it for a long time. "You could drop me off at school every morning, and I could take a bus home."

There came the briefest hesitation. "Is your mother on you again?"

She clutched the cell. She knew he'd understand. "She always takes Ashton's side. I have to wash dishes while he plays with that stupid soccer ball."

"I'll talk to her about it. Don't worry. Now Daddy has to go, but I'll see you next Saturday. Night, Gabby."

"But, Daddy—" Her eyes closed on hearing the dial tone.

Gabrielle shut off the phone, got up to put it in her backpack so she wouldn't forget it, then crept back to bed. Her father still might let her come live with him. He hadn't said no. He'd become angry on her behalf.

A moment of unease slithered down her spine. Perhaps she should have asked him not to mention to her mother the day and time she'd called. Not wanting to take a chance and call him again, Gabrielle decided to call him tomorrow and explain. He'd understand. She could always count on him.

Feeling better, Gabrielle closed her eyes. Unlike her mother, her father loved her. And soon she'd be living with him.

Robert took another tour through the fitness center. There was a new woman who'd been giving him the once-over for a couple of weeks now. He'd been playing it cool, but he was definitely interested.

He watched her lift the five-pound weights, the slight bounce of her full breasts, the way the shorts fit her thighs, cupped her butt, her woman's softness. Man, he had it good. He couldn't have picked a better profession. He got as much action as he wanted and got paid at the same time.

He stopped in front of the brunette he'd been watching. "You're doing well, Doris, but then you were already in good shape."

"A woman has to take care of herself," she purred, giving him a slow once-over.

He let his gaze travel back over her. He'd perfected looking over a woman without leering. "I can't see a thing that needs improving on."

She smiled, ran her tongue seductively over her bottom lip. "Do you offer the services of a personal trainer?"

Better and better. "You're looking at him. Why don't you come into my office when you're finished and we can talk."

"I'll do that."

Robert walked away. Another woman to fill his needs as Gina never could. In his office, he checked his stash of condoms, the chilled bottle of wine in the refrigerator, then went to sit behind his desk.

He glanced at the picture of Gabrielle and Ashton in the silver frame they'd given him for Father's Day. He hadn't been able to be with them long the last time because he'd had a date. He cared about them, but he had his whole life to be with them. This was his time, and he was going to live life to the fullest.

Women loved that he'd been married, had children, sympathized with him that his wife didn't understand him.

A knock sounded on the door. "Come in."

The door opened and the woman he'd been talking to entered. He moved to greet her and locked the door behind her. Yeah, life was great, and on his terms.

"At your service, Doris." His hand went to her breast.

TWELVE

Alec had a sleepless night. This time it wasn't the face of the man he'd killed who haunted him but Celeste's, beguiling one moment, indifferent the next. Sitting up in bed, he planted his feet on the floor, his head in his hands.

She was driving him crazy. Last night after he'd left her he'd sat in his car a good fifteen minutes before his hands were steady enough to drive. If one kiss made him rock hard, how much more would sinking into her satin heat do?

Groaning, Alec pushed upward and headed for the shower. Stepping inside the tile enclosure, he turned the five jets on full blast. They wouldn't help, but for the moment it was all he could do. Celeste was addictive; one taste and you wanted more.

Only he couldn't have more. Once had been too much, and she'd known how it affected him. She'd stood there, her lips moist and tempting after their kiss, and calmly told him good night.

His eyes closed, his palms pressed against the wall of the shower, Alec took one calming breath after the other. If she could act cool, then so could he.

But his body ached, wanted. Lifting his head and opening his eyes, he reached for the soap and washcloth. *Get it together, Dunlap*. No woman had ever thrown him and none ever would.

Big talk. So why could he so easily visualize her here with him, the water running off her silken skin, his hands and mouth following, wringing cries of pleasure from her lips, lips that he thought about on his body more and more?

In a foul mood, he viciously twisted the knobs to turn off the water. Thinking like that wasn't going to help.

Stepping out of the enclosure, he reached for the large white bath towel from a stack on the counter. He rubbed the fluffy cotton cloth briskly through his hair, took a few swipes over his body, then wrapped it carelessly around his waist. He reached for his briefs and heard a noise.

His head jerked up. It was only half past six. Celeste didn't come until around eight. He went to the nightstand. Opening the drawer, he reached for his service revolver. As if his hand hit an impenetrable wall, he stopped inches away. His fist clenched with rage, with fear he didn't want to face.

Resisting the urge to slam the drawer shut, he went to the fireplace and picked up a poker. Quietly he crept to the partially open bedroom door, flattening himself against the wall so he could look into the hallway.

He didn't hear anything else, but he wasn't about to think it was his imagination. He wasn't that jumpy. Someone besides him was in the house. The maid and housekeeper weren't returning to get the house in order until two days before Maureen and Simon were due to return.

He could call the police, but he had no intention of answering questions about why he had a poker in his hand instead of a gun. He eased into the hallway. His room was at the end of the hallway. He couldn't get a clear view of the stairs.

He started down the hall, his bare feet soundless on the runner, the poker gripped like a baseball bat ready to swing. Reaching the end of the hall, he peered over the stairs. Nothing.

Then he heard a noise again. This time from Maureen and Simon's room. Their three-week-long trip away had been well publicized. Thinking about Celeste last night, Alec had failed to set the alarm for the morning. Since he slept so poorly he was always up early to cut it off before Celeste arrived.

Chastising himself, he eased down the hallway to the open door of the master suite. A quick peep into the room revealed nothing. He stepped inside and heard a clinking sound coming from the bathroom. His hand tightening on the poker, he advanced in that direction. *You picked the wrong house, bud.*

Ready to swing, Alec stepped through the door connecting the bathroom. And froze. This time for a completely different reason.

"Celeste!"

Celeste shot up from crouching on the floor, wheeling as she did. Her eyes wide, she pressed her hand to her chest.

"What are you doing here?"

"I—I—" she stammered, glancing from the poker at his side back to him.

"Talk," he rasped, trying to combat the adrenaline rushing though him, mixed with arousal.

For once she couldn't seem to get the words out. Alec frowned. She couldn't possibly be afraid of him. He took a step toward her, felt the towel slip. Saw her eyes widen, not with fear but sexual curiosity—and reached to catch the towel a second too late.

"Oh, my," she whispered, her eyes staring at a part of him that hungered for her; then she turned away, which probably saved both of them

Grumbling, Alec snatched up the towel, tried and failed to secure it around his waist. "I'll be back," he rasped, and left. In his room he replaced the poker, pulled on his briefs, sweatpants, and a T-shirt. No way was he going to get on his jeans in his condition.

When he returned, she was sitting on the floor outside the bathroom with a bottle of water clenched in her hand, her head bowed. Crossing to her, he hunkered down in front of her. "I'm sorry I scared you."

Her head lifted. "You didn't scare me."

In her eyes he saw every one of his wicked fantasies fulfilled, every desire satisfied. "Celeste." They moved at the same time. Their lips met, a gentle pressure, a soft sigh of remembrance.

Gathering her in his arms, he eased them down on the floor. The heat of the kiss built as their mouths and hands sought each other. His hand slid under her T-shirt, felt the silken skin, the warmth that pulled him. He wanted her to feel him, feel what she did to him. With a deft roll, she was on top, her legs between his.

She stiffened. Alec was about to lift her away when she

relaxed again, her hands in his hair tightening, her tongue meeting his thrust for thrust.

Fire and ecstasy. He reached for control or he'd take her. His body clamored for release that he knew he'd find but couldn't take when he knew she deserved so much more.

He pulled his mouth away, rolled until they were side by side, then just held her, waiting until both of their bodies retreated from the jaws of arousal. He couldn't stop touching her. He wouldn't deny himself that much. His hand stroked her hair: The heavy strands drifted like silk though his fingers.

He thought of it spread out on his pillow and shook the image away. "What is it about you that gets to me?" he said, realizing too late that he'd voiced his thought aloud.

Her head lifted. She stared down at him with eyes that still shimmered with desire. "If I could answer your question, perhaps I could figure out why you get to me. No man ever has before."

He stared at her, the implication sinking in. His eyes clamped shut. *Damn.* Even as his brain told him to release her, his hold tightened. Who would have thought a woman with beauty, brains, a body to make a man whimper, could have reached the age of—

"How old are you?"

She pushed against him until she leaned far enough away so she could see his face. An imperious brow lifted. "A gentleman never asks a lady her age."

He didn't know why he wanted to laugh, to hug her. Celeste could act haughty, imperious, but he felt her heart beating as wildly out of control as his. "Your mother taught you that?"

"My grandmother. We might be third-generation Puerto

Rican, but she followed the old traditions," Celeste told him, a frown forming on her face.

"She wouldn't approve of this, I guess?" he asked, already feeling the emptiness of his arms as Celeste pushed away. Accepting his fate, he helped her to her feet.

"Thank you," she said primly. "I should get back to grouting the bathroom floor. I have an appointment at my office at twelve."

Now he frowned. "You're going to do it by yourself?"

"Yes. Willie's knees can't take the bending two days in a row." Celeste finished strapping on her knee pads. "The man I usually use had another job and I couldn't wait on him."

He should just leave, but his feet weren't moving. "I thought decor—" He stopped and amended at one of her sharp looks. "Interior designers just thought of the ideas and then hired and oversaw the work."

"Most of them do, but I like hands-on."

His unruly mind took her comment in an entirely different direction. He certainly liked her hands on him. From the way the pulse beat in the base of her throat, she had the same thought.

"I, er, better get to it if I'm going to be on time. I have to go home, shower, and change first."

She was making it harder to leave, and him harder. Innocent and irresistible. Who would have thought it? "I'll leave you to it." He turned.

"I cooked too much for breakfast, so I put a plate in the refrigerator for you. I don't like wasting food."

He swung back, but she had disappeared into the bathroom. He didn't understand her, couldn't get her out of his mind. She aroused his body, his curiosity. She gave with no thought of receiving, fought to help a man she'd just met, kissed him as if her life depended on it. She was also one hell of a cook, and he was suddenly hungry. "Thanks."

"You're welcome. Bye, Alec," she called from inside the bathroom. "We both have work to do."

True, but that didn't seem to keep him from wanting to stay. He hadn't gone too far down the stairs before he thought he knew the reason he lingered. As long as he thought of Celeste he didn't have to think his lifelong dream as a police officer might be over, of the face of the man he'd killed.

His appetite vanished. Instead of continuing to the kitchen, he went to his room and changed into his work clothes. Dressed, he glanced at the closed drawer of the nightstand. His life was in turmoil. It was no time to think about having an affair, but in this, as with the shooting, he couldn't push those thoughts away.

But he would. He had to.

"You think he'll come, Mom? He said he'd try."

Gina forced a smile and stared down at Ashton in his uniform and protective gear as they crossed the grassy park heading to the soccer field. Her heart ached for Ashton because he had given up on his father ever coming to one of his games, but not Max. "He said he'd try, but he's a busy man."

Ashton looked around. "I saw his car. It's gray like Coach Sams'. Do you see a car like that?"

"No, Ashton," Gina said. "But there are a lot of cars here."

"Come on, Ashton," called the coach on the field. "Warm-up time."

"You'll keep an eye out for him, won't you, Mom, because I have to keep my eyes on the ball."

Gazing down at the earnest face of her son, Gina wanted to hug him. A no-no while he was in uniform. "I will. I'll sit at the top of the bleachers so I'll have a good advantage."

"Ashton!" called the coach.

"Gotta go."

"Good luck," Gina called as Ashton ran on the field. Her smile slipped. She thought of calling Robert to ask him to come but already knew the answer. He'd cite Saturday as a busy day, that next weekend he was picking up the children.

Speaking to the family and friends of team members, Gina climbed the metal bleachers. She was on the fourth one before her breathing began to be labored. By the time she reached the eighth and top one, she was blowing hard. Sitting on the metal seat, she pressed her hand to her booming heart.

She should have brought a bottle of water. She could go back down the stairs and get one out of the chest reserved for parents, but then she'd have to climb the bleachers again.

Definitely not worth it. She'd be fine in a few minutes, sooner since the game was starting. She stood to her feet, yelling along with everyone else for their team. "Go, Yellow Hornets! Go, Ashton!"

The opposing team gained possession of the ball and headed downfield. Her gaze went to Ashton, swaying slightly, ready to defend the net. Her heart thumped as it always did. He loved being the goalie, but it was such a crucial position. And she never liked when the ball, as it did now, zoomed toward the net and Ashton had to block it with his small body.

He deftly blocked the ball. The cheers went up again. Gina had never been good at sports, but thank goodness both of her children were athletic and not clumsy like their mother.

"Your son is good, Gina," Carla Patterson commented as the game progressed and Ashton kept the other team scoreless. Her son Richie was a forward on Ashton's ream and had scored the only point in the game.

"So is Richie," Gina commented. "The team will really miss him when he moves to another age group to play."

Carla glanced up over her shoulder. "I can tell you I'm not looking forward to him playing with bigger boys. His father is all for it. Look at him down there on the sidelines." She laughed. "It's a wonder Coach Sams doesn't bar him from the games."

Gina's gaze wandered to where the coach and a group of men stood. Richie's father wasn't the only father there. The men showed their support of their sons while Robert made excuses. True, not all the fathers of the boys on the team came, but most of them did. Ashton had to notice that his father had been only twice and left in less than half an hour. He was another no-show today, and the game was almost over.

"Wonder who he belongs to?" Holly, one of the other mothers sitting beside Carla, asked.

Gina wouldn't have paid the comment any attention if she hadn't been looking for Max and remembered the impact he had on Celeste. And, if she was honest, on her as well. Searching the area, she saw Max—tall, athletic, graceful—coming down the sidelines. Her heart did a crazy thump. She frowned, wondering if there was something wrong with her heart.

"You'd better not let Ben see you ogling a man," Carla told the other woman with a laugh.

"He's so intent on the game he'll never notice, but if he

did . . ." Holly leaned over and whispered something in Carla's ear and they both laughed.

Gina could just imagine what Holly had said. Something sexual probably. Looking at Max getting closer to them, Gina couldn't blame her. Intimacy was an important part of marriage, as Pastor Carter had preached.

Gina should have known something was wrong with their marriage when Robert moved out of the bedroom, saying he needed a firmer mattress for his back, that he didn't want to disturb her when he came in so late from work.

She had been gullible and too trusting.

Max paused parallel to Ashton as his team took the ball back down the field. She saw Ashton's wide smile. He waved to Max. Max waved back. She could almost hear Max's warm chuckle.

Holly and Carla both turned to look up at her, a speculative expression on their faces. "He's a client," Gina felt compelled to say; then she stood, waving to Max although it was impossible for him not to see her on the short bleachers.

Since most of the men were on the sidelines, preferring to leave the seats to the women, Max drew a great deal of attention as he made his way to her. Courteous as always, he spoke and said "excuse me" several times before he stood beside her.

"Hi." He grinned.

"Hi," Gina said, grinning back. She might have kept the grin on her face if those around her hadn't let out a wild yell. Her attention snapped to the field.

One of the other team's best scorers was taking the ball downfield, dodging Ashton's teammates with deftness and skill. Ten feet away from the goal, he shot the ball. Ashton batted it away, keeping the other team from tying the score.

"Go, Ashton!" Max yelled, applauding wildly. "I don't feel so bad now. He's a great player."

"Thank you, and thank you for coming," she said.

"I told him I'd make it if I could. I try to keep my promises. Sorry I'm late. I came as soon as my cousin and his wife left." Taking her arm, he sat down, drawing her with him. "I hired a couple of men to help me move the furniture as you suggested. It looks good."

"Great. I can't wait until Monday to see it."

"You don't have to wait that long. I figured, after we do the grocery shopping, I could take you by so you can see it today," he said.

To be wanted. "I'd like that. I wish—" she began, then caught herself before she said she *wished his father kept his promises.* From the sympathetic look on Max's face, he knew what she'd been about to say. She felt exposed and tucked her head.

He leaned over and whispered, "Ashton has you."

Her head lifted. Max stared back at her, his black eyes direct, gentle with understanding. She felt the strange sensation in her chest again. "Thank you."

"Ashton is an incredible kid. He had to learn from someone." Max gave his attention back to the game.

Gina thought of Gabrielle, sullen and disrespectful. Who had taught her to be that way? Gina shook the thought away and stared back out at the field. Her concentration kept being fragmented between the man beside her and the game.

She didn't think it was intentional that he sat so close to her, that only a whisper of space separated them. Still, she felt the warmth, the muscular strength, and a strange feeling of being protected. Idiotic notions, but they were there nonetheless.

"Hold, Ashton!" the coach yelled. "Hold and this is our game!"

Gina, Max, and the crowd stood to their feet. The same player carried the ball downfield again, shooting it to his teammate, who shot it back. The player spun, straightened, then three feet from the net kicked the soccer ball. Ashton dove for the ball. It hit him squarely in the chest. He went down. The whistle blew.

The crowd, already on their feet, cheered loudly. The game was over.

Gina's hand clenched Max's arms. "He's not getting up! He's not getting up!" She frantically pushed her way through the celebrating crowd. The noise gradually abated as people realized Ashton was still down. The coach and others ran to the field.

By the time Gina reached the edge of the field, she was winded. Max, holding her arm, stopped. "Please go," she urged.

Thankfully, he didn't argue. He raced toward the crowd now gathered around Ashton. Praying every step, Gina pushed her body forward. She'd heard of players receiving a direct hit to their chest and it stopping their heart. Protective gear hadn't helped. Tears crested in her eyes. *Please, not Ashton.*

"Let me through." When people didn't move, she pushed them aside. "I'm his mother." Finally, they moved. Not knowing what she'd see, she felt tears sting her eyes, clog her throat.

She wasn't paying attention to any of the faces; her child was her entire focus. He had to be all right. The last person moved and she almost dropped to her knees. Ashton was sitting up with his coach on one side of him and Max on the other.

Max looked up. "He's all right, Gina. He just had the wind knocked out of him."

Relief swept though her. Tears crested, then rolled down her cheeks. "Ashton," her voice wobbled.

"Mama," he said, his lower lip trembling, his face damp with perspiration.

She dropped to her knees, dragging him into her arms, hugging him, rocking him. "Ashton! Ashton!"

"He's all right, Mrs. Rawlings, and he kept us undefeated," the coach said. "With players like Ashton, we're going to win the division championship."

Gina clutched her son tighter. "You can't possibly think I'll let him play again."

The coach blinked. "What?"

Gina tried to stand without releasing Ashton. She felt a strong hand at her elbow, effortlessly helping her to her feet. *Max.*

"Now, Mrs. Rawlings, Ashton is all right," the coach soothed.

"And he's going to stay that way," she said, her voice and body trembling as she held Ashton close to her.

"Mrs. Raw—"

"Perhaps it's best to discuss this later," Max said to the coach before leading her away. "Do you feel like driving or should I take you home? We can come back later and pick up your car."

"I— I'd appreciate it if you'd take us home."

"This way to my car."

Gina didn't release Ashton until Max opened the back door to his Pathfinder. She sat Ashton on the seat and climbed in beside him. Her hands trembled so badly Max had to help buckle them both in before he gently swiped his large hand down her arm.

"He's all right, Gina. In another hour or so he'll be ready to tell his friends about the save of the century." Max reached past her and brushed his hand over Ashton's head. "Quite a save."

Gina watched a smile spread across Ashton's face, his body straighten the tiniest bit away from hers. Closing the door, Max went around to the driver's side and got in. He'd effortlessly calmed the mother and reassured the son.

"Thank you," she said, capturing his attention in the rearview mirror.

"I'm just glad I was here for you and Ashton." He put the car in gear. "I'll have you home in no time. Unless Ashton would like a detour to pick up a pizza or a hamburger. If your mother agrees."

"I—" Gina began, but her son cut her off.

"I could eat a pizza, Mama," Ashton said, his face expectant.

Gina stared at her son, then at Max as his warm laughter chased away the last of her fears. "I guess it would be all right."

Ashton's grin matched Max's. "I feel better already."

For the first time since she'd seen Ashton so still on the field, Gina smiled, and it was all due to the man smiling back at her.

THIRTEEN

Alec knew it was a bad idea, but he hadn't been able to talk himself out of doing it. He'd never done it before, but somehow it seemed right. So why was he so nervous?

His hand tightened on the handle of the bag in his hand. He watched Celeste shut the back door of her van and walk to the driver's side.

He'd been trying to work up his nerve for several minutes, ever since he'd gotten back and seen her preparing to leave.

It was now or never. He stepped from around the corner of the house. "Celeste."

She turned, a bashful smile on her beautiful face. He wondered if she was thinking of the torrid kiss or seeing him hard and ready for her.

"Hi, Alec. I was just leaving."

"For your appointment?" he asked, trying to keep his mind on the matter at hand.

"Yes." She glanced at the plain stainless-steel watch on her slim wrist. "I'll have just enough time."

A shy Celeste was a novelty. She'd been so self-assured all the time, testing his control to the limits. It was reassuring to see that he wasn't the only one struggling to figure out what the hell was going on between them. "I hope you planned time to eat." He lifted the take-out bag from Sticky Fingers toward her.

Her eyes widened with surprised pleasure. "You bought me lunch?"

He felt like sticking his chest out and tucking his head at the same time. He'd never been this conflicted about a woman in his life. And he'd been dating since he turned sixteen. "It seemed the right thing to do at the time."

"Thank, you, Alec." Taking the bag, she brushed a soft kiss against his cheek. "I am hungry."

"Enjoy."

"I will. Did you pick up your lunch as well?" she asked.

Why did it always please him so much that she thought of his welfare? "And dinner."

"Wise move." She lingered, looking at him as if she wanted to say more, then climbed inside the van. Starting the motor, she let the window down. "I'll see you in the morning."

He didn't lie to himself. He wished it were sooner, wished it were in a wide bed with soft sheets draped in moonlight. "Drive safely."

"I will." Putting the van into gear, she backed out of the driveway and pulled off.

Alec watched until the van was out of sight. *Be careful, Alec. I've got a feeling Celeste could mean more trouble than you expected, but she could also mean more pleasure than any man has a right to experience.*

Her heart thudding in her chest, her hands unsteady, Celeste threw a last fleeting look at Alec in the driveway before she turned the corner at the end of the street. He excited her, made her body shiver with desire.

It had taken all her willpower to keep the image of him, splendidly naked and magnificently aroused, at bay while she grouted the bathroom. Of course she didn't have anything to compare it to, but somehow she just *knew*.

Stopping at the signal light, she glanced over at the take-out bag. He was taking care of her. Just as he had done when he thought she might be endangering herself. Being stubborn and a man, he wouldn't see it that way, of course. To him, he was just returning the favor.

But she had known a lot of selfish, self-centered people in her day who took with both hands, with no thought of giving back. Alec cared. Or was she confusing caring with lust?

The light changed to green and she pulled through. Was she confusing herself into thinking he felt the same way? Was the sexual tension an aphrodisiac that unduly influenced her?

She didn't have the answers. She just knew that she had no intention of turning her back on the sizzling attraction between them or trying to help Alec deal with his needless guilt. Both were risky, both demanded her total commitment, both could reap pain or pleasure.

Only time would show which.

. . .

Gina stuck her key in the front door of her house, but before she could turn the key, the door was snatched open. Gabrielle stood in the doorway. All Gina could think of was that she wasn't ready for another confrontation.

Gabrielle stepped around her mother to Ashton, who stood behind her. "You all right? Lazette said you got knocked out or something."

Ashton worked his small shoulders a bit in embarrassment. "It just winded me."

Gina decided to ignore how Lazette, Gabrielle's classmate who lived several blocks over, had contacted her. It was more important that Gabrielle seemed really concerned. "He's fine."

Gabrielle stared down at her brother a few minutes as if wanting to make sure.

"He felt revived enough to order pizza," Max commented.

Gabrielle's gaze snapped up to Max holding the three boxes of pizza and a handled bag. Her lips pursed. "I bet you bought him his favorite?"

"It's pepperoni personal pan-size, and I have it all to myself," Ashton said with a grin.

Gabrielle turned away. "I might have known."

Gina's hand itched to grab her daughter and shake her until her teeth rattled. Stepping into the foyer, Gina closed the door after they were all inside. "There's also a sausage one for you."

Her daughter stopped, whirled, her disbelieving gaze going to her mother.

Max casually handed her the personal-size box on top. "I recall how I always wanted a pizza for myself. Your mother also said you liked salad, so we got you one."

Gabrielle just held the box.

"And I got barbeque wings. Mama said we can share them," Ashton said.

"Gabrielle," her mother urged.

Gabrielle looked as if she were still having trouble taking it all in. "Thank you, Mr. Broussard."

"You're welcome. And if you or Ashton want to try the beef pizza your mother and I are sharing, feel free," Max said. "Now, we'd better eat before this gets cold."

In a matter of minutes, Gina had paper plates, drinks, and the food on the table. Seated, she said grace and served Max. "Thank you. I haven't had a pizza in years."

Both children stared at him as if he were from another planet. Max smiled good-naturedly and gazed across the table at Gina. "But if I had a choice I'd definitely prefer your mother's cooking."

Gina flushed with pleasure. "Thank you."

"Mama's a good cook, but I like pizza, too," Ashton said, taking a huge bite of his pepperoni pizza.

"Me, too," Gabrielle said, digging into her garden salad.

"Not me, and I'm looking forward to more of her meals." Max bit into his pizza. Chewed. Swallowed. "Definitely no comparison to your mother's cooking. Ashton, you and Gabrielle are two lucky children."

Gabrielle shrugged. Ashton took another hearty bite. Gina and Max shared a look. "A woman is never appreciated in her own country," she said.

"Because they've always had you to care for them." Max sipped his iced tea. "Let them eat a couple of my or Aunt Sophia's meals and they'd change their minds in a hurry."

Gina bit into her pizza and pondered what Max said. He

was probably right. The children did take her for granted, just as Robert had. Only Max seemed to truly appreciate her.

The phone on the kitchen counter rang. Excusing herself, she picked up the receiver. It was one of Ashton's teammates wanting to know if he was all right. As Max had predicted, Ashton retold his story to the caller with relish.

Gabrielle rolled her eyes, then and at the following two calls for her brother. "To think I was worried about him."

"He was hurt, Gabrielle." Gina was just happy to see Ashton acting normal.

The phone rang again. Ashton grinned. Excusing herself, Gina picked up the receiver, then told her son, "This one is for me. Yes, Nettie, thank you. I'll check on the day and time and get back to you." Hanging up, she retook her seat.

"You do so much and all of it so well," Max said. "I'm glad we met."

So was she. And to think, if Celeste hadn't forced her to attend Journey's End's grand opening she and Max might not have met. The thought made her stomach clench. She picked up her glass of iced tea just as the peal of the doorbell sounded.

"I bet that one is for me," Ashton said, finishing off a boneless wing.

His prediction proved correct when Gina answered the door. The coach stood on the porch, his team cap in his hands. "Mrs. Rawlings, I just came by to check on Ashton, and to ask you to please change your mind about him playing."

"I wanna play, Mama." Ashton stepped beside her and slipped his hand into hers. "My team needs me. I'll be more careful. I promise. Please."

"We'll take it game by game," she said. The coach opened his mouth to argue but snapped it shut at Gina's stern look.

"See you at Monday practice, Ashton." Replacing his cap, he left.

"Thanks, Mom," Ashton said, still holding her hand.

"Just keep your promise of being careful," she told him.

"Promise."

They arrived back in the kitchen to see Max putting his paper plate and plastic cup in the trash. "I should be going. I can take you back to your car now or later."

Gabrielle and Ashton picked up their plates as well. "First let's get your grocery list filled."

"We can do it another time."

She shook her head. "Ashton is feeling fine. There are a few things I need to pick up for myself. You kids want to go with us or stay here?"

"Staying."

"Going."

Predictably, Gabrielle elected to stay; Ashton liked going with Gina. "All right. I'll get my handbag, and we can leave."

Max never thought he'd enjoy shopping and finally decided it was because of Gina and Ashton. She believed in Max, in Journey's End, and wanted its success almost as much as he did. She wanted his guests to feel pampered. He wondered if anyone had ever pampered her.

"I should be finished with your Web site tomorrow night, so you can see it when you come out Monday," he told her.

Her eyes lit up. She clutched the four-pound container of strawberries to her chest. "So soon?"

He smiled, pleased that he could make her happy. "I'm a slug compared to all that you've done."

She placed the fruit in the shopping cart that Ashton insisted on standing in front of Max and pushing. "The phone call I received while we were eating was from a friend of mine, Nettie Hopkins. She's a master gardener. I spoke with her a few days ago about my ideas to landscape the yard, and she liked them. If it's all right with you, she can come out tomorrow around eleven to look everything over."

"It seems all I do is say thank you."

"I enjoy helping." Gina stopped in front of the pears. "I thought, if you don't mind, we, I mean you, could try out the signature dishes on them."

"Them?" Max asked, pulling the shopping cart back after Ashton tried to make a skateboard out of it.

"She's one of the Invincibles, a wonderful group of widows. They're all consummate hostesses," Gina told him, her hand clutching a pear. "My aunt Ophelia is one of them and the woman who, along with my mother, taught me how to cook. The Invincibles like nothing better than a project. It wouldn't surprise me if all of them didn't show up except Maureen, the founder, who is the owner of the antique store I told you about."

Max heard the trepidation in Gina's voice, saw it in her face. She respected them, feared she'd never be as good. "You're a wonderful hostess yourself. Aunt Sophia and I marvel at your ability to see what needs to be done around the house so effortlessly."

"Journey's End is beautiful. It deserves to be shown at its best," she said.

"I couldn't agree more. With your help, we'll show the Invincibles the hospitality Journey's End is going to be famous for." He'd deliberately said "we." "Get whatever you need."

Nodding, Gina chose pears, avocados, mixed greens, sweet onions. "I'll make a srawberry-chicken salad in the bread basket serving bowl I told you about. The signature drink will be a southern favorite, iced tea with a twist, strawberry tea slush. For dessert, a strawberry tart with fresh whipped cream."

"I'm hungry already," Max said, meaning it. He hadn't been kidding. He wasn't much of a pizza eater. "But those dishes will take time. Why don't we do something simple?"

She smiled at him in that shy way of hers that made him glad she'd come into his life. "If you know what you're doing, simple foods can be elegantly served and easy to prepare. You can make each meal special."

"You do that and more," he said. "I can't imagine where I'd be if you weren't helping me."

"We've helped each other," she said, the tension gone from her face and body.

He only had to think for a moment. "Then I'm in your hands."

Flushing, Gina quickly turned away. Max wondered about her response, and what it would be like if he were in her hands in an entirely different way.

She'd been right. Something was wrong with her. While Gabrielle and Ashton, for the first time in weeks, played a video game without needing a referee, Gina sat quietly in her home office trying to figure out what that "something" might be.

When Max looked at her, her stomach became jittery. He smiled and she felt happy. She saw him and felt restless, as if she needed something and he was the only one who could give it to her.

Celeste might have the answer, but she was knee-deep in writing up proposals and doing research on her upcoming projects. She read men so easily—that is, until Alec Dunlap had come into her life.

What was it about a certain man that threw a woman's life into a tizzy?

The ringing telephone interrupted her thoughts. She tensed. Perhaps it was Max. Her head dropped into her palm. She had to stop thinking about Max. He was her employer, becoming a friend. Nothing more.

"Mama, answer the telephone!" Gabrielle yelled. To a teenager, an unanswered phone offered endless possibilities.

"Got it," Gina said, picking up the receiver. "Rawlings Travel Agency, where—"

"Why didn't you call and let me know Ashton had been hurt?" Robert yelled.

"I—"

"What kind of mother are you?" he snapped, cutting her off once again. "I had to hear it from the coach at the gym."

Gina's spine straightened. "What was the coach doing there?"

"Telling me, of course, and ensuring that Ashton continues to play soccer," Robert said. "He'll play. You aren't going to make a sissy out of my son."

His son that he took no time to be with. She'd take care of the coach later. "Frankly, it never entered my mind to call you," she said with a calmness she was far from feeling.

"What the hell is wrong with you? Do you know how that made me look?"

"Now the real reason comes out." She came to her feet, her anger growing. "This isn't about Ashton as much as the image you want to preserve."

"You—"

"You miss his practices, his games, his programs at school and church. You're late with child support. How was I to know you cared?" she asked, this time talking over him. "If you would have been there today, I wouldn't have had to call you."

"I told you, woman, somebody had to work. You sure aren't bringing in the dough," he said snidely.

She was tempted to tell him how wrong he was. Because of Max she had paid the water bill and now had a small cushion. "If business is so good, Robert, why are you always late with the child support?"

He backtracked faster than a snake slithering on his belly. "It takes a lot of money to run this place."

"Robert, since you're worried about Ashton, I suppose you're coming over to check on him," she said.

"Er, I'm at work. The least you can do is take care—"

Gina hung up the phone, refusing to listen to another put-down, another excuse. The phone rang almost immediately. She picked it up.

"Don't—"

She crashed the phone down. She stared at it, feeling a sense of power she never had in the past. She was so tired of trying to keep the peace with Robert for the children's sake, of trying to be everything to everybody, tired of being put down. And it stopped now.

She picked up the phone and dialed the coach's cell. It was picked up on the second ring.

"Hello."

"Coach Sams, this is Ashton's mother."

"Is Ashton all right?" he asked, concern in his voice.

"He's fine. If you want to remain his coach, you will never go behind my back and try to undercut my decision for him to play. I, and only I, make that decision," she said. "If it happens again, I'm sure I won't have any difficulty finding him another team to play with. Do I make myself clear?"

"Yes, ma'am. It won't happen again. I'm sorry."

"I accept your apology and hope there won't be a need to have this conversation again."

"No, ma'am, there won't," the coach said meekly.

"Good. Good night."

Today was the start of a new day for her in more ways than one. Pulling out the desk drawer, Gina reached way in the back and drew out two bags of miniature Baby Ruth candy bars. Standing, she pulled out three romance novels from her bookshelf and removed the newly opened bag of M&M's behind the books.

"Was that Daddy on the phone?" Gabrielle asked.

Teenagers also had selective supersonic hearing. Gina whirled. She started to stick the candy behind her back but tossed all of it on her desk instead. "Yes. He called to check on Ashton."

Gina picked up a can of honey roasted peanuts from behind a picture of Ashton and Gabrielle at the park and quickly added it to the stack.

"You think losing weight will bring Daddy back?" Gabrielle asked with such hope that Gina's heart ached for her.

"I'm not doing this for your father; I'm doing this for me.

I'm so out of shape that I couldn't get to Ashton when he needed me." She pinched the roll of excess skin on either side of her waist. "I didn't have this three years ago."

"You have gained weight."

Gina couldn't decide if her daughter was deliberately trying to annoy her or not. What the heck. Gina threw her arm around her daughter's shoulders and noticed again she was only about three inches taller. "You know, Gabrielle, you don't always have to say everything that pops into your mind, even if it is the truth."

"But if you did lose weight, I bet Daddy would notice," Gabrielle said, still optimistic.

Gina palmed her daughter's pretty face. "Gabrielle, wanting something doesn't always make it happen. Your father and I will never get back together. He has his life, and I'm building mine."

"But it's not right. Daddy should be here."

"Gabrielle," Gina began. When she saw the mutinous look on her daughter's face, Gina decided to change the subject. "The Invincibles are coming to Max's B and B to discuss the ideas I've suggested for landscaping the grounds. I'm preparing the food and I'd like your help when it's time to serve. It would mean a lot."

"I guess."

"Thank you." Gina watched her daughter, head down, hands stuffed in the pockets of her jeans, leave the room. Change wasn't going to be easy, but Gina wasn't giving up.

Max was up by seven Sunday morning. By eight, he had all of the fruits and vegetables Gina said she'd need for the brunch lined up on the counter and ready to wash. When she arrived around nine thirty she would find he'd done that much at least. He wasn't a man who liked sitting back and letting others do his work. He truly appreciated all she did for him and wanted to make sure she knew it.

Besides, she worked too hard and, from what he could tell, got very little appreciation. Ashton and Gabrielle weren't the brats Max had imagined, but neither did they seem to be grateful for what a wonderful, loving mother they had.

But perhaps they weren't alone. Since Max didn't know the first thing about food preparation except the basics and his aunt was just as lost, he'd called his mother, who had been overjoyed to help him. She was getting ready to go to early-morning church services, but she welcomed his call.

He told her the dishes Gina had planned and asked how he could help. He'd gotten off the phone thirty minutes later with at least an idea of how he could help Gina, and he'd discovered something else. His mother missed him, worried about him. His calls every week or so weren't enough. Her other three children and her two sisters might live in Memphis with her, but they didn't negate her need to keep in touch with her oldest child. She sounded happier than he'd heard in a long time. Before hanging up, he promised to call more frequently.

Finished washing the fruits and vegetables as his mother had suggested, he set up the long table he'd used to put brochures on at the grand opening. Next came a plastic tablecloth, followed by Sharon's white lace tablecloth. Max's large hands smoothed out the few wrinkles. Usually he felt her presence when he used her things, but not this time. Attributing it to nerves, he finished setting the table.

"Looking good," his aunt said.

"Morning. Thanks." He checked his watch. "I'm going to run to the grocery store to get some flowers. Mama's suggestion."

"I'll finish setting the table." Sophia moved back into the kitchen.

"Use the yellow stoneware. I'm going to get yellow and white flowers."

She chuckled. "Between Gina and my sister, you're going to be a male Martha Stewart."

He paused with the keys in his hands. "Gina's the one. I wish she would give herself more credit."

Sophia reached up for the plates in the cabinet. "I figure if she's around you long enough, it will happen. You have a way with people."

"You think she'll leave?" The thought bothered him. He felt a strange emptiness at the notion that he wouldn't see her every day.

"She does have a business of her own to run, doesn't she?" Sophia asked. "She has her own dreams to fulfill."

"I guess. Be back shortly," Max said, continuing out the door to the detached garage in the back. He hadn't thought of Gina leaving. Somehow when he thought of Journey's End, he thought of her.

Guilt slammed into him before he took another step. His eyes shut. His head bowed. The B and B had been his and Sharon's dream. As his aunt had pointed out, Gina had her own dream. How could he have forgotten that even for a second?

Straightening, he got into the Pathfinder, started the motor, and backed out. He'd do well to remember whose dream he wanted to see come alive.

. . .

Gina pulled up at Journey's End and, as usual, Max came out almost immediately. Despite her jittery stomach, she had to smile. He wore a long white apron with a lobster on the front.

Opening her door, she stepped out of the car. "Hello, Max. Great apron."

"Good morning, Gina, Gabrielle, Ashton. Need any help?"

Gina's smile wavered. Max hadn't smiled back at her. She thought she knew the reason. "Yes, thank you. In the trunk." She activated the lock and went to the back of the car. "Don't worry, Max. They'll love Journey's End."

Without looking at her, he lifted the cardboard box. "I'm sure they will."

"I'll get the door, Max," Ashton said, and ran ahead of him.

"What's wrong with Mr. Innkeeper?" Gabrielle asked, staring after Max.

"He's worried about the impression the B and B will make on the Invincibles, and I guess about my ideas to landscape the grounds," Gina said, handing Gabrielle the gallon container of freshly brewed tea. She'd add the other ingredients just before she served the strawberry tea slush.

"But he was the one bragging about your cooking last night, about everything you did," Gabrielle pointed out, her expression defiant.

Gina's stomach, already jittery, knotted. She reached to pick up the small cooler containing the chicken breasts she'd marinated. "Maybe he changed his mind."

"He'd better not," Gabrielle said, and started toward the house.

Gina straightened at the angry note in her daughter's voice. She opened her mouth to call Gabrielle back, but Max, with

Ashton on his heels, came out of the door. As Max passed Gabrielle, she turned to glare at him.

Gina picked up the cooler by the handle and closed the trunk. The happiness she'd felt earlier was gone.

"I'll take that."

"I have it. Ashton, can you please get the door for me."

"Sure, Mama."

Going up the steps and into the house, Gina pushed the hurt out of her mind. She had a job to do.

"Is there anything I can do to help?" Max asked, standing in the doorway of the kitchen. Gina and Gabrielle had been busy in the kitchen since they arrived almost an hour ago.

"No, thank you." Gina, mixing salad greens on the counter, spoke without turning.

"We don't need you," Gabrielle said coldly.

Gina glanced up at Gabrielle, then went back to what she'd been doing. "Max, your guests should be arriving soon. Why don't you go wait for them."

"Aunt Sophia is already on it," he said without moving. He'd watched Gina for the past ten minutes. She flittered around the kitchen like a nervous butterfly. And Gabrielle kept throwing him dirty looks.

"Everything looks good," he tried again. Gina had never been this jumpy cooking in the past.

"My mama knows what she's doing," Gabrielle said. "There's no need to watch her."

"Gabrielle," Gina admonished, putting the salad in the refrigerator. "Please go check on Ashton."

"I was about to finish making the tea," Gabrielle protested.

"I'll do it." Gina removed the gallon of tea and shut the door after her. "The Invincibles should be here soon."

Max stood in the kitchen, watching Gina ignore him, aware that he had set them on this course, and he felt like he'd kicked a small puppy.

"They're here!" Sophia yelled.

"Come on," he said, noticing Gina's hesitation before she set the tea on the counter.

"Of course." Taking her apron off, she draped it over a chair at the breakfast table. Stepping past him, she went to the front door.

Four women emerged from a spotless vintage Mercedes. He guessed their ages ranged from mid- to late sixties. Each was well dressed, with understated jewelry and a spectacular hat.

"Welcome to Journey's End. Thank you for coming," Gina went down the steps.

"You initially only invited Nettie to look over the grounds. I was thrilled you decided to extend the invitation to the rest of us."

"I'm glad you could come." She made the introductions of her aunt Ophelia, Nettie Hopkins, the master gardener, and the other Invincibles, Donna Crowley and Betsy Young. "Max and his aunt will show you inside, and I'll bring refreshments out to the sunroom and serve."

Max offered his arm to Nettie. "It will be my pleasure."

The older woman put her arm lightly on his. "You have to be from the South."

"Memphis, born and bred." He slowed as they went up the steps.

"We won't hold that against you," Ophelia said.

In the sunroom, he paused. There were only six place settings. He looked at his aunt. She shrugged her shoulders.

"Gina and the children aren't joining us?" Ophelia asked, her voice tight.

"I thought they were," Max said, frowning.

Gabrielle entered, carrying a pitcher of tea and a basket of crackers. Directly behind her Gina carried the salad. Compliments flowed from each of the women on seeing the serving bowl made out of bread.

"Thank you." Gina took the pitcher from Gabrielle and finished filling the tall tea glasses. "I'll let you get acquainted during brunch, then afterward I can show Nettie the plans and walk her over the grounds. I'll check back periodically to see if you need anything. Please be seated."

No one sat. The Invincibles, aptly named, Max thought, looked at him as if he were cow dung. But more than that was the slight quivering in Gina's voice. "There seems to have been a mistake," he said.

Taking the pitcher from her unsteady hand, he placed it on the table and pulled out the head chair. "If anyone is going to be served, it is going to be you and Gabrielle. You did all the work." He pulled out another chair. "Gabrielle."

The teenager unfolded her arms and took the seat.

"But—" Gina began.

"I'll pull Ashton away from the TV in the study and get him to wash up. Please," Max said. He'd beg if he had to.

Her throat moved several times, as if she were having difficulty swallowing. "Thank you."

"No. Thank you," he said, then straightened. "Aunt Sophia, I'll get more chairs, if you'll get the place settings."

"It will be my pleasure." Sophia left the room.

"Good." Max smiled fondly at Gina, silently asking her forgiveness.

In a matter of minutes, everyone was seated around the table. Max picked up his tea glass and stood. "I'd like to propose a toast to Gina Rawlings. Her intuitive knowledge and warmth have helped me in countless ways at Journey's End. The tea, the delicious food you're going to eat today, will become the signature dishes of Journey's End. To Gina." He stared down at her. Her eyes were huge in her pretty face. Moisture sparkled in her chocolate brown eyes. "A woman of immeasurable worth, charm, and grace."

"To Gina," those sitting around the table chorused. Even Gabrielle and Ashton repeated the toast, although Gina's son giggled.

Gina blushed, but her smile was back. Max was going to do everything in his power for it to remain.

FOURTEEN

It had been difficult, but Celeste was ready when Alec rang her doorbell Sunday morning. After much debate, she'd chosen an off-the-shoulder yellow knit top and white cropped pants. The yellow top complemented her olive-hued skin, but the way the top bared one shoulder tempted a man to think about what was beneath and contemplate seeing for himself.

Of course, it was a wicked thought, and one that had never entered her mind until yesterday, when Alec's kiss made her crave more, crave him in the most decadent way. It went without saying that her patent and leather shoes matched her tote and were the exact same color as her yellow top.

She wanted to look sexy for Alec and sophisticated and classy to his family. She hoped they liked her, hoped he'd think she was desirable and not be able to wait to get her alone and rip off the top. She sighed and picked up her tote from the sofa. Of course, that wasn't going to happen. They had a long way to go before any ripping occurred—if at all.

She opened the door. Temptation stared back at her. Midnight black eyes raked over her in one encompassing, hot sweep, turning her legs to the consistency of wet noodles. Heat zipped through her as she did her own looking.

Oh, my! Not only was he built like a pagan god; he was gorgeous to boot. The white knit shirt delineated his muscled chest, the knee-length navy pants his strong thighs. His long, narrow feet were bare in navy deck shoes that had seen a lot of use. Looking at him, she wanted to do some ripping of her own.

"Hello, Alec," she greeted despite the crazy thoughts in her head, and hoped her voice sounded casual.

"Celeste. You're ready."

"You sound surprised." She stepped onto the porch to close the door. He didn't step back. The contact of her body against the muscled hardness of his sent a frisson of heat and desire shooting through her. She gasped. Her gaze flew up to his and found his eyes trained on her mouth, his nostrils flared.

She couldn't move. Didn't want to move. No, that was a lie. She wanted to close the distance between them, wanted his mouth on her, wanted it with everything within her.

"Alec." Her voice was the barest whisper of sound.

His head lowered. Her breath caught. Muttering, he stepped off the porch. "We don't want to be late."

"O— of course." She turned away to lock the door as much as to take a few calming breaths. She might have underestimated the power of the sexual pull between them. If she wasn't careful, this could get out of control in a hurry.

With a smile on her face, she joined him on the sidewalk.

He stood as still as a shadow, his expression hard. "Does your brother live far?"

"No." He bit out the word. Opening the passenger door for her, he slammed it shut as soon as she was seated.

As he rounded the truck, another thought struck. Perhaps it wasn't sexual tension. After all, she wasn't that experienced. All right, she had no experience with this. No sexual spark was precisely the main reason she had called off her three engagements.

She waited until he got inside the car. "Alec, if you don't want to take me, I'll call and explain that something came up and you'll be off the hook."

He started the motor. She opened her car door.

His hard gaze snapped to her. "What the—" Reaching across her, he slammed the door shut, but in doing so his bare arm grazed her breasts. She sucked in her breath, his hissed through clenched teeth.

Cautiously she slanted a look at him. Both hands gripped the steering wheel as he stared straight ahead. His chest rose and fell rapidly, as if he had run a race. Since she was having her own breathing issues, she understood his reaction completely.

He *was* fighting the attraction. She wasn't sure how she felt about that, but she did know they were going to be around his family for the next few hours and they couldn't be this jumpy. "Thank you again for the food. I was in my office until ten last night and then I worked at home until around one this morning. The first appointment was with an older couple who recently purchased a three-story house on East Bay. They want it completely redecorated. We drove over there, and it is an amazing property."

Alec put the truck into gear and pulled off. She relaxed. "Despite what Patrick said, I baked a batch of tea cakes to take on the boat. I always get hungry when I'm on the water. My parents have a beach home in Galveston. Not that with my father's busy practice they have time to go there very much."

"Law?" Alec threw the one word at her when he stopped at a signal light.

"Cardiovascular specialist," she told him. "He studied under Dr. DeBakey, the famed father of cardiovascular surgery. I love my job, but I miss my family in Houston."

He pulled off. He seemed intent on the traffic more than on her or what she said.

"You must know what I mean," she said as he drove into the entrance of the underground parking garage of a beautiful upscale condominium on the Ashley River.

He didn't answer until he'd parked. "There is nothing that compares to family, but sometimes you need the space."

"I thought that once, but when it all came down to it, what I really needed was the support and love of my family," she said, not shying away from the pain and sorrow she'd carry for the rest of her life.

He looked at her, impatience in his eyes where she'd once seen desire. "Yeah, I'm sure something major happened. Maybe you couldn't find the right dress for the prom?"

His derision angered her. "You can be such an ass." Opening her door, she got out and slammed it shut.

He got out and slammed his as well. "Don't slam my door."

Smiling, she opened it, eased it closed a few inches, then slammed it shut. "Oops!"

He rounded the vehicle. She put her hands on her hips, her eyes narrowed. He copied her pose.

"Having problems, big brother?"

Celeste whirled to see a younger, gorgeous version of Alec

walking toward them. Mischief shone from his dark eyes; laughter tumbled from sensuous lips. The man was a walking dream.

"Rafael Ricardo Dunlap at your service." Performing a short bow, he took her hand. "And you are?"

"Cut the crap, Rafael," Alec snarled.

Rafael ignored his brother, and Celeste decided to follow suit. "Celeste de la Vega."

Rafael kissed her hand. "Charming name for an exquisite woman, and reminiscent of my grandmother's country, where women are honored and adored."

"Rafael!"

Rafael tucked her hand into the crook of his arm. "Shall we go upstairs? I want to see you in sunlight and perhaps later by candlelight."

Celeste sighed. If Alec said those things to her, she'd be a goner. His brother was lethal.

"Celeste, you're with me, or did you forget!"

She felt the sudden tension in the air, the stillness of Rafael, who had only been playing around. "I didn't forget, but you seemed to have forgotten quite a few things." She pulled her arm free from Rafael. "Please thank Patrick and Brianna for the invitation, but I have a headache. Good-bye."

Rafael caught her arm when she started to move away. "I'd take you home if I thought it was necessary. I'll see you both upstairs." He looked at Alec. "I've always been proud of you."

Alec closed his eyes, rammed his hands into his pockets. Nodding to her, Rafael went to the elevator, punched the button. It opened almost immediately. He entered and the door closed.

Indecision held Celeste still. No one had to tell her that Alec regretted his outburst. The Dunlap brothers were close.

That meant they didn't steal each other's girlfriends. Rafael's remark about being proud of Alec must have cut deeply.

"Rafael loves you."

Alec's eyes opened. "I was jealous," he ground out, each word seemingly more difficult and more unbelievable than the last. "I trust him with my life."

The quick remark wouldn't come. The attraction had caught both of them unaware. Yet while she accepted it, wanted to nourish it and watch it grow, Alec wanted no part of it, of her. That hurt, but not as much as the reason behind him wanting to turn his back on something she felt could be beautiful.

"So what do you want from me?"

His ragged laughter echoed off the wall of the underground garage. "You really don't want to know the answer to that question."

"Tell me, and let me be the judge."

He came to her, heat and anger mixed with arousal. "I want you to lie down and open your—"

A car door slammed. He shook his head, then shoved his hand viciously through his hair. He walked away, then turned back. "You make me crazy. You make me want you until I can't think of anything else!"

"I want you to want me because I want you. At times I can't think of anything else," she said, her voice trembling as much as her body.

A man and a woman passed and got on the elevator.

Alec reached for Celeste, then let his hands fall, shaking his head as if to clear it. "There are things in my life . . . I . . . I have to sort through. You, this, just makes things more complicated."

"Why?"

"Don't push this, Celeste. Just leave it alone."

He looked tired. Without thinking, she brushed her hand over his head, smoothing back a lock of errant hair. She was tempted to curve her hand on the nape of his neck and bring his lips to hers. Instead, she curved her arm through his. "Let's go upstairs and have a good time. We worked hard last week and this week promises to be more of the same. We deserve this."

He took two steps before he stopped and stared down at her. "Today. Just today. There's no tomorrow for us."

Although she ached inside, she smiled. "Then let's make it one to remember."

Almost from the moment Alec and Celeste entered Patrick and Brianna's apartment, he realized that he hadn't been as good at hiding his problem as he'd thought. Besides Rafael, Alec's oldest brother, Sam, and his wife as well as his niece, Brooke, and her husband, John, were there. It was telling that Alec hadn't been aware of their coming. They were all worried about him.

His brothers might be able to hide it, but not the women. During brunch their touches lingered. They tried to stuff food into him just as Celeste had. He only marginally relaxed when they'd eaten and the men stepped outside on the terrace.

"It's happening again," Rafael said.

"What?" Alec asked, only half paying attention. The women were in the kitchen cleaning up. They'd all talked to Simon and Maureen, who were having a wonderful time, shortly before they'd sat down to eat. Afterward, everyone was going out on Patrick's boat.

Alec could hear Celeste's warm laughter mixed with the

other women's. She'd won them over as easily as she did everyone else. He wasn't sure how it happened, but instead of dreading being around his family because he didn't want to worry them, he'd been more aware of Celeste, the way the knit top kept slipping off her shoulder, how he'd like to take it off, and—

"Pay attention, Alec." Rafael elbowed him in the side.

"What?" Alec asked impatiently. He'd tried to apologize earlier for his actions in the garage, but Rafael, in his usual good-natured manner, had brushed it off.

"It must be something in the water, since you aren't living here in the condominium." Rafael scraped the last bit of apple cobbler and ice cream from his bowl. "I might have to stop visiting or stick to bottled water."

"As if any woman would want you," Patrick said playfully.

"She'd have to be hard up in the worst way," Sam agreed. Both men laughed.

"He's a goner for sure," Rafael said matter-of-factly. "Oh, well. I look good in a tux."

Alec slowly straightened from leaning against the frame of the French doors on the terrace. He looked at his three brothers and Brooke's husband as the implications of his brothers' words finally sank in. "Now, wait a minute."

Brooke's husband slapped Alec on the back. "Welcome to the fraternity."

Rafael shuddered. "One I never want to join."

"Wait a darn minute." Alec held up both hands. "I just met Celeste."

Patrick curved his arm around his brother's shoulders. "I knew almost from the time I met Brianna. How about you, Sam?"

"Same here." Sam smiled and looked toward the kitchen. "Turned me down flat three times in a row, but I knew she was the one and only for me."

"It takes some of us longer," John said. "But once you stop fighting it, you wonder what took you so long."

A strange panic hit Alec. "You have this all wrong. We're just dating. Patrick invited her."

"And you can't keep your eyes off her." Rafael's eyes narrowed. "Although I can't blame you. She's beautiful, and the way that top—"

Alec wasn't aware of the guttural sound he was making until Rafael laughed. "My job is done. I think I'll go get some more cobbler and one of those cookies Celeste baked." Whistling, Rafael went inside.

"He's wrong," Alec said, staring at the other men.

"Time will tell. I'm going to check on Brianna," Patrick said. "I don't want her overdoing."

"Brooke won't let her do too much. I'll go with you," John said. Both men went inside.

Alec went to the railing and looked out. The day was beautiful, the sky endless and blue. The calm waters of the river stretched out before him. It was a beautiful day to be alive.

"At certain times in a man's life he shouldn't be alone." His brother came up beside him. "I'm glad you have Celeste."

Alec looked at Sam, but his oldest brother stared straight ahead. He didn't have to ask what Sam meant. "I'm fine."

Sam turned, his gaze direct. "You know how it was when we almost lost Patrick. The anger, the helplessness, then thanking God that his life had been spared. No matter what, I'm glad you came home that morning. Just remember that." Turning away, he went inside.

Alec stared out at the marina again. In his mind, he knew what his brother said was true. In the academy they taught you how to handle confrontations without using your weapon, but that once it was pulled, you had to be ready to use it. It all boiled down to who went home.

"Alec?"

At the anxious sound in Celeste's voice he turned. "Is Brianna all right?"

"Yes." Celeste stepped out on the terrace, placing her hand on his chest. "I just came to tell you we're about ready to leave."

"Then let's go."

She didn't move. "Fun today, remember?"

That was the problem. He remembered too much. "Let's go."

"You, Max, have the once-in-a-lifetime task of creating a garden without walls that will be enjoyed by others long after you're gone," Nettie said as she stood on the acreage surrounding Journey's End. "It will definitely enhance the appeal of your bed-and-breakfast, but more than that it will be a place of quiet beauty, tranquility, and contemplation. You couldn't have selected a more apt name for your establishment than Journey's End."

"Then you think my plans will work?" Gina asked, her face bright and eager.

Max liked the look. Thank goodness he had come to his senses before he hurt her further.

Nettie took Gina's hands in hers, a smile on her kind face. "It will be spectacular. The wisteria arbor in the center with a small table to relax works beautifully. Creating steps and perching planters on either side of them going down to the water is brilliant. So is the idea for a few more well-placed trees."

"Gina has been on point with all of her suggestions for the B and B," Max said, with praise in his voice that he had no intention of hiding again. "I don't know what I would have done if she hadn't agreed to help."

Gina blushed prettily. "Thank you."

"It will be a Herculean task, but the rewards will be immeasurable." Nettie glanced around the yard. "The thing is to plan out everything, including the colors you want reflected, before you purchase one plant."

Max smiled down at Gina. "I've heard that before. We worked on it, but Gina wanted your stamp of approval before we started."

Ophelia laughed. "A man who listens."

Gina and the others joined in.

"Thank all of you so much for coming."

"Thanks for welcoming all of us," Donna said. "The food was fabulous. I want to bake that bread basket for the next Invincible meeting."

"I certainly plan to get the recipe for the strawberry tea." Betty glanced at Max, then Gina. "I promise not to tell anyone outside of the Invincibles."

"Certainly," Max said.

Gina couldn't stop grinning. "It will be my pleasure. Thank all of you."

Nettie reached for Gina's hand again. "You're quite welcome, but you already laid out the foundation. You're a smart woman."

Gina's eyes widened a bit at the compliment. "I— Why, thank you."

"You're welcome," Nettie said.

"She certainly is," Ophelia said. "I'm proud of her."

Gina swallowed. "Thank you, Aunt Ophelia."

"Just telling the truth." Ophelia glanced at her watch. "We'd better get going. We have a tea at the church to attend."

"I used to love going to teas," Sophia said.

"Would you like us to let you know of the next one?" Nettie asked.

"I think I'd like that," Sophia said.

"Consider it done," Ophelia told her.

"I'll walk you back." Max caught the older woman's arm, felt the slight weight, but her steps were steady, her gaze clear and direct. Opening the passenger door of the Mercedes, he helped her inside and closed the door. "Please come again. The door of Journey's End will always be open."

"After tasting the signature strawberry dishes, don't be surprised if you get a call one Saturday afternoon to expect guests for Sunday brunch." Ophelia opened her door.

"I'll hold you to that, but you don't have to call." Max doubted they'd listen. The women were too polite and too well-bred to just drop by. "I welcome you to come by and see the progress."

"Please do come back," Sophia said. "It will be a pleasure having you here again."

"We might take you up on that. Good-bye." Opening the door, Ophelia got inside the car. Starting the motor, she backed up. With a wave, she straightened and drove away.

Max turned to Gina immediately. "You did it!"

"We did it," Gina said. "But there's still a lot of work to be done." She spoke to Sophia. "You mentioned you wanted a retreat. I want to show you an idea I had."

Gina led Max and his aunt to the side of the house with the

garage. "You can add a surface of stone leading from the back porch to here. It will be easy to install pre-made bamboo lattice panels around the air-conditioning units to hide them and plant passion vines to lace over the panels. A tri-level fountain will drown out the noise of the units and help you relax. We can landscape the area with smaller-scale plants that will be low maintenance and add color. Well, what do you think?"

"What I've always thought." Max hugged her to him. "You're amazing."

Gina's eyes widened. He felt her heart rate increase.

"I'm sorry. That shouldn't have happened," Max said, his gaze on Gina's stricken face, all too aware of his aunt slipping away.

"It— it's all right," Gina said, her hand fluttering to her hair. "I'd better be going as well."

He'd scared her. "You haven't seen your Web site yet. Perhaps Gabrielle and Ashton can give me their take on it."

"A— all right."

"Good." Max breathed a bit easier and made sure he kept a respectable distance from her as they entered the house. In the study, he found Ashton watching a soccer game on television and Gabrielle talking on the phone.

Gabrielle saw Max, came upright from reclining on the sofa with her feet off the cushion. "Gotta go." Trying to appear innocent, she quickly hung up the phone.

Max didn't care about her being on the phone. She was cautious and suspicious of him. He just hoped her mother wouldn't be as well. He was all too aware that Gina had lagged behind him as they came into the house.

"Gabrielle, I want you and Ashton to give me your opinion of the Web site I created for your mother."

Gabrielle's gaze went to her mother. The teenager shrugged. "Sure."

Ashton left his TV program. "I wanna help, too."

Seeing that Gina had finally entered the room, Max sat at his desk and moved the mouse. The first thing he did when he came downstairs each morning was turn his computer on. After a few seconds his screen saver, a picture of Journey's End, appeared.

"Could you do that to mine?" Gina asked from two feet away.

"Sure. I'll have your site up in a moment, and you can sit down and navigate it." A few more entries and the site came up. He turned to look at her rather than the screen.

"It's beautiful," she said, edging closer.

"I thought I'd use rotating pictures of the ocean, beach, tropics, the city, and mountains to suggest all the places to travel. A person can select their mode of transportation, their destination, look for special deals. I'll put a counter on so you'll know the traffic. What do you think?"

"It's wonderful," she told him, her gaze going back to the computer. "I don't know how I can thank you."

He brushed aside her words. "It's small in comparison to what you've done for me." He turned to Ashton and Gabrielle. "Let's ask the experts. Well?"

"It's a definite improvement over what Mama had," Gabrielle said.

"Gabrielle, I thought we had the conversation about not speaking your mind even when it's true," Gina deadpanned.

"Max asked for our honest opinion."

"I did," he said, glad for once that Gabrielle appeared to have stopped glaring at him and being suspicious of him, which gave him a thought. It probably helped that, during dinner, he'd convinced Gina to let the children call him by his first name. "Many adults will be traveling with children; what do you two think would make the trip better?"

Gabrielle looked at Ashton. "Not to be bothered by her little brother."

"Or big sister," Ashton came back.

"So," Max said, trying to keep the peace, "if your mother offered free music downloads, electronic games, or interactive books for the children, would that work?"

Gabrielle and Ashton looked expectantly at their mother, who turned her horrified gaze to Max. Knowing Gina didn't have extra money, he talked fast. "You can give five-dollar gift cards for the music downloads, and the interactive books can be found at the dollar store to start with. The electronic games come later, and only with trips that have a considerable profit margin."

"Max, I think you just saved yourself from eating your own cooking," Gina said.

It was almost nine thirty before Gina got Ashton and Gabrielle to bed. Max had named the section for the interactive books Ashton's Place and the music selections Gabrielle's Picks. Both were excited about being on the site and talked nonstop all the way home. Gina had been glad, because her own thoughts were in such turmoil.

She needed time to think, to remember Max's impulsive hug. He'd apologized. She wished he hadn't. Too restless to sit, she paced in her bedroom. His arms felt good around her. The beating of his heart was comforting and exciting at the same time.

She picked up the phone and punched in Celeste's phone number, chewing on her bottom lip.

"Hello," Celeste answered before the phone rang a second time.

"You must have been sitting by the phone," Gina said.

"I was," Celeste admitted. "I rather hoped Alec would stop trying to ignore this thing we have between us, but . . ."

"I'm sorry." Gina sat on the side of her bed. "We aren't having much success where men are concerned."

"We? Explain yourself, *chica*."

Gina picked at the navy comforter. "I, er, I'm not sure I can."

"Just start talking, and we'll sort it out."

"I— I have these strange feelings toward Max, and this afternoon he hugged me."

"Yes!" Celeste shouted. "I knew it!"

"He apologized, but sometimes I get the strangest feelings when he looks at me," Gina confessed, then told her about the afternoon. "He's kind, considerate. He's careful to include Gabrielle and Ashton. Maybe I'm putting too much into this."

"And maybe you're not," Celeste said. "Alec is fighting the chemistry between us with all he has. I plan to fight just as hard to break down his resistance. I just haven't figured out what to do next."

"We're a pair," Gina said. "A short time ago I was miserable, feeling like a failure."

"And I hadn't met a man who turned my knees to jelly and made me want to do wicked things to him," Celeste mused.

"When you finish with Maureen's house, I'm ready to look at redecorating around here."

"Hallelujah," Celeste cheered. "You have the samples of

fabrics. Since they're last season's I can work a deal so your budget won't even feel it."

Gina realized something. "You knew how tight finances have been, didn't you? That's why you insisted I go talk to Maureen and Traci about their travel plans."

"If I hadn't had referrals, my interior design business would have never gotten off the ground," Celeste said. "The main thing is that you came through."

"Max built me a fantastic Web site that should help increase business."

"If that happens, will you have time to continue helping him?"

Gina hadn't considered the possibility. "I like helping Max."

"Then for the time being do both," Celeste advised. "Have him put your cell phone number on the Web site, and you add it to your answering machine recording. That way prospective clients can always reach you."

"I'll do that. Good night, and good luck tomorrow."

"Good night, and the same to you."

Gina hung up the phone, thinking she'd need more than luck.

Monday morning Celeste parked beside the walkway leading to Maureen's front door and drummed her fingers on the steering wheel. She still didn't have a concrete plan, and it didn't appear as if she were going to come up with one. If she were just dealing with breaking down Alec's resistance to dating her, that would be one thing, but a lot more was involved.

She understood that Alec was dealing with the guilt of taking a man's life. Until Alec reconciled that, he didn't want a woman clouding the issue. What he didn't understand was that she wanted to be there for him, that she understood what he was going through. She wanted to help. She wanted to see the carefree Alec she'd caught glimpses of in the past, and she was honest enough to admit she wanted the passionate one as well.

A soft rap on her window jarred her out of her thoughts. She jerked around, unable to hide her disappointment. Opening her door, she stepped out of the van. "Good morning, Willie."

"You certainly are the chipper one this morning." The older woman folded her arms. "One guess as to the reason."

"You'd be right." Celeste went to the back of the van for her toolbox and set it on the driveway. "He's a hard nut to crack."

"But my money's on you." Willie picked up the toolbox. "You're not giving up, are you?"

"Nope." Celeste picked up a medium-sized ice chest and closed the door. "But I must admit I'm not sure what to do next."

"You'll think of something."

"When? To take a quote from you, 'Time's a-wastin'." Opening the front door, she let them inside. "I'll put our lunch in the fridge."

"Did you bring his, too?" Willie asked.

"No, I didn't." For the first time Celeste gave a semblance of a smile. "He told me not to, so I didn't. Yesterday I learned from his brothers that Alec is a terrible cook, has the phone number of every imaginable place to eat on his cell and house phone. He's going to miss my cooking."

"And that means he's going to think of you and miss you," Willie said with a grin. "That sounds like a plan to me."

Celeste's smile faded. "But it's not enough."

"You've got weeks to think of something," Willie told her. "It will come to you."

"I suppose." Celeste went to the kitchen. She wrinkled her nose at the smell of burnt food. The handle of a skillet jutted from a sink of soapy water. Apparently Patrick had been on target about Alec's cooking skills, or lack thereof. He'd probably burned his breakfast. Stubborn man.

Going to the refrigerator, she opened it. Except for the few staples she'd purchased and several bottles of water, the shelves were bare. At least there was no beer. Opening the chest, she placed her and Willie's lunch of shrimp salad inside. Next came the two generous slices of lemon pound cake, the whipped cream and raspberries that would go on top, and bread sticks.

Shutting the door, she turned and went still. Alec. He was half-turned away from her. From his position, she couldn't tell if he had seen her and decided to leave or had changed his mind about leaving. Last night he'd stood off the porch while she opened her door. As soon as she'd said good night and gone inside, he practically ran to his car.

"Good morning, Alec."

He straightened. "Good morning, Celeste."

"I was just putting away our lunch." She rushed on when his eyes narrowed. "For me and Willie. Shrimp salad with lemon pound cake. I had a good time yesterday. You have a wonderful family."

"Yeah."

Alec certainly didn't do small talk.

"Willie is waiting. Bye." Celeste walked close enough to Alec for him to smell the exotic perfume she'd worn just for this moment. She wanted him to remember and yearn. From the sudden acceleration of his breathing, his clenched fists, he did.

A few steps past him, she began humming. She might be inexperienced, but she recognized when a man wanted her.

The day had just gotten brighter.

FIFTEEN

Gina waved the children off to school at a quarter past seven Monday morning. Ashton didn't care if she walked him to the car; Gabrielle thought it signaled she was still a baby. Since she and her daughter were enjoying peace for the first time in weeks, Gina stayed on the porch.

Closing the door, Gina smiled. She had Max to thank for that. Gabrielle had become Gina's champion, but it had also shown her that Gabrielle appreciated her as well.

Out of habit more than anything, Gina went to check her e-mail. She'd turned the computer on while she prepared breakfast. She had dial-up to save money, and therefore it took forever for her machine to boot up.

Entering her password, she thought of how well Sunday had gone. Yes, people appreciating you meant a great deal. E-mail popped up and she clicked on the symbol, automatically sliding the cursor to the bottom of the screen. Delete and Spam got the most action.

She blinked, then leaned closer to the computer screen. She couldn't believe her eyes as she counted the business e-mails, then counted again. The seven e-mails requesting information on various trips didn't go away. Excitement rushed through her. She smiled, then laughed aloud.

"Max, you did it!" She reached for the phone to call him, then decided to tell him in person, just as soon as she answered the requests for travel information.

An hour later, she arrived at Journey's End. For the first time Max didn't greet her. She pushed away her slight disappointment. The man had more to do than watch for her. Getting out of her car, she rushed up the sidewalk and onto the porch. She couldn't wait to tell him about the great response she'd gotten from her Web site.

Sophia answered the doorbell. "Good morning, Gina. Come on in."

"Good morning, Sophia." Gina stepped inside, then followed Sophia to the kitchen. "Where's Max?"

"He left for the home improvement store about fifteen minutes ago." Sophia waved Gina to a seat at the kitchen table and sat down. "Can I get you a cup of coffee?"

"No, thank you." Gina eased into the straight-backed chair. "He went without me," she said, then tried to backtrack as she heard the pitiful way she sounded. "I mean, I'm just surprised he decided to start today."

From the knowing look on Sophia's face, she wasn't buying Gina's explanation. "He just went to buy a couple of books, talk to the people there about the arbor for the wisteria."

"He agreed with my suggestion to make that the centerpiece of the gardens," Gina said.

"It's his tribute to Sharon," Sophia said, staring straight at Gina and picking up her coffee cup. "In fact, she's the reason for Journey's End."

Gina felt a strange tightness in her chest. "Sharon?"

"His deceased wife."

Gina had known Max was a widower but not the name of his wife. Nameless, she hadn't seemed real, but a name gave her a presence.

"They loved each other very much," Sophia said softly. "He was lost when she died suddenly of a brain aneurysm. She'd always talked of running a bed-and-breakfast after they retired. We feared we'd lose him, too, afterward. Nothing seemed to matter to him . . . until he remembered her dream for them."

"I envy her that kind of love," Gina whispered before she thought. Robert had left her with a smile on his face, never looking back or missing one thing they'd shared.

"Then you're ungrateful and selfish," Sophia said, setting her cup down with a clink.

Gina's shoulders snapped back against the chair. "W— what?"

Pushing her cup and saucer aside, Sophia planted her arms on the table and leaned forward. "At least you had a man who at one time loved you. You know the intimacy of a man, the joys a man can bring. So the blessing didn't last. You have two beautiful children as a result. I never had either."

Not knowing how to respond, Gina didn't say anything.

"So you're a single parent. So what?" Sophia shoved her hand in Gina's direction. "You're young and healthy with a roof over your head, a car to drive, and good friends who support you. You can make a new life. I'm sixty-five. I'm too old to have children, haven't had a date in twenty-five years, and no prospects in sight. If it wasn't for Max, I'd be back in Memphis growing old in a big house with only the echo of my voice to keep me company."

Gina's heart went out to the older woman. Reaching out, Gina placed her hand on hers. "Nettie is sixty-nine, a widow, and is keeping company, as she calls it, with a widower. It's not too late to find someone."

The corners of Sophia's mouth tilted upward slightly. "Nettie remains an attractive woman, cultured, of average height. My face is broad, I say what I want, and stand five nine in my stocking feet." She leaned back in her chair.

"I'm the oldest of four daughters," Sophia went on to say. "I took after my father's mother, Big Ella. She could pick a thousand pounds of cotton a day, dipped snuff like a man, and cursed like a sailor. My sisters are beautiful and always had a boyfriend. I'm the odd one. That's why it pisses me off to hear a woman whine about how some man or life has treated her. When she does that, she forgets her blessings."

"I'm sorry. You're right," Gina said slowly. "Every time something has gone wrong since the divorce I blame my ex-husband, blame myself for not making the marriage work. I never looked at it any other way."

"You were too close with too many things coming at you," Sophia told her. "But you're getting there. You're not the same woman who came to the open house with a bit of desperation in her eyes."

"Because of Max," Gina admitted freely.

"His belief in you or hiring you?" Sophia asked.

"Both. He helped me when I didn't know where to turn," she explained. "Celeste or my family would have helped financially, but I wanted to do it on my own. Like you, I'm the exception in the perfect family, the only one who has failed or messed up countless ways. This time I wanted to stand on my own and succeed."

"You're doing that, and you're helping Max."

"They must have been very happy," Gina mused.

"They were, but like a lot of young people they thought they had forever." Sophia got up and rinsed her cup in the sink. "You get my age and look back and ask where the time has gone. You begin to count each day as precious, taking nothing for granted, living each day to the fullest." She retook her seat. "Live your life in the present, not in the past."

For some odd reason Gina felt tears clog her throat, but there was a smile on her face. "Looking back, you can't look forward."

Sophia beamed at Gina as if she were one of her star pupils. "Exactly."

The back screen door opened and banged shut. In a few moments, Max entered, carrying an armload of magazines. Gina's heart sighed, then sped up. "Good morning, Max." He looked handsome in a white polo shirt and jeans that fit his muscular legs lovingly.

"Good morning, Gina. I went to get some magazines for us to look at to select the plan for the arbor." He pulled out a chair beside her and scooted closer until only a scant inch separated them. "I met a couple of handymen there who said they could build anything we want."

Gina stared down at the magazine on the table, wondering if Max was aware he'd used "we" and "us." Did he view her as someone who was helping him honor the dream and memory of his wife or as a woman he genuinely cared about?

"The arbor has to be strong if it's to support the wisteria, one of the men said," Max went on to say. "I'm thinking a natural look to blend in. What do you think?"

Gina glanced up into black eyes that made her heart sigh again, remembered looking forward, not backward. "I like it."

He smiled back, then looked down at the magazine. "I want to get started by the end of the week. In the meantime, I saw some pots already filled with flowers at the home improvement store that we could get to make the front porch and the back look more inviting."

Gina shook her head. "For the front of the house, potted plants would look great, but I've always liked non-traditional planters like wheelbarrows, a child's wagon, or an old washstand for the yard. They give the yard more character and interest. By planting the flowers in pots ourselves for the front, we could ensure we keep to a color theme," Gina said, purposefully using the "we." "And it would be less expensive."

"Yes, ma'am." He laughed and turned the page.

She looked at his aunt watching them, a pleased smile on her face. "But first we're going to create Sophia's outdoor retreat."

"No," Sophia said, shaking her head. "The grounds come first."

Max stood and went to her. "You come first. Without you, I wouldn't be here. I wouldn't have found myself."

Tears sparkling in her eyes, Sophia hugged him. "Without you, where would I be?"

Leaning away from her, he brushed the tears away from her eyes. "Looks like we rescued each other." He glanced around at Gina. "The nice thing about that is you never know who is rescuing whom."

Gina felt the warmth of his gaze, tried for all of two seconds to make herself believe he was just being nice. Then she smiled back. If she was going to be a fool, at least it was over a man she admired.

Late Monday afternoon, Alec placed a piece of flashing on the center footing, then wedged the last section of a four-by-four to rest on it to finish the base of the structure of the gazebo just as lightning flashed, followed by the boom of thunder. Dark gray clouds swept across the sky. Pulling a tarp over the lumber, Alec headed inside. For once, the weatherman's prediction of a storm was right.

Inside the house, Alec closed the door just as the rain hit in blinding sheets. Locking the door, he picked up the work shoes he'd taken off and continued through the living area.

"Oh, no!"

Hearing Celeste's yell, he dropped the shoes and hit the stairs running and almost barreled into her as she rounded the corner of the stairs. "What is it?" he asked, his gaze going beyond her as he looked for the cause.

"The rain. I had intended to be gone by now," she told him. "I got caught up in a phone call with a client and forgot about the time. I intended to be home before this hit."

Alec relaxed, but his fingers remained on her warm, bare skin just above her elbow. "Looks like you didn't make it."

She shot him a look of annoyance, then pushed against his chest. "What an astute observation, Officer Dunlap."

He watched her run lightly down the stairs, her toolbox in her hand. How could one woman annoy him and make him want to rip off her clothes and take her to bed at the same time?

She jerked open the front door. "Great. Just great!"

Alec stopped just behind her. The smell of rain mixed with her unique scent. He'd like nothing better than to make love to her in the rain; their passion would be just as powerful.

"Oh, well." Ducking her head, she started out the door.

Alex caught her arm, dragging her back before she had taken more than a couple of steps. Still, the blowing rain dampened her knit top and jeans. "What do you think you're doing?"

"Trying to go home," she told him.

"Are you crazy?" he asked, aware his voice had risen and unable to do anything about it. "You can't see a foot in front of you. Low places are probably flooded by now."

Her small chin lifted imperiously. "I planned to wait until it died down."

"And in the meantime you'd be wet and chilled sitting in the van," he told her. "What kind of sense does that make when you can wait inside?"

"I didn't want to be in your way," she said.

His hand unclamped. He stepped back. Horror washed across his face. "You think that badly of me?"

She rolled her eyes. "Men! And they call women flighty." She closed the door, set her toolbox on the floor, and put her hands on her hips. "You've made it clear that you don't want me around."

"I don't want you injured," he said; just the thought made his chest ache.

"I never thought you did." Turning, she opened the door, then shut it. "It hasn't let up, so it seems you have a temporary guest. I think there are some things you need to know."

She wasn't going into a storm. He could handle anything else. "Such as?"

"I'm afraid of the dark."

He almost laughed until her gaze darted away.

"At home I have a backup generator, flashlights with extra batteries in every room of my house." She slipped her hands into the pockets of her jeans. "I was kicked out of the Girl Scouts because I refused to go camping."

Alec couldn't imagine bold, take-charge Celeste afraid of anything. She had certainly stood toe-to-toe with him and not batted her lush lashes.

"What do you plan to do with me?"

He could think of all sorts of pleasurable things to do with her, but he was sure she hadn't meant the remark sexually. Pity. "Come with me." Not waiting for an answer, he went to the kitchen and opened a drawer. Taking out a flashlight that was almost as long as her arm, he handed it to her.

Closing her hand around the flashlight, she clicked it on, then shone the beam of light into her face before cutting it off. "Thank you."

"You're welcome. I'm going to take a shower." He paused in the doorway. The well-built house muted the storm, but he could still see the crackle of lightning, imagine the shuddering boom of thunder that followed. "Will you be all right until I get back?"

"Strangely, storms don't bother me," she told him. "Go on, but don't be surprised to see me if the lights go out."

He recalled all too well standing before her, fully aroused, aching with desire. He'd walked away then; he wasn't so sure he could again. Especially with her looking at him as if she wanted him. Turning back, he went to pick up his shoes again, then ran up the stairs as fast as his legs would carry him, because if he didn't, he'd reach for her and this time he wouldn't let her go.

Alec undressed with jerky motions in his room and stepped under the jetted spray of the shower. No matter how hard he tried not to, thoughts of Celeste there with him in the darkened enclosure as they used their hands and mouths to learn each other's bodies, listened for the sighs and moans of pleasure to learn what pleased the most, crept into his mind.

He cut the shower short, unsure if he'd done so because he was afraid she might actually join him or afraid he wouldn't be able to resist her if she did. Dressed, he went back downstairs to the kitchen.

And found it empty. A loneliness he didn't want to feel settled over him. He picked up the note by the flashlight on the island.

The rain slacked off, so I'm leaving. Thanks for the shelter. The lights didn't flicker once. Pity!
Celeste

He laughed, a rusty sound that ended in a groan. Her honesty made him rock hard. And it was only going to get worse.

Talking to her mother on her cell phone, Celeste opened her back door to the ringing of her landline. "Hold on, Mama." She picked up the extension in the kitchen. "Hello."

"I just wanted to make sure you reached home all right."

"I did. Thanks, Alec," she said, although she wanted to tuck her head on remembering the note she'd left.

"Your lights on?"

Heat infused her body. "Yes."

"Good. Night."

"Good night, Alec." Celeste slowly hung up the phone, then

remembered her mother. "Mama, I'm home safe, so I'll talk to you later."

"Who's Alec?"

Celeste shook her head. Her mother had the ears of a bat. "The brother-in-law of a client."

"Which one? Why is he calling you?"

In her room, Celeste pulled off her knit top. She was in for it now. "You don't know him. It stormed here, so he wanted to make sure I reached home all right."

"That was nice of him. Is he young? What does he do?" her mother asked.

"Mama, he's just a guy. I'd really like to get out of these wet clothes and take a bath."

"All right," her mother said. "Don't forget to take your vitamin C before you go to bed and drink honeyed green tea with lots of fresh lemons."

Celeste had to smile as she untied her shoes. Her mother fussed over all of them. "I won't, Mama. Kiss Dad for me. I love you both."

"Then bring home a nice young man for Christmas."

Celeste hung her head. Her mother also had a one-track mind at times. Perhaps she should have let the call go to voice mail. "Mama, please."

"You'll thank me one day. Good night, Celeste."

"Good night, Mama."

Finished undressing, Celeste headed for the bathroom. A picture of Alec, naked, muscular, and magnificent, flashed before her. If the lights had gone out would she have gone to him? She'd never know, and that annoyed the hell out of her.

. . .

Max enjoyed his time with Gina more and more. Her bright laughter and quick smile made his days brighter. She wasn't afraid of work. She tried so hard to please everyone. And, at times, that annoyed him. She was so smart and so ready to help others.

"I think we did a good job." Hands on her hips, she stared down at the bricked area beneath their feet. When he didn't answer she looked back over her shoulder at him.

The evening sun slanting over the house caught the highlights in her reddish black hair, the brightness of her chocolate eyes, the softness of her red lips.

"Max?" She frowned and turned fully toward him. "You all right?"

He couldn't help it. He touched his knuckled fingers to her cheek. Her skin was as soft and touchable as he'd imagined. Her eyes flew wide, but she didn't step back. *Good.* "You always worry about other people. I wonder who worries about you."

She looked away, but not before he saw the stricken look on her face. His hands clenched.

"We've made good progress the last three days with Aunt Sophia's retreat," he said, wanting to restore their earlier camaraderie. "We should be finished by Friday night. What do you say we treat ourselves and go to a movie?"

Her head lifted. Surprised delight stared back at him. "You want to take me to a movie?"

"Yes." He took a chance and laced her fingers with his so there would be no misunderstanding. She wore the gloves he'd insisted on as they laid the brick, but he felt her tremble, saw the lips he thought of more and more do the same. He wanted to press his own mouth there. It amazed him how much.

She swallowed, looked down, then up over his shoulder before meeting his gaze. "I'd like that very much."

Resisting the growing temptation to kiss her, he squeezed her hand. "You pick out what to see. We'll check the schedule before you leave today, and go from there."

"I'd like that." She pulled her hand free and took off her gloves. "Ashton's practice should be almost over and I have to pick him up and then Gabrielle."

"We all keep you pretty busy." He reached for her gloves, then went up the back steps to open the screen door.

"I like being busy." Inside, she washed her hands over the sink and dried them with a paper towel. "I'd take this over the day before I met you any day."

He stuck his hands under the water she'd left running. "Your Web site still bringing in prospective clients?"

"*Clients,*" she emphasized the word. "Ashton was so excited that a couple wanting to come for the Christmas holidays loved his idea of a travel package for their twin boys his age."

The pride and satisfaction looked good on her. She'd come a long way since they'd met. He picked up the ice chest. "If things get too hectic, just say so."

Opening the refrigerator, she took out two plastic containers and placed them in the chest he held open. "I like the way things are now. I just wish I had more time to—" She stopped, tucked her head, and dove back into the refrigerator for the third and last container.

"To what?" he prompted when she put the ice chest lid down without elaborating. "Gina, if I'm taking too much of your time, all you have to do is say so."

Shoving his hand away, she took the handle. "It's not that."

He planted his body directly in front of hers. "Then tell me.

It obviously has something to do with time, and I consume a lot of it."

"Max—"

"Tell me."

"Exercise," she blurted. She stepped around him and quickly went out the back door.

"Well, you've done it now," Sophia said from the doorway.

"Damn." He rushed out after Gina, barely catching her, and only then because she was too polite to ignore his frantic calls for her to wait. He raced to the driver's side. She stared straight ahead. He hoped the blinking of her eyes and clenching of the steering wheel didn't mean she was about to cry.

Crap. Any male with common sense knew women were sensitive about their weight. To him, she looked good the way she was.

She swallowed. Swallowed again.

"I'm sorry, Gina. I just wanted to make sure you weren't neglecting yourself." He rubbed his hand over his face. "You take care of everyone before you take care of yourself. You showed that at the brunch for the Invincibles, by helping me, by being there for your children. I just wanted to make sure you had time for yourself. Please don't leave angry."

Her head leaned forward until it rested on the steering wheel. Max opened the door, taking her arms and gently turning her toward him. "Please, Gina, look at me."

Slowly her head lifted. The tears and ravaged eyes weren't there. "I've never met a man like you."

His hand tenderly cupped her face. "I guess you bring out the best in me."

She clasped her hands in her lap. "Robert gave me a stationary bicycle two years ago. I've only been on it once. Guess I should have taken the hint."

"I run five miles every morning, but it's something I've gotten used to. Aunt Sophia prefers to do calisthenics," he said. "What do you want to do?"

She shrugged. "Something. Anything."

"I've an idea. Why don't I check the bike out when I come over Friday to pick you up? Maybe I can devise a way to put a laptop on it so you can work and exercise at the same time."

"That would mean we're still on for Friday night?" she asked cautiously.

"Yes, it would," he told her, hoping he hadn't ruined things.

"I'll think about it. I have to go." She started the motor.

He wanted to argue but stood instead. "If I didn't think you'd be late, I wouldn't let you go until it was settled and Friday night still on."

She jerked her head back around and stared at him a long time. "It's important to you?"

"Extremely. I'd very much like to take you out."

"In that case, we're back on." Closing her door, she backed out of the driveway.

Max shot his fist into the air. "You won't be sorry!" he yelled, grinning for all he was worth.

SIXTEEN

Gina pulled into Maureen's driveway with a flourish. Brakes squeaked as she came to a stop. Opening the door, she reminded herself to have them checked first thing in the morning. "I won't be but a moment."

"Why are you stopping here?" Ashton asked from the backseat.

"I'm expecting a phone call," Gabrielle said.

"I won't be long," Gina told them, and stood.

"I'm hungry," Ashton told her.

"Me, too."

Gina almost relented and got back in the car. No. This was for her. "Your dinner is in the cooler in the trunk. All I have to do is warm it up in the microwave." With that, she went to the door and rang the bell. She threw an anxious glance over her shoulder. The car trunk was up. She could see the top of

Gabrielle's head, and since she couldn't see Ashton in the backseat, she surmised he was with her.

They weren't going to be happy to see the veal cutlets, but Gina hoped the peach cobbler would help. She turned back around, debating whether she should go around the back. She'd called Celeste as soon as she'd left Max and said she had something important to tell her and was coming by.

Gina was about to go back to the car for her cell phone when the door opened. Her mouth opened, but nothing came out.

"Can I help you?"

Her mouth snapped shut. It wasn't every day you saw a man so well built with unsmiling eyes. "Hello. I'm Gina Rawlings. I'm here to see Celeste."

He stepped back. "Please come in. I'm Alec Dunlap. She's probably upstairs. Third door on the right."

"Thank you, Alec."

With the barest nod, he continued toward the kitchen. Gina stared after him for a moment, then hit the stairs. "Celeste."

"Gina." Celeste appeared on the landing, meeting her midway. "What has you so excited?"

"Max asked me out to a movie Friday night," she said.

Celeste squealed. Gina joined her, both women jumping up and down.

"What is going on?" Alec asked, one stocking foot planted on the bottom step.

"Girl talk, Alec," Celeste said, still grinning.

"Might have known it," he said, and went back toward the kitchen.

Celeste longingly followed each step until he disappeared.

"He's still being difficult?" Gina asked.

"Impossible." Celeste sat on the landing, pulling Gina down with her. "He hasn't said more than five words to me since he called to check on me the night of the storm. Wish I could say the same for Mama. She's called every day, asking about Alec."

Alec came back into view with a bottle of water in his hand. He never looked up.

Celeste's lips tightened. "He's just being stubborn." She firmly turned to Gina. "I want to hear all the details."

Gina, aware of two impatient children, told her, "It's not a real date or anything."

"Sounds like a date to me." Celeste grinned. "I'll drop by after work Friday and check on Ashton and Gabrielle, so you can just concentrate on having fun."

"I'm not sure I know how to do that or how to act." Gina came to her feet.

"I'll call you tonight and give you some pointers." Hooking her arm through Gina's, Celeste started down the stairs. "One of us might as well use my expertise."

Gina stopped at the front door. "You wouldn't let me give up. I won't let you."

"Who said I'm giving up?' Celeste opened the door. "I'm just strategizing. Good-bye."

"Good-bye." Gina rushed back to the car. Opening the door, she caught the unmistakable whiff of peach cobbler. Gabrielle had a book in front of her face, a dead giveaway. Ashton was quiet and bent over his drawing pad. "Is there any peach cobbler left?"

Gabrielle's book came down, Ashton's head came up. They started talking at once. Each blamed hunger. "Well, since you're both so hungry, I'm sure you'll eat your brussels sprouts, unlike the last time."

Grinning, then laughing at their groans, Gina pulled out of the driveway. Life was becoming fun again.

"You can't go out with him. What will Daddy think?" Gabrielle asked from beside Gina in the den. Several feet away, Ashton was stretched out in front of the television watching a Disney movie.

Gina looked at her daughter's angry face and wanted to put her head down and bawl. Why couldn't she make Gabrielle understand that whatever she and her father had shared was over, that as strange as it might seem, she wanted to go out and have fun?

"Gabrielle, your father has no say in what I do," Gina said. Wasn't it bad enough that she hadn't even lost an ounce, was worried about how she looked, if she had put too much into tonight with Max?

Her face mutinous, Gabrielle folded her arms. "He should. Max shouldn't be coming here."

"I like Max," Ashton said from his perch in front of the television.

His sister glared at him. "You're too young to understand, so be quiet."

"You can't make me."

Gabrielle turned on him and smiled coldly. "Wanna bet? Mama is leaving me in charge."

Her son's worried gaze flew to his mother. "Are you, Mama?"

Thank goodness for Celeste. "Not for long. Celeste is coming over."

Ashton stuck out his tongue.

Gabrielle followed suit.

The doorbell rang. Gina hurried to answer. She loved her children, but at the moment she wanted to be with an adult. She opened the door.

"Hello, Gina."

"Hello, Max." And Max was the adult she wanted to be with. The man looked positively mouthwatering. "Come on in and have a seat. I'll get my purse."

"You look very nice."

"Thank you." She closed the door. So he hadn't called her pretty; she'd get over it. In the den, she glanced around for Gabrielle.

"Hi, Ashton."

Ashton got up and ran to Max. "Hi, Max. Mama said you're taking her to a movie."

"That's right." Max squatted down to eye level. "I'll take good care of your mother."

"I know, but Gab—"

"Ashton," Gina cut in. They were going to need another talk about repeating conversations. "Where is your sister?"

Ashton shrugged. "I dunno."

"Max, I'll just go tell Gabrielle we're leaving," Gina said.

"Take your time." Max took a seat on the sofa. "How was practice this week?"

"Great. We play another hard team tomorrow," Ashton said. "My daddy is coming to watch me play."

"You must be excited," Max said.

Ashton nodded. "This time he promised."

Gina didn't want to hear any more. She went upstairs to

Gabrielle's room. The door was closed. Gina knocked softly. "Gabrielle. Max is here. Gabrielle, you have to come downstairs."

The door opened. Gabrielle leaned weakly against the door. "I don't feel so good."

All irritation left Gina. Shortly after Robert left, Gabrielle began having headaches. The doctor said they were due to stress and prescribed over-the-counter medication. Gradually they had tapered off. The last one was more than a month ago. Gina felt her daughter's forehead. Cool. "You were fine a minute ago."

"I'm sick now." Irritation in her voice, she wrapped her arms around her waist. "You can still go on your date. I'll go watch Ashton." She started past her mother, her steps slow, her head bent.

"No." Gina caught her arm. "You go to bed. I'll get your medicine."

"I can't watch Ashton in bed."

"I'm not going." Gina helped Gabrielle back into her room. Setting her on her bed, Gina got Gabrielle's pajamas. "Can you get undressed by yourself?"

Something flickered in her eyes; then she tucked her head. "Yes, ma'am."

"I'll be back." Gina went down the stairs. She heard Max's and Ashton's laughter before she entered the room. "Max."

His head came up. He stood. "Is everything all right?"

"Gabrielle has a headache. I won't be able to go." She twisted her hands. "I'm sorry."

He crossed to her. "So am I. Can I do anything to help?"

Somehow she smiled when she wanted to cry. "No, thank you."

Tenderly he brushed his hand down her arm. "I'll see myself out; good night."

"Good night," Gina croaked as she watched Max leave.

"You look sad, Mama," Ashton said.

"I'm fine," she said. "I'm going to take Gabrielle her medicine. Be good for Mama."

"I will," Ashton said. "Max said we males have to take care of women. He said I should help you."

Ashton stared up at her so seriously, Gina felt a pang in her heart. Max thought of her when no one else did. For now, it was enough.

It took Max thirty-four minutes to carry out his preparations and get back to Gina's house. He rang the doorbell and waited.

Gina opened the door, happiness widening her eyes. "Max."

He held up the bags in his hands. "G-rated movies, popcorn, candy, drinks. Looks like our movie date is still on."

Her lips trembled, then firmed. "Please come in."

"Thanks." He stepped inside the foyer. "How is Gabrielle?"

"Better, I think. She's resting in her room." Gina closed the door.

Max seriously doubted if Gabrielle was really ill. The illness must have occurred suddenly. There was no way Gina would have even thought of going out with her daughter sick. "Maybe she'll be well enough to join us later."

"Max, you're back!" Ashton shouted with glee when he saw Max.

"And I didn't come empty-handed." He held up the sacks in his hands. "With your mother's permission, we're going to pop popcorn and watch a movie. *Charlotte's Web* is first up."

"Can we, Mama?"

"Yes."

Ashton took off for the kitchen. Max leaned over and whispered as he passed Gina, "Once Ashton is asleep, I have a more grown-up movie."

In the kitchen, Max insisted Gina take a seat. "This I can do." Five minutes later he had the popcorn, candy bars, and drinks on a tray. With Ashton standing beside him, he slipped the movie into the DVD player. Sitting down beside Gina on the sofa, he picked up the tray.

Ashton squeezed in between them. "This is great. Daddy was always too busy to watch a movie with us."

Max carefully kept his eyes straight ahead and handed the popcorn to Ashton. "Share with your mother."

"I will." Ashton grabbed a fistful, then handed the popcorn to his mother. She took a couple of popped kernels.

"I'm going to check on Gabrielle."

Max watched Gina go, wondering if she'd used checking on Gabrielle as an excuse to leave. Minutes passed, then another. He had begun to wonder whether Gina was returning when she came back with Gabrielle. The teenager gave him a hard look, then curled up in a high-backed chair across the room.

"Hi, Gabrielle. Glad you're feeling better."

Gina stroked her hand over her daughter's head. "Do you want candy or a soft drink?"

"A Sprite."

"I'll get it." Gina left and returned shortly with the can of soda and a glass of ice.

Gabrielle uncurled enough to move a coaster on the end table near her. Gina opened the soft drink, filled the glass, gave it to

Gabrielle, and placed the can beside the coaster. Brushing her hand over her daughter's forehead again, Gina took her seat.

Max glanced at Gabrielle, who stared back at him. She might have won that round, but Max had no intention of giving up on seeing Gina.

"Mama had a date last night," Gabrielle told her father before he was barely inside the front door of the house Saturday morning.

"Gabrielle," Gina said, annoyed with her daughter. "It was hardly a date. You and Ashton were there."

"We saw movies and had popcorn," Ashton said with his usual high spirits.

Robert laughed and patted his daughter on the head as if she were five instead of thirteen. "If she can find a man, your mother should date."

He intended the remark to sting her pride. She smiled. "You'd be surprised."

"You can't mean that, Daddy," Gabrielle wailed.

"Your mother isn't getting any younger," Robert said snidely.

Gina looked at her ex, from his balding head to his long feet. He wore a white T-shirt with the name of his gym on the back, white shorts, and tennis shoes to show off the muscular build he was so proud of. "I'm a year younger than you, and have more hair."

He blinked. Smiling sweetly, Gina opened the front door. "Have a good time."

Robert took off for his convertible, with Gabrielle following closely. Her hand on Ashton's shoulder, Gina walked him to his father's car. Gabrielle acted as if she couldn't wait to be gone.

On the sidewalk, Gina hugged Ashton, bid Gabrielle good-bye. Robert had started around to the driver's side when Max pulled up in his SUV and parked behind the late-model Cadillac.

"Is this one of your coaches, Ashton?" Robert asked.

"It's Max," Ashton said, happily meeting Max halfway.

"Good morning, Gina." Max ruffled his hand across Ashton's head. "Hi, partner. Gabrielle, glad to see you look as if you're feeling better this morning."

Robert frowned. "Who are you?"

"It's him," Gabrielle said, glaring at Max. "The man Mama is dating."

The incredulous look on her ex-husband's face was priceless. His eyes bugged as Max came to stand beside her. Gina felt like laughing and she let it rip. It was glaringly obvious that Robert hadn't thought that a handsome, well-built man who was four inches taller than him and who had a headful of thick black hair would be interested in her. Robert was peacock proud and hated his premature balding.

Gina looped her arm through Max's strong, powerful one. "Good-bye. Be careful and have a good time."

"I'll see you later at the game, Ashton. Have a good time, Gabrielle," Max said.

Robert cleared his throat. "I—er—I'm having staffing problems. I have to get back to the gym by one. I'm dropping the children off at Ashton's game."

Gina snatched her arm down and advanced angrily on Robert. "You promised Ashton. You can't do this again."

"Daddy, you promised," Ashton said. "I told all my friends."

Robert frowned at Gina. "You know I'd come if I could."

Gina bit her tongue to keep from calling him a liar. "When were you going to tell them?"

"They understand, don't you, kids?" Robert asked, getting inside the car.

Dutifully they mumbled, "Yes." Gina shook, she was so angry. "Robert—" She bit off the word when Max's fingers curled around her upper arm. "You'll hear from me about this."

"Get in the car, kids," Robert ordered. As soon as the children buckled up, he pulled off.

"He makes me so angry!" Gina gritted out. "He always has excuses. His visitation is every two weeks, but he seldom keeps them over an hour or two, if he comes at all. Can't he see he's hurting his children with his selfishness?"

"No. He can't." Taking her arm, Max took her back inside. Closing the door, he pulled her into his arms. She stiffened, then relaxed. "You're doing all you can to take up the slack. They'll see it one day, but for now all you can do is be there for them."

"I am so angry at him. For so long, I made excuses for him," she said.

Leaning her away, he lifted her chin. "You'll have ulcers and the sleepless nights, and he'll keep on doing the same."

"You almost sound as if you're defending him."

His arms dropped to his sides. "Not really. I was sort of like him. I always thought there was time."

"Your wife?" she asked softly.

"Yes." He gazed over her head as if he were seeing into the past. "She tried to get me to take time to travel, have children, have fun. I always put it off."

"I bet she always knew she could count on you, that you

encouraged and supported her," Gina said with absolute conviction.

He looked down at her. "She was a social worker at the local hospital. She worked hard to help her patients, even going so far as to buy them groceries, help pay rent out of our money. I never objected. Some took, but most of them were people who just needed a little help."

"You helped her make a difference," Gina said fiercely. "You talked, had dreams, dreams you're making a reality at Journey's End. You're kind, thoughtful. Robert is none of those things. He only comes because he has to, not because he wants to."

"For all of your sakes I truly hope you're wrong," Max said. "Ashton and Gabrielle need a father."

"He's too into himself to see it," Gina said, her anger building all over again.

Max gently shook her. "Stop working on your ulcer."

"Not easy," she said; then, tired of talking about Robert, she changed the subject. "Why are you here?"

"To look at your exercise bike. We didn't have time last night."

"We only got through one movie before Ashton fell asleep," she reminded him, going down the hall to her bedroom. "And Gabrielle kept glaring at you. No wonder you decided to leave early."

"She wants things the way they used to be."

"I know, and that's the number one reason why I haven't shipped her off to Siberia without a return address," Gina joked, then sobered. "She loves her father."

Max curved his arm around her, gave her a slight squeeze. "She loves you, too. She stuck up for you Sunday. And for helping set me straight she can glare at me all she wants."

"Like I said, I've never met a man like you." Gina stepped into the bedroom. Her gaze went to the bed. Suddenly she was glad that Robert had converted the small study off the den into a bedroom when he'd moved out of their bedroom almost a year before he left. "You were just worried about what Nettie would think of my plans."

"That wasn't the reason." He waited until she looked up. "I was thinking of you more and more instead of Sharon when I thought of Journey's End. I felt guilty and made you pay."

Her eyes widened.

"I forgot that Sharon, more than anyone, never asked more of me than I could give." His thumb grazed across Gina's lower lip; then he walked over to the exercise bike. "I wouldn't get on this thing, either. The small seat is a killer." He glanced over his shoulder. "Why don't you find a chore or two to do while I take this off so I can find a comfortable replacement?"

Yesterday she might have been embarrassed, thought of her broad hips, but Max had shown her he was interested in her and not her dress size. "All right."

"When I'm finished, if you'd like, you can follow me to my mechanic and he can check your brakes." Hunkering down, he took a screwdriver out of his back pocket. "They're squeaking."

Robert had never taken care of her car. Once she'd called him when she had a flat and, although he said he was coming, he hadn't. An hour later, a passing motorist had stopped and changed the tire. Afterward, her father had taught her how to change a tire herself. "I'd appreciate it."

"Afterward, we can act like tourists if we have time before we go see Ashton's game."

"He'll be so disappointed Robert won't stay," she said.

"You'll be there," he told her, staring at her over the bike.

"And so will you."

"Nothing could keep me away."

Smiling, feeling better, she left the room. Was it possible that she had finally gotten something right? She certainly hoped so.

Alec stared at the almost empty shelves of the refrigerator and thought of the shrimp salad and lemon pound cake that were there earlier. His stomach growled. He shut the door, went to the phone, and picked up the list of restaurants that offered takeout.

Twice he ran his blunt-tipped finger down the list that Celeste had left. Nothing appealed to him. Tossing the list aside, he folded his arms and stared out the window. Was it the food that was unappealing or that he couldn't stop thinking that Celeste had finally gotten the message that he didn't want to be bothered and left him alone. So why wasn't he happy about it?

Alec shoved his hand through his unbound hair. There was no reason to keep thinking about Celeste, missing her. Yet he did. She wasn't coming back until Monday. The thought made him feel an emptiness he wasn't comfortable with, but no matter what, he couldn't push it away. It was ridiculously easy to visualize her face, exquisite and mischievous, remember the arousing taste of her mouth, the silken texture of her skin.

He groaned at his body's quick arousal, the sharp ache he knew could only be satisfied by one woman. He could fight it, but he wouldn't win. If he were to have any peace before Monday, he needed to see her. He now had her cell and home phone numbers, knew where she lived. Yet he couldn't just drop by or call after asking to be left alone. There had to be a good reason.

With her busy schedule, she could be anywhere. Was she thinking about him or had she relegated him to the past? He liked that thought even less.

"Dunlap, you're losing it."

Perhaps the reason for him being unable to get her out of his mind was that he felt obligated to her. One meal didn't make up for all the times she'd fed him. Maybe if he did something for her, he'd get some peace. The idea had merit, but what?

The solution came to him almost instantly. He reached for the receiver and dialed.

"Hello."

"Brianna, great. This is Alec."

She laughed. "Hi. You sound excited."

He frowned, then forged ahead. Pregnant women were overly emotional. "I need your help."

"I'm sorry, Alec, but I can't help you talk Helen out of your birthday party," Brianna said.

"No, it's not that," he told her. He'd already gotten a stern talk from Sam about the party, but it wasn't needed. Alec loved Helen like the sister he'd never had. He'd never disappoint her.

"Then I'm in."

"It's about Celeste," he said, and explained what he needed.

"I'm on it, Alec. I'll call you back as soon as I can."

"Thanks, Brianna. Bye." Alec hung up the phone and waited.

"Hello, Celeste."

The last person Celeste expected to see when she answered the door was Alec. She'd thought of him, missed him fiercely, but this time she was determined to stay away.

"Can I come in?"

"Yes." She moved aside to allow him to enter. Alec stepped inside, than abruptly halted, his sharp, somewhat accusing gaze jerking toward her. She didn't moan in frustration, but it was a near thing. She'd completely forgotten she had a guest. "Enrique Santiago, Alec Dunlap."

Enrique, suave, handsome, and lithe, moved toward Alec with elegant grace, his hand extended. Always protective of her, he had followed her when she went to answer the door. "Dunlap."

"Santiago."

The handshake was brief, but the men continued to stare at each other. Not since her early college days when guys were crawling out of the woodwork to date her had something like this happened. "Alec, I was just about to get Enrique a glass of wine. Would you like anything?"

"No."

"Please have a seat." She waved him toward the den. "I won't be but a minute."

"I just wanted to give you this." Alec handed her the pink gift bag.

Taking the bag, Celeste pushed aside the white tissue paper, then let out a loud whoop. Impulsively she hugged Alec. "Thank you."

The tension left his face, and he almost smiled. "Dalton signed it for you."

Celeste hugged the book to her chest. "An ARC for *Sudden Prey*. The book isn't supposed to be out until January."

"Dalton's publishing house is sending out copies for early reviews. I figured I owe you." Alec glanced at Enrique and his face harshened again. "I'll let you get back to what you were doing."

Celeste didn't gasp or hit Alec over the head with her new

book for his insinuation. She simply walked to the door. "I won't keep you."

He stared at her for a long moment, then started toward her.

"I'm the one who should be going," Enrique told her. When he was even with Alec, he said, "You don't deserve her," and kept walking until he stood in front of Celeste.

"You don't have to go," she said, meaning it. Their engagement hadn't worked out, but they remained friends.

His smile was the saddest she'd ever seen. "You don't know how badly I wished that were true. I hoped that one day you would wear my ring again." He glanced at a fuming Alec. "I see now that it will never happen."

She had never wanted to hurt him. Her heart had chosen, and there was nothing she could do about it. "You're a wonderful man, Enrique."

"Just not the man for you."

"No."

His long, elegant fingertips brushed across her cheek with exquisite gentleness. He ignored the guttural sound coming from across the room and waited until Celeste threw a worried glance in Alec's direction, then looked back up at him. "You never looked at me the way you look at him."

"I'm sor—"

"No, don't say it. There has always been honesty between us," he chided gently. "Your heart chose—not wisely, I think." He glanced at Alec. "Jeans and scuffed boots. He isn't worthy of you."

"Don't let us keep you," Alec said.

Enrique, one of the most successful and influential lawyers in the state, coolly looked at Alec. "You won't."

Celeste laughed, then sobered. "There is a very lucky woman waiting out there for you."

"But I wanted you." Bending, he kissed her on the cheek. "Good-bye."

Celeste closed the door behind him, then leaned her head against it.

"Are you all right?"

"No," she whispered, and heard the roar of a powerful engine, Enrique's Ferrari.

"You want to sit down or for me to get you a glass of water?" Alec asked, clearly anxious.

Lifting her head, Celeste faced him. Why this man and not Enrique, a man who adored her, would lay the world at her feet, would pamper and spoil her?

"Celeste?"

"I don't know if I like either of us right now." The book clutched in her arm, she went to the kitchen and opened the refrigerator door. "We hurt a wonderful man."

"We?"

Celeste shut the door without getting the pitcher of lemonade. "We. He saw the way I looked at you, the way you growled when he touched me, and he realized I'd never love him the way he deserved."

Alec looked as if he'd been sucker punched. "You're seeing him?"

"Up until six months ago we were engaged, for three months."

"You were engaged?" he asked.

"He was engagement number three. You should know that each of them would take me back in a heartbeat. So don't think you're Mr. Hot Stuff." Placing the book on the counter, she opened the refrigerator, took out the pitcher, and filled a glass. She took a long swallow.

"I already know men want you." His hot gaze raked her. "Men can't seem to keep their eyes off you."

"You don't seem to have that problem."

He crossed to her in seconds, his hard, muscular body surrounding her, pinning her against the cabinet. "I probably want you more than all of them put together." His hand cupped her cheek. "Unlike Enrique or any of the others, I've tasted your passion, felt you moan beneath me."

Breath became harder for her to draw in. "H—how do you know they haven't?"

"Because if they had, they'd do whatever it took to taste, to feel that way again." His mouth fastened on her, claiming, devouring. Celeste met the passion and the fury in the kiss. She wanted, needed this.

Alec held her away, his breathing hard and labored. "Why is it that if I see you, I want you? Why can't I forget you?"

His words hurt. "If you don't want to be here, leave. You know the way out." Picking up her glass, she went into the den and took a seat on the sofa. Remote in hand, she turned on the flat-panel television, flicking through the channels, anything to drown out the noise of the front door closing.

She jumped when his hands settled on her shoulders from behind. "You haunt me."

Her head fell forward. Misery welled within her. She didn't want the attraction between them to make him unhappy.

"But you give me the only measure of peace I have, the only time when I don't see his face," he said, the words tortured. "I ended a man's life, a man who had a wife, a man who was about to become a father. Two weeks before I came here, I drew my weapon and couldn't fire it. I can no longer do the job I love. I'm a danger to myself and anyone on duty with me unless I get my head on straight."

Her heart ached. She tried to turn, but he held her fast. "I know how you feel," she said slowly.

"You can't possibly know how I feel," he told her, lifting his hands from her. "The worst thing that has probably happened to you is a broken nail."

Setting the glass down with a hard thud, she rounded the sofa. She pushed her face in his. "You don't know what the hell you're talking about, Alec Dunlap! You aren't the only one who has ever regretted taking a life. You did yours in the line of duty to save your partner and yourself. I took a life because I wanted to party and got drunk."

His eyes widened; his mouth became unhinged.

Cold, chilled to the bone, Celeste wrapped her arms around her body. "Elaine Mathis was my best friend since kindergarten. We did everything together. We were inseparable and elated when we were accepted as pre-med majors at the University of Texas at Austin. We had just finished our freshman year and came home for the summer."

"Celeste, don't." Alec pulled her into his arms, holding her tightly. "I'm sorry, honey. So sorry."

She heard him but couldn't stop the words. "We went to a pool party. We'd had a hard year, and I figured it was time to have some fun." She shuddered. "I was too drunk to drive my car, so Elaine put me in the backseat and started home. She never made it. They think she fell asleep at the wheel. She—she hit a light post. Out cold in the back, I came away without a scratch. I've never drunk alcohol since."

His hold tightened. "Having you relive that isn't worth you trying to help me."

Tears glistened in Celeste's eyes for Elaine, for him. "I quit school, became depressed. If it hadn't been for my family, I wouldn't be here today."

"Celeste, no," he groaned.

"I just wanted the pain and guilt to go away. Yolanda came into my bedroom before I could hide the sleeping pills I'd been saving. It's the only time I've ever seen her angry." Celeste placed her head on Alec's chest, felt the unsteady beat. "It wasn't your fault. It takes time for that to sink in. Give yourself time."

He didn't say anything, just picked her up and sat down on the sofa, cradling her shivering body against his. "Thank you for trying to help me. It wasn't easy, yet you did it. I'm grateful."

She lifted her head to look at him. "I hear a 'but.'"

His hand tenderly brushed tears from her face. "You weren't to blame. It was a tragic accident. I'm directly responsible."

"The second he shot the guard, then your partner, and then tried to shoot you, he became responsible. You had no choice."

He didn't want to talk about it. It wouldn't do any good until he was ready. He pressed her head back on his chest, gently stroking her hair. "So, Ms. de la Vega, tell me about the other two engagements."

"What would you like to know?"

SEVENTEEN

"We're really going on a dinner cruise?" Gabrielle asked, obviously trying to act nonchalant, but the sparkle of excitement in her eyes gave her away.

"Yes." Max parked, then went around to open Gina's door. After the game he'd told them he had a surprise and would pick them up at six.

"Thank you," Gina said, getting out of the vehicle.

Max nodded, aware she was thanking him for more than the door. Gabrielle and Ashton needed a diversion after being left by their father. Both had looked miserable at the soccer field. Ashton's coach had to take him out after he let a ball get by him. It had taken a lot of talk on Gina's part to get his head back up, his spirits revived. He'd gone back in and kept the other team from scoring again while his team scored four goals.

Gina grabbed Ashton's hand as he started past her for the

boarding area. "You stick close to me. No running, and I don't want you leaning over the rail."

"Yes, ma'am," he said, looking at the cruise ship as people stood in line to board. "I bet I can draw this."

"I bet you could." Max waited until slow-walking Gabrielle joined them. "What's your hobby?"

"I don't have one," she said.

"She used to write poems," Gina said. "They were very good. I wish she hadn't stopped."

"There hasn't been much to write about." Her shoulders hunched.

Max didn't have to see Gina's face to know her daughter's words hurt. "Gabrielle, it sounds as if you might be able to help me out."

She slanted a suspicious look at him. Gina caught Ashton as he tried to climb up on the rail.

"Your mother has made the guest rooms more inviting, but I've noticed in a lot of establishments each guest room has a name or theme," Max said, embellishing on his idea as they boarded the boat and found an empty space to stand on the first level. "Do you think you could help me out and come up with names? I thought I'd put a gold plate on each door. On it would be your name."

Her eyes rounded to the size of saucers. "You'd really put my name on it?"

"Yes." He put his hand on Ashton's shoulder as he tried to pass him. "It would give the place a classy touch."

"I'll think about it," Gabrielle said, leaning on the rail beside her mother as the ship slowly pulled out to sea.

"Thanks. If it's all right with your mother, I can pick you all up tomorrow afternoon and you can come over and view the rooms." Max lifted Ashton up with one arm so he could see over the railing.

"All except you picking us up, it's fine." Gina put her arm around Gabrielle's shoulder. "We can come over after church and I can give Sophia another lesson in preparing the signature dishes."

"It's no trouble picking you up," Max said. "It will give you a break from driving and it will give me a chance to finish working on your bike. Anyone want to go up on the third level of the observation deck? The view is better."

"Me," Ashton said.

Max chuckled. "I thought so." He looked at Gina. "I won't let him get hurt."

"I know. I trust you." Giving him a tender smile, she started toward the stairs with Gabrielle beside her.

With Ashton secure in his arms, Max followed. The day might have started off badly for them, but he had one more surprise that he hoped would lift Gabrielle's and Gina's spirits.

A little over an hour later, they were shown to their table. The dining room was climate controlled, with brass fixtures, ten-foot ceilings, and Oriental carpeting. They were barely seated before a man appeared to present Gina and Gabrielle each with a long-stemmed red rose.

Gina's eyes widened with undisguised pleasure. "What a wonderful surprise, Max. It seems I'm always thanking you."

"I'm glad you like it," Max said.

"I—" Gabrielle's hand trembled. "Thank you."

"You're very welcome." Max picked up his menu. "Let's order, shall we."

. . .

"May I have this dance?"

Gina stared up at Max and wanted with all her heart to take the hand he offered. After they had finished their dinner, a woman had come onstage to sing about a lost love. The dance floor had quickly filled.

"Mama can't dance," Gabrielle said from her seat next to her mother. Gina couldn't tell if her daughter was just stating a fact or she didn't want her mother dancing with Max.

"Your mother is a very smart woman," Max said, his long-fingered hand and warm gaze never wavering. "I can teach her."

"I don't like to dance," Ashton said, loud enough for diners several feet away to hear.

"Gina does," Max said with all the confidence of a man who knew what he wanted.

Gina felt her heart race. How could Max understand her need to forget her worries and just have fun once in a while when Robert never had? The answer was simple: Max wasn't selfish.

Not daring to look at Gabrielle, Gina placed her hand in Max's, felt his strong, confident grip as he led her to the dance floor, then curved his arm around her waist. She sighed without realizing it as he pulled her gently into his arms. Their bodies didn't touch, but she felt the pull, the heat.

Her gaze lifted to his, and she knew he could easily see the desire in her eyes that she no longer wanted to hide.

His back to their table, his fingers stroked the small of her back. "One day we'll dance without an audience."

"I'd like that," she said, a bit breathless. Max made her feel light-headed, giddy, as if she'd drunk too much champagne.

"How about next Saturday night? Dinner, dancing, just the

two of us?" he asked, his feet and body moving so smoothly she followed him without thinking. "I'll make reservations."

A date. There would be no confusion this time. "I'll get a sitter just in case."

The side of his sexy mouth kicked up and Gina felt the familiar sweet ache in her stomach. "Like I said, you're a smart woman."

She tilted her head to one side in a flirtatious manner. "It's about time, don't you think?"

"Look out, world."

She smiled up at him, feeling lighter with each passing moment. Life had certainly taken a turn.

Monday evening, Gabrielle climbed the stairs of Journey's End behind her mother, Max, and Ashton. Gabrielle's knees shook the tiniest bit. She shouldn't be nervous. She didn't like Max all that much, so it would be no big deal if he didn't care for the names for the guest rooms she'd worked on so hard to come up with last night.

It was a matter of pride, she decided. She wanted him to see that she was smart, smart enough to know he was trying to take her daddy's place. She wasn't going to let that happen.

He probably thought giving her the rose would win her over, but he couldn't be more wrong. She might have been pleased on the dinner cruise ship at first, but that was before he'd danced with her mother. He was definitely putting the moves on her. He might as well give up. Gabrielle wasn't going to let it happen.

Yesterday they'd had an OK time at the B and B after church, but she wasn't as easily won over as Ashton and her mother. Ashton was a kid and didn't know any better. Her mother had acted all gooey because Max had removed the narrow seat on her exercise bike and put on a larger, padded one and rigged up a place in front to place Gabrielle's father's old laptop.

She bet her father could have done the same thing if her mother had said anything. Gabrielle had told Gina so, but all she'd said was that she hadn't had to ask Max.

Going down the hallway, Gabrielle had to admit Max did a lot. But she knew her daddy would, too. It was just that he was so busy at his job. Her daddy loved her and she loved him. It was up to her to see that her mother didn't get all mushy on Max.

Max stopped in front of the first guest room. "You thought of the names so quickly. I can't wait to hear what you've come up with."

Gabrielle's knees shook even worse. They were all looking expectantly at her, even her brother.

"Go on, Gabrielle," her mother said. "I'm anxious myself."

"Come on, Gabrielle," Ashton said. "Max said he'd kick the ball with me when you finished."

It was now or never. *Show him you're smart.* She took a deep breath. "The Orchid Suite, for the largest room, and for the other three the Rose Room, the Southern Room, and the Ashley River Room." Gabrielle looked at her mother smiling proudly at her and her knees steadied. "There are roses on the bedspread of the main bedroom. My teacher has an orchid on her desk, so you could put one in the room. I figure we could find objects and pictures to make the names go with the rooms."

Max grinned. "Perfect, but I might have known. Your mother is incredible, so why shouldn't her daughter . . ." Max paused and glanced down at Ashton. "And son be the same way."

"They're lovely names, Gabrielle." Her mother beamed. "Elegance linked with charm." She turned to Max. "I'm sure I can find theme decorations to reflect the rooms' names."

"And once you do, I can do a video of the door with the nameplate, then film inside the room." Max put his hand on Ashton's shoulder. "The Rawlings family has really helped out."

"Not me," Ashton said, his head bowed.

Max hunkered down next to Gabrielle's little brother. "I had hoped you'd help me and your mother finish measuring the grounds for the gardens."

His head came up. "I can do that."

"I knew I could count on you." Max pushed upward. "In the meantime, what do you say we put our skills against the women? I bet we can get the soccer ball past them."

"In your dreams," Gabrielle said before she thought, then jerked toward her mother and waited for the reprimand for speaking to an adult that way.

"You tell him, Gabrielle." Her mother put her arm around Gabrielle's shoulder. "I've practiced enough with Ashton. So bring it on."

He's going to make it, Sharon.

Arms folded, Sophia watched Max and Ashton play soccer against Gina and Gabrielle. In lieu of a goal they'd set two clay pots several feet apart. Neither team had scored, but that didn't seem to matter to the happy group.

"They're having fun."

Startled, Sophia swung around at the male voice—Southern and filled with good humor. Standing before her was a tall, slender gentleman in gray slacks and a crisp white shirt and gray bow tie. His full head of hair and mustache were gray as well. He looked like a bearded Sean Connery, with every bit of the charm and charisma.

"I'm sorry. I didn't mean to frighten you," he said, and extended his hand. "Profess— Albert Cummings. I live next door."

"Sophia Durand," Sophia said, and shook his hand. The grip was firm but gentle. "Are you in education?"

"Was," he said, smiling again. "Retired last term from the College of Charleston after fifty years of teaching English. I decided to do some of the things I've always wanted before it was too late."

Sophia nodded. That had been her thought as well. "I retired last semester after forty-four years with the Memphis School District. The last twenty as principal."

"They'll miss us," he said, and chuckled.

"They certainly will." Sophia liked his easy smile, the bright laughter. Laughter had her turning toward the game.

"Your family?" Albert asked.

"Partially. Max, the man trying to keep the ball away from the girl, is my nephew. The woman in front of the goal on the other end is Gina Rawlings, a friend. Ashton and Gabrielle are her children."

"It seems only yesterday that I could run that fast, was that limber," Albert said with a smile in his voice.

She looked at him. People usually didn't like to talk about the limitations age had imposed on them. "In my mind, it seems only yesterday that I graduated from college, bright and eager to meet the world."

"You met it, and succeeded."

She turned to him. "Why would you say that?"

"Because you didn't go on and on about how difficult it was to teach students who don't want to learn, as many of my colleagues do." He folded his arms. "It's our job to teach the unteachable. Not an easy task, but one that can and should be rewarding."

Sophia stared at him. "My friends think I'm a throwback because I think the same way."

He leaned closer. She smelled his pleasant aftershave, an intoxicating mixture of spices. "Perhaps it's time you had new friends."

Sophia's eyes widened. Was this distinguished man flirting with her? Dear lord, she hoped so.

"Hi there. I'm Max Broussard."

Sophia jumped again. "Ah, Max. This is Albert Cummings, our next-door neighbor."

The men shook hands. "I didn't mean to interrupt your game. I just returned after an extended trip abroad and was looking the place over outside when I saw you playing," Albert explained.

"You didn't interrupt. It's nice to meet a neighbor," Max said. "No wonder I didn't see a car."

Albert's lips twitched. "And you wanted to check me out. I assure you, my intentions weren't sinister."

"Of course not," Sophia said, a bit put out with her favorite nephew and not shy about showing it.

Max said to Albert in an aside, "If I were thirty years younger, I'd be in big trouble."

"You still might be," Sophia said. A man hadn't flirted with her in—never.

Gina and the children joined them. "Professor Cummings?"

A pleased smile spread across Albert's face. "Gina Malone. It's good seeing you. How have you been?"

"Fine." Gina introduced her children. "You look well."

"Thank you." Albert glanced at Sophia, then Max. "I won't keep you."

"If you have time, why don't you join us for a glass of strawberry tea slush, Journey's End's signature drink?"

"Journey's End?" A faint line radiated across his brow.

Max inclined his head toward the Victorian. "My bed-and-breakfast."

"It's charming enough for one," Albert said. "I'm thankful you rescued the place. Although the house had been in the same family for three generations, when the previous owners moved into a retirement home their children decided to sell. Hopefully, you'll start a new tradition."

Sadness touched Max's features for an instant, and Sophia knew he was thinking about Sharon. Then he glanced at Gina and the shadow disappeared. "I'm going to try. How about that tea? Of course, your wife is invited as well."

"I'm not married," Albert said. "Thank you; I would like to join you."

You're forgiven, Max. "Albert, I'd love to hear about your travels. I was in Paris ten years ago."

Albert took her arm. "The City of Lights is still beautiful. Like all beautiful things age enhances."

Sophia sighed inside. Max was definitely forgiven.

"Sophia, I think you have an admirer," Gina said as she helped Sophia clean up the kitchen. Albert had stayed for dinner and just left. Max and the children were in the study.

"I hope so." Sophia paused in drying a glass serving dish that had held lime jerked pork chops. "He's so good-looking and charming. And look at me, tall and plain."

"Good men, the kind that stick, look beyond what's on the outside," Gina said with feeling. "I admit I'm not the greatest judge of a man's character, but if Max thought Albert was trying to run a game, he wouldn't have invited him for dinner again." Sophia didn't have to know that Gina had seen the longing way Sophia looked at Albert and thought to help her out the way she had helped Gina.

Sophia placed the dish in the cabinet. "Max is a good judge of character. It's just that I waited so long for a man to smile at me the way Albert did this afternoon. I'm afraid I might turn out to be one of those desperate women people pity."

"You might also find something you've dreamed of for so long." Gina placed the dishcloth over the faucet. "It's scary taking steps when you can't see where your foot is going to land. Trust is hard, but some risks are worth taking."

"But what would he want with me when he can be choosey?" Sophia asked, real fear in her voice.

"Only Albert can answer that question." Gina had asked herself the same question about Max. "I don't know why some people click and others don't. I just know it happens. As I said, it's scary stepping out on trust, but I'm finding the rewards far outweigh the risks."

Sophia looked at Gina a long time. "You've grown so much."

"I pray I have. I'd still be floundering if it wasn't for Max. Gabrielle still worries me, but we're getting there, I think. For some of us, this life's journey isn't a smooth one."

"The pupil becomes the teacher." Sophia nodded. "Great rewards sometimes require great risks."

"Exactly," Gina said. "This is our time, Sophia. We have to seize the moment or we'll regret it for the rest of our lives."

"Max."

"Max," Gina said. "If you tell him, I'll never cook another meal for you."

Sophia held up both hands. "You really went for the jugular. My lips are sealed."

"Until Albert unseals them," Gina said, then pressed her hands over her lips, giggling. "Sophia, I'm sorry. It just slipped out."

"You didn't say anything I wasn't thinking." Sophia's eyes narrowed. "He'd better not turn into a frog or I'm driving nonstop to New Orleans for a voodoo doll to put a nasty hex on him."

"You're kidding, aren't you?"

Sophia hooked her arm through Gina's and started from the kitchen. "My motto has always been 'don't get mad; get even.'"

Gina thought for a moment. "If the children's father doesn't get his act together, mind if I ride shotgun?"

"Glad for the company."

Ever since Saturday night, Alec hadn't been able to stop thinking of what Celeste had gone through. He wanted to kick his butt for all the times he had carelessly thought of her not having any serious problems in her life. She had, and he'd forever be thankful to God that her family had helped her conquer her demons.

Every time Alec thought of her stashing sleeping pills, his

stomach churned. He'd called her twice on Sunday just to hear her voice, had piddled around Maureen's kitchen until he saw Celeste Monday morning.

She'd taken one look at him, his eyes anxious, and palmed his face. "I'm fine, and we both have work to do."

He knew that logically, but he couldn't help checking on her later in the day. He'd used the excuse that he'd lost the names of the helpers she'd suggested. She'd called them herself and arranged for both to come by later that day.

"Anything else?" she asked, a smile tugging her lips.

"I guess not."

"Good. Traci and Ryan are coming by tomorrow and I want to have the curtains hung by then."

He looked past her to the ladder. "I could stay—"

Celeste pushed him out the bedroom door. "You still have to finish the roof and railing."

"I've decided not to brick the gazebo. Instead I'm going to match the wood shingles on the roof of the main house. The unfinished cedar will age and blend in naturally," he told her. "It will have accent lighting, so Maureen and Simon can entertain at night if they want."

She folded her arms. "You decided to take my advice."

He shrugged. "You are an interior designer."

"So let me get back to work. Good-bye, Alec." She closed the door.

He'd gone back outside to wait for the men she'd called. With only a week left, he needed all the help he could get. And when the time came, he'd return to Myrtle Beach.

As he opened the terrace doors and put on his shoes, he knew he'd leave a part of himself behind as well because he'd leave Celeste.

. . .

Celeste threaded the lush silk onto the rod, trying to keep her mind on what she was doing and not on Alec. His concern for her, his need to ensure she was all right, touched her. Yet concern wasn't love.

"You all right?" Willie asked.

"Getting there," Celeste told Willie, who worked on the other curtain. They had a total of eight to put up.

"He's tougher to get through than I thought," Celeste's assistant commented. "But the looks he gives you are hot enough to start a forest fire."

Celeste worked her shoulders, trying, failing, to push away the memory of his hot kiss, his feverish hands on her. He'd held her so tenderly Saturday night, done his best to distract her, yet he hadn't changed his mind about their relationship. Friends, never lovers. She'd kept it light and playful this morning, figuring that would help both of them get through the day.

"Daylight is burning."

Giving herself a shake, Celeste continued threading the material on the two-inch wooden rod. Her heart had chosen. Thus far, it didn't appear as if it had chosen well.

"Anyone for ice cream?" Max asked, rising to his feet in the dining room of Journey's End Tuesday night.

"Me! Me!" Ashton said, practically jumping out of his chair.

"I guess I wouldn't mind," Gabrielle said, coming to her feet.

Gina followed suit. "Only if it's lemon custard."

"You got it." Max pulled Gina's chair back, then shoved it beneath the table. "How about you, Aunt Sophia? Albert?"

"No, thank you," Sophia said. Being alone with Albert was worth missing a banana split.

Albert, who had come to his feet when Gina stood, smiled. "No, thank you. I'll stay and keep Sophia company."

Max took Gina's arm. "We're off. If you change your mind, I have my cell."

Sophia waved them away, silently thanking Gina. Sophia hadn't missed the little nudge she'd given Max shortly before he made his announcement.

Albert retook his seat as Gina left the room. "That was a wonderful meal."

"Gina cooked everything." Sophia casually picked up her coffee cup. "I'm learning to cook, thanks to Gina, but I have a long way to go."

Albert lifted a brow. "Why learn now?"

Fair question. "Gina made it look so easy, plus I like helping Max, and she has her own travel business to run."

"I might need her myself." Albert sipped his coffee. "I'm leaving for Egypt Sunday, but there are several other trips I want to take."

Sophia didn't know which disturbed her more, Albert not commenting on her inability to cook or his upcoming trip. "You don't think it's odd that a Southern woman my age can't cook?"

The corners of his beautiful brown eyes crinkled. "I have two younger, very different sisters. I learned not to compare people. I don't play sports, don't particularly like watching them. However, I could play chess for hours."

"I haven't played chess in years."

"Then we'll have to remedy that, and soon."

Sophia smiled across the table at Albert, wondering if she

was being foolish to hope that finally it was her turn to find that special someone.

"If Albert hurts her, I'll break his neck," Max growled, his ice-cream cone forgotten as he and Gina walked side by side near the pier, the children in front.

Gina bumped him playfully with her shoulder. "She wants this chance, Max."

He slanted Gina a look. "I know, but she has no experience."

"With a good man, it doesn't matter." Catching his hand, she brought the cone nearer, then swirled her tongue around his dripping vanilla ice cream.

Max stared down at her, his eyes narrowing; then his tongue slowly followed. Heat burst through Gina. "Saturday night can't get here fast enough for me."

"Me, either," she replied breathlessly, wondering what Max tasted like, positive she'd find out.

EIGHTEEN

Wednesday afternoon, Ryan and Traci couldn't say enough about the redesign of the master suite. Usually Celeste soaked up the accolades like a sponge. Not today. The reason wasn't lost on her.

By tomorrow afternoon, she'd have no reason to be here. And when that happened Alec would be lost to her.

Her arms wrapped around herself, she stared out the window of the suite. Through the trees, she caught glimpses of the wood shingle roof, the cupola of the gazebo. Alec was so close yet so far away. She'd finally come to the conclusion that she couldn't push, drag, or manipulate him into giving them a chance. The decision had to be his, freely given.

Yet the thought of never being in his arms again, never tasting his mouth again, never feeling the erratic beat of his heart, saddened her as nothing else could.

She placed her hand on the window. "Alec."

"Celeste."

She whirled and he was there, gorgeous, devastatingly male, his eyes troubled. "I didn't hear you."

He took a hesitant step inside the room. "Ryan and Traci came by to see the gazebo."

She smiled when she wanted to weep. "You don't have to tell me how much they liked it."

"You haven't seen it in a while."

"I can see the cupola, the shingled top," she said playfully, wishing Willie would return from getting a bottle of water.

His hands clenched and unclenched. He glanced around the room. "You did a good job here. It's beautiful, just like Ryan and Traci said."

"Thank you."

"I— They said you'd planned on finishing up tomorrow."

She wrapped her arms around her waist. "Yes. Simon and Maureen arrive back Saturday evening. Traci and Ryan have planned a party for them at their house."

"Are you going?"

She wanted to believe she heard longing in his voice. "She invited me, but I thought I'd let Maureen and Simon see the suite for the first time by themselves. I'm babysitting later."

He slowly nodded. "So, after tomorrow, we won't see each other?"

"Probably not." The words almost stuck in her throat.

His hand shoved through his silky black hair. She'd never get to do that for him. "I— If I don't see you, take care of yourself."

"You do the same." They stared across the short distance separating them, neither aware of how to close the space.

He turned, looked over his shoulder as if he needed one last glimpse of her to carry with him always, then continued out the room.

Celeste wasn't aware she was crying until she felt the moisture on her cheeks. "Good-bye, Alec."

Sophia answered the door Wednesday afternoon and tried with all her might not to sigh with relief, grin like a fool. She'd been so afraid that Albert wouldn't come back. "Albert, what a pleasant surprise. Please come in."

"Hello, Sophia." Albert stepped into the foyer. "I hope you'll forgive my bad manners for dropping by twice without calling."

"Of course. We're neighbors." Sophia waved Albert to a seat in the living room, glad the beautiful new curtains were hung, wondering if he'd hinted for her phone number.

Albert waited until she sat on the sofa, then sat beside her. She jumped up almost immediately. "I'm sorry. Would you like something to drink? Tea? Coffee?"

"No, thank you. Actually, I wanted to ask you something." Sophia sat down. "Of course."

"I have tickets for the opening night of the symphony orchestra Saturday night and would be honored if you'd go with me."

She blinked, stared at the handsome man inches from her. Her heart raced. Her stomach felt hollow. Did she need a voodoo doll or dare she hope? She sat up straighter, squared her shoulders. "Albert, I'm flattered more than you can know, but I have to ask, why me?" Sophia said, refusing to lower her gaze.

His brows drew together. "The question should be, why not you?"

She shook her head, her pulse skittering as he took her

hands in his. The skin wasn't as tight as she'd wished, but thank goodness it wasn't dry and ashy. "That's not an answer."

His gaze narrowed on her face, as if trying to come up with an explanation she'd understand. She could easily imagine him doing the same thing in the classroom. "Intelligence can be just as attractive as outer beauty."

Her heart clenched. She wanted to tuck her head, but she had asked for this.

His hands moved to her shoulders, gently shaking them. "Stop trying to analyze. Forget your psychology courses. Sometimes things just aren't logical. You just have to go with your gut."

Just like Gina had said, but . . . "I don't want to call you a liar, but what you're saying is hard to believe. I have three beautiful sisters. You saw Max, and then there is me. I'm plain and undatable."

His observant eyes narrowed. "You're a woman of substance. Have you ever tried to have a conversation with a person who didn't get what you were trying to say?"

"Yes, but—"

"Do you know how exhilarating it is to not have to explain what you said, or how frustrating to quote a verse from a beloved poem and see the blank look?" he asked. "You get it."

She wanted to believe. "But how can you know I'll understand or be familiar with the poem?"

His hands on her shoulders gentled. "Sophia, my dear. Sometimes you just know."

It seemed she wouldn't be driving to New Orleans after all. "I'd be delighted."

"Good. I was hoping you'd want to share my last night with

me before I leave." He stood, bringing her with him. "Would you prefer to have dinner before or after?"

"Dinner?"

"The symphony starts at seven," he told her. "I wasn't sure if you preferred to eat late or early."

"Late," she said. There was no way she wasn't going to get the full effect of this date, and that meant dining late.

"I'll pick you up at six thirty." He squeezed her hands. "Now I must go. I'm meeting some colleagues for an early dinner or I would have liked to have stayed."

Oh, my. "I would have liked that."

"Me, too."

They stood, inches apart, staring at each other for several seconds before Sophia reluctantly withdrew her hand. "I'll see you to the door."

"Until Saturday."

"Until Saturday."

Grinning, Sophia watched Albert get into a Volkswagen Bug and drive away. Retrieving her purse and car keys, she went outside where Max, Gina, and two men were staking out the garden beds. "Max, I'm going shopping."

Max pushed to his feet, pulling off his work gloves and shoving them into the back pocket of his jeans. "I guess you accepted Albert's invitation."

Surprise lifted her brow. "How did you know?"

"He stopped by to assure me he'd take care of you," Max said. "I told him I'd be watching."

Sophia started to laugh, then saw Max's serious expression. "Please tell me you're kidding."

"Which part?"

"Both," she said.

Max's mouth flattened into a thin line. "He seemed all right or I wouldn't have invited him to dinner, but that was before I knew he wanted to date you. I don't want some man taking advantage of you."

"And I don't want to die an old maid who's never been kissed," she said, silently adding *among other things*.

Max shifted restlessly and refused to meet her gaze.

Sophia touched his arm. Since her nephew was a smart man, he was probably thinking about those other things. "I love you for wanting to protect me, but don't you think it's time I get a chance to experience what other women have? Even if it doesn't turn out the way I'd like, I would have had moments I could look back on and not feel odd and unlovable."

Max took her shoulders. "You're neither."

The corners of her mouth lifted slightly. "But I've felt that way. I want this chance."

Max nodded. "But if he messes up or crosses the line . . ."

Sophia would be disappointed if Albert didn't at least try to cross that line. "If that happens, I have a way of taking care of him. Now I have some shopping to do."

Thursday afternoon, Celeste stood on the threshold of the suite, her critical eyes examining every detail from the beautiful curtains to the scrumptious bed waiting for the newlyweds. Simon and Maureen had fought for and found their happiness; she and Alec wouldn't be so lucky.

Closing the door, she went down the stairs. She wanted the newlyweds to open the door and be enchanted; she wanted the bedroom to be their place of refuge and passion. Her steps quickened on the stairs. They'd have what she couldn't.

Opening the front door for the last time, she went to her van and started the motor. She'd left the key on the nightstand as they'd discussed. Refusing to look at the side of the house for Alec, she put the vehicle into gear, glanced into her rearview mirror, and saw Alec's truck drive up behind her. Her heart raced in spite of her good intention not to hope, not to feel.

In the mirror, she watched him get out, his long-legged stride bringing him closer and closer. She rolled down the window.

"Hi. Glad I caught you." He held up the handled bag from Sticky Fingers. "I figured you'd be tired, so I picked up your dinner. You have time to see the gazebo before you leave? I'm finished except for coating the floor and steps with a clear varnish."

He was nervous. He'd never talked that much or that long. He was giving her all he could. She shut off the motor. "I hope you didn't forget my double fudge sundae."

"I'll never forget anything about you."

The depth of emotions in his words caused her hands to clench. "Neither will I about you."

He opened her door. "It won't take long."

Because otherwise it would be too painful for both of them. She stepped down and stared up at the only man she'd ever wanted, the man her heart had chosen, the man she would never call her own.

He put the take-out bag on the seat and closed the door. Without touching or speaking, they took the same path they'd taken weeks ago. Only this time they walked side by side, careful not to touch. This time it was Alec who paused by the camellia bushes.

"Are you going to keep trying to get them to grow?"

"I don't know." She glanced at the lush pink flower, then him. "I don't like giving up on something I want, but sometimes you have no choice."

"No, you don't." He continued on the path.

Celeste took only a few steps before she saw the gazebo against the backdrop of the flowering trees and vines in the garden. "It's beautiful, Alec. They'll love it." She went up the steps, looked up at the rafters.

"You helped."

"You did the hard work. You should be very proud."

His eyes narrowed on her face. "You're a very special woman."

She reached for him. He stepped back, regret in his eyes. "Sometimes the choices you make aren't the ones you want, but you have to live with them. Be happy, Celeste."

Despite the pain in her heart, she smiled. He didn't need any more guilt. "You, too, Alec. Good-bye."

Stepping past him, she continued to her van. She was almost there when he passed her. Once inside the truck, he backed out of the driveway. Celeste did the same, refusing to cry again. At least not until she reached home.

"Are you all right?" Max asked Gina. They were seated in one of the most exclusive restaurants in the city, with a view of a beautiful courtyard, yet Gina seemed distracted. She'd only picked at her lobster and steak. "Is it Gabrielle?"

"No. I'm sorry." She bit her lip. "My best friend is going through a rough time."

Max placed his hands on hers. "Is there anything I can do to help?"

"No." She placed her other hand on top of his. "Thanks for asking. I wish I could have seen Sophia before she left on her date."

Max shook his head. "I don't think I've ever seen her so happy."

"The right man can do that for a woman."

He leaned closer. He certainly hoped she included him. "Would it appear too forward if I said I wanted to be alone with you?"

She briefly tucked her head. "We could have dessert at my house."

"I'll signal the waiter."

In a matter of minutes, they were on their way. Max planned on waiting at least until they'd eaten dessert before kissing her, but when Gina dished up ice cream over the pecan pie the image of her tongue swirling the ice cream the other day hit him hard and he got hard.

He might have made it if she hadn't gotten ice cream on her finger and stuck it in her mouth to lick it off. He groaned. Her startled gaze flew up to him. Embarrassment flickered in her eyes. She reached for a napkin. "I'm sorry."

"I'm not." Taking her hand the same way she had his the day on the pier, he smeared it with ice cream, then licked it off, all the time his eyes on her, watching hers grow larger, her breathing labored.

"That was good, but I can think of one thing that tastes better." Putting her hands on his shoulders, he pulled her into his arms until their bodies were flush.

He breathed a sigh of relief when she came willingly. "I need to kiss you."

"Then don't keep either of us waiting."

His mouth closed over hers. Hers opened willingly. He'd been right. Nothing had ever tasted so right. His arms held her closer, reveling in the softness of her body pressed against the hardness of his. One thing he hadn't counted on was the desire for the growing urgency to take, to give, to make her his in every possible way.

He started to ease back. She moaned into his mouth, hers greedily taking from his, her hands clutching him closer.

Caught up in the swirling vortex of her opening for him, giving to him, he pulled her closer instead of letting her go. He couldn't. Not yet.

His hand closed over her breast, felt the nipple tighten, push against his hand. Gina arched subtly, asking for more. Catching the tab of the zipper of her dress, he pulled it down as far as it would go, to the small of her back. With a brush of his fingers, the lightweight black material slid off one cinnamon-hued shoulder, then the other. He stepped back. The dress fell to the floor.

Gina stilled as if she just realized what had happened. Max dipped his head, his teeth closing on the distended nipple through the lacy bra.

"Max," she moaned, her hands pressing his head closer, her body trembling.

He wanted to feast on her, pleasure her. "Bed," he rasped; picking her up, he hurried toward the bedroom. A dim light shone on the nightstand, illuminating the turned-down bed. Sitting her down, he quickly divested himself of his clothes and put on the condom he'd earlier slipped into his pocket, then picked her up again, felt her shiver.

Concerned, unsure whether her reaction was fear or arousal, he sat down, then tilted her face to his. "This won't go any further if that's what you want."

She tucked her head. "I—"

His fingers lifted her head again. "Is this one of those times I shouldn't ask what's the matter?"

"The sheets are new."

He wanted to shout, to strut. He caught her face with both hands. "I want you, Gina. You don't know how much it pleases me to know you want me, too."

Her hands lightly clasped his wrists. "I figured you'd show me."

He laughed. Hers mixed with his. He tumbled back in bed, taking her with him. Before the sound died, his mouth was on her, showing her the depth of his desire, how much she meant to him. His mouth traced along the delicate curve of her throat, the beckoning swell of her breasts.

"You're beautifully made." His tongue laved one turgid point, then the other, his hand sliding over her stomach, finding silken skin, the elastic top of her panties. He slipped his hands underneath, felt her desire.

"Max." She trembled in his arms, the aching hunger in her body growing each second. Restlessly she moved her hips, wanting him there.

The heel of his hand pressed against her, somehow making the ache better and worse. She burned for him. Her legs closed, shamelessly trapping his hand there.

His mouth came back to hers, his tongue flickering against hers. She relaxed her legs, then felt his finger stroke the most intimate part of her, once, twice. Her hips moved against his hand, reaching, searching; then his hand was gone, and she wanted to cry out.

But then Max was looming over her, his face tight with desire. "The first time I want to be inside you."

Slipping his hands beneath her hips, he brought them together. Gina closed her arms around his shoulders, her legs around his waist. Unimaginable pleasure spiraled through her.

He began to move, his hips surging into her. She met him thrust for thrust, reveling in the delight of being in Max's arms, their bodies locked together in passion and need. Soon she felt her body tighten; she thought fleetingly of pulling back to prolong the ecstasy she'd only dreamed about, but her hunger was too fierce, the pleasure too great.

With a hoarse shout of her name, Max took both of them over. For endless moments she lay beneath him, content as she'd never remembered being.

Lifting his head, he stared down at her. "I always knew you were amazing."

She kissed his chin, stroked his chest lightly dusted with hair. "I don't have to pick the children up until the morning."

His eyes devoured her. "Absolutely amazing," he said, taking her mouth again.

Alec couldn't sleep. He'd only been able to sleep in short intervals since he'd said good-bye to Celeste on Thursday. He'd tried to fake it for Simon and Maureen's homecoming party Saturday night with all of his family and the Invincibles but knew he'd failed. He missed Celeste.

Oddly, Rafael didn't tease him, just handed him a slip of paper with the names of a florist, a swank restaurant, and a jeweler and said, "You'll figure out which one you need or maybe all three."

Alec had shoved the paper into his jeans pocket and tried to keep a smile on his face. He didn't need any of them.

Pretending became even more difficult as everyone came back to look at the gazebo. He'd accepted Simon and Maureen's praise, their hugs, watched them walk to the center and "christen" it with a kiss. He cheered with the rest of the family, despite the misery he felt.

He'd gone to bed early to leave the house to Maureen and Simon, but he didn't even think of closing his eyes. Therefore, he was awake when an electrical storm blew into Charleston shortly around four Sunday morning.

Through the window he saw the fierceness of the lightning lighting up the sky. The lamp on the bedside table flickered. "Celeste."

Sitting on the side of the bed, he reached for his cell phone, punched in five numbers before he aborted the call. What if she was asleep and he woke her up? Standing, he went to the window. Rain lashed against the pane; wind viciously swayed hundred-year-old trees.

The light flickered again. *I'm afraid of the dark.*

He punched in her phone number and paced while he waited for an answer.

Her flashlight and cell phone beside her in the bed, Celeste tried to read *Sudden Prey*. Ashton and Gabrielle were asleep in the separate guest bedrooms Celeste kept for her parents and sister. Gina had called twice to ensure that Ashton and Gabrielle were all right, to ask if she should come get them.

Since it was four in the morning and Celeste heard Max's voice in the background and the weather was so bad, Celeste had forbidden her from needlessly endangering herself when the children were fine. She had the electric company's emergency repair number on speed dial; she'd checked her home generator and her flashlights.

She was fine physically. Emotionally was another story. After reading the same paragraph for the third time, she placed the book on the bedside table. Usually she devoured Dalton Ramsey aka Edgar Gunn books. Tonight she was too restless and too consumed with thinking about devouring someone else.

The ringing of the cell phone was a welcomed distraction. "Gina, Ashton and Gabrielle are fine."

"It's Alec."

Clutching the cell phone, Celeste sat up straighter. "Alec, are you all right?"

"That's what I called to ask you. Your lights on?"

"Oh, Alec." She didn't even think of lying, because she knew he'd come. The weather was too bad to drive in. "I'm fine. The generator is working, and I have a flashlight with me."

"Smart. Sorry I disturbed you."

"You didn't," she told him, wanting to prolong the conversation. "Maureen and Simon called earlier. They had fun at the party, and really liked what we did."

"They're happy."

"When are you leaving?" she asked, sliding her legs over the side of the bed.

"Early this morning. I report for duty at eight Monday."

There was a tightness in his voice that hadn't been there earlier. "You can do it, Alec. I believe in you."

"No matter what, knowing that helps. Good night, Celeste."

"Good night, Alec. Safe travel." Celeste hung up the phone and knelt at her bed to say a prayer for Alec.

. . .

Gina couldn't stop smiling. She practically floated up Celeste's walk Sunday morning and rang the doorbell. Making love with Max had been . . . fantastic. She now knew what women were talking about when they whispered about curled toes and off the chart.

Celeste opened the door; her usual smile wasn't there. Gina's happy mood took a nosedive. "Are you all right?"

"I'll get there." Stepping back, she closed the door after Gina entered. "Ashton and Gabrielle just woke up. I thought it best to let them sleep as late as they wanted."

Gina flushed, her smile returned. "Thank you for taking care of them."

"No problem." Celeste leaned in closer to whisper, "I want details later," then she straightened to say, "They enjoyed the wide-screen TV and cable, and I enjoyed them."

"Hi, Mama," Ashton greeted, running to her. "Celeste let me help bake chocolate-chip cookies and we watched her TV." He spread his arms wide. "Can we get one that big?"

"There's nothing wrong with the size we have." She hugged him to her just as Gabrielle came into the room with her backpack dangling from one shoulder. Gina hadn't been prepared for her daughter's close scrutiny but met it with a smile, refusing to feel regret or guilt about her night with Max.

"Good morning, Gabrielle."

"Good morning," Gabrielle greeted.

"I'm hungry." Ashton stared up at Gina. "Can we go to Max's house and eat and play soccer?"

"We're going home." Gina steered him toward the door. She

wasn't sure if she was sophisticated enough to be around Max *and* the children this soon. "Thank Celeste and let's go."

They did as requested and Gina opened the door; then she looked back at Celeste and smiled. "You have another visitor."

Celeste stepped around Gina and the children and stared at Alec, who stood a few feet from her porch with a blooming pink camellia in a large terra-cotta pot. "Alec."

"We'll get out of your way. Nice seeing you again, Alec." Gina hustled the children down the walk.

"Morning," Alec greeted the passing trio, his gaze snapping back to Celeste.

She came down the steps. "Is that for me?"

He shifted, a bit embarrassed. "Yes. I didn't like the idea of you giving up. You're too brave."

Her fingertip gently touched the blossom. "Thank you." Her voice quivered. "Please put it on the porch. I never thought of one in a pot."

Putting the plant down, he straightened and handed her the magazine he'd stuck in his back pocket. "The man at the nursery said this would help."

Celeste accepted the book, folded her arms around it. "I thought you'd be home by now."

"I couldn't leave." He shifted again. "I didn't like the idea of you giving up. You deserve all the good things life has to offer."

"So do you." She took his arm, felt his muscles bunch. "The least I can do is serve you a cup of coffee."

"I—"

She talked over him. "You'll be on your way in less than five minutes." Ignoring his resistance, she led him into the house and to the kitchen. "Have a seat." Filling a coffee mug, she turned. "Alec, sit. I won't bite."

"That's the problem. I dream of you doing just that."

Her hand trembled. Coffee sloshed over the side of the red mug.

"Careful." Quickly crossing to her, he took the mug. Grabbing a paper towel, he took her hand in his, turning it over. "You didn't burn yourself, did you?"

"No," she said, and waited until he lifted his eyes to hers. "But nothing could burn as much as the need to have your hands on me."

In the blink of an eye, his body changed. Frank desire stared at her, his breathing accelerated. His hands softened; then he lifted them to tenderly cup her cheek. The pad of his thumb grazed her trembling lip.

She bit.

Air hissed through his teeth as he sucked in a breath. With a quick fierceness that might have startled her if she hadn't wanted him so badly, he pulled her into his arms, his mouth replacing his thumb, his tongue thrusting into her mouth, plundering, taking, giving. Celeste grabbed a fistful of his hair and held on, riding, feeding the storm of the kiss.

She felt his calloused hand on her waist, gliding up to close over her breast that had begun to feel heavy, to ache. She burned with the heat of desire.

Suddenly he released her. She cried out in protest until she realized he'd done it so he could jerk her knit top over her head. Her bra dropped to the floor. His breath gushed through his slightly parted lips as he stared as if mesmerized at her.

A man had never seen her before. Instinctively she crossed her hands over her breasts.

"Please, no," he said, the words guttural. He moved her arms aside, then brushed the backs of his hands across each nipple. She shuddered. "Exquisite."

Unable to breathe, she watched him slowly lower his head toward her nipple. The heat of his breath, then the moisture of his mouth, the gentle clamp of his teeth, the swirl of his tongue against the turgid point, caused her knees to give way.

He caught her to him. "You're the most perfect thing I've ever seen." Picking her up, he started out of the kitchen.

She knew what he searched for. "Last door on the right."

In her bedroom, he didn't put her down until he'd tumbled with her into the unmade bed. She wanted to feel him against her. Grabbing the hem of his shirt, she pulled it over his head just before his mouth took hers again.

The assault of the glorious weight of him, the heat of his skin, the drugging taste of his kiss, filled her with a consuming desire. She wanted, ached.

His hand swept under the short skirt, on the inside of her thigh until it reached the junction of her legs. She moaned when he cupped her woman's softness, trembled like a wide-tossed leaf.

With trembling hands, she fumbled to unbuckle his belt, and became frustrated when she couldn't undo the thing. He took over, easily doing what she couldn't. It had required him to re-move his hands from her, but when she felt the full naked length of him on her, pinning her to the mattress, she counted the cost worth it.

He stared down at her, his beautiful midnight eyes glazed with desire. "I want you, need you."

Tenderness and love welled inside her. "I'm yours."

His mouth claimed her, fierce and tender at once. His

calloused hand palmed her breast. Her body was on fire. She squirmed against him, held him tightly to her.

His hand swept down her stomach; his fingers lifted her thong, finding her damp and needy. Moaning, she arched into him as intense pleasure spiraled through her. The lazy sweep of his tongue matched the motion of his fingers.

His mouth moved to the curve of her cheek, her ear, unleashing a new stream of need. "I want to be inside you more than my next breath."

Celeste moaned again, wanting the same with each quaking breath. He slipped her thong from her. Gloriously male, he towered over her. "I can't wait." The urgency of his voice caused her to shiver anew.

His mouth lowered to begin a maddening foray over her heated body. A nip here, a swirl of his tongue there, a suckle here, until she quivered with need.

She was dimly aware of him putting on a condom; then above her again, he began to ease into her. The fit was tight, but her desire eased his entry until he filled her. Her arms held him tightly, as she knew that he'd shown considerable restraint and care of her. The slight pain had been worth this. She wanted more.

She arched her hips. Alec answered. He kissed the side of her neck and began to move, slowly at first, then faster. She was caught up in a frenzy of ecstasy with Alec. She let herself go, tumbling, reaching. When she fell, Alec was there with her.

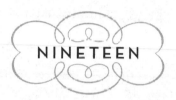

NINETEEN

Gina was five minutes from her home when her cell phone rang. She picked it up from the console and flipped it on. "Rawlings Travel Agency, carefree travel for a carefree vacation."

"Gina Rawlings, please."

"This is she," Gina answered, turning into her street.

"This is Nurse Radford calling from Mercy Hospital."

"What?" Gina's euphoria evaporated.

"Robert Rawlings was brought by ambulance to Mercy Hospital's emergency room this morning. He asked that you be notified."

Gina threw a quick look at Gabrielle in the passenger seat. "What's wrong with him? What happened?"

"All I can say is that it's serious but not life threatening. The doctor will tell you more when you get here. Good-bye."

Gina hung up, then pulled over to the curb and shut off the motor. "Your father is all right, but he's in the hospital."

Gina didn't want to be in the emergency room searching for Robert. He had no part in her life, but she only had to look at the frightened faces of her children to know the connection would always be there even if he ignored it.

"I don't see Daddy," Gabrielle said, her hand clasped tightly with her brother's.

"He's probably in a room." Gina went to the busy desk, waiting behind an elderly woman in a wheelchair until it was her turn. "I'm looking for Robert Rawlings. I was contacted by a nurse who said that an ambulance had brought him here."

The heavyset African-American woman glanced down at a clipboard in front of her. "Cubicle Ten through that door." She inclined her head and slapped a name tag that said "Visitor" on the counter. "Return it when you leave. I'll buzz you through to the door on the right."

"Thank you." Gina went back to the children, their eyes wide and frightened. "I'm going back to see your father."

"I want to go."

"Me, too."

She wasn't letting them see their father until she learned how badly he was hurt. "I know. I'll just go back and see how he's doing. Gabrielle, take care of your brother."

She nodded, her arm going around his trembling shoulders. "You'll tell Daddy we're here."

"Yes." Her fingers unsteady, she ran her hand over Gabrielle's head, touched Ashton's damp cheek. "I'll be back as soon as I can." Wishing she didn't have to leave them alone, she went back to the patient cubicles. Various moans, soft conversation, and loud laughter came from behind curtained walls. Those less fortunate were on stretchers in the hallway. She heard Robert's curse before she located his cubicle.

Unsure of what she'd find, she eased back the curtain.

"My leg is killing me. I want something for pain," he demanded. His elbows dug into the mattress, he tried to raise himself up. His left leg, propped on two pillows, was bruised and swollen from the knee to his ankle.

"We can't give you any more medication at the moment," a robust redhead in a scrub uniform said. "Your leg is broken. We're going to put on a soft cast."

"Dammit, I want a pain shot!"

"Robert," Gina said, stepping farther into the room. "How did this happen?"

"That's a stupid question even for you, Gina," he spat. "It doesn't matter. What matters is that I'm in pain."

Chastised in front of the woman, Gina said, "Then I won't stay. Gabrielle and Ashton wanted you to know that they're here."

"Go. You're useless anyway," he snarled. "My leg hurts like a bitch."

Gina had a perverse urge to bump the bed as she turned to leave. Common sense prevailed and she went back to the waiting room. Gabrielle and Ashton were huddled on a leather sofa looking lost and afraid. She quickly went to them. "Your father broke his leg. They're going to put on a cast."

"Karin in my class broke his leg. We all got to write on the cast," Ashton said.

"Daddy is going to have a cast, too," Gina said. "He's going to be fine."

"You're sure?" Gabrielle asked, her lips trembling, her eyes filled with tears.

Sitting beside Ashton, Gina reached past her son and hugged her daughter. "I wouldn't lie to you. I tell you what. Why don't we find the vending machine to get you something to eat?"

"What if Daddy needs us?" Gabrielle asked.

If only her father was as concerned about her. "I'll tell the receptionist where to find us." Standing, Gina started toward the desk. Her cell phone rang. Reaching inside, she got in line again to speak with the busy receptionist. "Hello."

"I just wanted to hear your voice."

"Max." Her voice trembled.

"What is it?" he asked sharply. "Are you and the children all right?"

His first thought had been for them. She had finally gotten it right. "Robert broke his leg and is in the emergency room. We're here now."

"Which hospital?"

"Mercy."

"I'll be there as soon as I can. Don't worry. Bye."

Gina slipped the phone back in her purse. "Max is coming, but we have time to get you something to eat at least."

"I'd rather stay here in case Daddy needs us," Gabrielle said. "You can go."

Gina brushed her hand over her daughter's hair. She deserved a father who loved her and put her first. "I don't want to leave you."

"I'll be fine," she said, but her lower lip trembled.

"We'll all wait." She led them to a seat in the waiting room with a clear view of the sliding glass door of the entrance. "When Max gets here he can take Ashton to get a bite to eat."

"You think Daddy's hungry?" Ashton asked in a soft whisper.

"No, sweetheart, he's not." She pulled him into her lap. "He's not hungry at all." *What he is, is selfish.*

Fifteen minutes later the steel double doors leading back to the cubicles swung wide. A slender black man in green scrubs came around the corner pushing Robert, his left leg extended on the raised footplate of a wheelchair.

Gabrielle jumped up and ran to him, stopping by his side, tears in her eyes. "I was scared."

"Your father is going to be fine," Gina said, unsure whether Robert remained in a surly mood. He grimaced in pain, his left hand clutching his upper thigh.

Awkwardly Robert patted her hand. "I'm hurting now. I just want to go to bed and take another pain pill."

"Are you the family?" asked the man standing behind the wheelchair.

"Yes," Robert answered before Gina could say otherwise.

"I'm Nurse Harris." He handed her a sheet and a prescription. "Mr. Rawlings fractured his left tibia. He'll be in the soft cast until the swelling goes down enough for a permanent cast. Keep the leg elevated as much as possible. He has an appointment to see the orthopedic doctor again Friday." He handed Gina a pair of crutches.

"Whoa. Wait a minute." Gina held up her hands, not taking the crutches. "You should be talking to someone else. We're divorced."

Nurse Harris silently stared at Robert.

"We've only been divorced a short time." Robert briefly shut his eyes. "I can't believe you'd be so petty as to refuse me coming home when I'm in such pain."

"You can't come home with me," Gina said, aware they were drawing attention and not caring.

"Mama, you have to let him come home!" Gabrielle wailed, her voice carrying, tears running down her cheeks.

"I'll help, Mama," Ashton said.

Despite the pain Robert said he was experiencing, he looked smug. "At least my children have compassion."

Gina gritted her teeth. She'd never wanted to do bodily harm so badly to any person as she did now to Robert. He was using the children, but she wasn't letting him get away with it. "More than you have."

Her words wiped the smugness from his face, but her children stared at her, their hearts in their eyes. This couldn't be happening; then she saw the entrance door open and Max was there.

"Max," she breathed the word, but he heard her and quickly came to her side. He threw a glance at Robert. "Hi, Gina. Hi, partner, Gabrielle."

"What are you doing here?" Robert asked, his voice surprisingly strong for a man in pain.

"Gina needed me," Max said, curving his arm around her shoulder.

"We don't need you," Robert said hotly. "Or is he the reason you don't want me back?"

"You left—"

"Gina," Max said softly.

With difficulty, Gina reined in her temper. "There must be someone else you can call."

Robert bowed from the waist and put his face in his cupped hands. "I'm in so much pain, I can't think."

"Mama, please let him stay," Gabrielle pleaded. "I'll take care of him. I've been doing good with my chores."

"Mama." Ashton edged closer to his father. "I'll help you, Daddy."

Gabrielle swiped tears from her eyes. "I can go stay with you, Daddy, and help take care of you."

"No!" Gina shouted, feeling the situation slipping out of her hands. "You can come back, just until we figure out an alternative."

Robert lifted his face, reached for Gabrielle's hand, and put his arm around Ashton's shoulder. "I knew I could count on my children. You haven't turned your backs on me."

"We love you, Daddy," Gabrielle said, clutching her father's hand.

Gina was trapped unless she wanted her budding relationship with Gabrielle to take a nosedive. In Gina's presence Robert had never held Gabrielle's hand or hugged Ashton before. He was playing this for all that it was worth. "My car is parked out front."

By the time Gina pulled into her driveway she wanted to stuff a sock in Robert's mouth. He complained constantly—she stopped too quickly, hit every bump in the road, turned a curve too quickly. It wasn't any better by the time she and Max managed to get him inside and on the sofa.

"I need a drink."

"I'll get it, Daddy." Gabrielle and Ashton both took off for the kitchen.

"You can go now." Robert glared up at Max.

Max turned to Gina. "Have you and the children eaten yet?"

"Didn't you hear me?" Robert snapped.

Gina had had enough. She leaned down to within an inch

of his face. "This is my house. Max is an invited guest. If you don't like it, you're welcome to leave."

"Here you are, Daddy." Gabrielle handed him a glass of water. "Ashton has iced tea."

Robert's lips pressed together in a hard line. Gina didn't know if it was because he wanted alcohol or because of what she'd said; she didn't care. "That was nice of them to think of giving you a choice, wasn't it, Robert?"

He traded glares with her and Max before taking the tea Ashton held and took a sip. "I want to go to bed."

Gina's gaze snapped to Max. His jaw clenched, but he remained silent. "Gabrielle, could you start fixing sandwiches for lunch? Ashton, please help."

"I want to stay," Gabrielle said, stepping closer to her father.

Patience, Gina reminded herself. "I know, but we have to eat. You said you'd help if he came here. That means doing what I tell you the first time."

She didn't move.

"I could use some food," Robert whispered.

Gabrielle took off with Ashton on her heels. Robert folded his arms, a little smile on his lips.

Gina planned to wipe it off. "You're in your bed."

"What!" He jerked, then grimaced. "You can't be serious."

"I am." Gina glanced toward the kitchen. "Surely you didn't think I'd give up my bed for you."

Robert shot a defiant look at Max. "You wouldn't have to give it up."

Gina gasped. Max clenched his fists. "This sofa makes into a bed. You're not that far from the half bath off the kitchen. If this isn't agreeable—" She picked up the phone on the end table and held it out to him. "You can call someone else."

"I never thought you could be so mean." His head fell forward until his chin touched his chest.

She replaced the phone. "You know what, Robert? I really don't care what you think. If it weren't for Gabrielle and Ashton, you wouldn't be here."

"What about my prescription?" Robert lifted his head and moaned loudly. "I need my medicine."

"I'll go," Max said.

Gina held out her hand to her ex. "Your credit card and insurance card."

Robert picked up the plastic bag the hospital had put his tennis shoes and socks in, took out his billfold, and extended the cards to Max. "Just my medicine."

Taking the cards, Max faced Gina. "You need anything?"

"No. I'm glad you're here."

He reached out his hand toward her face, only to let it fall before making contact. "I'll be back as soon as I can."

Robert waited until the front door closed. "Be careful, Gina. Men can be users."

She fixed him with a hard gaze. "That's one of many lessons you taught me that I don't plan to forget." Leaving him with his mouth open, she went into the kitchen.

Max had met few people as selfish and manipulative as Robert Rawlings. Gina's ex alternated between complaining, having Gabrielle and Ashton wait on him, and shooting Max killer looks. It might be un-Christian, but Max wanted him gone. He said as much when Gina walked him to the door and they stepped outside later that evening.

She shook her head. "You can't want him gone any more

than I do, but you see how Ashton and Gabrielle are worried about him, can't do enough for him. He might not have been there for them, but they're going to be there for him."

She looked tired. Part of the reason was they'd spent most of the night making love. The other part was a loudmouthed fool. "I wish we were alone."

"Me, too." She briefly tucked her head. "I might not make it tomorrow."

Fear coursed through him. He caught her arm. "Don't let him con you, too."

"I'm immune, but he's going to need a couple of days to get used to the crutches," she told him. "I'd rather be here if he needs me than have him fall and have to stay longer."

"I'm not sure that's not his plan," Max told her. At her puzzled look, he continued, "He's been watching you for the past hour."

"Because he's angry at me for telling him off," she said.

"More like a man who's thinking he might have made a mistake."

Gina scoffed. "He walked out on me, Max."

"Then. But I've got a feeling he's beginning to second-guess what a fool he was. You've moved on and he doesn't like it. But if he thinks he can walk back in, he'll have to get by me first," Max said fiercely, taking her into his arms, forgetting who might be watching.

"And that would take some doing." She placed her hand on his chest. "I wish we could go someplace for just five minutes."

His hand covered hers. "You don't want to leave the children."

She smiled up at him. "How come you understand me so well?"

"You're a good mother." He kissed her hand. "It won't be

the same working in the garden not knowing you're in the house or on the way."

"Please tell Sophia I expect to hear that she's mastered the crust for the tarts when I return."

He placed a soft kiss on her forehead. "I'll be thinking of you. If you need me or just want to scream, call."

"I will." On tiptoes, she brushed her lips across his, then she went back inside.

Max stared at the closed door for a few moments, then went to his Pathfinder. He wished he didn't have the bad feeling that he'd found a woman he could love just to lose her. Gina wanted to have a good, loving relationship with her children. Robert knew that and had used it to his advantage. Gabrielle wanted her father and mother back together. They were under the same roof. Max had a bad feeling that that was exactly where Robert and Gabrielle wanted him to stay.

Celeste came awake, instantly missing the warmth of Alec. He'd left while she was asleep. She opened her eyes and sat up to see the tiny sheet of paper on the night table. Darkness had fallen. The bedside lamp was on. Alec could be so sweet and so irritating—like now. She was tempted to ball the note up, but she was aware she'd never be able not to read what he'd written.

You're everything I ever dreamed of, every wish, every fantasy. I want you to know that, for me, this was real. You'll be a part of me forever. Think of me sometimes.

Good-bye,
Alec

The tenderness she'd felt evaporated. She leaped out of bed. What kind of man wrote such a tender note and then told the woman good-bye? He either loved her or was running a game.

The answer hit her, buckling her knees and sending her plopping back on the bed. *Alec loved her.* The knowledge overwhelmed her. Tears prickled her eyes. She'd done it. Almost.

Standing, she went to her closet. Loving a person meant taking risks, but Alec was worth it. He was the only man for her. She just had to convince him. He wasn't getting away from her.

She was in the bathroom running her bath before it hit her. You miss what you don't have. Alec had to want her as much as she wanted him. She'd give him a week to realize he couldn't live without her; then she was going after him if he didn't come to his stubborn senses first.

The perfect time would be the birthday party that Sam and his wife were giving for Alec. And she knew the perfect present.

"What about Daddy's jammies?" Ashton asked, his eyes round with worry, later that night.

"He can sleep in his clothes," Gina answered, trying to get the children to bed.

"How is he going to take a bath?" Gabrielle asked, sitting cross-legged on the floor next to her father.

This time, Gina was stumped for an answer.

"Your mother can help me," Robert said with a grimace. "Gina, can you fix my pillow and get me a pill?"

"I'll do it," Ashton said. Gina caught Ashton by the collar of his pajama top. "You can help." Bending, Gina slowly lifted Robert's leg, allowing Ashton to straighten the pillows. "Good job. We'll get your father a glass of water to take his medicine, and then you're going to bed."

She helped Ashton with the water in the kitchen and followed him back into the den. Robert's and Gabrielle's heads were close together. Seeing Gina, he twisted away. Her daughter came to her feet. Gina frowned, wondering what they were talking about.

"Here's your water, Daddy."

Gabrielle opened the pill bottle and shook out two white tablets into her father's waiting palm.

Robert took the medicine, then said, "I didn't realize how much I missed you until lately. Despite the pain, it feels good being here."

Gina rolled her eyes. "Time for bed. No argument. I'll be up in a minute." She watched them kiss their father, then slowly trudge up the stairs. "Robert, your stay here is limited. Remember that."

"I'm just thankful you let me stay," Robert said. "If you don't mind, can you go to my place and get some of my things? Or I can have my assistant bring them over. I'd like an update on the gym in any case, and she can do both. The apartment manager can let her in."

A picture of the well-toned woman in Robert's arms flashed into Gina's mind. "I don't want any of your women here."

"Strictly business," he said, lying back and closing his eyes. "I'm going to try and sleep. Good night."

She stared at him a few minutes longer, then went to her room. Undressing, she bathed and climbed beneath the covers.

Memories of Max there with her washed over her. She hugged the pillow, smelled his scent. They weren't likely to be together for a while, but when they were they'd make up for lost time. Smiling, Gina drifted off to sleep.

During second period at school, Gabrielle borrowed the cell phone of a friend and went into the girls' bathroom. Her hand clenched; her stomach churned. She wanted her family back the way it was, but she was scared.

Her daddy said he needed her, the family needed her. She had to make the call early, before her mother and Max had a chance to talk. She couldn't let her family down. Her daddy was counting on her. Before she completely lost her nerve, Gabrielle pressed in the number she'd memorized.

"Journey's End," Max answered.

Gabrielle's mouth dried.

"Hello."

She wiped her hand on the side of her skirt. "Max, this is Gabrielle."

"Is everyone all right?"

Don't be fooled, her father had warned her last night and again this morning. *Max doesn't care about you or Ashton. He's just using you to get to your mother.* "We're super; that's why I called. My parents are getting back together. You don't need to call or come by anymore."

Silence.

"Max, are you there?" She bit her lips. What if he called her mother? Her daddy said he wouldn't, but if Max did, her daddy told her to say Max lied.

"I'm here, Gabrielle. Your mother loves you; never forget that. Good-bye."

The line went dead. Gabrielle shivered. She'd done it. She'd saved her family, so why did her stomach still feel queasy?

TWENTY

Robert was getting on her last nerve. If he wasn't complaining, he was demanding. By ten Monday morning, Gina wanted to scream and would have if she hadn't briefly spoken with Celeste and Sophia earlier. Celeste sounded like her old self and Sophia like a woman on the brink of falling in love.

Hearing the doorbell, Gina got up from the desk in her office and went to answer it. A tall, attractive light-skinned black woman with red hair in a stylish nylon black and white sweatsuit stood on the porch, a small suitcase in her hand.

"Yes?"

"Good morning. I'm Kathy Owens, Robert's assistant," she said. "You must be Gina."

Gina returned the smile, glad it was a different woman than the one she'd seen the day Robert asked for a divorce. "Yes. Please come in. Robert is in the den." Showing the woman in to Robert, Gina excused herself and went back to her office, glad Robert had someone else to make demands on.

However, less than an hour later Robert yelled for Gina to help him to the bathroom. "Can you help me take a bath?"

"I'll help you to the bathroom and you can take a sponge bath," she said.

"Come on, Gina," he cajoled. "I can't reach all the places."

"Take it or leave it!"

"I never thought you'd treat me this way," he said, his head tucked so low his chin touched his chest.

"That makes two of us." She waited until his head lifted. "I never thought you'd divorce me, but I got over it. Make up your mind, Robert. I have work to do."

"The sponge bath."

Helping Robert to the bathroom, Gina spread a towel over his lap, maneuvered his shorts off, and propped up his leg. Preparing the sink with hot water, she gave him a washcloth.

"I remember a time you would have enjoyed washing me." His gaze dropped momentarily to his lap.

"It's a good thing for you that I've forgotten the past and the way you treated me and the children, or I would have left you in the emergency room. Call when you're ready to go back to the couch." Opening the door, she went to her office to call Max. She needed to hear his voice.

"Journey's End," Sophia said, excitement ringing in her voice.

"I guess we won't be taking that trip to New Orleans after all?" Gina quipped.

"You got it. Albert called me from the airport to tell me good-bye again, and to remind me not to forget our chess date when he returns in two weeks," Sophia said. "As if I would."

Smiling, Gina took her seat behind her desk. "I'm so glad things are working out for you."

"Me, too. I just hope he doesn't meet some woman or begin to question why he's interested in me while he's away," Sophia said, her laughter sounding a bit forced.

"Albert impressed me as a man who knows what he wants," Gina said, meaning every word.

"I hope so," Sophia said. "We'll miss you around here. Our first guests arrive Friday afternoon."

Disappointment slumped Gina's shoulders. "I know. I'll try to get by, but I'm not sure. The last test batch of the signature dishes tasted fantastic."

"You were here with me, but nothing beats a failure but a try." Sophia laughed. "At least they're longtime friends and love us."

Gina chuckled as well. "You'll do fine. Is Max around?"

"He's outside in the garden as usual. I'll get him."

"Thank you." Gina relaxed back in her chair, aware of the dreamy smile on her face and not caring one bit.

"Hello, Gina."

"Max," Gina almost purred the name. "Thanks again for yesterday. You saved my sanity."

"I was glad I could help," he said. "Since I know how busy you're going to be, you don't have to come back at all. I've taken too much of your time as it is."

Her heart lurched. Her skin chilled. "What?"

"You were great, but with the first guests arriving Friday, it's even more important that I pay strict attention to Journey's End, and you have your business and now your ex to care for, so you'll be busy as well. I don't want to take up any more of your time."

"I— I don't understand," she managed.

"I'll put your final check in the mail this afternoon. Thank you for helping turn Journey's End into a place I'll always be proud of."

He no longer wanted her. Her throat stung. Her eyes burned.

"Please tell Ashton and Gabrielle good-bye for me," he said. "Good-bye, Gina."

Clutching the phone, Gina felt tears sting her eyes, her body tremble. Max didn't want her. How could that be after Saturday night?

"Gina, I need a fresh glass of water!" Robert yelled.

Closing her eyes, Gina tried to make sense of the conversation she'd had with Max. She couldn't have been that wrong about him. She couldn't.

"Gina!"

Getting a dial tone, she called Celeste. "Please be there."

"Serendipity."

When she heard Celeste's voice, tears rolled down Gina's cheeks. "Max broke up with me."

"What!"

Gina sniffed, wiped away tears with the back of her hand. "Just now on the phone."

"I'll be there in fifteen minutes."

Gina hung up the phone and reached for a tissue. "Max," she whispered, and let the tears flow.

"Gina!"

For the second time in her life, a man she loved had dumped her. The second time hurt a thousand times worse. Putting her head on her desk, she gave over to the tears.

· · ·

"Tell me one good reason why I shouldn't come over there and rip you a new one?" Celeste snapped as soon as Max answered the phone.

"Since I deserve it, I can't." The phone clenched in his fist, he walked to the screened-in porch.

"You— What did you say?" she demanded.

"Take care of Gina. I—" He shook his head. Everywhere he looked, the gardens, the pier, the house, he was reminded of Gina there with him, reminded of what he'd never have.

"What's going on, Max? I just hung up from talking to Gina. She's devastated. What kind of game are you playing?"

"I can't explain, Celeste, but I want only the best for her."

"Crap!" she spat. "I am so tired of men talking nonsense. If you care about someone, you tell them. You have a problem, you discuss it and work it out."

"Sometimes, no matter how much you want to do that, it's impossible."

"You men need to get a grip. Once I straighten Alec out, you're next."

The line clicked dead. Max continued to stare out the screen. He didn't know who Alec was, didn't particularly care.

He did know that Gabrielle had lied, but he realized that she would always be a wedge between him and Gina. A mother shouldn't have to choose. He loved Gina enough that he wouldn't even consider asking her to. Pitching the phone on the padded chair, he headed to work in the garden. As he walked to the flower bed, he no longer felt the excitement, the sense of accomplishment.

Without Gina by his side, nothing would ever be the same again.

. . .

"There's something else going on with Max," Celeste told Gina the moment she got her alone in the bedroom with the door closed. Not for anything did Celeste want Robert to realize what had happened.

Gina's lower lip quivered. "You're sure?"

"Positive." Celeste pushed her toward the bathroom. "Put some cold compresses on your eyes and rest. I'll take care of Bigmouth and start dinner."

"Celeste, you have work to do."

"If I needed you, where would you be?" she asked, already knowing the answer. "To everyone, you have a headache."

"Maybe Max is worried about the grand opening this weekend?" Gina said.

"Could be." Celeste marched Gina into the bathroom. "I don't want to see you until the kids get home." Closing the door, Celeste went to the den. "Gina has a headache. There's a new sheriff in town. One who won't be run ragged. Do I make myself clear?"

"No wonder you can't keep a man," Robert quipped.

"That's right. I can be as mean as a snake." Grinning, she grabbed the end of the pillowcase enclosing the pillow his leg was propped on. "Want to try me?"

Robert's eyes bugged.

"I didn't think so." Celeste straightened and went into the kitchen.

After much debate, Gina decided to casually let Gabrielle and Ashton know during dinner that Max wouldn't be coming around any longer. Celeste had left to meet a client shortly after the children came home.

Trying to keep from crying again, Gina gave the reason she hoped more and more was the truth—he was busy with his B and B. The disappointment on Ashton's face had made her heart ache. From Gabrielle there was nothing. But for the first time in Gina's memory, after dinner her daughter helped clear the table and wash the dishes without being asked.

"Ashton, turn that thing down. I'm trying to rest," Robert bellowed from the den.

Gina rushed into the room to see Ashton with his head down. "Robert, what do you think you're doing talking to him that way?"

"Trying to rest," Robert said. "The TV is too loud. Ashton understands, don't you, son?"

Coming slowly to his feet, he nodded. "I'm sorry, Daddy."

"There's only one TV, Robert," Gina reminded him. "They're allowed to watch TV once they've finished their homework and chores."

"They don't mind letting me rest, do you?" Robert asked.

"No, Daddy." Gabrielle put her hand on Ashton's shoulder. "You want me to kick some balls to you?"

He looked at his daddy. "I guess."

Steaming, Gina waited until they were outside. "This is their house, Robert. You have to make allowances for them, not the other way around. I don't want to hear you yell at Ashton again, or you're out of here."

"He's my son, Gina. I wouldn't do anything to hurt him." Leaning back on the sofa, Robert closed his eyes. "This pain is making me surly." His eyes opened and he stared at her. "But the accident made me see things more clearly. I should have never left you and the children."

"What?"

He reached for her hand. "Gina, can you forgive me and give me another chance?"

She was stunned. "You can't be serious?"

"I am." He let his hand fall. "I know we can't make love, but let me move back in bed with you. You see how Ashton and Gabrielle want me here. We can be a family again."

She stared at him on the ugly black leather sofa he had insisted they buy and saw him for the selfish man he was. "Robert, when you left, I cried. I blamed myself when I should have blamed you. Now I thank you. I don't love you. I don't hate you. You're just the children's father. When you can maneuver better, you're leaving."

Feeling free, Gina left the room and saw Gabrielle in the kitchen with a bottle of water in her hand, anger in her eyes. "Gabrielle."

"Why can't it be the way it was?" she asked, her voice quaking.

"Because we don't love each other," Gina told her with a new calm.

"You could," Gabrielle told her.

"No. We couldn't, and I refuse to try again."

Whirling, Gabrielle went out the back door. Gina didn't even think of going after her. She loved her daughter, but she was not going to dictate how Gina lived her life.

By Wednesday, Gina could think of Max and not get misty. Thursday saw her determined not to give up on him. Aware of how much the grand opening meant to Max, Gina called and luckily got Sophia on the phone. Assured that Max was outside, Gina walked Sophia through the signature dishes, plus a welcoming meal and brunch on Sunday.

Helping made Gina feel a part of Journey's End. She refused to think she and Max couldn't resolve whatever the problem was.

Robert didn't have any visitors besides his assistant every day. Perhaps that was why he was so cranky. He should have one friend who cared. The children had taken to avoiding the den. He didn't appear to notice or care that they spoke to him when they came home from school, then didn't come back until time for bed.

Gina certainly noticed that Gabrielle and she were at odds again. Why she couldn't figure out. She yearned for the closeness they once had shared, before the divorce. Unfortunately, Gabrielle was growing closer to Robert and further from Gina.

And there was nothing she could do about it.

Sunday afternoon, Celeste was ready to go after Alec.

She decided on bare and flirtatious and pulled out a backless white sundress with a floral-print flared skirt. Sam and his wife were having Alec's birthday party at their house and had invited her. She was going.

Shortly after one that afternoon, she pulled out of the driveway and headed for the freeway. Alec wasn't getting away from her. She glanced at the sheet of paper that Helen had written her name and address on that day at Patrick and Brianna's place. Celeste was familiar with Myrtle Beach but not the area

Helen and Sam lived in. She wasn't worried. Her navigation system wouldn't let her get lost.

In a little over an hour, Celeste saw the Myrtle Beach sign welcoming visitors. She refused to listen to the little voice that said she might not get the welcome she expected from Alec. If he gave her any problems— and she was sure he would—she'd just show him the note he'd written.

She patted her pocket, felt the paper, her trump card. Flicking on her signal, she exited Highway 17, looking for a convenience or grocery store. She didn't want to arrive empty-handed at the party. She grinned. She'd give Alec his present in private. Laughter bubbled from her lips.

Spotting a convenience store at the end of a strip shopping center, she signaled to turn and parked in front. She reached into her purse and grabbed her wallet. The top was down, but there were only two other cars in front of the small store. She'd only be a minute.

Pushing the tinted glass door open, she started to the back. Alec would be surprised to see her. Grabbing a twelve-pack of Pepsi, she placed it on the counter. "I'm getting another," she said to the young woman behind the cash register.

The woman's eyes were wide and fixed behind Celeste. Fear instantly coursed though her. Slowly, she turned. Two feet in front of her stood a disheveled man with a dirty overcoat and a gun in his hand. It was pointed straight at her.

Alec's "small" birthday party had fifty or more people milling around Sam and Helen's huge backyard. Beneath the trees were several tables, but most of the people seemed content to wander and eat. As usual, Sam had cooked enough barbeque for anyone who wanted to take a plate home afterward. Helen had all kinds of salads and vegetables lined up. Alec hadn't seen it yet, but he was sure there was a cake someplace.

He felt every one of his thirty-five years and then some. Most of those attending were on the police force. They were laughing or playing cards or horseshoes, enjoying themselves. Alec couldn't. Standing with a can of soda in his hand, he never felt less like celebrating.

He missed Celeste. Hated that he had hurt her. His hand clenched on the can. He'd known he'd have to walk away, yet he'd made love to her anyway. He hadn't been able to do otherwise. If he had a weakness, it was Celeste.

A week felt like years. He'd returned to work, did his job, but the joy he once felt was no longer there. And it had nothing to do with the possibility that he might have to draw his weapon again. It had to do with an emptiness inside him that he feared would never be filled unless he had Celeste in his life again. Absently he wondered how long before the ache in his gut went away, how long before he felt alive again.

He'd picked up the phone countless times to call her and always hung up. He couldn't offer her any kind of life unless he was a whole man. Not for anything would he begin a relationship with her knowing that one day or night he might not come home because he couldn't draw his weapon at a crucial moment.

So far he and Tony were doing investigative fieldwork on a double homicide. An officer in homicide could go weeks without drawing and even longer without firing his weapon. But the chance was always there. Alec just prayed he'd be able to do his job.

"Alec."

He turned, alerted by the grave sound of his brother Sam's voice. Alec's blood ran cold. The last time his brother had worn that dire expression was when Patrick had been wounded. Patrick stood beside Sam and Simon. Brooke's husband was there as well. Earlier, Rafael had been charming some woman. All of them were off-duty. "What's wrong?"

"Let's go inside." Taking Alec's arm, Sam led him back into the house but he didn't stop until they stood in the front by Patrick's truck. Patrick slid in and started the motor. Simon climbed into the backseat.

"What I'm going to say isn't going to be easy," Sam said, opening the passenger door.

Alec's gut knotted as a patrol car, lights running on top, pulled up beside the truck, and suddenly he knew. He grabbed his brother's shoulders. "Just tell me Celeste is all right."

"We don't know. A patrol car answered a silent alarm. When he got out of his car, a man in an overcoat came out and fired two shots before disappearing back inside the store."

Alec's head briefly fell; then he quickly got inside the truck. "Tell me the rest on the way."

Sam climbed inside. Patrick gunned the motor. "The call I went in earlier to take was from Anderson in burglary. They found a woman's handbag on the seat of a silver convertible BMW registered to Celeste de la Vega. Inside were a checkbook, a notepad, and a sheet of paper with my and Helen's address and phone number."

Fear, then rage gripped Alec. He wanted to scream his fury. Aware that he couldn't help Celeste or those with her if he let those emotions control him, he slowly pulled it together. "Is Rafael going to negotiate?" Alec asked, his voice calm.

"He left as soon as I told him," Sam said. "He's the best. Brooke's husband is staying with the women."

Rafael was the top police negotiator on the Myrtle Beach police force, but they all knew there were those variables that no one could foresee—like a druggie or a mental patient. Who else would wear a coat on a day the temperature was in the eighties?

Siren blaring, lights flashing, the patrol car sped through a red light. Patrick was right behind it. Alec's hands clenched in his lap. "Her family. Have they been notified?"

"Anderson was going to call as soon as he got off the phone with me," Sam said.

Alec felt Simon's hand on his shoulder. He had been in the burglary division before he transferred to Charleston. "He's good, Alec. SWAT is probably already there."

"Get Anderson on the phone. I want to call her parents and her sister. They have to be going out of their minds with worry," Alec said.

"Way ahead of you." His brother handed him a notepad with a phone number and his cell phone.

Alec stared at the phone. What would he say? How could he help them?

"Just say what you feel," Patrick said. 'We're almost there."

Alec punched in the numbers. "Hello—"

"Are you related to Alec?" a female voice interrupted.

Caller ID. "This is Alec. Is this Celeste's sister or mother?"

"Thank God," the woman said. "I'm Yolanda, her sister. I told my parents that you would bring her and the others with her out safely."

"I'm going to do my best. We're almost there, Yolanda. I have to go, but I just wanted you to know that—" They pulled up into the shopping center. Police cars and TV vans were everywhere. So was an ambulance. Alec swallowed the knot in his throat. "I love her. I'll call."

Disconnecting the cell phone, Alec jumped out behind Sam. Running, they reached the command center. Behind a patrol car, Rafael stood with a microphone in his hand. At Alec's questioning gaze, he didn't say a word. He didn't have to. His hard expression spoke volumes.

There was no way a SWAT sniper could get a clear shot with the dark-tinted windows. Unless Rafael could talk the man into surrendering, people could die.

"Come on, Floyd. Let's think this through," Rafael said calmly. "Nobody is hurt thus far, and we want to keep it that way."

"Are you listening to me?" a shaky male voice bellowed, the sound coming through the speaker. "I want a gassed-up car here in five minutes, or I'm going to start killing people."

"Floyd, we're working on your demands, but these things take time. How many people are in there with you?"

"Five, so you'd better listen and stop jerking with me!" he yelled.

"I wouldn't do that, Floyd. You have the power, but you have to realize that you have five precious bargaining chips. A smart man like you would keep every one of them unharmed."

Silence.

Alec pointed to himself, then toward the store. Rafael shook his head and clicked back on his microphone. "Floyd, as I said, you're in control here. You have the power to end this peacefully. With a good lawyer, you'd be out on the streets in no time."

"I ain't going back to jail. You heard me. You just get that car here, or I'm going to kill her."

TWENTY-ONE

Alec broke and ran for the store. Patrick and Simon wrestled him to the ground.

"Let me go."

"Getting yourself killed is not going to help Celeste or any of the other people in there with her," Simon said. "She and her family are depending on you to bring her out safely."

Rafael gritted his teeth and turned toward the storefront. "Floyd, now you're not thinking like the smart man I know you can be," he said. "Act rashly and you aren't giving us a reason to keep talking. Don't forget, I'm working on that car for you."

"It shoulda been out here by now. I gotta get out of here."

"I understand, Floyd. You just let the hostages go and we can talk."

"You trying to play me for a fool. I oughter shoot one now."

Alec came to his feet, his pleading eyes on Rafael.

"Remember, you have the power, but you have to use it like the smart man you are," Rafael said. "The car is almost here, but I need to make sure everyone inside is all right first. I need to send a policeman inside."

"Nobody comes inside unless they want a bullet!" Floyd yelled.

Unbuttoning his shirt, Alec turned and met Anderson, the burglary division chief. "You're off-duty and not in this division, Dunlap."

"I'm asking, Captain Anderson. Begging, if it comes to that," Alec said. "If the woman you loved was in there, wouldn't you want to be the one to go in?"

"The object is not to give him another hostage," Anderson said.

"He won't get one," Alec said with steely determination.

Captain Anderson stared at Alec for a few more seconds, then said, "Get me a vest and an ankle piece."

Alec pulled off his shirt and fastened on the bulletproof vest. He straightened after fastening the ankle piece.

Patrick handed over his 9mm. The gun had more stopping power than the .35 on Alec's ankle. "Just in case."

Alec stuck the gun in the small of his back and pulled back on his shirt. He was ready; he just hoped he had the opportunity.

Celeste wouldn't give up hope. She had too much to live for. Her legs out in front of her, her back to the plate-glass window where the robber could watch them and the police, she prayed. Beside her was a young girl who looked about sixteen. She sobbed quietly now. When the robber had shot at the policemen, she'd become hysterical. The man threatening to shoot her only escalated her hysteria.

Celeste had to shake her to get her to stop. The man's unsteady hand on the gun, his mumbling to himself, weren't good signs that he was lucid enough to think clearly.

On the other side of the teenager was the store clerk, a woman in her mid-thirties with frizzy red hair. The other two were young men in their early twenties.

"I'll kill them!" Floyd yelled into the phone, pointing the gun at the teenager again. For some reason, he seemed to have fixated on her. "If you want a dead cop, then send him in."

Celeste's heart thumped in her chest. Alec was out there. She didn't know if hostage negotiators gave their full names or not, but she was sure Rafael gave the robber his to let her know that Alec was outside. She hoped he'd called her parents. Her mother would have finally met Alec. Celeste touched the note in her pocket and refused to think she wouldn't be there when they met in person.

"You think I won't off one of them? You think I'm bluffing? I want that car!"

"Floyd, it's like this," Rafael said calmly. "No car unless I'm one hundred percent sure that everyone inside is all right. You're asking for everything and not willing to give anything in return. This is a give-and-take situation."

"I've got the gun!" he yelled.

"We know that, Floyd, but it's getting close to five, and that means traffic is going to be a bear," Rafael told them. "You want us to clear the way, but that's going to take more time. You let him come in for a quick look and you're on your way in under five minutes."

Silence.

Alec didn't have to glance at his watch. Rafael always hooked a watch to his belt loop at the start of negotiations. Ninety-eight minutes had passed since Alec had arrived on the scene. Helicopters whirled overhead. Two were police, but the others were with the news media. They could only get so close, but with the high-powered lenses on their cameras they didn't have to do much more. He was aware the hostage situation was being carried live on at least one TV station.

He'd talked to Yolanda less than ten minutes ago and her local news in Houston wasn't carrying the standoff. The story hadn't gone national. Her mother and then her father had gotten on the line, begging him to bring Celeste safely back to them. He promised he would. He refused to think he wouldn't hold her again, hear her teasing laughter again.

"If there is an accident on Highway Seventeen, things are not going to go smoothly for you, Floyd," Rafael told him. "You could be sitting in a fully fueled car in the next five minutes. It's up to you, Floyd."

"Send him in, but if he's packing he's going back out feet-first!"

Rafael stared at Alec. "Don't do anything foolish."

Hands raised, Alec stepped from behind the police car. It was up to him now. He'd wanted this, refused to think of the last time he'd had to pull his gun. One-handed, he opened the door, pausing long enough for the sniper across the street to maybe get the robber in his sights.

The man either was too smart or just had dumb luck. He was too far back for the sniper to take him out. Alec cursed under his breath. The man stood thirty feet from the entrance. The five hostages were positioned in front of him.

Alec saw Celeste at once. Her eyes were huge in her face. His gut knotted; his heart raced. *Hold on, baby. I'm here, and I'm taking you home to your family.*

She appeared unharmed, as did the other hostages. As Alec did not want to bring attention to her, his gaze passed over her and stayed on the thin-faced man with a gun pointed at him. His hand trembled, perspiration beaded on his face, and it wasn't just because of the overcoat. Alec had seen too many addicts coming down from a high not to recognize one.

"My car."

"I haven't gotten a chance to make sure they're all right," Alec said with a calmness he was far from feeling.

"Talking time is over." Floyd grabbed the young girl in front of him by the hair and shoved the gun against her temple. "A car, or I put an end to her worthless life."

"Please, don't kill me! Please! Please!" the teenager screamed, crying uncontrollably.

"Let her go. You'll get what you want," Alec told him.

The two men and the woman hunched their shoulders, bent their heads, cowering in fear, but they remained in front of the gunman. Celeste stared at Alec, then calmly turned to the man. "I'm dating a policeman. If you take me, your chances are much better of getting out of here alive."

"No!" Alec shouted, taking a frantic step toward her.

Shoving the teenager away, the man grabbed Celeste, hooking his arm beneath her neck. "Well, looks like we have lover boy in person."

"Let her go," Alec said, his voice deadly quiet.

"Now why would I do that?" Floyd laughed, an evil, croaking sound. "Like the man said, I'm in control. Time to die, cop." He pointed the gun at Alec.

Cupping her balled fist, Celeste drove her elbow as hard as she could into the man's stomach and yelled, "Pancake!" Celeste and the other hostages flattened themselves on the floor.

With a grunt, the robber staggered backward, then straightened with a snarl and aimed his gun at Celeste, who was on the floor in front of him.

Fear and adrenaline pumping through him, Alec pulled the 9mm from the small of his back and fired in one smooth motion. The man fell backward. Gun still drawn, Alec stepped past Celeste and the other hostages. Kicking the gun from the man's lax fingers, Alec crouched down. Despite the single bullet hole in the man's chest, Alec checked for a pulse. None.

"All clear!" Alec shouted, and pushed to his feet.

The words barely left his mouth before the front door burst open. His brothers rushed inside, followed by other policemen. The hostages scrambled to their feet and ran for the front door.

Adrenaline still rushing through his blood, Alec saw Celeste being hugged by his brothers near the store's entrance. In five long strides, he reached her. Fury and fear riding him, he jerked her out of Rafael's arms. "What the hell do you think you were doing? Don't you ever—" was all he managed before he crushed her to him. "Don't ever."

Celeste held him just as tightly. "I knew you'd save us," she said, her body trembling as much as her voice.

"Thank you," croaked a young male voice. "You saved us."

Alec reluctantly released Celeste. Three former hostages, two men and a woman, stood there. They all were looking at Celeste.

Alec's arm tightened. She'd been foolishly brave. He wanted to tie Celeste to him and make sure she remained safe.

Celeste smiled up at Alec. "I told the person next to me that my fiancé would come for me and to flatten like a pancake when I gave the signal."

"She knew you'd come," the woman said. "We passed the word to each other while he talked on the phone."

The vice around his chest eased. "Fiancé?"

"Yes," Celeste said firmly, then straightened. "I need to call my family."

"Already done," Simon said. "I told them you'd call as soon as you could. Be prepared for the television cameras."

"Television cameras. Oh, my goodness!" She turned to Alec. "How do I look? Mother will disown me if I don't look my best."

Patrick chuckled. "Only a woman."

"And she's all mine," Alec said. Curving his arm around her waist, he led her outside, his brothers flanking them. They were met by the flash and glare of cameras, reporters clamoring for a statement. Celeste, Alec, and his brothers kept walking to Brianna, Maureen, Helen, Brooke, and her husband, who had arrived. The other hostages weren't so inclined to ignore the media. Even the teenager, sitting in the back of an ambulance, seemed to have recuperated enough to talk to reporters.

Alec didn't care. He had all he needed.

"I'm never going to forgive you," Celeste said.

Since she was naked in his arms and in his bed and they'd just made love for the second time, Alec figured he wasn't in too much trouble. He kissed her forehead, grazed his fingers over the tattoo at the base of her spine. Fifteen minutes ago his lips had been there. "You looked beautiful."

"My mother said I should have combed my hair." Raising up on her elbow on his chest, she gazed down at him. "I told her it was my fiancé's fault."

He arched a brow. "I might forget a lot of things, but not being a fiancé."

"I can see you're the type of man who will forget birthdays and anniversaries." She walked her fingers up his chest. "I'll have to put the dates in your day planner."

"So when did this happen?"

She took his face in her hand. "The moment after I read the note you left. I was coming to remind you." She momentarily closed her eyes. "Waiting for you to come, I clung to that note, to your love. You're the one thing I can't do without. I refused to think I wouldn't live to see you again."

He clutched her to him. "You're braver than anyone I know. You helped me move on." His forehead touched hers. "I want to start living in the present, not the past. I want to wake up with you, have you annoy me, thrill me, love me." He lifted her head, pushed her hair from the face he'd love through eternity. His lips brushed gently across hers.

It was time.

"Just so I won't be one of those husbands who forget, let's make it official, because I plan to be the kind of husband a very special and courageous woman like you deserves. Celeste de la Vega, will you marry me?"

Her lips trembled, then firmed. "Yes. And just so you know, I plan to be the kind of wife a very special brave man deserves, and love you until you holler."

His eyes darkened. "What if I make you holler first?"

Her dark eyes twinkled with sensual promise. "You can try."

Hooking one arm around her, he sat up and glanced at the clock on the nightstand. "We have six hours until we have to catch the plane to Houston to meet your family."

"What are we waiting for?" she asked, tumbling him back into the bed.

Determined not to let Max dumping her affect her business, Gina worked harder than ever. Finding that customers liked the gift ideas for their children, she expanded to baskets of fruit waiting in the staterooms of those taking cruises, a small fruit and cheese tray in hotel rooms, champagne—or chocolate-covered strawberries for those who didn't drink—for couples celebrating a special occasion.

"Gina! Gina!"

Gina's fingers paused over the computer keyboard as she finished the e-mail to a prospective client. The couple who described themselves as a "youthful sixty" were looking for a B and B for their fortieth wedding anniversary. Gina hadn't hesitated to recommend Journey's End.

She missed Max more each day instead of less, but at least she was learning to work through her pain. Oddly, it was Max who had taught her to be stronger, more self-sufficient, to be her own woman.

"Gina, I can't get my pillow straight."

She hit "send," refusing to yell back to Robert that she was busy. He was getting pretty good walking on his permanent cast. His orthopedic doctor had advised non-weight-bearing for five more weeks. She'd give Robert another week—if she could stand him—and then he was out of her house. If it weren't for the children, he'd be out of her life as well.

Perhaps Robert living with her was the reason for Max to end their relationship, and not the grand opening this weekend. Sophia had called her Sunday morning to let her know things were going well, the food a hit. From Max there was nothing. Neither of them mentioned his name.

Gina could keep on guessing or ask Max, and that was exactly what she planned. She was going to be as bold as Celeste in going after the man she wanted, but without the danger.

Shutting down the computer, Gina shuddered. She still got chills just thinking about the attempted robbery yesterday. The television camera had caught Celeste and Alec, arms wrapped around each other, as they left the convenience store with his brothers, then with the wives of his brothers, Brooke and her husband, and Rafael watching fondly. Gina had thanked God and shed a tear at the happy reunion. Celeste, like Maureen and the other women, had found lasting love.

Besides Celeste's hair being a little mussed, she'd looked ecstatic and stunning. Her engagement to Alec had put that look on her face. They'd talked for a few minutes last night and this morning before she and Alec caught a plane for Houston. Alec had asked for a transfer to the Charleston Police Department so Celeste wouldn't have to make the commute to Myrtle Beach.

Standing, Gina picked up her purse and went into the den. Robert vainly attempted to reach the pillow propped under his leg. Walking over, she straightened his leg. "I'm going to pick up Ashton and Gabrielle."

"What about the car pool?" he asked.

"Parent-teacher conference today," she said. "I told you."

He rubbed his thigh. "The pain medication must have made me forget."

It was a lie. He took the medication at night to help him sleep; then he didn't wake up until well after ten, which suited her. The less she was around or talked to Robert, the better.

"I'll be back in a couple of hours." She started from the room.

"Gina, have you given any more thought to our getting back together?" he asked.

She paused. "Robert, we've had this discussion. I don't want to have it again. By the end of the week, you should have progressed enough to be on your own. The children have planned a farewell dinner for you Friday night, and afterward I'm taking you to your apartment or your assistant can pick you up."

"You won't give us a chance?" Robert almost whined. "If we made love, you'd see."

She laughed. "Robert, it's over. There's nothing there. The only reason you're here is because you had no place else to go." She adjusted the strap of her purse. "It's your life to live it as you please, but there should be someone who cares about you besides Ashton and Gabrielle."

"I've got lots of friends," he snapped. "My assistant for one."

You pay her, Gina thought, then decided to let it go. *His life, his problem.* "I have to go or I'll be late."

Going to the garage, she got into her car and backed out. Life had certainly changed. Robert had left to build a new life and chase women; he now wanted her to take him back.

Never.

There was a verse in the Bible that God would make your enemies your footstools. Robert wasn't her enemy—at least not any longer. But his life apparently wasn't what he wanted, whereas her future was brighter than she'd ever imagined. Each day she grew more confident, felt more in charge of her life. If the situations with Max and Gabrielle could be resolved, Gina's life would be near perfect.

Parking at Ashton's school, Gina went to meet his teacher. As expected, the caring and innovative woman in her early twenties praised Ashton's academic and social skills. After picking him up from the after-school program, Gina went to get Gabrielle from her school a block over.

"Hello, sweetheart. How was school today?" Gina greeted Gabrielle when she opened the passenger's door.

"Hello. OK, I guess." Closing the door, Gabrielle set her bulging backpack at her feet, buckled her seat belt, and stared straight ahead.

"We had a fire drill," Ashton said. "Our teacher said we were the quietest and best behaved of all the classes."

Gina threw a worried look at Gabrielle and pulled away from the curb. "Did your school have a drill as well?"

"Yes, ma'am."

"Gabrielle, you've been quiet the past week. You know you can talk to me if you have a problem," Gina told her.

"What would I have a problem about?" Folding her arms, she stared out the window.

"That's what I'm asking you," Gina said.

"I told you already."

Gina couldn't let it go. There was something bothering Gabrielle. She didn't cater to her father like she did when he first came back. "Are you worried about your father?"

"Please, just leave me alone. You're always on my case."

"Gabrielle, that's not the truth."

"Wow!" Ashton exclaimed. "Look at all those police cars."

Gina looked. A strange truck and three police cars with flashing lights were parked in front of her house. Neighbors were on the sidewalk and in their yards gawking.

"Daddy?" Gabrielle whispered.

"He was fine when I left." Gina braked sharply in the driveway. "Stay here with your brother until I find out what is going on." Thankful for once that Gabrielle didn't argue, Gina raced to the front door. Jamming her key into the lock, she went inside.

Raised voices greeted her. She rushed to the den, where all the loud voices were coming from. "What's going on?" Besides Robert and his assistant, there were four policemen and a strange man in the room.

Everyone turned to her. One of the policemen approached. When he moved, Gina saw Kathy with her fisted hand clutching her blouse between her breasts. Robert looked ready to bolt.

"Who are you?" asked the policeman.

"Gina Rawlings. This is my house."

"I guess what they say is true," said the barrel-chested man in jeans and a long-sleeved plaid shirt. He looked about fifty, weighed at least 270, had a prominent nose in his light-skinned, unattractive face. "The wife is always the last to know. Robert and my soon-to-be-ex-wife have been having an affair for the past two months."

"What?" Gina yelled, her gaze flickering between Robert and his assistant.

"Honey, no, you have it all wrong," Kathy said, her face and voice frantic. One of the policemen kept her from going to her husband.

"I guess your blouse came open by itself," the husband sneered.

"I— I wasted a soft drink on it," she said, licking her lips. "You came in just when I was trying to dry it."

Gina was enraged at Robert's duplicity, but something the husband said caught her attention. "How did you get in my house?" she asked the man.

He pulled a key out of his pocket. "I made a duplicate of the one Robert gave Kathy."

"You gave that woman a key to my house? You worthless bastard!" Gina shouted as she rounded on Robert.

"Now, Gina." Robert held out one hand and tried to hobble backward without his crutches. "You know I couldn't do anything with my leg broke."

"Cowering from a woman." The man stared at his scared wife. "If you want him, you can have him. If he hadn't called the police and you hadn't gotten in the way, his other leg would be broken."

Robert tried to back up and stumbled. If the policeman hadn't caught him, he would have fallen.

The man laughed. "You thought you were so slick trying to keep both of us on a string. You bet on the wrong man, Kathy. My cement business is thriving, but playboy here spends too much time running after women to make a profit."

Kathy whirled on Robert. "Is that the truth? You said you were raking in the money."

"What about you?" Robert yelled back. "You said you had filed for divorce. If you hadn't asked me to carry you like some simpering teenager, I wouldn't have tripped and broken my leg."

"You should have been in better shape and not so clumsy!" Kathy shot back.

Kathy's husband folded his arms and smiled. "Looks like there's trouble in paradise."

The woman swung back to her husband. "I don't want him, honey. It was a mistake."

"I don't want you," Robert said, looking smug. "Gina and I are getting back together."

"Shut up, both of you!" Gina shouted. "You're disgusting. I can't believe you're so morally low and crass to discuss your shoddy affair in front of us." She turned to the policeman nearest her. "Please get them out of my house."

"You want to charge him for breaking and entering?" the policeman asked.

"Yes," Robert said loudly.

"No," Gina said, glaring at Robert. "This is my house, and I say no. I want my key back." She held out her hand.

"Sorry." The man gave her the key. "We're both better off without them. Thanks, and good-bye."

"Honey, please!" Kathy cried, trying to catch up with her husband as he hurried out the door. The last policeman closed the door behind him.

"Gina, Kathy's husband had it all wrong," Robert said, trying to hop to her with one crutch. The other one was across the room.

Ignoring him, Gina went to the kitchen for a black plastic bag. Opening the wicker basket where she kept Robert's things in the den, she began stuffing his possessions inside.

"Gina, please. You have to listen."

"I'd advise you to shut up, Robert, or I'll put you on the sidewalk instead of taking you to your apartment." Finished, she took her house key off his key ring and handed him his other crutch. Not once had she thought of changing the locks. "I know it's a foreign concept, but think of the children for once, and keep your selfish mouth shut. You've decided to go home early. You love and thank them for all they've done."

Gripping the plastic bag, she opened the front door and started for her car in the driveway. One of the police cars remained parked at the curb. She supposed he wanted to stay in case he received another call about a disturbance.

She spoke to the children as soon as she opened the back door and placed the plastic bag inside. Gabrielle was in the backseat with Ashton. Silently they climbed out the other side. "Your father is fine, but he's decided he wants to go home. Right, Robert?"

"Yeah. I won't be able to drive, so I won't be around for a while," he said.

"That's all right." Gabrielle pulled a silent Ashton closer. "Good-bye."

"Good-bye," Ashton said.

Robert's surprised stare matched Gina's. Neither child appeared unhappy to see him leave early. He had himself to blame.

"Get in."

Sitting down, Robert maneuvered his left leg into the car and shut the door. Gina pulled off.

A short while later she stopped at the manager's office of Robert's apartment complex. Getting out, she placed the plastic bag on the sidewalk, then opened his door.

"Gina, please listen."

"Get out, Robert."

As soon as he managed to stand, Gina closed the car door. Going around to the other side, she got in and sped off.

Her anger hadn't abated by the time she arrived home. At

least the police car and the gawking neighbors were gone. Pulling into the garage, she let down the door and went inside. Her main concern was Ashton and Gabrielle.

She found them sitting side by side on the sofa. Gabrielle had her arm around her brother's shoulder. Both looked scared. Gina's temper spiked, but she controlled it and hunkered down in front of the children.

"It's all right." She placed a hand on each of their legs. "Everything is going to be all right."

"The man and woman were shouting at each other and saying bad words. Is that why Daddy wanted to go home early?" Ashton asked.

Gabrielle glanced at her mother, then away. Ashton might be too young to understand what had happened but not Gabrielle or the neighbors. Gina had never felt more helpless. "It was time."

The doorbell rang. Ashton jumped up and ran toward the door. Gina came to her feet and rushed after her son. "Ashton, no!" She didn't want to talk to any nosey neighbors.

Unlocking the door, Ashton pulled it open. "Hi, Max."

"Max," Gina whispered, her heart doing a familiar dance of delight. His jeans and shirt were sweaty and dirt stained. He apparently hadn't taken time to change clothes before coming over.

"Hi, champ." Picking Ashton up, he went to Gina. His hand swept her hair from her face. "Are you all right?"

Gina only had to look at Ashton clinging to Max to know he or Gabrielle had called him. Embarrassed, feeling stupid, she clung to her pride. *The wife was always the last to know, and mistress makes three.* "I'm fine. Thank you for coming, but I don't want to keep you from working."

Max's gaze flickered to Gabrielle, then back to Gina. "Nothing that can't wait. Why don't I take all of you to dinner? You can come back with me to Journey's End. While I get cleaned up, you can visit with Aunt Sophia and see the progress on the garden."

"We could pick up something on the way," Gabrielle said. "Mama, why don't you go comb your hair? I'll keep Max company."

"I drew a picture for you, Max. I'll go get it."

Max set Ashton on his feet, his gaze going back to Gina. "Your hair looks fine to me."

The embarrassment faded. Max never expected more of her, always saw the best in her. "Gabrielle, I think I've told you about not saying everything that comes to your mind."

"I'll remember next time," she said.

"See that you do." Hugging her daughter, Gina went to her bedroom.

"I wasn't sure you'd come," Gabrielle said, staring at her feet.

"If Gina or Ashton or you need me, you can always count on me." He stared in the direction Gina had taken. "I care about your mother."

Gabrielle's head lifted. "She likes you, too." She folded her arms but kept her gaze level. "Daddy told me to call you and tell you they were getting back together."

"You wanted your family the way it used to be. I understand, but I hope we can be friends. Your mother wouldn't do anything that would come between you and her."

"She hasn't been happy since you stopped coming around. I thought Daddy wanted us to be a family again, but he was seeing that married woman." Gabrielle swallowed. "All the neighbors saw."

"Some men aren't smart enough to appreciate what they have," Max told her gently. "I was faithful, but I didn't appreciate the time my wife and I had. I learned the hard lesson not to take anything or anyone for granted. I want us to be friends."

"Because of Mama?"

"Partially, but I also want to get to know you better," he said. "You're smart and you love your family, just like your mother."

Gabrielle bit her lip, momentarily tucked her head. "You didn't rat me out with Mama. Ashton, although a pain, likes you. I guess I could give it a try."

Ashton raced back into the den with a large sheet of paper clutched in his hands. Following behind him and pleased to see him happy, Gina never considered reprimanding him for running in the house.

"I drew this for you, Max." Ashton held out the paper, his small face wreathed in a huge smile.

Max took the sheet. He stared at the drawing a long time before lifting his head. "Thanks, Ashton."

"May I?" Gina asked. Gabrielle had already leaned over to see what was on the paper. The crayon drawing depicted a man and a little boy playing soccer against a woman and a girl.

"It's for your refrigerator," Ashton told him proudly.

"I'll put it up as soon as we get to Journey's End." He carefully rolled the drawing. "Everyone ready?"

"Ready," Gina said, following Max and the children out the door. He had his hand on Ashton's head, his head bent toward Gabrielle. Gina stared at them a few moments, hoping, praying, that her daughter was willing to give him a chance.

Seating the children in the back, Max held the passenger door open for Gina. She was about to get in and saw her neighbor across the street watching them.

Gina waved. "Hello, how are you doing?"

"Ah, fine, Gina," answered the startled young woman. "And you?"

"Couldn't be better," she said, a grin on her face, finally getting into the SUV.

Max realized he didn't have much time. Ashton and Gabrielle had school tomorrow. Gina would want to get Ashton in bed by eight thirty.

Max waited until they had consumed their takeout, cleaned up the kitchen. "Gina, could I talk to you outside for a moment?"

"Sure."

Taking her arm, Max led her out the front door. On the steps were large planters of ivy, begonia, and sweet peas.

"You've accomplished so much," she said softly.

"I thought of you every hour of every day you were gone," he said.

She faced him. "I could have been here."

Tricky subject. His hands settled on her waist. "You had a lot to contend with. I didn't want to add any more."

Her hands rested on his chest. His heart rate went crazy. "Max, you know there's such a thing as being too noble."

"I finally figured that out." He pulled her closer so their bodies touched from the waist down. "If I had all the time in the world, if you weren't a part of my life I'd be a miserable man."

"I was so lonely without you, but I planned to hunt you down as soon as Robert left." Her lips tightened. "He used me."

"And paid the price. He lost you, and the children saw a side of him that he'll have a difficult time trying to erase."

"Gabrielle called you, didn't she?"

"She was worried about you." His hand curved around Gina's neck. "Apparently she had never seen you so angry. I think she'll be coming around enough to accept me in your life, in all of your lives eventually. Would you like a short or long engagement?" he asked.

"Short."

"Right answer." His lips settled on hers, kissing her as if she were the most precious, most desirable woman in the world.

Life was good and his journey with his new family wasn't an end but a wonderful beginning.

READING GUIDE QUESTIONS

1. It is difficult for anyone to learn their marriage is over. Gina had to face this harsh reality and accept it before she could move on. What do you think Gina's first clue should have been that her marriage to Robert was doomed?

2. After Robert asked for a divorce, Gina went to his gym later that day—determined to get him to change his mind, determined to do whatever it took to save her marriage. Her efforts failed in the worst, most embarrassing and demoralizing way. If you had been in Gina's position would you have acted differently? How would you have handled the situation at the gym?

3. Because the stigma of divorce in today's society is gone, divorces are on the rise. If you were faced with the possibility of a divorce, what is the one thing you couldn't forgive? If children were involved would you stay for them, but not forgive or forget?

4. Gabrielle wanted her family back the way it was, and acted like a spoiled brat. In her defense, she loved her father and was scared. Why do you think girls in general love—and forgive—their absent, non–child-support-paying fathers?

5. Gina's best friend, Celeste, never liked Robert or thought much of him as a man, yet she never voiced her feelings to Gina. Do you agree with Celeste's decision? Why or why not?

6. Celeste and Alec were instantly attracted to each other, but Alec fought the attraction. Celeste refused to let him shut her out. Have you ever gone after a man? How did it turn out? Do you now regret that decision?

7. Max thought he had time in his marriage to do all the things that he and his wife planned. He was proven painfully wrong. Did reading his story make you re-think your priorities to always put those you love first?

8. There is a rising number of single, older females in this country. It was fun watching Sophia warm to the

possibility of finally finding love. Do you believe that you can be too old to fall in love?

9. What is the one thing that you will take away with you after reading *And Mistress Makes Three*?